T0214683

Lecture Notes in Computer Science 11444

Commenced Publication in 1973
Founding and Former Series Editors:
Gerhard Goos, Juris Hartmanis, and Jan van Leeuwen

More information about this series at http://www.springer.com/series/7407

Christian Hochberger · Brent Nelson ·
Andreas Koch · Roger Woods ·
Pedro Diniz (Eds.)

Applied Reconfigurable Computing

15th International Symposium, ARC 2019
Darmstadt, Germany, April 9–11, 2019
Proceedings

 Springer

Editors
Christian Hochberger
Technical University of Darmstadt
Darmstadt, Germany

Brent Nelson
Brigham Young University
Provo, UT, USA

Andreas Koch
Technical University of Darmstadt
Darmstadt, Germany

Roger Woods
Queen's University Belfast
Belfast, UK

Pedro Diniz
INESC-ID
Lisbon, Portugal

ISSN 0302-9743   ISSN 1611-3349 (electronic)
Lecture Notes in Computer Science
ISBN 978-3-030-17226-8   ISBN 978-3-030-17227-5 (eBook)
https://doi.org/10.1007/978-3-030-17227-5

Library of Congress Control Number: 2019936513

LNCS Sublibrary: SL1 – Theoretical Computer Science and General Issues

This Springer imprint is published by the registered company Springer Nature Switzerland AG
The registered company address is: Gewerbestrasse 11, 6330 Cham, Switzerland

Preface

The 15th International Symposium on Applied Reconfigurable Computing (ARC) was held in April 2019 at TU Darmstadt in Germany. It is highly appropriate that ARC came to Darmstadt as TU Darmstadt was the first university worldwide to create a Chair for Electrical Engineering, awarded to Professor Erasmus Kittler in 1882.

Even closer to ARC's key focus on reconfigurable computing are two globally renowned research and high-tech institutions, both located in Darmstadt: The GSI Helmholtz Centre for Heavy Ion Research is a hotbed of high-energy physics research, employing a number of accelerators, detectors, lasers, and storage rings for advanced experiments. Discoveries made at GSI include six new elements, among them Darmstadtium (Ds, atomic number 110). Many of the scientific instruments employ reconfigurable devices such as field-programmable gate arrays (FPGAs), which are the key subject of ARC, in critical functions.

A similarly keen interest in the use of FPGAs is also prevalent in the European Space Agency (ESA), which operates its European Space Operations Centre (ESOC) in Darmstadt. FPGAs are investigated by ESA in Darmstadt both for ground as well as for space use, e.g., as components for compact CubeSats. In the course of ARC 2019, excursions to both of these fascinating institutions were part of the symposium's program.

The main program of the symposium was formed by 20 full papers and seven poster presentations. They were selected from over 50 submissions from all around the world. The selection was driven by a thorough review process with more than 200 reviews in total, which resulted in a competitive process. Besides these high-quality scientific papers, one tutorial and an invited talk complemented the program.

We hope that you find the selected papers interesting and useful for your own research or development!

February 2019

Christian Hochberger
Brent Nelson
Andreas Koch
Roger Woods
Pedro Diniz

Organization

General Chairs

Andreas Koch   TU Darmstadt, Germany
Roger Woods   Queen's University Belfast, UK

Program Chairs

Christian Hochberger   TU Darmstadt, Germany
Brent Nelson   Brigham Young University, USA

Proceedings Chair

Pedro Diniz   INESC-ID, Lisboa, Portugal

Steering Committee

Hideharu Amano	Keio University, Japan
Jürgen Becker	Universität Karlsruhe (TH), Germany
Mladen Berekovic	Universität zu Lübeck, Germany
Koen Bertels	Delft University of Technology, The Netherlands
João M. P. Cardoso	University of Porto, Portugal
Katherine (Compton) Morrow	University of Wisconsin-Madison, USA
George Constantinides	Imperial College of Science, Technology and Medicine, UK
Pedro Diniz	INESC-ID, Lisboa, Portugal
Philip H. W. Leong	University of Sydney, Australia
Walid Najjar	University of California Riverside, USA
Roger Woods	Queen's University of Belfast, UK

In memory of *Stamatis Vassiliadis* [1951–2007], ARC 2006–2007
Steering Committee member.

Program Committee

Hideharu Amano	Keio University, Japan
Zachary Baker	Los Alamos National Laboratory, USA
Juergen Becker	Karlsruhe Institute of Technology, Germany
Nikolaos Bellas	University of Thessaly, Greece
Mladen Berekovic	TU Braunschweig, Germany
Joao Bispo	University of Porto, Portugal

Marco Domenico Santambrogio	Politecnico di Milano, Italy
Yukinori Sato	Toyohashi University of Technology, Japan
Antonio Carlos Schneider Beck	Universidade Federal do Rio Grande do Sul, Brazil
Yuichiro Shibata	Nagasaki University, Japan
Dimitrios Soudris	National Technical University of Athens, Greece
Theocharis Theocharides	University of Cyprus, Cyprus
George Theodoridis	University of Patras, Greece
David Thomas	Imperial College, London, UK
Nikolaos Voros	Technological Educational Institute of Western Greece, Greece
Chao Wang	University of Science and Technology of China, China
Markus Weinhardt	Osnabrück University of Applied Sciences, Germany
Roger Woods	Queen's University Belfast, UK
Yoshiki Yamaguchi	University of Tsukuba, Japan

Sponsors

The 2019 Applied Reconfigurable Computing Symposium (ARC 2019) was sponsored by:

Contents

Image/Video Processing

High-Level Synthesis

CGRAs and Vector Processing

Applications

Fault-Tolerant Architecture for On-board Dual-Core Synthetic-Aperture Radar Imaging

Helena Cruz[1,2], Rui Policarpo Duarte[1,2(✉)], and Horácio Neto[1,2]

[1] INESC-ID, Rua Alves Redol, 9, Lisbon, Portugal
[2] Instituto Superior Técnico, University of Lisbon, Lisbon, Portugal
{helena.cruz,rui.duarte,horacio.neto}@tecnico.ulisboa.pt

Abstract. In this research work, an on-board dual-core embedded architecture was developed for SAR imaging systems, implementing a reduced-precision redundancy fault-tolerance mechanism. This architecture protects the execution of the BackProjection Algorithm, capable of generating acceptable SAR images in embedded systems subjected to errors from the space environment. The proposed solution was implemented on a Xilinx SoC device with a dual-core processor. The present work was able to produced images with less 0.65 dB on average, than the fault-free image, at the expense of a time overhead up to 33%, when in the presence of error rates similar to the ones measured in space environment. Notwithstanding, the BackProjection algorithm executed up to 1.58 times faster than its single-core version without any fault-tolerance mechanisms.

Keywords: Synthetic-Aperture Radar · BackProjection Algorithm · Approximate computing · FPGA · Dual-core · SoC

1 Introduction

There is an increasing need for satellites, drones and Unmanned Aerial Vehicles (UAVs) to have lightweight, small, autonomous, portable, battery-powered systems able to generate Synthetic-Aperture Radar (SAR) images on-board and broadcasting them to Earth, avoiding the time-consuming data processing at the receivers.

SAR is a form of radar used to generate 2D and 3D images of Earth which is usually mounted on moving platforms such as satellites, aircrafts and drones.

This work was supported by national funds through Fundação para a Ciencia e a Tecnologia (FCT) with reference UID/CEC/50021/2019, and project SARRROCA, "Synthetic Aperture Radar Robust Reconfigurable Optimized Computing Architecture" with reference: PTDC/EEI-HAC/31819/2017, funded by FCT/MCTES through national funds, and POCI - Programa Operacional Competitividade e Internacionalização e PORLisboa - Programa Operacional Regional de Lisboa.

SAR can operate through clouds, smoke and rain and does not require a light source, making it a very attractive method to monitor the Earth, in particular, the melting of polar ice-caps, sea level rise, wind patterns, erosion, drought prediction, precipitation, landslide areas, oil spills, deforestation, fires, natural disasters such as hurricanes, volcano eruptions and earthquakes.

Space is a harsh environment for electronic circuits and systems as it can cause temporary or permanent errors on them. Therefore, systems designed for spacecrafts or satellites must be reliable and tolerate space radiation. The main radiation sources in space are: high-energy cosmic ray protons and heavy ions, protons and heavy ions from solar flares, heavy ions trapped in the magnetosphere and protons and electrons trapped in the Van Allen belts [3,15,20]. These radiation sources are capable of deteriorating the electronic systems and provoking bit-flips, leading to failures in electronic systems [2,11,14,16]. Fault tolerance mechanisms are used to increase the reliability of these systems at the expense of extra mechanisms, processing time and power.

BackProjection is an algorithm for SAR image generation that is capable of generating high quality images. BackProjection is considered the reference algorithm for image formation since it does not introduce any assumptions or approximations regarding the image. However, it is a very computationally intensive algorithm. Therefore, typical fault-tolerance mechanisms will introduce a huge penalty on its performance.

System-on-Chip (SoC) Field-Programmable Gate Arrays (FPGAs) were chosen as a target device because of their power efficiency, performance and reconfigurability, which are very important characteristics for space systems. Furthermore, the use of a SoC FPGA will enable future developments of dedicated hardware accelerators to improve the performance of the system.

2   Background

2.1   Synthetic-Aperture Radar

SAR is a form of radar used to generate 2D and 3D high resolution images of objects. Unlike other radars, SAR uses the relative motion between the radar and the target to obtain its high resolution. This motion is achieved by mounting the radar on moving platforms such as satellites, aircrafts or drones, as illustrated in Fig. 1. The distance between the radar and the target in the time between the transmission and reception of pulses creates the synthetic antenna aperture. The larger the aperture, the higher the resolution of the image, regardless of the type of aperture used. To generate SAR images, it is necessary to use an image generation algorithm, such as the BackProjection Algorithm, described below.

2.2   BackProjection Algorithm

The BackProjection algorithm takes the following values as input: number of pulses, location of the platform for each pulse, the carrier wave number, the radial

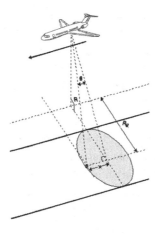

Fig. 1. Example of geometries involved in a SAR system.

distance between the plane and target, the range bin resolution, the real distance between two pixels and the measured heights. The BackProjection algorithm, from [1], performs the following steps for each pixel and each pulse:

1. Computes the distance from the platform to the pixel.
2. Converts the distance to an associated position (range) in the data set (received echoes).
3. Samples at the computed range using linear interpolation, using Eq. 1 [13].

$$g_{x,y}(r_k) = g(n) + \frac{g(n+1) - g(n)}{r(n+1) - r(n)} \cdot (r_k - r(n)) \tag{1}$$

4. Scales the sampled value by a matched filter to form the pixel contribution. This value is calculated using Eq. 2, and dr is calculated using Eq. 3, as in [13].

$$e^{i\omega 2|\vec{r_k}|} = \cos(2 \cdot \omega \cdot dr) + i\sin(2 \cdot \omega \cdot dr) \tag{2}$$

$$dr = \sqrt{(x - x_k)^2 + (y - y_k)^2 + (z - z_k)^2} - r_c \tag{3}$$

5. Accumulates the contribution into the pixel. The final value of each pixel is given by Eq. 4 [13].

$$f(x,y) = \sum_k g_{x,y}(r_k, \theta_k) \cdot e^{i \cdot \omega \cdot 2|\vec{r_k}|} \tag{4}$$

Table 1 summarizes the algorithm's variables and their meaning.

Table 1. Variables and their meaning

Variable	Meaning
$g(n)$	Wave sample in the previous adjacent range bin
$g(n+1)$	Wave sample in the following adjacent range bin
$r(n)$	Corresponding range to the previous adjacent bin
$r(n+1)$	Corresponding range to the following adjacent bin
r_k	Range from pixel $f(x,y)$ to aperture point θ_k
dr	Differential range from platform to each pixel versus center of swath
x_k, y_k, z_k	Radar platform location in Cartesian coordinates
x, y, z	Pixel location in Cartesian coordinates
r_c	Range to center of the swath from radar platform
$f(x,y)$	Value of each pixel (x,y)
θ_k	Aperture point
r_k	Range from pixel $f(x,y)$ to aperture point θ_k
ω	Minimal angular velocity of wave
$g_{x,y}(r_k, \theta_k)$	Wave reflection received at r_k at θ_k

Algorithm 1.1. BackProjection algorithm pseudocode.
Source: PERFECT Manual Suite [1].

```
1: for all pixels k do
2:      f_k ← 0
3:      for all pulses p do
4:          R ← ||a_k − v_p||
5:          b ← ⌊(R − R0)/ΔR⌋
6:          if b ∈ [0, N_bp − 2] then
7:              w ← ⌊(R − R0)/ΔR⌋ − b
8:              s ← (1 − w)·g(p,b) + w·g(p,b+1)
9:              f_k ← f_k + e^{i·k_u·R}
10:         end if
11:     end for
12: end for
```

The pseudocode to compute the aforementioned steps is shown in Algorithm 1.1. k_u represents the wave number and is given by $\frac{2\pi f_c}{c}$, where f_c is the carrier frequency of the waveform and c is the speed of light, a_k refers to the position of the pixel, and v_p, corresponds to the platform position.

The BackProjection algorithm implementation used in this study was taken from the PERFECT Suite [1] and is written in C. This suite also contains three input image sets: small, medium and large, which produce images of sizes 512×512, 1024×1024 and 2048×2048 pixels, respectively.

2.3   SAR Image Quality Assessment

The metric used to evaluate the quality of a SAR image is the Signal-To-Noise Ratio (SNR). The SNR measures the difference between the desired signal and the background noise, see Eq. 5. The larger the SNR value, the greater the agreement between the pixel values. Values above 100 dB are considered reasonable [1].

$$SNR_{dB} = 10\log_{10}\left(\frac{\sum_{k=1}^{N}|r_k|^2}{\sum_{k=1}^{N}|r_k - t_k|^2}\right) \tag{5}$$

- r_k - Reference value for k-th pixel.
- t_k - Test value for k-th pixel.
- N - Number of pixel to compare.

2.4   Fault-Tolerant SAR Image Generation

Precise fault-tolerant mechanisms consist of repetitions of the same operations in one or more units and evaluate which is the most voted result, regarding it as the correct one. The most common one is Triple Modular Redundancy (TMR) and consists of having three entities calculating the same value and have a voter entity compare the results. The most common output value is assumed to be the correct one. This mechanism is explained in [8,10]. In the aforementioned mechanism more than twice the power is consumed, and a latency overhead is always required.

Fault-tolerant versions of SAR image generation algorithms are presented in [8,10,19]. [10] proposes a fault tolerance mechanism for the Fast-Fourier Transformer (FFT) algorithm based on range and azimuth compression by implementing Concurrent Error Detection (CED) and using weighted sum, and also implements scrubbing. [19] also presents a mechanism for FFT algorithm based on a weighted checksum encoding scheme. [8] describes a Fault-Management Unit which is responsible for the following functions: a scrub controller to periodically reload the FPGA configurations data, a fault detection circuit to periodically test the hardware, a switching circuit responsible for removing a faulty processor and replace it by an alternative processor, and a majority voter circuit, which is responsible for comparing the results of a TMR mechanism used during the SAR algorithm execution.

2.5   Approximate Computing Fault Tolerance

If small variations in the computation of image processing algorithms are introduced, they may not be perceptible at all. Therefore, such algorithms allow some deviations from the correct value while still having valid images. In this context, this paper proposes a novel fault-tolerance mechanism which relies on approximations of the computations when in the presence of errors.

Reduced-Precision Redundancy (RPR) is used to reduce the overhead introduced by TMR by using a full-precision computation and two reduced-precision

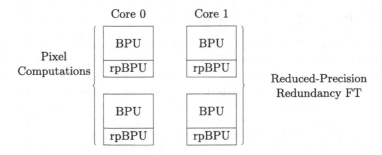

Fig. 2. Workload distribution of the developed fault tolerance mechanism between the CPU cores.

computations. RPR can be implemented in hardware, following an architecture similar to TMR, or software, following an architecture similar to temporal redundancy. The full-precision computation corresponds to the "original computation" and the other two computations to approximations. Computing the approximations reducing the overhead of the redundant computations, hence it is more efficient than calculating a full-precision values. However, the overhead of the voting process is kept constant. Examples of applications that use RPR are [12,17].

In [4], the authors proposed a mechanism for Single Event Upset (SEU) mitigation, which relies only on the comparison of the full-precision result against only one approximation, obtained from a Look-Up Table (LUT). Due to the lack of precision, only the Most Significant Bits (MSbs) are compared. It they are equal, the full-precision result is passed to the output of the arithmetic units, otherwise, the approximate result is used. While it is not possible to determine which unit is the acting as the faulty one, the full-precision computation is always more prone to error than the reduced one.

3   Dual-Core Fault-Tolerant SAR Imaging Architecture

3.1   Proposed Architecture

In the BackProjection algorithm, the pixel computations are the most intensive set of computations.

The calculation of each pixel, or Backprojection Unit (BPU), is done in parallel, which means each core computes one pixel at a time. For this reason, it is protected by RPR, reducing the total overhead in the system. A scheme of the architecture of the fault tolerance mechanism is displayed in Fig. 2, where it is possible to observe which parts of the Backprojection (BP) algorithm are protected. The approximations are calculated after the full-precision computations. The approximation computation and the error detection are represented in Fig. 2 as Reduced-Precision Backprojection Units (rpBPUs).

Table 2. Dual-core execution times in function of the number of pixels per batch. The longer execution per batch number is displayed in bold in the table.

	Original	Pixels in batch			
		4	8	16	32
Core 0	—	**240.4 s**	**240.6 s**	**241.5 s**	**241.7 s**
Core 1	—	239.9 s	239.3 s	241.0 s	239.4 s
Total	477.4 s	480.3 s	479.9 s	482.6 s	480.4 s

3.2 Algorithm Parallelization

In this algorithm, the pixel computations have no dependencies, therefore, they can be computed in parallel. The workload was divided between the cores statically since dynamic load-balancing introduces overhead in the system. The results of this test are presented in Table 2, where the execution time is presented in function of the number of pixels per batch. The tested number of pixels per batch was 4, 8, 16 and 32.

From Table 2 it is possible to conclude that the number of BPUs per batch does not have a significant influence on the total execution time since it is smaller or equal than 1%. It is also possible to observe that the workload is relatively balanced, since there are not any accentuated differences in the execution times of each core. This leads to conclude that dynamic load-balancing is not necessary and that the batch number is also indifferent. The final chosen number of units per batch was 4, since it resulted in a similar execution time on both cores.

3.3 Modified Reduced-Precision Redundancy

This work uses a modified version of the RPR mechanism, which computes only one approximation (rpBPU) after computing the full precision result (BPU) to perform the comparison. The architecture of the modified RPR mechanism is presented in Fig. 3.

Both full-precision and reduced-precision values are compared by computing their difference. If the difference is greater than an acceptable threshold (T) from the reduced-precision value, it is assumed the value is incorrect and the reduced-precision value is used instead. If not, the full-precision result is assumed correct and is used. The reduced-precision value is copied to the output when an error is detected because it is calculated in a shorter amount of time, and thus it is less likely to have been affected by a fault. The reduced-precision values are calculated using the aforementioned optimizations.

3.4 Algorithm Profiling

To produce a reduced computation of the BPU it was necessary to profile the source code to determine which were the most time consuming operations.

Moreover, the operations that last longer are the ones that are more prone to be subjected to error. In future work, this profiling will also be important to determine which operations to port into a hardware accelerator.

For profiling, the software implementation of the BackProjection algorithm ran on the target device, Zynq FPGA from Xilinx, with the small image as input. It took approximately 8 min to generate this image, using the o3[1] optimization level. Other image sizes required processing times greater than 156 min. The implementation of the algorithm was profiled using **gprof**[2]. Table 3 shows the percentage of time dedicated to the most time consuming instructions in the BackProjection algorithm.

Table 3. BackProjection algorithm profiling.

Operation	Execution time (%)
Sine	42.05
Cosine	42.54
Others	15.41

The trigonometric functions are responsible for over 80% of the execution time of the algorithm, which means that the potential for the reduced-precision redundancy mechanism lies within these functions. The rest of the algorithm, including input and output operations, is executed in under 16% of the time.

3.5   Trigonometric Functions Optimization

The optimizations for the trigonometric functions tested are described below and the results are presented in Table 4.

- COordinate Rotation DIgital Computer (CORDIC) algorithm [18];
- Taylor Series;
- Wilhem's LUT[3];

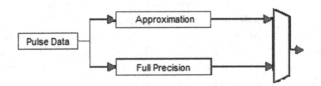

Fig. 3. The architecture of the modified RPR fault-tolerance mechanism.

[1] https://gcc.gnu.org/onlinedocs/gcc/Optimize-Options.html.
[2] https://ftp.gnu.org/old-gnu/Manuals/gprof-2.9.1/html_mono/gprof.html.
[3] https://www.atwillys.de/content/cc/sine-lookup-for-embedded-in-c/.

Table 4. Comparison of the results produced by different optimization algorithms for the trigonometric functions.

Design	Variation	Time [s]	SNR [dB]
Baseline		477.4	138.9
CORDIC	10 iterations	238.8	60.5
	15 iterations	262.7	90.5
	20 iterations	286.3	120.2
	25 iterations	311.3	136.1
	30 iterations	335.1	136.3
Taylor Series	4 terms	186.0	71.8
	5 terms	192.3	103.8
	6 terms	201.5	133.6
	7 terms	210.4	135.3
Wilhem's Look-Up Table	n/a	123.2	69.1
Libfixmath	Taylor I	179.3	54.5
	Taylor II	158.8	33.6
	LUT	134.8	99.2
Ganssle	3 coefficients	163.5	66.3
	4 coefficients	167.3	105.2
	5 coefficients	170.7	118.3
	7 coefficients	176.5	134.8
	7 coefficients	179.8	135.3

- libfixmath[4];
- Ganssle optimizations [9].

Observing the results on Table 4, the following conclusions can be drawn. All optimizations are indeed faster than the original version, which was expected. However, most of these optimizations lead to a large precision loss.

The implementation of the CORDIC algorithm used to test was developed by John Burkardt[5]. CORDIC is the algorithm with the worst performance, with all its tested versions being slower than any other version of another algorithm.

The results obtained from the Taylor Series algorithm were outperformed by the Ganssle methods, both in SNR and execution time.

The Wilhem's Look-Up Table method was the fastest overall and outperformed some variations of the other algorithms. It is a good alternative in systems with very limited memory since the LUT table occupies 66 bytes only, however, if memory does not represent an issue, the libfixmath library is a better alternative.

---

[4] https://github.com/PetteriAimonen/libfixmath.
[5] https://people.sc.fsu.edu/~jburkardt/c_src/cordic/cordic.html.

Besides the LUT variation, `libfixmath` provides two functions based on Taylor Series. These two variations are outperformed by the Ganssle optimizations and even the author's Taylor Series implementation, with worse performance and less precision. `libfixmath` LUT variation is one of the best options for the BackProjection optimization.

The Ganssle optimizations are a good alternative to replace the trigonometric functions in the BackProjection algorithm. The first variation, the one that uses 3 coefficients to calculate the final result, is outperformed by both the LUT methods. Nevertheless, the other variations provide higher precision without a significant increase in the execution time. There are two functions that vary only in the type of variables they use: single precision or double precision. Double precision is more subject to errors since it requires more bitwise calculations and the gain in precision is not significant to the point of being worth computing them in prone to error environments. The 4-coefficient variation does not provide much more precision when compared to the `libfixmath` LUT function and the execution time increases by more than 30 s, making the former a better alternative. The 5-coefficient variation provides more precision with an execution time increase of less than 36 s. The 7-coefficient (implemented with single precision) function provides a precision very similar to the original, with a difference of only less than 4 dB in the SNR, and an increase of less than 43 s.

To sum up, the functions that represent a better option for the BackProjection algorithm optimization are the `libfixmath` LUT and the Ganssle variations of 5 and 7 coefficients. These three functions are used in the implementation of the RPR mechanism.

4   Implementation Results

The research design was implemented on a Pynq-Z2 board from TUL. This board contains a Zynq XC7Z020 device from Xilinx, an external 512 MB DDR3 memory, and I/O peripherals. The Zynq device contains a Programmable Logic (PL) and a Processing System (PS). The PL corresponds to a Xilinx 7-series FPGA. The PS main components are a dual-core ARM Cortex-A9 processor and a memory controller.

4.1   Precision Optimization Evaluation

Algorithm 1.1 was implemented using three precision reduction optimizations: the `libfixmath` LUT and the 5 and 7-coefficient Ganssle trigonometric functions. The execution times of the complete architecture for each of these optimizations is presented in Table 5. As can be observed, the architecture implemented using the `libfixmath` is 1.58 times faster than the serial original version of the algorithm. Regarding the 5-coefficient Ganssle algorithm, the execution was 1.50 times faster than the original and the 7-coefficient Ganssle algorithm was 1.49 times faster than the original version. When compared to the dual-core version of the BackProjection algorithm, the final architecture using the

Table 5. Comparison between the execution times depending on the optimization.

Design	Baseline (single core)	Baseline (dual core)	Libfixmath	Ganssle 5-coef.	Ganssle 7-coef.
Exec. time [s]	477.4	240.4	301.5	317.3	319.7

Table 6. Results of RPR with Agressive Fault-Injection.

Optimization	libfixmath	5-coefficient Ganssle	7-coefficient Ganssle
#1	55.4	37.9	−62.3
#2	63.4	79.8	103.3
#3	−inf	82.1	94.7

libfixmath LUT method, the 5-coefficient and 7-coefficient Ganssle algorithms introduce an overhead of 25%, 32% and 33%, respectively.

4.2   Solution Evaluation

To test the developed architecture, a set of tests were performed. The fault injection was implemented in software and at compile-time by introducing bit-flips according to a specific distribution. Measurements performed in the L2 space were reported in[6] and on average there is one SEU per day. However, other locations in space induce more bit-flips.

Regarding the Reduced-Precision Redundancy mechanism, the objective was to observe the final quality of the generated images, using the SNR, in the presence of faults. To test the this mechanism, the following tests were implemented. To inject faults, a fault injection function was called after every statement and a bit-flip could or not affect the last modified variable. The frequency of the bit-flips depends on the test.

- **Test RPR With Aggressive Fault Injection.** The average occurrences of bit-flips in space is 1 per day. To evaluate the mechanism on a more aggressive scenario, with worse conditions, this fault injection follows a normal distribution with a mean value of 40 and a standard deviation of 5. The results of this test are presented in Table 6.
- **Test RPR With 1440, 2880 and 8640 Bit-Flips per Day.** Considering the average of bit-flips, a worse-case scenario was tested: an average of 1440 bit-flips per day, or one every 60, 30 and 10 s, respectively. The bit-flip affects a random bit in a random variable. The results of this test are presented in Table 7.

Each of the RPR tests was executed three times for each of the optimizations implemented: libfixmath, 5-coefficient and 7-coefficient Ganssle algorithms.

---

[6] http://herschel.esac.esa.int/Docs/Herschel/html/ch04s02.html.

Table 7. Results of RPR with 1440, 2880, and 8640 bit-flips per day.

		Optimization			
		`libfixmath`	5-coefficient Ganssle	7-coefficient Ganssle	
1440	#1	138.9 dB	138.8 dB	19.9 dB
	#2	138.6 dB	138.5 dB	134.8 dB
	#3	138.8 dB	138.8 dB	138.8 dB
2880	#1	97.8 dB	67.9 dB	109.9 dB
	#2	8.3 dB	129.1 dB	34.4 dB
	#3	90.3 dB	101.1 dB	83.3 dB

5   Discussion

The overall results for the executions with injection of 1440 bit-flips were close
to the original SNR value of the image, except the first execution of the 7-
coefficient Ganssle algorithm. The other iterations deviated from the original
value a maximum of 4.1 dB and an average of 0.65 dB, when in the presence
of errors. The low SNR value of the first iteration of the 7-coefficient Ganssle
algorithm is justified by the fault injection in random variables. Certain variables
are more critical than others, for example, the final result of the approximation
has a greater impact on the final image quality.

Most of the results for very aggressive error rates were not considered acceptable, since the SNR values are inferior to 100 dB. Two iterations, the third of
`libfixmath` and the first of the 7-coefficient Ganssle algorithm were either minus
infinite or a negative value, which generate a blank image.

The overall SNR values obtained for 2880 bit-flips are inferior when compared
to the results of 1440 bit-flips, which was expected since the rate of bit-flips
doubled. The 5-coefficient Ganssle algorithm provided the best results of this
test: two out of three SNR values are considered acceptable and the other has a
SNR almost half of the original value. The results obtained using the 7-coefficient
Ganssle algorithm generate one acceptable image. For this test, the optimization
which provided the best results was the 5-coefficient Ganssle algorithm.

The rate of 8640 bit-flips represents a fault injection of 10 bit-flips per second. At this rate the proposed mechanism was not successful at detecting and
correcting faults. The values in the results table are **nan**, $-\infty$ or negative values,
which generate a blank image. A SNR equal to **nan** happens when a bit-flip
affects a floating-point variable and the resulting value is not considered a valid
floating-point representation. Regarding the SNR of $-\infty$, the calculation of this
metric involves a logarithm operation, which equals $-\infty$ in C when calculating
the logarithm of 0. The mechanism became ineffective due to the elevated rate
of bit-flips, leading to the conclusion the mechanism is only able to tolerate a
certain rate of faults.

6 Conclusions and Future Work

This work explored the research and development of a fault-tolerant architecture for SAR imaging systems capable of generating SAR images using the Backprojection Algorithm in a space environment.

The modified RPR mechanism proposed avoids the use of more costly mechanisms, such as TMR, while taking advantage of the dual-core processor on the Zynq device to improve performance. The main drawback of this mechanism, is the inability to detect or correct control errors.

The final architecture consists of a dual-core implementation of the Backprojection Algorithm, protected by the modified Reduced-Precision Redundancy mechanism. Depending on the optimization used, the overhead of the fault tolerance mechanism ranges from 25% to 33% when compared to the dual-core version of the Backprojection Algorithm.

In spite of the limitations of a software implementation the modified RPR mechanism, the algorithm was tested under pessimistic conditions, different from the average use scenario. Furthermore, the developed architecture with an approach of RPR was demonstrated to be a good alternative for intensive space applications. Future work involves exploring optimization techniques such as the ones described in [5–7].

References

1. Barker, K., et al.: PERFECT (Power Efficiency Revolution For Embedded Computing Technologies) Benchmark Suite Manual. Pacific Northwest National Laboratory and Georgia Tech Research Institute, December 2013. http://hpc.pnnl.gov/projects/PERFECT/
2. Baumann, R.C.: Radiation-induced soft errors in advanced semiconductor technologies. IEEE Trans. Device Mater. Reliab. **5**(3), 305–316 (2005). https://doi.org/10.1109/TDMR.2005.853449
3. Claeys, C., Simoen, E.: Radiation Effects in Advanced Semiconductor Materials and Devices. Springer, Heidelberg (2002). https://doi.org/10.1007/978-3-662-04974-7
4. Duarte, R.P., Bouganis, C.: Zero-latency datapath error correction framework for over-clocking DSP applications on FPGAs. In: 2014 International Conference on ReConFigurable Computing and FPGAs (ReConFig14), pp. 1–7, Deceember 2014. https://doi.org/10.1109/ReConFig.2014.7032566
5. Duarte, R.P., Bouganis, C.S.: High-level linear projection circuit design optimization framework for FPGAs under over-clocking. In: 2012 22nd International Conference on Field Programmable Logic and Applications (FPL), pp. 723–726. IEEE (2012)
6. Duarte, R.P., Bouganis, C.-S.: A unified framework for over-clocking linear projections on FPGAs under PVT variation. In: Goehringer, D., Santambrogio, M.D., Cardoso, J.M.P., Bertels, K. (eds.) ARC 2014. LNCS, vol. 8405, pp. 49–60. Springer, Cham (2014). https://doi.org/10.1007/978-3-319-05960-0_5
7. Duarte, R.P., Bouganis, C.S.: ARC 2014 over-clocking KLT designs on FPGAs under process, voltage, and temperature variation. ACM Trans. Reconfigurable Technol. Syst. **9**(1), 7:1–7:17 (2015). https://doi.org/10.1145/2818380

8. Fang, W.C., Le, C., Taft, S.: On-board fault-tolerant SAR processor for space-borne imaging radar systems. In: 2005 IEEE International Symposium on Circuits and Systems, vol. 1, pp. 420–423, May 2005. https://doi.org/10.1109/ISCAS.2005.1464614

9. Ganssle, J.: The Firmware Handbook. Academic Press Inc., Orlando (2004)

10. Jacobs, A., Cieslewski, G., Reardon, C., George, A.: Multiparadigm computing for space-based synthetic aperture radar (2008)

11. Maki, A.: Space radiation effect on satellites. Joho Tsushin Kenkyu Kiko Kiho **55**(1–4), 43–48 (2009)

12. Pratt, B., Fuller, M., Wirthlin, M.: Reduced-precision redundancy on FPGAs (2011). https://doi.org/10.1155/2011/897189

13. Pritsker, D.: Efficient global back-projection on an FPGA. In: 2015 IEEE Radar Conference (RadarCon), pp. 0204–0209, May 2015. https://doi.org/10.1109/RADAR.2015.7130996

14. Sinclair, D., Dyer, J.: Radiation effects and cots parts in smallsats (2013)

15. Sørensen, J., Santin, G.: The radiation environment and effects for future ESA cosmic vision missions. In: 2009 European Conference on Radiation and Its Effects on Components and Systems, pp. 356–363, September 2009. https://doi.org/10.1109/RADECS.2009.5994676

16. Tambara, L.A.: Analyzing the impact of radiation-induced failures in all programmable system-on-chip devices (2017)

17. Ullah, A., Reviriego, P., Pontarelli, S., Maestro, J.A.: Majority voting-based reduced precision redundancy adders. IEEE Trans. Device Mater. Reliab. **PP**(99), 1 (2017). https://doi.org/10.1109/TDMR.2017.2781186

18. Volder, J.: The cordic computing technique. In: Papers Presented at the 3–5 March 1959, Western Joint Computer Conference, IRE-AIEE-ACM 1959 (Western), pp. 257–261. ACM, New York (1959). https://doi.org/10.1145/1457838.1457886

19. Wang, S.J., Jha, N.K.: Algorithm-based fault tolerance for FFT networks. IEEE Trans. Comput. **43**(7), 849–854 (1994). https://doi.org/10.1109/12.293265

20. Ya'acob, N., Zainudin, A., Magdugal, R., Naim, N.F.: Mitigation of space radiation effects on satellites at low earth orbit (LEO). In: 2016 6th IEEE International Conference on Control System, Computing and Engineering (ICCSCE), pp. 56–61, November 2016. https://doi.org/10.1109/ICCSCE.2016.7893545

Optimizing CNN-Based Hyperspectral Image Classification on FPGAs

Shuanglong Liu[1](✉)(iD), Ringo S. W. Chu[2], Xiwei Wang[3], and Wayne Luk[1]

[1] Department of Computing, Imperial College London, London, UK
{s.liu13,w.luk}@imperial.ac.uk
[2] Department of Computer Science, University College London, London, UK
ringo.chu.16@ucl.ac.uk
[3] China Academy of Space Technology, Beijing, China
wangxiwei@gmail.com

Abstract. Hyperspectral image (HSI) classification has been widely adopted in remote sensing imagery analysis applications which require high classification accuracy and real-time processing speed. Convolutional neural networks (CNNs)-based methods have been proven to achieve state-of-the-art accuracy in classifying HSIs. However, CNN models are often too computationally intensive to achieve real-time response due to the high dimensional nature of HSI, compared to traditional methods such as Support Vector Machines (SVMs). Besides, previous CNN models used in HSI are not specially designed for efficient implementation on embedded devices such as FPGAs. This paper proposes a novel CNN-based algorithm for HSI classification which takes into account hardware efficiency and thus is more hardware friendly compared to prior CNN models. An optimized and customized architecture which maps the proposed algorithm on FPGA is then proposed to support real-time on-board classification with low power consumption. Implementation results show that our proposed accelerator on a Xilinx Zynq 706 FPGA board achieves more than $70\times$ faster than an Intel 8-core Xeon CPU and $3\times$ faster than an NVIDIA GeForce 1080 GPU. Compared to previous SVM-based FPGA accelerators, we achieve comparable processing speed but provide a much higher classification accuracy.

Keywords: Hyperspectral image classification · Deep learning ·
Convolution neural network · Field-programmable gate array

1 Introduction

Hyperspectral images (HSI) contain spectrum information for each pixel in the image of a scene, and can be used in finding objects and identifying materials or detecting processes [4]. Hyperspectral images are widely employed in many

---

The first two authors contributed equally.

C. Hochberger et al. (Eds.): ARC 2019, LNCS 11444, pp. 17–31, 2019.
https://doi.org/10.1007/978-3-030-17227-5_2

applications from airborne and satellite remote sensing mission [19], to oil spill detection [16], early cancer diagnosis [15] and environmental monitoring [14]. HSI classification involves assigning a categorical class label to each pixel in the image, according to the corresponding spectral and/or spatial feature [2]. With the advent of new hyperspectral remote sensing instruments and their increased temporal resolutions, the availability and dimensionality of hyperspectral data are continuously increasing [12]. This demands very fast processing solutions for on-board space platforms in order to reduce download bandwidth and storage requirements [19], making reconfigurable hardware such as FPGAs very promising to perform and accelerate HSI classification methods.

Among the approaches explored for HSI classification, convolutional neural network (CNN) based methods such as BASS Net [17] and HSI-CNN [13] are favourable over the others because of their greatly improved accuracy for some popular benchmark datasets, with the ability to use extensive parameters to learn spectral features of a HSI. However, these CNN-based algorithms have great computational complexity due to the large dimensionality of hyperspectral images. Besides, prior CNN models used in HSI classification may not be hardware efficient to be deployed on embedded systems such as FPGAs without any modifications since they are not specially designed for FPGAs.

In order to address the above challenges and achieve fast processing speed on embedded devices, this work proposes a novel CNN architecture based on BASS Net [17], and our model is more hardware efficient for implementation on FPGAs while maintaining similar accuracy as the original BASS Net. Besides, we propose and optimize the hardware architecture to accelerate our proposed network in FPGA by parallel processing, data pre-fetching and design space exploration. Compared to previous SVM-based FPGA accelerators, the proposed accelerator has almost the same scale of processing speed on the same scale of FPGA device, but provides a lot higher accuracy results.

The main contributions of this work are summarized as follows:

- A novel network for HSI classification which takes into account hardware efficiency, and thus achieves real-time on-board HSI classification with both high accuracy and fast processing speed (Sect. 3);
- A highly optimized hardware architecture which maps the proposed CNN model onto FPGAs, and it processes all the layers in on-chip memories to enable high throughput of real-time HSI applications (Sect. 4);
- Evaluation of the proposed accelerators on a Xilinx ZC706 FPGA board across four popular benchmark datasets. Our accelerator achieves an overall classification accuracy of 95.8%, 99.4%, 95.2% and 98.2% respectively which largely outperforms previous SVM-based FPGA accelerators, and it achieves around 10 to 25 us/pixel processing speed which is about 80× and 3× faster than the respective CPU and GPU designs (Sect. 5).

2   Background and Related Work

2.1   Hyperspectral Imagery

Unlike traditional RGB image, hyperspectral images are typically represented as a data cube in dimension (x, y, λ), where x and y represent spatial dimensions with space information of pixels, and λ represents the third dimension with spectral information for distinguishing different materials and objects.

Hyperspectral image (HSI) classification is the task to assign a class label to every pixel in an image. Several approaches have been explored in literature for HSI classification. K-nearest neighbors (k-NN) based methods use Eucledian distance in the input space to find the k nearest training examples and a class is assigned on the basis of them [17]. Support Vector Machine (SVM) based methods introduce dimensionality reduction in order to address the problem of high spectral dimensionality and scarcity of labeled training examples, with SVM classifiers used in the reduced dimensional space. Although these methods adopt parallel processing [19] and are suitable for FPGA-based acceleration, they often behave weakly in terms of the classification accuracy when tackling large datasets [17].

2.2   CNN-Based HSI Classification

Recently, deep learning based methods have achieved promising performance in HSI classifications [3] due to their ability to use extensive parameters to learn features. Deep learning methods [20] utilize spectral-spatial context modeling in order to address the problem of spatial variability of spectral signatures. These methods often use convolutional neural networks (CNNs) for feature learning and classification in an end-to-end fashion. CNNs adopt extensive parameter-sharing to tackle the curse of dimensionality. They extract and learn representative features via multiple times of back propagation. Using features is more effective than rule-based algorithms for recognition tasks.

One of the most popular CNN models for HSI classification is BASS Net [17]: a deep neural network architecture that learns band-specific spectral-spatial features and gives state-of-the-art performance without any kind of data-set augmentation or input pre-processing. While this algorithm leads to high classification performance due to efficient band-specific feature learning, the model is very computationally intensive, which often requires huge amount of resources and energy. Nevertheless, this network has parallelism in many computational blocks and thus can be prallelized in hardware platforms such as FPGAs. However, the BASS Net is not suitable to be deployed on embedded systems without modification. The main challenge is that the CNN architecture does not have identical layer parameters, which increases the difficulty of designing generic hardware modules that support varying parameters. For example, there are 1-D convolutional layers with different kernel sizes such as 3×1 and 5×1 implemented using spectral information and 2-D convolutional layers applied using spatial information. Fully-connected layers are also applied after all convolution layers for summarization and output classification probability. Because of these reasons, direct mapping of this algorithm to FPGAs may not be efficient and cannot satisfy the requirement of real-time processing without the proposal of algorithm adaptions and efficient hardware architecture.

2.3 Related Work

Prior work includes deploying SVM-based HSI classification on FPGA for acceleration and utilizing GPUs for algorithmic speed up on CNN-based methods. There is exhaustive literature on accelerating the traditional algorithms such as SVMs using FPGAs. Wang et al. [19] proposed a novel accelerator architecture for real-time SVM classification. The accelerator uses data flow programming to achieve high performance and can be usd for different applications. Tajiri et al. [18] proposed a hyperspectral image classification system on FPGA, by introducing the Composite Kernel Support Vector Machine and reducing the computational complexity. These former accelerators achieve real time processing speed but they do not achieve high classification accuracy and therefore are not favoured over CNN-based methods.

Recently CNN-based HSI approaches have been proposed by many researchers. Santara et al. [17] presented an end-to-end deep learning architecture that extracts band specific spectral-spatial features and performs landcover classification. Luo et al. [13] proposed a novel HSI classification model to reorganize data by using the correlation between convolution results and to splice the one-dimensional data into image-like two-dimensional data to deepen the network structure and enable the network to extract and distinguish the features better. Lee et al. [5] built a fully convolutional neural network with a total of 9 layers, which is much deeper than other convolutional networks for HSI classification. To enhance the learning efficiency of the proposed network trained on relatively sparse training samples, residual learning was used in their work. However, all of these efforts have only focused on the improvement of the accuracy of these algorithms on CPU or GPUs, the performance of their models have never been reported or considered in prior works. Therefore, it is unclear if these algorithms are suitable for on-board platforms and it is not straightforward to map them into embedded devices for real-time processing.

To the best of the authors' knowledge, this is the first work that proposes FPGA architecture for CNN-based HSI classifications. Our FPGA-based accelerator achieves high accuracy, fast processing speed and lower power consumption, which is suitable for on-board space platforms.

3   Proposed CNN-Based HSI Classification Model

Deep neural network architectures such as BASS Net are based on pixel-wise classification results of the input image. That is to say, for each pixel, the input to the network is the pixel X_i from the image with its $p \times p$ neighbourhoods (for spatial context) in the form of a $p \times p \times N_c$ volume, where N_c is the spectral bands of the dataset scene, i.e., the number of channels of the input image, and p is called the patch size. The output of the network is the predicted class label y_i for X_i. Leng et al. [6] studied different strategies to take account of neighbour pixels and extract smaller spectral cube with labelled central pixel from a HSI for training samples. These strategies are single pixel, four neighbour pixels and eight neighbour pixels, i.e., the patch size is 3, as shown in Fig. 1.

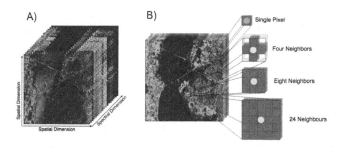

Fig. 1. (A) Hyperspectral Image cube. (B) Extraction of data cube with labeled at central pixel from a raw HSI.

3.1 Structure Description

We propose our network based on the structure of BASS-Net [17]. The motivation behind the network is that it uses significantly fewer parameters compared to other models and exhibits parallelism at inference stage. We further modify the model such that it is more efficient for FPGA implementation. The patch strategy is altered to 24 neighbours, i.e., the input patch size is 5 (see Fig. 1) to adapt our model as it performs even better on HSI classification procedures. The proposed model processes through the following three stages at both training and inference, as shown in Fig. 2.

Spectral Feature Selection and Band Partitioning. In this step, the $p \times p \times N_c$ input volume is taken as input by a 3×3 or 1×1 spatial convolution for feature selection; then the spectral dimension of the output is split into N_b bands with equal bandwidth and passed as input to the second step for parallel processing;

Spectral Feature Learning. This step applies N_b parallel networks, with one for each band: the input is first flattened to one dimension along the spatial dimensions; a 3×3 convolution filter is applied in the spectral dimension to learn spectral features; the outputs of the parallel networks are then concatenated and fed into the summarization and classification stage.

Summarization and Classification. This step summarizes the concatenated outputs of the band-specific networks of the previous stage by using a set of fully connected layers, each of which is followed by a ReLU layer. A C-way softmax layer performs the final classification by calculating the conditional probabilities of the C output classes.

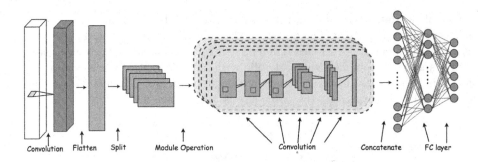

Fig. 2. Overall structure of our model architecture.

3.2 Hardware Adaptations

There are some tunable parameters in the network architecture for different design choices: the input patch size p, the number of parallel bands N_b in the second stage and the convolutional kernel in the first stage. Compared to BASS Net, three major changes are introduced for hardware efficiency and accuracy improvement:

(1) We utilized 3×3 CNN filters in stage 1 for spatial dimension learning, which amplifies spatial signatures and are identical to the convolutions in stage 2;
(2) 1-D convolutions of kernel size 3×1 and 5×1 in stage 2 are all replaced by 2-D 3×3 fixed kernel size for generic hardware module design and reuse, thus the accuracy is improved due to the increased parameters;
(3) In stage 2, the data are flattened along the spatial dimension and split into N_b segments along the spectral dimension. We choose N_b from 2, 4 or 8 for easy parallel processing in FPGA technology.

For block 1, we also apply 3×3 convolution for input patch size of $5 \times 5 \times N_c$ or 1×1 convolution for input patch size of $3 \times 3 \times N_c$. One of the strategies is chosen for different datasets in order to have a trade-off between the accuracy and processing speed.

Our final network[1] parameter configurations are summarized in Table 1, and the final choices of N_b for different datasets are described in Sect. 5.1.

3.3 Training Process

Regularization Methods. Trainable parameters are shared across each band in block 2 in order to minimize hardware resources and design space. Bands must be placed sequentially to allow back-propagation and avoid gradient vanishing problem. Dropout is applied on the fully-connected layers in block 3 to prevent over-fitting.

---

[1] https://github.com/custom-computing-ic/CNN-Based-Hyperspectral-Image-Classification.

Table 1. The proposed CNN-based HSI network with input patch size 5×5 and $N_b = 4$.

Input patch size: $5 \times 5 \times 220$ and $N_b = 4$					
Layer		Type	Input volume	Output volume	Kernel
Block 1	layer 1	3×3 conv	$5 \times 5 \times 220$	$3 \times 3 \times 220$	$3 \times 3 \times 220 \times 220$
Split into N_b bands along spectral dimension and each is run in Blcok 2					
Block 2	layer 1	3×3 conv	$9 \times 55 \times 1$	$7 \times 53 \times 2$	$3 \times 3 \times 1 \times 2$
	layer 2	3×3 conv	$7 \times 53 \times 2$	$5 \times 51 \times 4$	$3 \times 3 \times 2 \times 4$
	layer 3	3×3 conv	$5 \times 51 \times 4$	$3 \times 49 \times 4$	$3 \times 3 \times 4 \times 4$
	layer 4	3×3 conv	$3 \times 49 \times 4$	$1 \times 47 \times 4$	$3 \times 3 \times 4 \times 4$
The output of N_b Blocks concatenated					
Block 3	layer 1	Fully Connect layer	752×1	120×1	752×120
	layer 2	Fully Connect layer	120×1	9×1	120×9

Loss Functions. We employ cross-entropy loss function as error measure. The training process aims to minimise the loss value to obtain a distribution that is the best capture of the data set. Given a training dataset: $\{X_i, y_i\}_{i=1}^{N}$, the designated loss function is described as:

$$\mathcal{L}(p, \hat{p}) = -\sum_{i=1}^{N} p(x) \log \hat{p}(x) \tag{1}$$

where $p(x)$ is the probability distribution of our models, and $\hat{p}(x)$ is the actual distribution that represents the dataset.

Optimizer. We used Adaptive Moment Estimation to update kernel weights and biases with initial learning rate 0.0005, $\beta_1 = 0.9$ and $\beta_2 = 0.999$.

4   Proposed CNN-Based HSI Accelerator

4.1   Hardware Architecture

Based on our proposed network, we design the hardware architecture of the FPGA accelerator for CNN-based real-time HSI classification shown in Fig. 3. The proposed CNN accelerator design on FPGA is composed of several major components: the computation units (CONV and FC modules), on-chip buffers, external memory and control unit. The processor (PS) configures the parameters of the layers for the two computation units through the control unit. CONV and FC are the basic computation units for the CNN-based HSI classification algorithm. Due to the limitation of the on-chip memory size, the input data and weights of all the layers are stored in off-chip memories and transferred to on-chip buffers when processing each layer. All intermediate data for processing are stored in on-chip buffers to avoid frequent off-chip memory access. Therefore, the required on-chip buffers need to store at least the input and output data size of one layer, since these on-chip buffers will be reused when the next layer is processed.

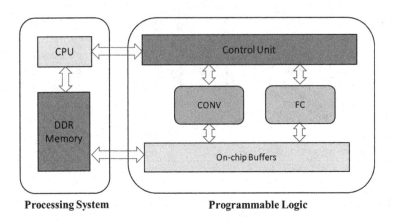

Fig. 3. The architecture of the FPGA-based CNN accelerator which integrates 2 computation units: CONV and FC.

4.2 Convolution and Fully-Connected Design

Our convolutional and fully-connected layer architectures are inspired by the design in [21]. The CONV unit contains several computational kernels running in parallel, and each kernel consists of 9 multipliers followed by an adder tree to implement the 3×3 2-D convolution operation. Multiple kernels are utilised for parallel channel and filter processing and the total number of kernels represents the parallelism of the CONV unit (P_C). Besides, we implement 1×1 convolutions in the CONV kernel by reusing the 9 multipliers and bypassing the adder trees. Therefore, the degree of parallelism of 1×1 CONV is 9 times of P_C.

The operation of the FC kernel is to perform dot product between the reshaped input feature vector and the weight matrix. The FC kernel also contains several multipliers to calculate the dot product between each row of the weight matrix and the feature vector in parallel. The number of multipliers in the FC kernel represents the parallelism of the FC unit (P_F).

4.3 Optimizations

In this section, we describe the optimization techniques used for the FPGA-based HSI accelerator design in order to increase the system throughput. The optimizations to the FPGA-based accelerator mainly focus on: (1) fully utilising the existing hardware resource to reduce the computation time by parallel processing [8], and (2) increasing the data reuse to reduce the communication time to off-chip memories [7].

Data Pre-fetching and Pipelining. We adopt the parallel processing of multiple data and filters inside the CONV and FC kernel to increase the data reuse and reduce computation overhead. However, there is another overhead involving the transfer of the weights from DDR memory to the computational units. These weights actually do not need to be stored in on-chip buffers as they are only used once which is different from input data. To reduce this overhead, weights are pre-fetched before processing in order to overlap weight transfer time and computation. Figure 4 shows the timing of several computation and weight transfer phases.

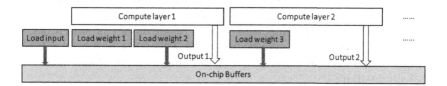

Fig. 4. Computation and weights transfer flows.

To compute the first layer, we first load input data and weights of layer 1 and 2 from DDR memory to on-chip buffers. At the same time, the computation of layer 1 can start as soon as the weights of layer 1 are valid since the input data are already in on-chip buffers; after the computation of layer 1, the output of layer 1 has already been stored in the on-chip buffers and the weights of layer 2 have loaded to the memories, so we can process layer 2 immediately after finishing layer 1 and at the same time we load the weights for the next stage, i.e., layer 3. As a result, the total execution time only needs to cover the transfer of the input and the final output, and the computational time. All the weight transfer time is overlapped in the computation stage, and there is no waiting time between computations of two consecutive layers.

Data Quantization. The main benefit of accelerating CNN models in FPGAs comes from the fact that CNNs are robust to low bitwidth quantization [11]. Instead of using the default double or single floating point precision in CPU, fixed-point precision can be used in FPGA-based CNN accelerator to achieve an efficient design optimized for performance and power efficiency [9,10]. In this work, we implement our proposed design with 16 bit fixed-point which has been shown to achieve almost the same accuracy as floating point in the inference stage, in order to allow optimizations for high parallelism mentioned in the above section. It should be noted that there is no significant accuracy loss in the HSI classification result when reducing the precision from 32-bit floating point to 16-bit fixed-point quantized version for the inference process, as long as the training stage adopts 32-bit floating point.

Design Parameter Tuning. We tune the hardware design parameters of the accelerator mentioned above based on the network input size and structure, in order to fully utilize the computation resources (DSPs) and achieve the optimal performance for the proposed CNN accelerator. This process involves adjusting the computational resource allocations, i.e., P_C and P_F between the CONV unit and FC unit to achieve minimal computation time.

This step in essence covers design space exploration (DSE). The design parameters used in the network and the hardware accelerator are summarized in Table 2. In our approach, we first adjust the network parameters in the training stage to verify the accuracy results. Then for a given set of network parameters, we develop a tool with the Nonlinear programming solver *fmincon* in Matlab Optimization Toolbox to automatically generate the optimal hardware design parameters in terms of the processing speed. Based on our approach, we can easily extend our network to support different HSI datasets and achieve the corresponding optimal speed. Therefore, it largely improves the design quality and designer productivity.

Table 2. Network and hardware accelerator parameters for design space exploration.

Data-set variables	
C	Number of classes in the HSI dataset
N_c	Spectral bands or input volume channels
Tunable network design parameters	
N_b	Number of split band in Block 2
ps	Input patch size
Tuable hardware design parameters	
P_C	Parallelism of CONV unit
P_F	Parallelism of FC unit

5   Evaluation

In this section, the accuracy of our proposed network is compared to other CNN-based algorithms and some traditional methods. The performance of our accelerator is also compared to prior FPGA-based accelerators.

5.1   Benchmarks

Four benchmark datasets[2] are used to evaluate our proposed model and accelerator. These include Indian Pines scene, Salinas scene, Kennedy Space Centre (KSC) scene and Botswana scene. The first three datasets were acquired by the

---

[2] These datasets can be obtained from http://www.ehu.eus/ccwintco/index.php?title=Hyperspectral_Remote_Sensing_Scenes.

NASA Airborne Visible Infra-Red Imaging Spectrometer (AVIRIS) across Indiana, California, Florida, and the Botswana dataset was acquired by the NASA EO-1 satellite over Botswana. The spectral bands used for these datasets after removing bands covering the region of water absorption are 220, 224, 176 and 144 respectively. The classes and spectral bands of each dataset are summarized in Table 3. Some classes are dropped during training due to limited samples. We randomly select 15% as training samples, 5% as validation samples and the reminder as testing samples. The network parameter configurations after tunning in the training stage are also summarized in Table 3.

Table 3. Dataset variables and their corresponding network configurations.

Dataset	Classes	Spectral bands (N_c)	Block 1	N_b	Patch size
Indian Pines	11	220	1×1	4	3×3
Salinas	16	224	1×1	8	3×3
KSC	13	176	3×3	8	5×5
Botswana	14	144	3×3	8	5×5

5.2   Experiment Setup

The proposed accelerator is developed using Verilog HDL. The hardware system is built on Xilinx Zynq ZC706 board which consists of a Xilinx XC7Z045 FPGA, dual ARM Cortex-A9 Processor and 1 GB DDR3 memory. The whole system is implemented with Vivado Design Suite. The ARM processor in the Zynq device is used to initialize the accelerator, set the layer parameters and transfer the weights of each layer. All designs run on a single 250 MHz clock frequency.

For comparison, the respective software implementations run on CPU and GPU are using the deep learning software framework Tensorflow [1] in CentOS 7.2 operating system. The CPU platform is Intel Core Xeon 4110 CPU@2.10 GHz with 8 cores. The GPU platform is NVIDIA GeForce 1080 (Pascal) with 2560 CUDA cores and 8 GB GDDR5 256-bit memory).

5.3   Classification Accuracy

We first evaluate the overall accuracy (OA) of the proposed accelerator for the four benchmark datasets. Here the average per-class accuracy is omitted for each datasets due to lack of space. Table 4 shows the results of the comparison of the proposed framework with other traditional and deep learning based methods. From the table, we can see that our proposed network achieves nearly the same accuracy compared to BASS Net and even better overall accuracy for the Botswana dataset. It is not surprising that our proposed framework outperforms all the other traditional methods (k-NN and SVM) on all the evaluated four data sets in terms of accuracy.

Table 4. Classification accuracy (%) comparison of the proposed network and other methods on the benchmark datasets.

OA (%)	k-NN	SVM	BASS Net	Proposed
Indian Pines	76.4	89.8	96.7	95.8
Salinas	86.3	93.1	98.9	98.9
KSC	79.5	89.1	95.3	95.2
Botswana	81.6	85.4	98.1	98.7

5.4   Resource Utilization

Table 5 shows the resource utilization (LUTs, FFs, DSPs, etc.) of our proposed accelerator when implemented in the target Zynq device. The implemented accelerator contains 64 CONV kernels and 256 FC kernels, i.e., $P_C = 64$ and $P_F = 256$. From Table 5, we can see that the computational resource, i.e., DSPs are almost fully utilized and the allocation is balanced between the CONV and FC modules. The on-chip memories are sufficient to store the total amount of input data and output data, since the intermediate data size is relatively small for the proposed network (see Table 1). This is because the CNN-based HSI method is doing pixel-wise processing and we can process each pixel in on-chip buffers.

Table 5. FPGA resource utilization of the accelerator.

Resources	LUTs	FFs	DSPs	BRAMs
Used	46866	108991	832	210
Total	218600	437200	900	545
Utilization	21.4%	24.9%	92.4%	38.5%

5.5   Performance Comparison vs. Other Processors and Accelerators

We then compare the performance of our FPGA-based accelerator in FPGA platform with other platforms (CPUs and GPUs). The CuDNN libraries and batch processing are used for optimizing the GPU solution, and the compilation flag -Ofast is activated for the CPU implementation. The results are shown in Table 6. As a reference, we also show the execution time of BASS Net in CPU and GPU. The BASS Net is not implemented in FPGA platforms due to the reasons mentioned in Sect. 2.2. Our accelerator achieves the processing speed of 25.2, 26, 16.4 and 11.2 us/pixel respectively for the four datasets. Compared to the GPU, the average speedup is about 3 times. Compared to the CPU, we achieve more than 70× speedup. It should be noted that CPUs and GPUs are not realistic to be mount on a satellite or a drone because of their high power consumption, and therefore their usability is very limited in space platforms.

Table 6. Speedup of our proposed accelerators vs. CPUs and GPUs.

Execution time (us/pixel)		CPU	GPU	FPGA
Indian Pines	BASS	1166	123	-
	Ours	2180	99.6	25.2
	Speedup*	86.5x	3.9x	1x
Salinas	BASS	1170	100.6	-
	Ours	2026	102	26
	Speedup*	78x	3.9x	1x
KSC	BASS	723	49.6	-
	Ours	1511	46.4	16.4
	Speedup*	92x	2.8x	1x
Botswana	BASS	808	53.5	-
	Ours	978	37.7	11.2
	Speedup*	87x	3.4x	1x

* The numbers in this row represent the speedups of our model run in FPGA platform compared to that run in CPU and GPU platforms.

Finally we compare our accelerator to other FPGA-based accelerators implementing SVM [18,19]. These two accelerator are implemented in an Altera Stratix V 5SGSMD8N2F45C2 FPGA on Maxeler MAX4 DFE [19], and in a Xilinx Kintex-7 XC7K325T-FF2-900 FPGA device [18] respectively. Due to these accelerators have different DSP numbers compared to ours, we also provide the speedups normalized by the number of DSPs. The results are shown in Table 7.

Table 7. Accuracy, Speed and Power consumption of our accelerator vs. other FPGA accelerators implemented based on SVM methods.

	Accuracy (%)	Speed			Power (W)
		Mpixels/s	Kpixels/s/DSP	#DSP	
SVM DFE [19]	85.4	1.01	0.6	1680	26.3
SVM Kintex-7 [18]	81.3	0.65	0.7	840	4.25[a]
Ours	98.7	0.09	0.1	900	9.0[b]

[a]This is the power consumption reported in [18].
[b]The power consumption of ours is measured from the board using a power meter.

Compared to the SVM-based accelerators, our accelerator is based on CNN model and therefore is much more computationally intensive due to the large complexity of the network in order for accuracy improvement. This is exactly the motivation that we accelerate the CNN-based HSI models on FPGA platforms. Nevertheless, our accelerator still achieves the same scale of speed in terms of both pixel per second and pixel per second per DSP. Besides, our accelerator has much less power consumption than the accelerator in [19]. Therefore, our proposed accelerator is more promising for embedded HSI applications with high accuracy and low power consumption requirement and on-board platforms.

6   Conclusion

This work proposes a hardware accelerator for CNN-based HSI applications on FPGA platforms. We first adapt the state-of-the-art BASS Net for hardware efficiency and accuracy improvement. Then we propose a hardware architecture to accelerate our proposed network to achieve real-time processing speed. Hardware optimization techniques are applied to customize and optimize our accelerator together with design space exploration. Experimental results based on public datasets show that our accelerator achieves notable accuracy improvement compared to previous SVM-based FPGA accelerators, and significant speedup compared to the respective implementation of our CNN model on CPUs and GPUs. Future work includes extending the network with other types of layers such as depth-wise convolution for enhancing accuracy and performance, and developing automatic tools to generate hardware designs for HSI applications.

Acknowledgement. The support of the UK EPSRC (EP/I012036/1, EP/L00058X/ 1, EP/L016796/1 and EP/N031768/1), the European Union Horizon 2020 Research and Innovation Programme under grant agreement number 671653, Altera, Corerain, Intel, Maxeler, SGIIT, and the China Scholarship Council is gratefully acknowledged.

References

1. Abadi, M., et al.: TensorFlow: large-scale machine learning on heterogeneous systems (2015). https://www.tensorflow.org/
2. Bioucas-Dias, J.M., et al.: Hyperspectral remote sensing data analysis and future challenges. IEEE Geosci. Remote Sens. Mag. **1**(2), 6–36 (2013)
3. Chen, Y., Lin, Z., Zhao, X., Wang, G., Gu, Y.: Deep learning-based classification of hyperspectral data. IEEE J. Sel. Top. Appl. Earth Obs. Remote Sens. **7**(6), 2094–2107 (2014)
4. Grahn, H., Geladi, P.: Techniques and Applications of Hyperspectral Image Analysis. Wiley, Hoboken (2007)
5. Lee, H., Kwon, H.: Going deeper with contextual CNN for hyperspectral image classification. IEEE Trans. Image Process. **26**(10), 4843–4855 (2017)
6. Leng, J., et al.: Cube-CNN-SVM: a novel hyperspectral image classification method. In: 2016 IEEE 28th International Conference on Tools with Artificial Intelligence (ICTAI), pp. 1027–1034 (2016)
7. Liu, S., Bouganis, C.S.: Communication-aware MCMC method for big data applications on FPGAs. In: IEEE International Symposium on Field-Programmable Custom Computing Machines (FCCM), pp. 9–16 (2017)
8. Liu, S., Mingas, G., Bouganis, C.S.: Parallel resampling for particle filters on FPGAs. In: IEEE International Conference on Field-Programmable Technology (FPT), pp. 191–198 (2014)
9. Liu, S., Mingas, G., Bouganis, C.S.: An exact MCMC accelerator under custom precision regimes. In: IEEE International Conference on Field Programmable Technology (FPT), pp. 120–127 (2015)
10. Liu, S., Mingas, G., Bouganis, C.S.: An unbiased mcmc FPGA-based accelerator in the land of custom precision arithmetic. IEEE Trans. Comput. **66**(5), 745–758 (2017)

11. Liu, S., et al.: Optimizing CNN-based segmentation with deeply customized convolutional and deconvolutional architectures on FPGA. ACM Trans. Reconfigurable Technol. Syst. (TRETS) **11**, 19 (2018)
12. Lopez, S., et al.: The promise of reconfigurable computing for hyperspectral imaging onboard systems: a review and trends. Proc. IEEE **101**(3), 698–722 (2013)
13. Luo, Y., et al.: HSI-CNN: a novel convolution neural network for hyperspectral image. In: 2018 International Conference on Audio, Language and Image Processing (ICALIP), pp. 464–469. IEEE (2018)
14. Martin, M.E., et al.: Development of an advanced hyperspectral imaging (HSI) system with applications for cancer detection. Ann. Biomed. Eng. **34**(6), 1061–1068 (2006)
15. Martin, M.E., Wabuyele, M.B., et al.: Development of an advanced hyperspectral imaging (HSI) system with applications for cancer detection. Ann. Biomed. Eng. **34**(6), 1061–1068 (2006). https://doi.org/10.1007/s10439-006-9121-9
16. Salem, F., et al.: Hyperspectral image analysis for oil spill detection. In: Summaries of NASA/JPL Airborne Earth Science Workshop, Pasadena, CA, pp. 5–9 (2001)
17. Santara, A., et al.: BASS net: band-adaptive spectral-spatial feature learning neural network for hyperspectral image classification. IEEE Trans. Geosci. Remote Sens. **55**(9), 5293–5301 (2017)
18. Tajiri, K., Maruyama, T.: FPGA acceleration of a supervised learning method for hyperspectral image classification. In: 2018 International Conference on Field-Programmable Technology (FPT). IEEE (2018)
19. Wang, S., Niu, X., Ma, N., Luk, W., Leong, P., Peng, Y.: A scalable dataflow accelerator for real time onboard hyperspectral image classification. In: Bonato, V., Bouganis, C., Gorgon, M. (eds.) ARC 2016. LNCS, vol. 9625, pp. 105–116. Springer, Cham (2016). https://doi.org/10.1007/978-3-319-30481-6_9
20. Zhang, L., Zhang, L., Du, B.: Deep learning for remote sensing data: a technical tutorial on the state of the art. IEEE Geosci. Remote Sens. Mag. **4**(2), 22–40 (2016)
21. Zhao, R., Niu, X., Wu, Y., Luk, W., Liu, Q.: Optimizing CNN-based object detection algorithms on embedded FPGA platforms. In: Wong, S., Beck, A.C., Bertels, K., Carro, L. (eds.) ARC 2017. LNCS, vol. 10216, pp. 255–267. Springer, Cham (2017). https://doi.org/10.1007/978-3-319-56258-2_22

Supporting Columnar In-memory Formats on FPGA: The Hardware Design of Fletcher for Apache Arrow

Johan Peltenburg[1]([⊠]), Jeroen van Straten[1], Matthijs Brobbel[1], H. Peter Hofstee[2], and Zaid Al-Ars[1]

[1] Delft University of Technology, Mekelweg 4, 2628 CD Delft, The Netherlands
j.w.peltenburg@tudelft.nl
[2] IBM Research, 11500 Burnet Road, Austin, TX 78758, USA

Abstract. As a columnar in-memory format, Apache Arrow has seen increased interest from the data analytics community. Fletcher is a framework that generates hardware interfaces based on this format, to be used in FPGA accelerators. This allows efficient integration of FPGA accelerators with various high-level software languages, while providing an easy-to-use hardware interface for the FPGA developer. The abstract descriptions of data sets stored in the Arrow format, that form the input of the interface generation step, can be complex. To generate efficient interfaces from it is challenging. In this paper, we introduce the hardware components of Fletcher that help solve this challenge. These components allow FPGA developers to express access to complex Arrow data records through row indices of tabular data sets, rather than through byte addresses. The data records are delivered as streams of the same abstract types as found in the data set, rather than as memory bus words. The generated interfaces allow for full system bandwidth to be utilized and have a low area profile. All components are open sourced and available for other researchers and developers to use in their projects.

Keywords: FPGA · Apache Arrow · Fletcher

1 Introduction

The domain of data analytics is becoming increasingly mature. Various solutions for e.g. scalable computing on large distributed data sets, easy to use data structuring interfaces, storage and visualization exist (e.g. respectively Spark [12], Pandas [3], Parquet [10], etc.). At the same time, the demand to process this data in a more efficient manner increases as well. To overcome limitations with serialization bottlenecks for heterogeneous software systems, an Apache project named Arrow [9] was launched to provide a common in-memory format for big

This work has been supported by the Fitoptivis European ECSEL project no. ECSEL2017-1-737451.

C. Hochberger et al. (Eds.): ARC 2019, LNCS 11444, pp. 32–47, 2019.
https://doi.org/10.1007/978-3-030-17227-5_3

data. The project provides libraries for (at the time of writing) 11 different languages to consume or produce data sets in the common in-memory format. This alleviates the need to serialize data stored as language-native run-time objects when performing inter-process communication between application components running in different language run-times. Zero-copy inter-process communication is made possible through the common data layer that is offered by Arrow.

FPGA accelerators may also benefit from this format. The no-serialization advantage has been exploited in an open-source, hardware-agnostic FPGA acceleration framework called Fletcher [6]. The goal of the project is to generate interfaces based on Arrow meta-data called *schemas* that provide an abstract description of the type of data in a tabular data set. Because the in-memory representation follows from the schema, an interface can be generated based on the schema that fetches the data based on a table index rather than a byte address, delivering exactly the data object expressed through the schema, rather than a bus word. This increases the programmability for the hardware developer - they can focus on the accelerator implementation rather than spending time on the platform specific interface and host-side software to shape data into a format useful for the accelerator.

In this paper we describe the internals of the hardware solution of Fletcher to support a set of common Arrow data types. This is challenging because on the one hand, schemas can widely vary, and on the other hand, platform specific interfaces can widely vary. Section 2 introduces the background. Next, we list some requirements for the hardware components of Fletcher in Sect. 3. The main contributions of this work can be found in Sects. 4 and 5. A vendor-agnostic hardware library that is used in Fletcher is introduced in Sect. 4. Section 5 shows how the components from the library are combined into designs that can read from Arrow data sets through a host-memory interface and reshape the data into a format desired by the schema. Functionality and performance for a large variety of schemas are verified in Sect. 6.

Related work not discussed throughout the paper is discussed in Sect. 7. We conclude this paper in Sect. 8.

2   Background

2.1   Problem Definition

To explain why the use of Arrow with FPGA accelerators is relevant, consider an example use-case of matching regular expressions to a column of UTF8-strings (a common operation performed on strings that are stored in databases or event logs). Evaluating regular expressions in hardware is known to be efficient and streamable with state-of-the-art work shows a throughput of 25.6 GB/s [7]. This significantly exceeds the available interface bandwidth (e.g. 8 GB/s for PCIe Gen3 x8).

However, to attach such an FPGA accelerator to a high-level language, language native strings need to be serialized to a usable format. The throughput of serializing approximately 1 GiB data set of language native strings in C++,

Table 1. Serialization throughput of various language run-times of 1 GiB of strings

Throughput (GB/s)	Language		
	C++ (gcc)	Java (OpenJDK)	Python (CPython 3.6)
Xeon E5-2686	0.55	0.83	0.27
POWER9 Lagrange	0.81	0.81	0.16

Java and Python in software on an Intel Xeon machine and an IBM POWER9 machine are shown in Table 1. From this table, it can be seen that the serialization throughput of language-native string objects to a usable format in FPGA is not in the same order of magnitude as host-to-accelerator bandwidth.

Using Fletcher framework for FPGAs allows exploiting the more efficient in-memory format of Arrow and allows large data sets to be streamed-in at system bandwidth. Fletcher is operational on two major FPGA platforms meant for data-center and cloud applications; the OpenPOWER CAPI [8] SNAP framework [4] and the Amazon Web Services (AWS) EC2 F1 instances [1].

2.2 Apache Arrow

Arrow data sets are typically tabular and stored in an abstraction called a RecordBatch. A RecordBatch contains several columns for each field of a record, that are in Arrow called *arrays*. These arrays can hold all sorts of data types, from strings to lists of integers, to lists of lists of time-stamps, and others. Arrays consist of several Arrow contiguous *buffers*, that are related, to store the data of a specific type. There are several types of buffers. In this work we consider *validity* buffers, *value* buffers and *offset* buffers.

Validity buffers store a single bit to signify if a record (or deeper nested) element is valid or *null* (i.e. there is no data). Value buffers store actual values of fixed-width types, similar to C arrays. Offset buffers store offsets of variable

(a) Schema:

Field A:
Float (nullable)
Field B:
List(Char)
Field C:
Struct(E: Int16, F: Double)

(b) RecordBatch:

A	B	C
0.5f	"fpga"	(42, 0.125)
0.25f	"fun"	(1337, 0.0)
∅	"!"	(13, 2.7)

(c) Arrow buffers:

Index	Buffers for:					
	Field A		Field B		Field C	
	Validity (bit)	Values (float)	Offsets (int32)	Values (char)	Values E (int16)	Values F (double)
0	1	0.5f	0	f	42	0.125
1	1	0.25f	4	p	1337	0.0
2	0	×	7	g	13	2.7
3			8	a		
4				f		
5				u		
6				n		
7				!		

Fig. 1. An example schema (a) of a RecordBatch (b) and resulting Arrow buffers (c).

length types, such as strings (which are lists of characters), where an offset at some index points to where a variable-length item starts in another buffer.

A RecordBatch contains specific meta-data called a *schema* that expresses the types of the fields in the records, therefore defining the types of the arrays, in turn defining which buffers are present. When a user wants to obtain (a subset of) a record from the RecordBatch, through the schema, we may find out what buffers to load data from to obtain the records of interest. An example of a *schema*, a corresponding *RecordBatch* (with three *arrays* and the resulting *buffers* are seen in Fig. 1.

Normally, an FPGA developer designs an accelerator that has to interface with a memory bus to get to the data set. That means the accelerator must typically request a bus word from a specific byte address. However, in the case of a tabular data set stored in the Arrow format, it is more convenient to express access to the data by supplying a table index, or a range of table indices, and receiving streams of the data of interest in the form of the types expressed through the schema, rather than as a bus word.

Because schemas can express a virtually infinite number of type combinations an implementation of the mechanisms must meet a challenging set of requirements. In the next section, we first describe the requirements of such an interface.

3   Requirements

Consider an accelerator to be the data sink in case an Arrow RecordBatch is being read. From the description in the previous section, a set of requirements for the generated interface can be constructed.

1. **Row indexing:** The data sink is able to request table elements by using Arrow table row indices as a reference. In turn, the data sink will receive the requested elements only.
2. **Streaming:** The elements will be received by the sink in an ordered stream.
3. **Throughput:** The interface can be configured to supply an arbitrary number of elements in a valid transfer.
4. **Bus interface:** The host-memory side of the interface can be connected to a bus interface of arbitrary power-of-two width.

The first requirement allows developers to work with row indices rather than having to perform the tedious work of figuring out the byte addresses of data (including potentially deeply nested schemas with multiple layers of offset buffers). Furthermore, it implies that elements are received in the actual binary form of their type, and not, e.g., as a few bytes in the middle of a host memory bus word (that are often 512 bits wide for contemporary systems). This allows the developer to not have to worry about reordering, serializing or parallelizing the data contained in one or multiple bus words.

The second requirement maps naturally to hardware designs that often involve data paths with streams of data flowing between functional units.

The third requirement allows multiple elements of a specific data type to arrive per clock cycle. For example, when a column contains elements of a small type (say a Boolean), it is likely the accelerator can process more than one element in parallel. This differs from Requirement 2 in the sense that the elements that will be delivered in parallel are part of the same request mentioned in Requirement 1. Furthermore, it can be that the top level element is a list of small primitive elements. Thus, one might want to absorb multiple of the nested elements within a clock cycle.

The last requirements allows the interface to be connected to different platforms that might have different memory bus widths. In the discussions of this work, we will generally assume that this width is set to 512 bits, since the platforms that Fletcher currently supports both provide memory bus interfaces of this size. However, Fletcher can also operate on wider or narrower bus interfaces.

4   Vendor-Agnostic Hardware Libary

Fletcher aims to be vendor-agnostic in order to thrive in an open-source setting. All designs are based on data streams. This requires custom streaming primitives that can perform the basic operations on streams. Commercial tools contain IP cores to support some (but not all) of these operations as well. However, to engage with an open-source oriented community, it is important to not force designs to use vendor-specific solutions. This causes the need for a custom streaming operations library that is maintained alongside Fletcher.

The most important streaming components are discussed in this subsection. The most basic primitives on which all other components are built, are as follows:

Slice   A component to break up any combinatorial paths in a stream, typically using registers.

FIFO   A component to buffer stream contents, typically using RAM.

Sync   A component to synchronize between an arbitrary number of input and output streams.

The throughput requirement mentioned in the previous section dictates that streams must be able to deliver multiple elements per cycle (MEPC). To support this, and other operations, the previously mentioned primitives are extended by the set of following stream operators:

Barrel   A pipelined component to barrel rotate or shift MEPC streams at the element level.

Reshaper A component that absorbs an arbitrary number of valid elements of an MEPC stream and outputs another arbitrary number of elements. This element is useful for serializing wide streams into narrow streams (or vice versa, parallelizing narrow streams into wide streams). The element can also be used to reduce elements per cycle in a single stream handshake or to increase (e.g. maximize) them. The implementation of the Reshaper uses the Barrel component.

Arbiter   A component to arbitrate multiple streams onto a single stream.
Buffer   An abstraction over a FIFO and a sync with a variable depth.

On top of the streaming components (especially the Arbiter and Buffer), a light-weight bus infrastructure has been developed to allow multiple masters to use the same memory interface. This bus infrastracture is similar to (and includes wrappers for) AXI-4, supporting independent read/write request and data channels and bursts.

Read/Write Arbiter   Arbitrates multiple masters onto a single slave.
Read/Write Buffer   Allows buffering of at least a full maximum sized burst to relieve the arbiter of any back-pressure.

5   Components to Match Arrow Abstractions

5.1   Implementation Alternatives

Designing an interface to Arrow data could follow different approaches. A flexible approach would have a small customized soft processor generate the requests based on a schema or some bytecode that is compiled on the host. In this way, any schema (reasonably limited in size) could be requested, and schemas can be changed during run-time.

However, this approach would have several drawbacks. First of all, it would introduce more latency as it takes multiple instructions to calculate addresses and generate requests. Moreover, as developers can create schemas with fixed-width types of arbitrary length, allocating streams for the "widest" case is impractical. If one would supply the implementation with support for some very wide fixed-width type (effectively limiting the schemas that can be expressed already), it would cause a relatively large amount of area overhead for schemas with narrow primitives. For example, consider a hard-coded 1024-bit stream of which some schema only uses one bit. As schema data can be of many varieties, the streams would require run-time reordering of the elements coming from bus words. This involves relatively expensive parametrizations of the Stream Reshaper to support all possible cases of aligning arbitrary elements. Elements themselves must be restricted to be smaller than 1024 bits and only a fraction of RAM spent on FIFOs in the data paths is effectively used.

The aggregate of these drawbacks causes the proposed interface generation framework to completely configure the generated interface during compile-time. For this purpose, we introduce highly configurable components that correspond to abstractions seen in the Arrow software-language specific counterparts.

5.2   Buffers

Readers. As explained in Sect. 2, Arrow *buffers* hold C-like arrays of fixed-width data. We implement a component called a BufferReader (BR). The BR is a highly configurable component to support turning host memory bus burst requests and responses into fixed-width type MEPC streams. It performs the following functions:

- Based on the properties of the bus interface and the data type, perform the pointer arithmetic to locate elements of interest in the Arrow buffer.
- Perform all the bus requests desired to obtain a range of elements.
- Align received bus words.
- Reshape aligned words into MEPC streams with fixed-width data types.

An architectural overview of the proposed implementation of two BRs (in combination providing a setup to read variable-length types) is shown in Fig. 2.

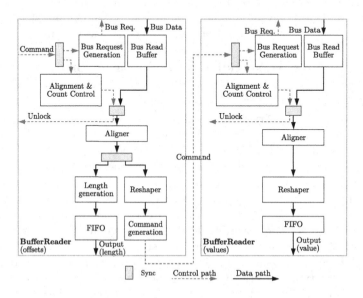

Fig. 2. A BufferReader for an offsets buffer (left) and a values buffer (right)

The top-level of a buffer reader contains the following interfaces, that are all pipelined streams:

Command (in)   Used to request a range of items to be obtained from host memory by the BR. Also contains the Arrow buffer address and a special *tag*.

Unlock (out)   Used to signal the completion of a command, handshaking back the command's original *tag*.

Bus read request (out) Used to request data from memory.

Bus read data (in)   Used to receive data words from memory.

Data (out)   A MEPC stream of data corresponding to an Arrow data type.

Reading from a values buffer, and reading from validity bitmap buffers (by instantiating a BR with element size one) is supported by the rightmost configuration of the BR as shown in Fig. 2.

Here, a command stream is absorbed by two units: a bus request generation unit and an alignment and count controller. The bus request generator performs all pointer arithmetic and generates bus burst requests. The alignment and count controller calculates, based on the width of the bus and the type of elements, how much a bus word must be shifted (especially for the first bus word received), since some first index in the command stream might point to any element in a buffer. It also generates a count of valid items in the MEPC stream resulting from alignment. This is also useful when last bus words in a range contain less elements than requested.

Even though first and last bus words might not be aligned or do not contain all requested elements, after aligning and augmenting the stream with a count, the reshaper unit will shape a non-full MEPC stream into a full MEPC stream.

Furthermore, when the last bus word has been streamed to the aligner, an unlock stream handshake is generated to notify the accelerator that the command has been completed in terms of requests on the bus.

Offset buffers require the consumer of the data stream to turn an offset into a length. In this way, the consumer (typically the accelerator core logic) can know the size of a variable length item in a column. Therefore, for offset BRs, two consecutive offsets are subtracted to generate a length. Furthermore, BRs support the generation of an output command stream for a second BR. To generate this command stream, rather than generating a command for the child buffer for each variable length item, the BR requests both the last offset and the first offset in the range of the command first, before requesting all offsets in a large burst. The first and last offset can then be sent as a single command to the child BR, allowing it to request the data in the values buffer using large bursts.

Command (out)   Used to generate commands for other buffers. This is useful when this BR reads from an Arrow offsets buffer.

Writers. Complementary to BRs, we also implement BufferWriters (BW) that, given some index range can write to memory in the Arrow format. They contain the same interface streams as BR, except the data flow is inverted. An architectural overview of the proposed implementation of two BW is observed in Fig. 3. Writing to a validity bitmap buffer or a values buffers requires the buffer writer to operate as follows (as seen on the right side of the figure).

When a command is given to the BW, the MEPC input stream is delivered to a unit that pre- and post-pads the stream to force the stream to be aligned with a minimum bus burst length parameter. Furthermore, it generates appropriate write strobes (only asserting strobes for valid elements). The elements and strobes are then reshaped to fit into a full bus word and sent to a bus write buffer. Note that sometimes it is unknown how long an input stream will be when the command is given. Therefore the command to the BW supports both no range or with range commands. At the same time this requires counting accepted bus words into the BusBuffer. A bus request generation unit uses this count to generate bus requests preferably when full bursts are ready, but if the

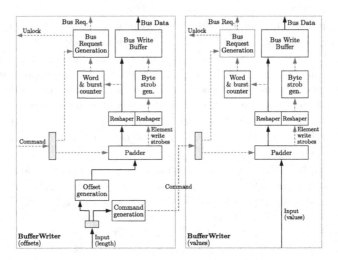

Fig. 3. A BufferWriter for an offsets buffer (left) and a values buffer (right)

input stream has ended, bus words are bursted out with minimum burst steps until the buffer is empty.

If the BW writes to an offsets buffer, it can be configured to generate offsets from a length input stream. This length input stream can optionally be used to generate commands for a child buffer. To achieve maximum throughput, the child command generation may be disabled, otherwise the child buffer writer will generate padding after the ending of every list in an Arrow Array containing variable length types.

5.3 Arrays

To support Arrow *arrays*, that combine multiple buffers to deliver any field type that may be found in an Arrow schema, we implement special components called ColumnReaders and Writers.

These ColumnReaders- and Writers instantiate the BRs and BW resulting from a schema field. They furthermore support:

- Attaching command outputs of offsets buffers to values or validity bitmap buffers.
- Arbitration of multiple buffer bus masters onto a single slave.
- Synchronization of unlock streams of all buffers in use.
- Recursive instantiations of themselves. This, in turn, supports:
  - Nested types, such as `Lists<List<Type>>`.
  - Adding an Arrow validity bit to the output stream.
  - Support Arrow *structs*, such as `Struct<List<Int16>, Float>`.

The ColumnReaders and ColumnWriters are supplied with a configuration string that conveys the same information as an Arrow schema. By parsing the

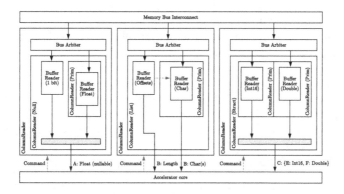

Fig. 4. Resulting ColumnReader configuration from the Schema in Fig. 1

configuration string, the components are recursively instantiated according to the top level type of the field in a schema. An example for the schema from Fig. 1 is shown in Fig. 4. Reading from the example RecordBatch (corresponding to the schema) will require three ColumnReaders. The manner in which they are recursively instantiated is shown in the figure. Here one can discern four types of ColumnReader configurations:

Default A default ColumnReader only instantiates a specific ColumnReader of the top-level type of the corresponding schema field, but provides a bus arbiter to share the memory interface amongst all BRs that are instantiated in all child ColumnReaders.

Prim A ColumnReader instantiating a BR for fixed-width (primitive) types.

Null Used to add a validity (non-null) bitmap buffer and synchronize with the output streams of a child ColumnReader to append the validity bit.

List Used to add an offsets buffer that generates a length stream and provides a first and last index for the command stream of a child ColumnReader.

Struct Used to instantiate multiple ColumnReaders, synchronizing their output streams to couple the delivery of separate fields inside a struct into a single stream.

Through the List and Struct type ColumnReaders, nested schemas may be supported. On the top level all streams that interface with the accelerator core are concatenated. A software tool named *Fletchgen* generates top levels for various platforms (including AWS EC2 F1 and OpenPOWER CAPI SNAP) that wraps around the ColumnReaders and ColumnWriters and splits the streams that are concatenated onto single signals vectors into something readable (using the same field names as defined in the schema) for the developer. A discussion of the inner workings of *Fletchgen* and the support for these platforms is outside the scope of this paper but the implementation may be found in the repository online [6]. The complement (in terms of data flow) of this structure is implemented for ColumnWriters. One additional challenge to ColumnWriters is that they require dynamically resizable Arrow Buffers in host memory, because it cannot always be assumed that the size of the resulting Arrow Buffers is known at the start of some input stream. This is an interesting challenge for future work.

5.4   Continuous Integration

All parts of Fletcher are open sourced. This allows all interested parties to submit changes to the hardware design. Part of improving the maintainability of the project includes bootstrapping of the build and test process in a continuous integration framework, where the simulator used is also an open-source project [2]. By using fully open-sourced tools in the collaborative development process, the threshold to get started with FPGA accelerators and Fletcher is lowered.

6   Results

6.1   Functional Validation

Because the number of schema field type combinations is virtually infinite (due to nesting), it is not trivial to validate the functionality of the framework. To obtain good coverage in simulation, a Python script is used to generate random schemas with supported types. The types decrease in complexity the deeper their nesting level, such that at some point the nesting ends with a primitive type. The resulting buffers are deduced from the schema, random content is generated and a host memory interface is mimicked. Random indices are requested from the simulated ColumnReaders, and their output streams are compared to the expected output. In this way, the correct functioning of over ten thousand different generated structures was validated.

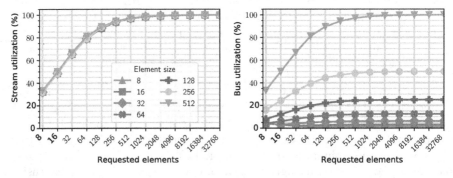

(a) Near-optimal output stream utilization   (b) Memory bus pressure

Fig. 5. Utilization for a ColumnReader for various fixed-width types versus command range (each line represents a different fixed-width type).

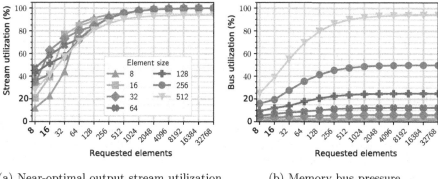

(a) Near-optimal output stream utilization   (b) Memory bus pressure

Fig. 6. Utilization for a ColumnWriter for various fixed-width types versus command range.

6.2   Throughput

ColumnReaders/Writers for Fixed-Width Types. The main goal of the hardware components of Fletcher is to provide the output streams with the same bandwidth as the system bandwidth, if the accelerator core can consume it. In other words, the generated interfaces should not throttle the system bandwidth because of a sub-optimal design choice (like a sub-optimal in-memory format or a sub-optimal hardware component).

We simulate the throughput of ColumnReaders and ColumnWriters, assuming that we have a perfect bus interconnect, i.e. the bus delivers/accepts the requested bursts immediately and at every clock cycle a valid bus word can be produced. We measure the bus utilization and stream output utilization (in handshakes per cycle during the processing of a command) for different fixed-width types, as a function of the range of Arrow array entries requested through the command stream. We furthermore assume the accelerator core can handshake the ColumnReader output or ColumnWriter input stream every cycle. The results of this simulation for a data bus width of 512 bits (as both platforms, AWS EC2 F1 and OpenPOWER CAPI SNAP, that Fletcher currently supports use this memory bus width) are shown in Fig. 5a and b, where the bus utilization and output stream utilization is shown, respectively, for various fixed-width types. Similar measurements for the ColumnWriters are seen in Fig. 6.

Initialization overhead and latency of both the ColumnReader and ColumnWriter is present when the command only requests a short range of entries. However, once the range grows larger (a likely scenario in most big data use cases where massively parallel operators on data sets such as maps, reductions and filters are applied), the stream utilization becomes near optimal. As long as the element width is smaller than the bus width, maximum stream throughput is achieved, and as long as the element width is equal to the bus width, maximum bus bandwidth is achieved. We may conclude that a ColumnReader for fixed-width types does not create a bottleneck if the accelerator core can absorb data at the system bandwidth rate. A developer using a ColumnReader can now express access to an Arrow Array in terms of RecordBatch indices and will receive the exact data type as specified through the schema on the stream, without degradation of the system bandwidth.

ColumnReaders/Writers for Variable-Length Types. We simulate throughput of a ColumnReader/Writer for an Arrow Array where the items in the Array are lists of primitive types. We choose the type to be a character (8 bits). We generate random lists between length 1 and 1024 and, in Fig. 7, plot the utilization of the bus and the input/output streams as function of the elements-per-cycle parameter of this ColumnReader/Writer. From these figures, we may observe that the value stream utilization is near-optimal, independent of the number of elements per cycle that it is configured for; as long as the memory bus can deliver the throughput, the accelerator core is fed at maximum throughput.

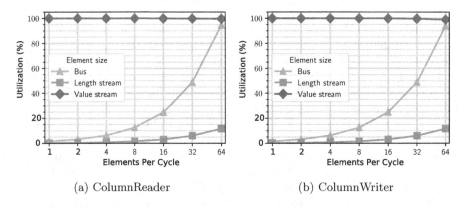

(a) ColumnReader   (b) ColumnWriter

Fig. 7. Bus and input/output stream utilization for an increasing elements-per-cycle parameter demonstrating utilization near 100%.

6.3   Area Utilization

For the same memory bus width as the supported platforms (512 bits), we synthesize ColumnReaders and ColumnWriters for various fixed-width types ($W = 8, 16, \ldots, 512$) and for various variable-length types ($W = 8$ with $EPC = 64$, $W = 16$ with $EPC = 32$, etc.) for a Xilinx XCVU9P device (that used in AWS EC2 F1 instances). The area utilization statistics are shown in Table 2.

The ColumnReaders/Writers require little area. Most configurations utilize less than one percent of the resources. Interestingly, ColumnReaders/Writers for small elements require more LUTs than wider elements on a wide bus. This is due to the reshaper and aligner units discussed in Sect. 5, requiring aligning and reshaping more MEPC stream element count combinations, increasing mux

Table 2. Area utilization statistics for a Xilinx XCVU9P device

Type	Resource	W = 8	W = 16	W = 32	W = 64	W = 128	W = 256	W = 512
Column Reader Prim(W)	CLB LUTs	0.30%	0.28%	0.26%	0.24%	0.22%	0.20%	0.21%
	CLB Registers	0.20%	0.20%	0.20%	0.20%	0.22%	0.24%	0.26%
	Block RAM (B36)	0.65%	0.65%	0.65%	0.65%	0.65%	0.65%	0.65%
	Block RAM (B18)	0.05%	0.05%	0.05%	0.05%	0.05%	0.05%	0.05%
Column Reader List of Prim(W)	CLB LUTs	2.34%	1.81%	1.46%	1.32%	1.03%	1.04%	0.78%
	CLB Registers	1.01%	1.01%	1.01%	1.01%	1.00%	1.00%	1.00%
	Block RAM (B36)	1.30%	1.30%	1.30%	1.30%	1.30%	1.30%	1.30%
	Block RAM (B18)	0.09%	0.09%	0.09%	0.09%	0.09%	0.09%	0.09%
Column Writer Prim(W)	CLB LUTs	0.20%	0.19%	0.19%	0.20%	0.20%	0.22%	0.23%
	CLB Registers	0.28%	0.28%	0.28%	0.28%	0.29%	0.31%	0.33%
	Block RAM (B36)	0.37%	0.37%	0.37%	0.37%	0.37%	0.37%	0.37%
	Block RAM (B18)	0.02%	0.02%	0.02%	0.02%	0.02%	0.02%	0.02%
Column Writer List of Prim(W)	CLB LUTs	1.03%	0.97%	0.91%	0.87%	0.80%	0.78%	0.52%
	CLB Registers	1.18%	1.12%	1.11%	1.11%	1.06%	1.06%	0.73%
	Block RAM (B36)	1.11%	1.11%	1.06%	1.06%	1.06%	1.06%	0.74%
	Block RAM (B18)	0.07%	0.05%	0.07%	0.07%	0.07%	0.07%	0.05%

sizes. Designers may chose to reduce this number in the ColumnReaders and Writers themselves, but this requires an asymmetric connection to the memory bus interconnect, effectively moving the alignment functionality to the interconnect. Register usage increases when element size increases, since register slices on the path to the accelerator core match the width of the elements. Block RAM usage is the same for all configurations, because this depends on the maximum burst length that has been fixed to 32 beats for all configurations.

7 Related Work

While Arrow is not the only framework following the trend of in-memory computation for big data frameworks (an overview can be found in [13]), it is a framework that is especially focused on providing efficient interoperability between different tools/languages. This allows the 11 languages supported by Arrow to quickly and efficiently transfer data to the FPGA accelerator using Fletcher.

Several solutions to abstract away memory bus interfaces are commercially available and integrated into HLS tools (such as Xilinx' SDAccel and Intel's FPGA SDK for OpenCL). However, they have no inherent support for nested types that Arrow schemas can represent, and usually work well only with simple, C-like primitive types and arrays. Loading data from nested structures involves pointer traversal and arithmetic which HLS tools do not deal with efficiently [11]. At the same time, after Fletcher generates an interface that delivers streams which HLS tools can operate on very well.

State-of-the-art frameworks to integrate FPGA accelerators with specific databases exist [5], although interface generation specific to the schema data type and serialization overhead are not discussed.

8   Conclusion

The goal of the Fletcher framework is to ease integration of FPGA accelerators with data analytics frameworks. To this end, Fletcher uses the Apache Arrow in-memory format to leverage the advantages of the Arrow project, including no serialization overhead and interfaces to 11 different high-level languages. To support the wide variety of data set types that Arrow can represent, and to convert these data sets into hardware streams that are desirable by an FPGA developer, this work has presented a bottom-up view of a library of vendor-agnostic and open-source components. These components allow reading from tabular Arrow data set columns, by providing a range of table indices, rather than byte addresses, to refer to records stored in the tables. Fletcher is effective at generating these interfaces without compromising performance. It takes very little area to create an interface that provides an accelerator core with system bandwidth for any configuration of the Arrow data set. Fletcher significantly simplifies the process of effectively designing FPGA-based solutions for data analytics tools based on Arrow.

References

1. Amazon Web Services: AWS EC2 FPGA Hardware and Software Development Kits (2018). https://github.com/aws/aws-fpga
2. Gingold, T.: GHDL VHDL 2008/93/87 simulator (2018). https://github.com/ghdl/ghdl
3. McKinney, W.: Python for Data Analysis: Data Wrangling with Pandas, NumPy, and IPython. O'Reilly Media Inc., Newton (2012)
4. OpenPOWER foundation: CAPI SNAP Framework Hardware and Software (2018). https://github.com/open-power/snap
5. Owaida, M., Sidler, D., Kara, K., Alonso, G.: Centaur: a framework for hybrid CPU-FPGA databases. In: 2017 IEEE 25th Annual International Symposium on Field-Programmable Custom Computing Machines (FCCM), pp. 211–218, April 2017
6. Peltenburg, J., van Straten, J.: Fletcher: a framework to integrate Apache Arrow with FPGA accelerators (2018). https://github.com/johanpel/fletcher
7. Sidler, D., István, Z., Owaida, M., Alonso, G.: Accelerating pattern matching queries in hybrid CPU-FPGA architectures. In: Proceedings of the 2017 ACM International Conference on Management of Data, SIGMOD 2017, pp. 403–415. ACM, New York (2017)
8. Stuecheli, J., Blaner, B., Johns, C., Siegel, M.: CAPI: a coherent accelerator processor interface. IBM J. Res. Dev. **59**(1), 7:1–7:7 (2015)
9. The Apache Software Foundation: Apache Arrow (2018). https://arrow.apache.org/
10. The Apache Software Foundation: Apache Parquet (2018). https://parquet.apache.org/
11. Winterstein, F., Bayliss, S., Constantinides, G.A.: High-level synthesis of dynamic data structures: a case study using Vivado HLS. In: 2013 International Conference on Field-Programmable Technology (FPT), pp. 362–365, December 2013

12. Zaharia, M., et al.: Apache spark: a unified engine for big data processing. Commun. ACM **59**(11), 56–65 (2016)
13. Zhang, H., Chen, G., Ooi, B.C., Tan, K.L., Zhang, M.: In-memory big data management and processing: a survey. IEEE Trans. Knowl. Data Eng. **27**(7), 1920–1948 (2015)

A Novel Encoder for TDCs

Günter Knittel[✉]

GSI Helmholtzzentrum für Schwerionenforschung GmbH,
Planckstraße 1, 64291 Darmstadt, Germany
G.Knittel@gsi.de

Abstract. We present a novel encoder design for FPGA-based Time-to-Digital Converters (TDCs) that use tapped delay lines. The encoder is the most challenging and problematic unit on such measurement devices. Recent developments in TDC methodology include the Wave Union principle, and encoders based on population count. These two methods can alleviate fundamental disadvantages of FPGA-based TDCs. However, it appeared to be problematic to combine the two methods. The contribution of this paper is a special arithmetic unit that allows us to combine these two methods into a fast and compact encoder.

The paper is a report on work in progress, real-world measurement results cannot be given at this point in time.

Keywords: TDC · Wave Union · Population count · Encoder

1 Introduction

TDCs are measurement devices that measure the time of occurrence of an electrical signal (typically leading edge, optionally also trailing edge and thus pulse length). TDCs are used in massive numbers in accelerator facilities such as at the GSI or at CERN, where they measure the time-of-flight (and derived parameters) of particles after a collision.

TDCs can be built in various ways, using a multitude of measurement methods. The most common platforms are ASICs and FPGAs. Examples of an ASIC implementation are *HPTDC* and *picoTDC* [1]. The picoTDC employs a Delay Locked Loop with 64 elements, that can further be divided into 256 time taps by a resistive interpolator. This results in a time resolution of about 3 ps. The architecture allows one measurement to be made per 1.28 GHz clock cycle. The chip offers 64 channels.

Although these specs can hardly be met using programmable devices, FPGAs are still an attractive platform because of their flexibility. On FPGAs, the dominant architecture is based on *tapped delay lines* (TDLs). The signal to be measured is fed into a delay line, consisting of a number of discrete delay elements whose outputs are put on the inputs of a row of registers. These registers (called *snapshot registers*) are clocked by a common clock. The result is a so-called *thermometer code*, which is an indication of the time that has elapsed between the arrival of the signal edge and the corresponding clock edge. The common clock

© Springer Nature Switzerland AG 2019
C. Hochberger et al. (Eds.): ARC 2019, LNCS 11444, pp. 48–57, 2019.
https://doi.org/10.1007/978-3-030-17227-5_4

also clocks a counter, whose value is the coarse time. The method is graphically explained in Fig. 1.

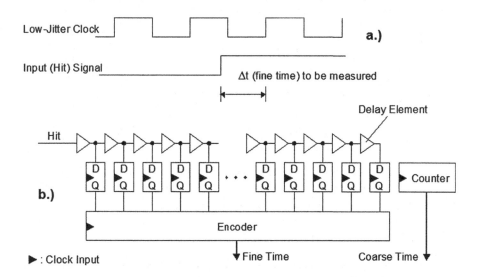

Fig. 1. a. Measurement principle. b. One measurement channel.

The task of the encoder is to transform the snapshot bits into a numerical value. This value is called the *fine time*. Most generally this is the problem of computing the position of the transition in the snapshot bits. Coarse time and fine time represent the time of arrival of the signal edge, which can be measured to a precision of a few (ten) picoseconds on current FPGA devices.

There are a couple of general design requirements for such TDL-encoder combos. Firstly, the clock period must be shorter than the total propagation time on the delay line, that is, the time it takes for a signal edge to propagate through the entire delay line. Otherwise, the edge can drop off the far end without ever being sampled. On FPGAs, however, the clock frequency cannot be very high, which sets a lower limit to the length of the delay line. A long delay line has a high number of snapshot bits, which increase the hardware expenses of the encoder. Nevertheless, the encoder should be able to produce one result each clock, allowing one measurement to be performed per clock as well.

On FPGAs, the best way to implement a delay line is to construct a long (ripple-carry) adder [3]. For highest performance, the carry signals are typically implemented using the fastest logic elements and wires that are available on a given technology. Thus, an adder chain offers the highest time resolution. A suitable input pattern is shown in Fig. 2. To give a rough idea about a typical TDL, in one of our previous designs the TDL consists of about 300 full adders and is sampled at 200 MHz.

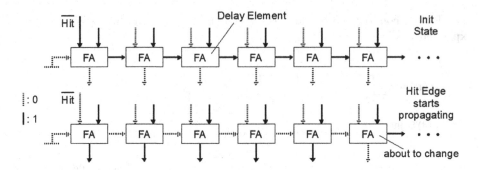

Fig. 2. Tapped delay line using a ripple carry adder.

While the principle is quite simple, there are a number of severe implementation problems associated with TDL-based TDCs, some of which are FPGA-specific, others are fundamental in nature, as discussed below.

1.1   Problems: Bins and Bubbles

By means of the specific chip layout of FPGAs, which typically group functional units into small clusters (known as *CLB, LAB, PFU* etc.), the delay on the carry chain from one adder to the next is not constant, but can vary strongly across the length of the TDL. This results in a large differential non-linearity (DNL). The common expression for this phenomenon is an *uneven bin width.*

The Wave Union principle [6] provides a significant improvement in DNL (see also [4]). Instead of entering the TDL itself, the input signal triggers a launcher which sends a sequence of edges down the TDL. The encoder must then determine the position of each individual edge, and the fine time is expressed as the sum of all positions.

The idea behind this is as follows. While one edge is stuck in a long bin for some time and does not increase the sum, another edge might be in a sequence of short bins and increase the sum at a high rate, leading to a higher time resolution. When this edge is in a long bin, the other edge might help out in the same way. This improvement is obtained while still using only one TDL. Hardware costs for the launcher are small.

However, having more than one transition in the snapshot bits complicates the encoder further. Either the hardware expenses grow, or the designer has to resort to multi-cycle operation, thereby increasing the measurement deadtime.

But this is not the only problem. Another severe problem for the encoder design is that there is typically no sharp transition in the snapshot bits. Instead, there can be short but arbitrary sequences of 0s and 1s around each wavefront (*"bubbles"*). There are two reasons for this. One is metastability due to simultaneous transitions on the data and clock inputs of the flipflops. There is no remedy. The other is skew on the clock distribution network, which can cause individual flipflops to sample the wavefront at the wrong time. There is no remedy as well, but it appears to be deterministic.

As a consequence, the position of the transition cannot be determined precisely. Instead, some sort of *"most plausible estimate"* would have to be found. Not only does this complicate the encoder design further, it also reduces measurement precision.

In [5] a solution is given for this problem, although only for TDCs using a single edge in the TDL. According to this work, the amount of delay can be expressed as the number of set bits (population count) in the snapshot pattern. The idea behind this is as follows. When the signal has traveled down the delay line for some time T_0 and produced a pattern with N set bits, $N + 1$ set bits can only occur *after* T_0. Thus the population count is a monotonic function in time and this is all that is needed.

An encoder based on population count can nicely be built as a tree of adders of increasing width. When using pipeline registers, the clock frequency can be very high.

1.2   Problem: Wave Union and Population Count

It is obvious that the Wave Union principle and population count encoding cannot be combined so easily. For example, if we use a short low-pulse to travel down the delay line, the population count is constant in first approximation regardless of sampling time. However, we can still combine the two methods if we somehow manage to compute two distinct population counts: one from the start of the TDL up to the pulse, and one from the pulse to the end of the TDL. The big problem is of course how to assemble the two subsets of snapshot bits efficiently and automatically irrespective of pulse position.

Further requirements for the encoder are:

- Single-cycle measurement
- High clock rate for a short TDL
- Compact design

The solution is given in the following section.

2   Solution

The presented solution is intended for a single low-pulse on the TDL, i.e., a Wave Union of a leading falling edge and a trailing rising edge. For the explanation we use the following parameters.

The TDL is $32 \times 7 = 224$ delay elements (full adders) long. It is conceptually divided into segments of length 7. For each of these segments, an individual population count (PC) is computed. Obviously, this population count ranges from 0 to 7 and fits into a 3-bit number.

The low-pulse that travels down the TDL must be such that at least one segment is entirely low at any arbitrary sampling time. Such segments are used as markers. For each segment, a flag Z is computed which is set if its population count is 0. $Z = 1$ indicates a marker. If there are more than one markers in the snapshot bits, they are assumed to be contiguous. In Fig. 3, an 18-bit low-pulse is established by injecting the hit signal at two positions. In this example, the hit signal has propagated through six adders at the time of sampling. Some bubbles are shown.

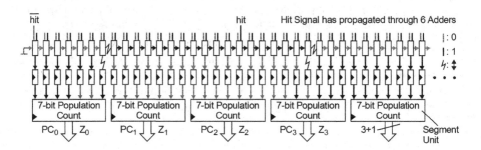

Fig. 3. TDL, snapshot registers, and segment units.

From PC_n and Z_n, two overall population counts are computed: the "lower" population count (LPC) from the start of the TDL to the first marker, and the "upper" population count (UPC) from the end of the TDL backwards to the first marker. The fine time is then of the form $T_f = LPC + (224 - UPC)$. In Fig. 3, LPC = 5 and UPC = 200.

We start the derivation with the lower population count. The design is based on the following observation: any set Z-flag sets all downstream segments to zero. This can be translated into the circuitry shown in Fig. 4. As can be seen, the bit pattern controls its own processing, a separate control unit is not necessary.

Clearly, the generic form is not well suited for implementation because of its slow speed of operation. However, the operations can be rearranged so that they are better suitable for pipelining.

Both the arithmetic sum and the OR-chain are associative. Thus we can first compute the sums of all pairs of population counts. The ORed Z-flags that enter each pair can then be applied to the sum. This can be repeated hierarchically to form a binary tree. This is shown in Fig. 5 for 8 segments.

As can be seen, the tree can be built from one parametrizable cell, which we call *special adder*. For TDLs of this length, the amount of logic in any pipeline stage is very small, so that a high clock frequency can be achieved.

For the upper population count UPC the same considerations as in Fig. 4 apply, except that the direction of the OR-chain is reversed, and the "left" population count of each pair is masked instead of the right one. The corresponding special adders are shown in Fig. 6. Clearly the two cells are identical, the desired functionality is established merely by proper connection of the input ports.

Using these cells two adder trees can be built, one for LPC and one for UPC. They operate in parallel so that one snapshot pattern can be processed per clock. Both trees are fed by the same set of segment units, so that the segment units

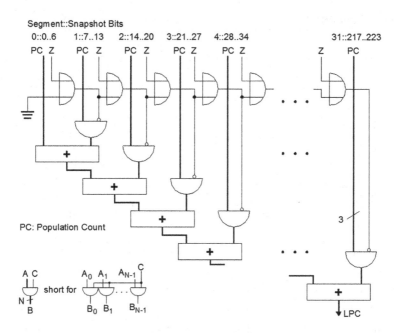

Fig. 4. Generic ALU computing LPC.

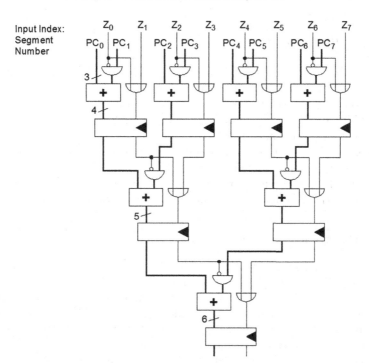

Fig. 5. Partial adder tree.

Special Adder Function
for Lower Population Count:

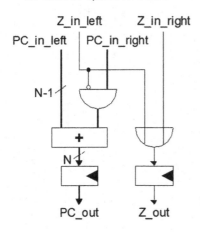

Special Adder Function
for Upper Population Count:

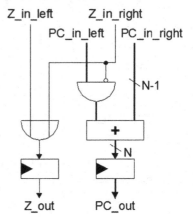

Fig. 6. Special adder.

are present only once. One full adder tree is shown in Fig. 7. Note that in Fig. 7, PC and Z have been merged into one bus for better readability.

3   Implementation

Because of the high number of measurement channels there is a strong pressure on the price per channel. Therefore, the goal of this work is to integrate a high number of channels on a truly low-cost platform: 48 channels on a Lattice LFE5UM-85F FPGA, which currently costs about 32€. For the pure TDC, a measurement channel would then be around 67 cents.

Having developed an efficient algorithm is half the battle, but an efficient implementation is equally important on FPGAs. Quite often one can experience wasteful use of chip resources by the design tools. What is needed are highly optimized functional units, and we have used *macros* to achieve this goal.

3.1   Working with Macros

Macros are collections of logic elements with fixed placement and optionally fixed routing. Macros are advantageous for large designs that mostly consist of replicated units. Then, prototype units can be manually optimized to the highest degree and replicated across the chip in identical form at the desired locations. Mapper, placer and router will obey user design input and not alter the internal macro structure. Macros can include other macros.

Designers can create macros by first implementing a regular design (including I/Os, clocks etc) and then transforming it into a macro, mostly by removing the

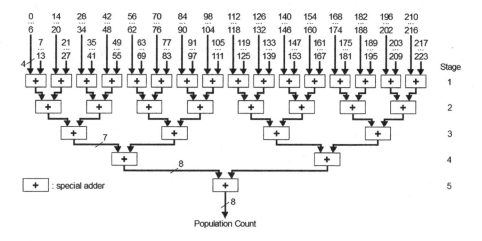

Fig. 7. One of two adder trees.

I/Os and changing the ports into internal pins. This is done using an FPGA editor such as the EPIC tool from Lattice.

Optimizing a design consists mainly of placing logic elements in the optimal location, if need be for individual LUTs and FFs, thereby achieving the highest density and clock rate. EPIC even allows individual wires to be routed.

On the downside, the design style approaches that of ASICs with their notorious high labor costs. Nevertheless, the encoder design was implemented using macros without compromises.

Figure 8 shows the floorplan of a macro containing the TDLs and encoders for two channels. The chip layout shows rows of DSP-slices and Embedded Block-RAMs, and inbetween slabs of so-called Programmable Functional Units (PFUs). Each PFU has 8 4-input LUTs and 8 FFs, grouped into four identical slices [2].

It can be seen that 8 channels can be placed within one slab, leaving some room for control logic and datapath elements (and control logic for FIFO memories). As a sidenote: the required wide multiplexer that funnels the data of all channels to an interface can be built from DSP-slices, which are not used for other purposes in the design.

Thus we are confident that 48 channels can be integrated on this low-cost FPGA device when using 6 slabs, leaving enough room for interface logic (such as JESD204B).

A collection of design specs that were achieved:

- Bounding Box: $61 \times 4 = 244$ PFUs
- Occupied PFUs: 235 PFUs
- Occupied Resources: 1880 LUTs, 1880 FFs
- Used Resources: 1814 LUTs, 1362 FFs
- Usage: 96.5% of LUTs, 72.4% of FFs
- Max. Clock Frequency: $\sim$375 MHz

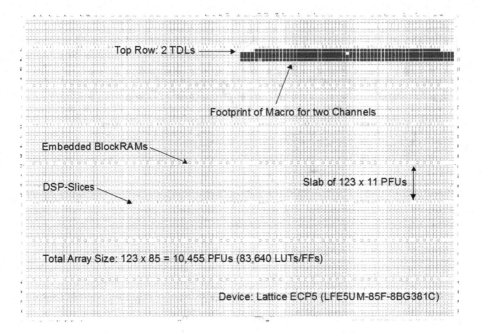

Fig. 8. Floorplan of macro with two channels.

We think that the achieved clock frequency is very high for this device (cf. [2], page 62). How much of this figure can be transported to the complete design remains to be seen, but it will most likely be enough for the TDLs of that length, according to our previous designs.

4   Conclusion

We have laid the groundwork for a high channel count, low cost TDC for use in particle detectors and many other applications. We have presented a novel encoder design that is capable of combining two state-of-the-art methods in TDC design: Wave Union and population count encoding. Still, the encoder is compact and very fast.

The final TDC, if our further design work is successful, might represent a very competetive system with respect to the price/performance ratio.

References

1. Horstmann, M.: Picosecond TDC Design. Ecole de microélectronique 2017 de l'IN2P3, Paris, 14–19 May 2017
2. Lattice Semiconductor: ECP5 and ECP5-5G Family Data Sheet. FPGA-DS-02012 Version 1.9, March 2018

3. Liu, C., Wang, Y.: A 128-channel, 710 M samples/second, and less than 10 ps RMS resolution time-to-digital converter implemented in a Kintex-7 FPGA. IEEE Trans. Nucl. Sci. **62**(3), 773–783 (2015)

4. Uğur, C., Korcyl, G., Michel, J., Penschuk, M., Traxler, M.: 264 channel TDC platform applying 65 channel high precision (7.2 psRMS) FPGA based TDCs. In: 2013 IEEE Nordic-Mediterranean Workshop on Time-to-Digital Converters, Perugia, Italy, 3 Oct 2013 (2013)

5. Wang, Y., Kuang, J., Liu, C., Cao, Q.: A 3.9-ps RMS precision time-to-digital converter using ones-counter encoding scheme in a Kintex-7 FPGA. IEEE Trans. Nucl. Sci. **64**(10), 2713–2718 (2017)

6. Wu, J., Shi, Z.: The 10-ps wave union TDC: improving FPGA TDC resolution beyond its cell delay. In: IEEE Nuclear Science Symposium, Dresden, Germany, 19–25 Oct 2008 (2008)

A Resource Reduced Application-Specific FPGA Switch

Qian Zhao[1](✉)(iD), Yoshimasa Ohnishi[1](iD), Masahiro Iida[2](iD),
and Takaichi Yoshida[1](iD)

[1] Kyushu Institute of Technology, 680-4 Kawazu, Iizuka-shi, Japan
{cho,takaichi}@ai.kyutech.ac.jp, ohnishi@el.kyutech.ac.jp
[2] Kumamoto University, 2-39-1 Kurokami Chuo-ku, Kumamoto, Japan
iida@cs.kumamoto-u.ac.jp

Abstract. Public cloud providers are employing more and more FPGAs
as hardware accelerators in data centers. For large applications that
requiring cooperation among multiple FPGAs, a network for connecting these accelerators is necessary. Most high-performance commercial
switches are designed for general purpose networks, so that have high
costs. On the other hand, FPGA-based programmable switches can be
customized with minimum necessary functions, but the high-performance
full-crossbar design requires too many resources to implement a many-
port switch on them. In this work, based on the fact that network topologies of a specific type of applications commonly follow a particular pattern, we show a method of designing and implementing an application-
specific switch with reduced resources on FPGAs. Our case studies show
that such resource reduced switches can implement a high-performance
network with low-cost commercial FPGAs.

1 Introduction

Employing FPGAs as hardware accelerators to enable high-performance computing in low-power consumption have been a noticeable trend in clouds [1].
When a large number of FPGAs are available in a cluster and more accelerators
require cooperation among multiple FPGAs, a high-performance, high-flexibility
and low-cost network for connecting these FPGAs become necessary.

In this work, the conventional network connected by network interface cards
(NICs) and the FPGA network are considered as the primary network and the
secondary network, respectively. Three network architectures are shown in Fig. 1.
And pros and cons of these architectures are listed in Table 1. Figure 1(a) shows
an FPGA mesh network, in which an FPGA connects to FPGAs neighboring
to it with Multi-Gigabit Transceiver (MGT) links [2,3]. A simple switch for
routing data across the mesh network has to be implemented in all FPGA nodes.
This architecture has advantages of low wiring cost, high bandwidth and low
latency for local nodes communications. As the physical wires connect only the
nearest neighbor (NN) nodes, it cannot implement wide range communications
efficiently. The NN network is widely used in high-performance computing (HPC)

© Springer Nature Switzerland AG 2019
C. Hochberger et al. (Eds.): ARC 2019, LNCS 11444, pp. 58–67, 2019.
https://doi.org/10.1007/978-3-030-17227-5_5

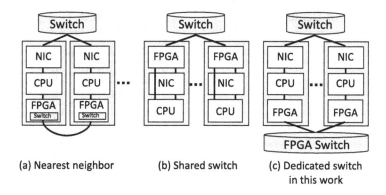

Fig. 1. Network architectures of FPGA attached systems.

Table 1. Pros and cons of networks.

	Topology flexibility	Wiring cost	Bandwidth Local	Bandwidth Wide	Latency Local	Latency Wide
(a) Nearest neighbor	×	△	○	×	○	×
(b) Shared switch	○	○	△	△	△	△
(c) Dedicated switch	○	×	△	○	○	○

applications, in which communications mainly occur between neighboring nodes. For cloud applications, a more flexible network solution is required.

Figure 1(b) shows a network architecture implemented in Microsoft Catapult V2 [1]. FPGAs share a common datacenter network with NICs so that connectivity between FPGAs is not restricted by physical wirings. However, the network bandwidth and latency using a shared switch are lower than Fig. 1(a).

Figure 1(c) shows an FPGA network with a dedicated switch proposed in this work. This architecture has merits of high-throughput, high-flexibility and fewer resource occupation of FPGA nodes. The main drawback is the additional wiring cost of the secondary network. In this research, we suppose the FPGA switch is used for connecting FPGA accelerators within the same server rack (ex. 42 nodes at maximum in a standard 42-U rack), so the wiring cost is manageable.

For an accelerator switch, its design targets are different from the primary network switch. Recent commercial switches have been designed with more functionalities such as network virtualization, deep packet processing, security, etc. However, additional features usually degrade performance. For an accelerator network, providing low-latency and high-bandwidth performance is more important than the functional diversity. Also, custom protocol support is necessary. It is difficult to implement complex protocol stacks within a hardware accelerator, so custom lightweight protocols are commonly adopted. The above two conditions cannot be satisfied by a commercial software-defined network (SDN) [4] processor.

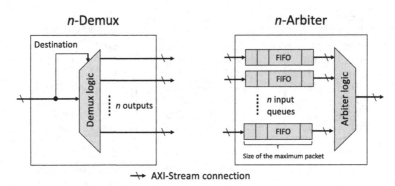

Fig. 2. Basic switch modules: demultiplexer and arbiter.

In this work, we use an FPGA to implement a high-performance and low-cost switch for the accelerator network, as shown in Fig. 1(c). Accelerator networks for cloud applications of the same class usually share the same topology such as a ring network, a 2D-Torus network, and a 3D-Torus network, etc. Benefit from the reconfigurability of an FPGA, we can generate a switch with the minimum function set required by an application, thus maximum resource efficiency and performance. Our contributions are as follows.

1. We propose an application-specific datapath design method for FPGA switch, which requires much fewer resources than a full-crossbar design but achieves the same performance.
2. We propose a CAD tool to generate application-specific switch. We use bit-stream caching and partial reconfiguration approaches to shorten the generation time of switch designs.

2   Proposed FPGA Switch

2.1   Basic Switch Modules

Two essential modules of a switch are demultiplexer (demux) and arbiter, as shown in Fig. 2. A demux module forwards a packet from the input to an output according to the destination of a packet. A commercial switch usually uses a programmable lookup module to index a destination for a packet with IP address. As we only consider a single-layer accelerator network, we code the switch conditions (an IP address or a custom node number) in the demux module to save resources. A custom protocol can be easily supported by redefining these conditions. An arbiter module is an input multiplexer, which reads a packet from input queues in a round-robin policy and forwards the packet to the output. Each input of an arbiter module has a BRAM (Block RAM) implemented FIFO (First-in, First-out) that can buffer a packet of the maximum size (1,500 bytes). These buffers consume most of the BRAM resources of a switch design. A packet

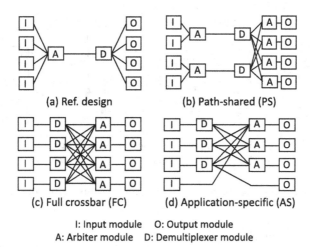

(a) Ref. design   (b) Path-shared (PS)

(c) Full crossbar (FC)   (d) Application-specific (AS)

I: Input module   O: Output module
A: Arbiter module   D: Demultiplexer module

Fig. 3. Examples of basic switch designs (a-c) and the proposed switch design (d).

processing datapath consists of demux and arbiter modules. In this work, the interconnections between these modules use AXI-Stream protocol with a data width of 256-bit (32 bytes). We note an n-output demux as n-Demux and an n-input arbiter as n-Arbiter.

2.2   Basic Switch Designs

Figure 3(a) to (c) show three typical switch datapath designs. Figure 3(a) is a basic switch that can forward packets from any input port to any desired output port with a single shared datapath, however, has low throughput and latency performance. Suppose a datapath with a 256-bit data width working at a 175 MHz clock; then the throughput is 44.8 Gbps, which is far from enough for the implementation of a standard 10GbE 48-port switch (480 Gbps required). Besides, since incoming packets are processed with the round-robin policy by arbiters, the latency will be degraded when the number of ports increases. In the worst case, the packet in the last scheduled datapath of an n-input arbiter has to wait for $n \times (1,500/32)$ cycles to be processed.

Figure 3(b) shows a method to enhance the internal bandwidth by providing more datapaths. Each datapath handles a part of packet requests, therefore near n times better performance can be achieved by implementing n datapaths. When the number of datapath n equals the number of inputs and outputs, we can get a full-crossbar switch shown in Fig. 3(c). A full-crossbar provides a dedicate datapath for each I/O port. Thus it has the highest performance. However, the resource utilization of a full-crossbar architecture grows in $O(n^2)$ according to the number of ports n increases, so it requires much more resources than designs of Fig. 3(a) and (b). Commonly, a full-crossbar based many-port switch requires more resources than most commercial FPGAs can provide, so it is not practical.

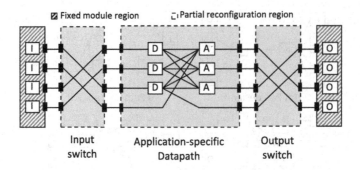

Fig. 4. Proposed switch with input and output switch blocks.

2.3 Proposed Switch Design

Applications of the same class usually share the same topology. Therefore, to implement a high-performance switch with an FPGA, we keep the number of datapath of a full-crossbar datapath but reduce unnecessary resources for a certain application to obtain an application-specific datapath, as the example shown in Fig. 3(d). Resource reduction can be achieved in two aspects. First, we can remove unnecessary datapaths of unconnected ports. For example, the first and the second demuxes of Fig. 3(d) have no connection to the fourth port so that can be removed. Second, after removing unnecessary paths, we can use smaller demux and arbiter modules with a required number of outputs or inputs. For example, the first and the second demuxes of Fig. 3(d) have three outputs, and the second and the third arbiters have three inputs. For the best case like a ring topology adopted in Microsoft Catapult V1 [1], each datapath only has one input and one output, so that all demux and arbiter modules can be removed to achieve the least resource utilization (e.g., the fourth path of Fig. 3(d)).

The proposed switch has to be reconfigured to implement networks for different applications. However, the compiling and reconfiguring of an entire FPGA requires a long time. The proposed switch can be optionally divided into few partial reconfigurable regions, and each of these regions can be individually compiled and reconfigured to save the time for implementation. As Fig. 4 shows, these partial reconfigurable regions include an input switch region, a datapath region, and an output switch region. For networks that can share the same datapath but with different I/O orders, only the input switch and the output switch have to be updated. These I/O switch blocks are implemented with fewer FPGA resources than the main datapath, therefore can be compiled and reconfigured in a shorter time. However, a very large application-specific datapath is difficult to be implemented in a reconfiguration region under current partial reconfiguration technology provided by FPGA vendors, as it usually occupies most regions on an FPGA.

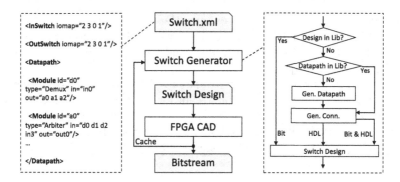

Fig. 5. Switch generation flow.

3   Switch Generation Tool

3.1   Design Flow

The target of the proposed design flow is to generate an application-specific switch automatically and efficiently, as shown in Fig. 5. A switch specification file of the XML format is used to describe a desired switch structure. The proposed switch generator reads a switch specification file and then generates a corresponding switch project. Then, we use a vendor FPGA CAD system to compile the switch project and generate bitstream. At last, a host system reconfigures the target FPGA with the generated bitstream. Next, we explain all the steps in detail.

The switch specification file showed in Fig. 5 gives a simple example that illustrating a part of the switch Fig. 3(d). First, the connectivity of the input switch and the output switch are described in the *InSwitch* element and the *OutSwitch* element, respectively. The numbers listed in *iomap* attribute mean the 1st, 2nd, 3rd, and 4th inputs are mapped to the 3rd, 4th, 1st, and 2nd outputs, respectively. In most cases, the *iomaps* of the *InSwitch* and the *OutSwitch* are the same. However, they are allowed to be different in the proposed tool. Next, datapaths are described by a *Datapath* element. Modules of demux and arbiter are listed as *Module* elements within the *Datapath* element. Each module has a unique *id*, which is used to describe connectivity between modules within the *in* attribute and the *out* attribute.

The design flow of the proposed switch generation tool is given on the right side of Fig. 5. A bitstream caching mechanism is implemented to shorten the switch generation time, specifically for a design or a datapath that have generated before. The entire flow is explained as follows. The switch generator reads a switch specification file, then searches the library for a switch of the same topology. If the cache exists, the tool exports the switch bitstream directly. Otherwise, the tool continues to search the library for a datapath that contains the requested topology using a simplified subgraph isomorphism solver. If the cache exists, the tool only generates RTL (Register transfer level) codes of the input switch and the output switch, then exports the switch project with the datapath block bitstream and RTL codes of I/O switch blocks. Otherwise, the tool generates RTL codes of the datapath block and I/O switch blocks, then exports an RTL level switch project.

After the switch project is generated, the FPGA CAD system is executed to compile the design and generate a bitstream for the target FPGA. Meanwhile, the switch specification together with the bitstreams of the switch level and the datapath block level are cached in the library for future use. For cloud applications, a central library will be effective for sharing switch designs among tenants.

3.2   Compiling and Reconfiguration Overhead

The main drawback of the proposed reconfigurable switch is the long compile time and reconfiguration time for new switches. For the best use case, the switch bitstream is pre-compiled during the design time of an application and can be repeated used during runtime. So there is no compile overhead at the runtime. During the reconfiguration, the FPGA switch will be stopped for a few seconds, which is considered acceptable for an accelerator network utilized by a single application. In practice, most cluster system for scientific computing applications satisfy such requirements.

For other cases, the proposed partial reconfigurable approach and caching mechanism can shorten the compile time. As applications of the same class usually share the same topology, the partial bitstream of the datapath can be cached and reused. If the I/O orders of accelerator nodes are different, only I/O switch blocks have to be regenerated, which is faster than recompiling the entire switch design. A challenge left for the future work is how to reconfigure the FPGA switch shared by multiple applications without disturbing each other.

4   Case Study

In this section, we compare the resource utilization of the proposed application-specific (AS) switch with a path-shared (PS) switch and a full-crossbar (FC) switch. All switches operate as a 10GbE switch using Xilinx 10G ethernet subsystem IP v3.1. The target FPGA board used for evaluation is Xilinx KCU1500, which is a middle-end FPGA with 64 MGT ports. The CAD tool we used was Vivado 2017.1.

4.1   Basic Module Evaluation

In this work, the demux module has no buffers, so the resource usage of demuxes with different output sizes are the same. The number of used LUT, FF, and BRAM for a demux are 177, 603, and 4.5, respectively. The resource usage of arbiters with input sizes from 4 to 36 are evaluated and listed in Fig. 6. We can see a linear growth of the resource usage of LUT, FF, and BRAM when the input size increases.

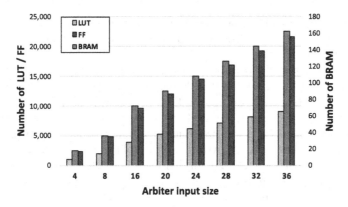

Fig. 6. Arbiter resource usage of different input sizes.

For the performance, the latencies of the proposed demux and arbiter are 3 clocks and 4 clocks, respectively. The latency of a datapath with one demux and one that used in FC and AS arbiter is 7 clocks. The clock frequency was 175 MHz, so the latency is 40 ns. On the other hand, a PS datapath has one demux and two arbiters, so the latency is 11 clocks. After considering the latency of I/O modules, the proposed FPGA switch still has a comparative performance with high-end commercial switches (commonly over 200 ns).

4.2   Torus Networks

Torus network cases used for evaluation were a 2D-Torus network of 6×6 scale (a 36-port switch is required) and a 3D-Torus network of $3 \times 3 \times 3$ scale (a 27-port switch is required). Torus networks are widely used in scientific applications such as cellular automata, FFT, etc. We compare the LUT, FF, and BRAM utilization of PS, FC, and AS designs. The datapath clock of all designs was

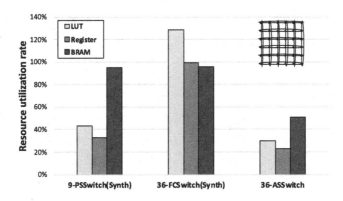

Fig. 7. Resource of 2D-Torus switch.

175 MHz. If a design can be successfully implemented, resource utilization data were derived from the routed design report. Otherwise, data were derived from the synthesized design report.

The results of the 2D-Torus network are shown in Fig. 7. For a PS design (Fig. 3(b)), since all 36 ports of 10GbE require 360 Gb/s bandwidth in total, a 9-datapaths (44.8 Gb/s per datapath) PS was generated. However, the implementation was failed because of high BRAM usage. A crossbar design can provide better performance than a PS design using individual datapaths. The FC design (Fig. 3(c)) that using 36-Arbiters and 36-Demuxes in all paths requires 29% more LUTs (LUTs are used for FIFOs when BRAM usage near 100%) than the target FPGA can provide. Since each node in a 2D-Torus network only connects to its nearing neighbor nodes in four directions, we can make an AS design with 4-Arbiters and 4-Demuxes instead of 36-Arbiters and 36-Demuxes. As a result, the AS design reduces 46.3% of BRAM utilization while keeping the same bandwidth and latency performance as the FC design. Besides, when the scale of the 2D-Torus network increases, the size an FC design increases in $O(n^2)$, on the other hand, the AS design, in this case, increases in $O(n)$.

The observed results of the 3D-Torus network are similar to the 2D-Torus network, as shown in Fig. 8. For a PS design, since all 27 ports require 270 Gb/s bandwidth in total, seven datapaths were implemented. Although the target FPGA can provide enough resources for the FC design, which uses 27-Arbiters and 27-Demuxes in all paths, the routing was failed for unsolvable congestions at last. Since each node in a 3D-Torus network only connects to its nearest neighbor nodes in six directions, we can make an AS design with 6-Arbiters and 6-Demuxes instead of 27-Arbiters and 27-Demuxes. As a result, the AS design reduces 50% of BRAM utilization of the FC design. We can see the proposed AS switch can implement the same performance as FC design, but the resource utilization is even fewer than the PS design. Besides, the network architecture using the proposed application-specific switch can provide high flexibility for various topologies required by cloud applications by updating datapath circuits.

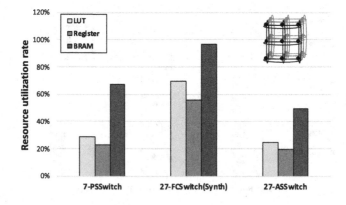

Fig. 8. Resource of 3D-Torus switch.

5 Conclusion and Future Works

In this work, we have shown that high-performance crossbar switch for accelerator networks can be implemented with commercial FPGAs by utilizing the application-specific resource-reduction technique. In the future work, we will implement more switch functions like traffic controlling with the application-specific method to achieve both functionality and performance. And then produce a switch prototype to examine this work with real-world applications.

References

1. Caulfield, A.M., et al.: A cloud-scale acceleration architecture. In: Proceedings of the 49th Annual IEEE/ACM International Symposium on Microarchitecture, October 2016
2. Tsurata, C., Kaneda, T., Nishikawa, N., Amano, H.: Accelerator-in-switch: a framework for tightly coupled switching hub and an accelerator with FPGA. In: Proceedings of International Conference on Field Programmable Logic and Applications, September 2017
3. Sheng, J.Y., Xiong, Q.Q., Yang, C., Herbordt, M.C.: Collective communication on FPGA clusters with static scheduling. ACM SIGARCH Comput. Archit. News **44**(4), 2–7 (2016)
4. Bosshart, P., et al.: P4: programming protocol-independent packet processors. ACM SIGCOMM Comput. Commun. **44**(3), 87–95 (2014)
5. Zilberman, N., Audzevich, Y., Covington, G.A., Moore, A.W.: NetFPGA SUME: toward 100 Gbps as research commodity. IEEE Micro **34**(5), 32–41 (2014)

Software-Defined FPGA Accelerator Design for Mobile Deep Learning Applications

Panagiotis G. Mousouliotis[(✉)] and Loukas P. Petrou

Division of Electronics and Computer Engineering,
Department of Electrical and Computer Engineering, Faculty of Engineering,
Aristotle University of Thessaloniki, 54124 Thessaloniki, Greece
pmousoul@ece.auth.gr, loukas@eng.auth.gr

Abstract. Convolutional neural networks (CNNs) have been successfully used to attack problems such as object recognition, object detection, semantic segmentation, and scene understanding. The rapid development of deep learning goes hand by hand with the adaptation of GPUs for accelerating its processes, such as network training and inference. Even though FPGA design exists long before the use of GPUs for accelerating computations and despite the fact that high-level synthesis (HLS) tools are getting more attractive, the adaptation of FPGAs for deep learning research and application development is poor due to the requirement of hardware design related expertise. This work presents a workflow for deep learning mobile application acceleration on small low-cost low-power FPGA devices using HLS tools. This workflow eases the design of an improved version of the SqueezeJet accelerator used for the speedup of mobile-friendly low-parameter ImageNet class CNNs, such as the SqueezeNet v1.1 and the ZynqNet. Additionally, the workflow includes the development of an HLS-driven analytical model which is used for performance estimation of the accelerator.

Keywords: FPGA accelerator · High-level synthesis ·
Mobile embedded systems · CNN · Deep learning application

1 Introduction

HLS tools [11] provide a higher level of abstraction in digital design and increased productivity when compared to more traditional design methods, such as the hardware description languages (HDLs). This increased productivity comes at the cost of limited design flexibility, compared to HDLs, plus a steep learning curve [1]. To make HLS-driven design more attractive, Xilinx introduced the SDSoC tool [8]. With SDSoC, the user marks for FPGA acceleration functions of the input C/C++ application code which are compiled to be run on the CPU side of the FPGA SoC.

© Springer Nature Switzerland AG 2019
C. Hochberger et al. (Eds.): ARC 2019, LNCS 11444, pp. 68–77, 2019.
https://doi.org/10.1007/978-3-030-17227-5_6

In order to develop mobile deep learning applications on an FPGA SoC, we accelerate mobile-friendly ImageNet class CNNs [5,9], which are characterized by small model size and, relatively, limited computational requirements. The characteristics of these CNNs translate in limited requirements in terms of BRAM and DSP FPGA resources; meaning that small, low-power, and low-cost FPGA SoC devices, such as the xc7z020clg484-1 FPGA SoC device, can be used.

Porting mobile-friendly CNNs onto small FPGA SoCs using SDSoC is not a straightforward procedure. Our contribution includes a workflow where: (1) CNNs are first described in a higher-than-C/C++-level language such as Matlab, (2) CNNs' feature-maps and parameters are quantized at 8-bit dynamic fixed-point format using Ristretto [4], (3) the quantized CNNs are implemented in C/C++, (4) the computational intensive functions of the C/C++ description are re-written in a HLS-compatible way in order to be accelerated, and, finally, (5) the SDSoC tool is used for developing an application and deploying it to a specific FPGA SoC board. In this work, we also improve and extent the design of the SqueezeJet [10] accelerator and use it to accelerate both SqueezeNet v1.1[1] [6] and ZynqNet [2] CNNs achieving 13.34 fps for the execution of the SqueezeNet v1.1 and 11.54 fps for the ZynqNet on the xc7z020clg484-1 FPGA SoC device. Finally, we show how the HLS performance estimation information can be used to develop an analytical model of an accelerator design. The results of the analytical model of our accelerator are the closest to the real accelerator latency measurements performed on the FPGA SoC device when compared with the performance estimation and the C/RTL Co-Simulation functionalities of Vivado HLS.

The rest of the paper is organized as follows: Sect. 2 presents related work. Our software-defined workflow is described in Sect. 3. Section 4 presents the SqueezeJet-2 accelerator design as an improved version of SqueezeJet. The development of our analytical model is presented in Sect. 5. Section 6 shows: (1) results related to the performance of our analytical model in terms of accuracy, and (2) results related to the performance of our accelerator in terms of latency and resources utilization. Finally, Sect. 7 concludes the paper and proposes future work.

2 Related Work

In this section we refer to works that could be used to develop mobile deep learning applications with FPGA SoCs. Mobile computer vision applications (automotive, drones, etc.) often pose real-time performance constraints translating in minimal latency or a batch size equal to one.

ZynqNet describes a CNN architecture and an HLS design for the acceleration of this network. ZynqNet derived from SqueezeNet by replacing the combination of convolutional and maxpool layers with a convolutional layer having increased stride [12]. This transformation simplifies the accelerator design; by implementing a convolutional layer and a global pooling layer, the ZynqNet accelerator can process the whole CNN except the last softmax layer. Convolutional layer

---

[1] https://github.com/DeepScale/SqueezeNet/tree/master/SqueezeNet_v1.1.

acceleration is achieved by calculating multiple output feature-map channels in parallel using processing elements (PEs) which fully unroll the calculation of a 3×3 kernel.

In Angel-Eye [3], a design flow for mapping CNNs onto embedded FPGA devices is proposed. This design flow includes a dynamic fixed-point quantization strategy, a software controlled hardware architecture with 3×3 convolution kernel support, and a run-time workflow which allows a single frame to be processed by multiple CNNs. Since real-time processing is of main concern, Angel-Eye uses a batch size of one in order to minimize latency.

In [14] a latency-driven design method is presented as an extension of the fpgaConvNet modeling framework [13]. This work models CNNs using the synchronous dataflow (SDF) model of computation. CNNs are interpreted as directed acyclic graphs (DAGs) whose nodes are mapped to hardware building blocks which are interconnected to form the final SDF graph. The SDF model of computation allows the generation of static schedules of execution and the calculation of the amount of buffer memory between the interconnected hardware building blocks. The SDF graph is partitioned along its depth and a single flexible reference architecture is generated which enables the execution of all the subgraphs. In contrast to Angle-Eye, this reference architecture is tailored to a specific CNN and it is optimized in terms of latency. Their framework produces synthesizable Vivado HLS code for the resulting architecture.

We follow a similar approach to ZynqNet by developing an accelerator which targets CNNs optimized for embedded mobile applications; the architecture of these CNNs can be easily adapted to run on FPGA SoCs. For this purpose, we improve the design of the SqueezeJet convolutional layer accelerator and we also add to it support for performing the maxpool operation. Similarly to Angel-Eye, we use Ristretto for 8-bit dynamic fixed point data quantization. Our accelerator is software controlled and it is using parallel operating PEs that execute concurrently 1×1 kernel convolutions which calculate multiple output feature map channels. Thus, it can support arbitrary convolution kernel sizes without limiting the utilization of the accelerator computing resources, which are valuable in embedded mobile FPGA SoC devices. We also use a batch size of one to minimize the latency and achieve real-time performance. Finally, we don't use a mathematically-driven design methodology as it is the case with fpgaConvNet, but we derive an analytical model for the performance estimation of our accelerator, which can be used for design improvements by means of design-space exploration.

3   Software-Defined Workflow

This workflow could be generalized and applied for the FPGA acceleration of any algorithm if a quantization framework existed which could handle a broad range of algorithms.

We used Ristretto [4], a deep learning quantization framework implemented as a Caffe [7] extension. Ristretto decreases the bit width of the feature-maps and parameters in every CNN layer and performs a CNN forward pass to get the accuracy; it keeps reducing the bit width up to a network accuracy threshold set by the user. We quantize both the SqueezeNet v1.1 and the ZynqNet CNNs down to 8 bits in both feature-maps and parameters using dynamic fixed-point arithmetic. The top-1 accuracy drop is 2.76% and 1.44% for the SqueezeNet v1.1 and the ZynqNet networks respectively.

We adapted and extended a SqueezeNet Matlab project[2] to support the forward pass of SqueezeNet v1.1 and ZynqNet in floating-point and dynamic fixed-point modes. Matcaffe, a Caffe Matlab interface, is used to generate the network parameters and inter-layer network data in order to compare the Caffe results against those of the Matlab implementation. The results from Ristretto are used in the Matlab implementation to generate the parameters for a dynamic fixed-point network model; we developed a Matlab script that can be used to save the generated network parameters to binary files.

Furthermore, we developed a C/C++ project which implements and tests the forward pass of the floating-point and fixed-point versions of the CNNs by using the binary files generated in the aforementioned Matlab project.

In the next step, the computationally intensive CNN layer functions, the convolutional and the maxpool, are re-written in an HLS-compatible way.

Finally, the whole C/C++ project is imported in SDSoC for testing and implementation.

4   Accelerator Design

4.1   SqueezeJet-2

SqueezeJet-2 is an improved re-design and extension of the SqueezeJet accelerator [10]; its improvements follow.

Support for Stride Values Larger than 1: The ZynqNet CNN uses convolutional layers with a stride equal to 2.

Single Accelerator Design: SqueezeJet used two accelerators; one for the first SqueezeNet v1.1 layer and another one for the rest of the layers. Our current implementation uses a single accelerator for all the CNNs' layers. To overcome the first layer's small input channel issue, we use a software solution that reshapes the input and the parameters of the first layer in order to increase the computation utilization of our accelerator.

Use of Double Buffering Technique: In this way, the communication latency of reading the input feature-map data is hidden behind the computation of the convolution operation.

Support for the Maxpool Operation: We re-arranged the SqueezeNet v1.1 layers to bring the maxpool layers before the merge layers. The idea is to make it possible for our accelerator to perform the calculations for both the convolutional and the

---

[2] https://github.com/mtmd/SqueezeNet_MATLAB.

maxpool layers without the need of sending data back to main memory. In the case where only the convolution operation is required, the maxpool operation is bypassed.

Use of the LUTs to Increase the Number of the Implementable Multiply-Accumulate (MAC) Units: Although the xc7z020clg484-1 FPGA SoC device includes 220 DSP blocks, we managed to implement 256 MAC units (16 PEs with each of them consisting of 16 MAC units) by making use of the resources related HLS pragma; we implemented half the MAC units using DSP blocks and the other half using LUTs. Unfortunately, the HLS synthesis tool is unable to map multiple 8-bit multiplications on a single DSP block.

Support for dynamic fixed-point arithmetic.

4.2   Cache Organization and Operation

Below, we provide details related to the SqueezeJet-2 cache organization and operation regarding the convolution operation; the description of the caches used for the implementation of the convolution operation follows.

_weights[PAR_FACT][Q_CHOxKxKxCHI_MAX]: Consists of a group of PAR_FACT caches of size Q_CHOxKxKxCHI_MAX. These caches result from the partitioning of the _weights array with a factor of PAR_FACT. This is done in order to have simultaneous access to these caches. Each of these caches is used by one of the PAR_FACT PEs, which is responsible to calculate Q_CHO output channels of a specific output pixel[3]. Because the weight and bias parameters will be reused in the calculation of every output-feature-map pixel, we store all the CNN parameters in the on-chip BRAMs. In case where this is not possible, we partition the parameters in the output-channel dimension and we calculate specific output-feature-map channels in every accelerator function invocation; in the end we merge the partial results in the output-channel dimension to get the final result.

_bias[PAR_FACT][Q_CHO_MAX]: This cache group holds the CNN layer's bias values and its use is similar to the one of the _weights cache group.

linebuf[K_MAX][WIxCHI_MAX]: This is a single cache of size K_MAX by WIxCHI_MAX. It is described in this way because when the kernel's height by width size is larger than 1×1, some feature-map lines will be reused as the line-buffer array "slides down" the input-feature-map.

linebuf_idx[K_MAX]: This is an array used as a "pointer" that determines the order of the line-buffer lines as they "slide down" the input-feature-map. This is done to avoid having an array of pointers-to-line-buffers because the HLS tool used cannot handle passing to functions pointer-to-pointer-to-arrays arguments.

linebuf_win0[KxKxCHI_MAX], linebuf_win1[KxKxCHI_MAX]: These are two caches which "slide horizontally" on the linebuf cache. We use two line-buffer windows instead of one in order to implement double buffering, which is used

---

[3] In this work, "pixel" is used to describe the set of all the channels that can be addressed with some specific spatial coordinates. This notion extents in the case of a feature-map line or a line-buffer line.

for overlapping communication with computation; the process of reading new input-feature-map data from the main memory while executing the convolution operation.

out_pix0[CHO_MAX], out_pix1[CHO_MAX]: These are two caches which hold an output-pixel result. We use two of them as part of the double buffering implementation.

Below, listing 1.1 shows the top level C/C++ HLS description of the convolution operation; pre-calculation of often-used terms, cache initialization, and HLS pragmas are omitted.

Listing 1.1. Top-level HLS description of the convolution operation

```
1   // For each output row
2   L_H_OUT: for ( uint8_t ho = 0; ho != h_out; ho++ ) {
3     // Shift line-buffer ''down'' in the input-feature-map.
4     // Fill the ''last'' line-buffer line with KxCHI values (K 3D pixels).
5     shift_linebuf( fmap_in, &iidx, linebuf, linebuf_idx, WIxCHI, KxCHI, kernel,
6       stride, ho, h_out, PADxCHI );
7     uint16_t lb_pixel_pt = KxCHI; // last line-buffer pixel ''pointer''
8     // Line-buffer window initialization
9     init_linebuf_win( linebuf, linebuf_idx, linebuf_win0, KxCHI, KxKxCHI, 0 );
10    // line-buffer pixel ''pointers'' for line-buffer windows
11    uint16_t pixel_iwp0 = ( SxCHI << 1 );
12    uint16_t pixel_iwp1 = SxCHI;
13    // For each output pixel (in each output row)
14    L_W_OUT: for ( uint8_t wo = 0; wo != w_out; wo++ ) {
15      if ( wo%2 == 0 ) {
16        // Calc pixel
17        pixel_calc( linebuf_win0, _weights, _bias, KxKxCHI,
18          Q_CHOxKxKxCHI, Q_CHO, out_pix0, ei, eo, ep );
19        // Update line-buffer line and line-buffer window
20        update_linebuf_win( fmap_in, &iidx, linebuf, kernel,
21          SxCHI, WIxCHI, &lb_pixel_pt, linebuf_idx, linebuf_win1,
22          KxCHI, KxKxCHI, &pixel_iwp1, PADxCHI, ho, h_out, stride );
23        // Write back to off-chip memory
24        write_back( fmap_out, &oidx, ch_out, out_pix1, wo, use_relu );
25      }
26      else {
27        // Calc pixel
28        pixel_calc( linebuf_win1, _weights, _bias, KxKxCHI,
29          Q_CHOxKxKxCHI, Q_CHO, out_pix1, ei, eo, ep );
30        // Update line-buffer line and line-buffer window
31        update_linebuf_win( fmap_in, &iidx, linebuf, kernel,
32          SxCHI, WIxCHI, &lb_pixel_pt, linebuf_idx, linebuf_win0,
33          KxCHI, KxKxCHI, &pixel_iwp0, PADxCHI, ho, h_out, stride );
34        // Write back to off-chip memory
35        write_back( fmap_out, &oidx, ch_out, out_pix0, wo, use_relu );
36      }
37    }
38    // Write back to off-chip memory leftover pixel
39    if ( w_out%2 == 0 )
40      write_back( fmap_out, &oidx, ch_out, out_pix1, 1, use_relu );
41    else
42      write_back( fmap_out, &oidx, ch_out, out_pix0, 1, use_relu );
43  }
```

The shift_linebuf() function "shifts" the line-buffer cache down the input feature map using a stride step. Then, using init_linebuf_win(), the first line-buffer window is initialized with line-buffer data. Two line-buffer window "pointers" are initialized with line-buffer addresses (indices) that will be used to fill the line-buffer windows with new data. The pixel_calc(), update_linebuf_win(), and the `write_back()` functions are executed concurrently taking advantage of the double buffering technique.

In our implementation, the SqueezeJet-2 accelerator exchanges data with the ARM CPU of the xc7z020clg484-1 FPGA SoC device using AXI buses. Specifically the interfaces used are: AXI General Purpose (GP) interface for simple arguments, such as input-feature-map size, kernel size, stride, etc., AXI Accelerator Coherency Port (ACP) for input/output-feature-maps which require to be cache coherent since they are used in CNN layers running in the ARM system, such as the merge layer, and AXI High Performance (HP) Port for weight/bias CNN parameters which don't require cache coherency. In the case of the AXI ACP and HP ports, simple DMAs are used for efficient data movement.

5   HLS-Driven Analytical Model

We derive our analytical model of performance estimation using HLS information such as pipeline depths, and function/loop call overheads.

The convolution operation's performance can be formulated by describing analytically the cost, in terms of cycle count, of the `precalc_terms()` function, the `init_caches()` function, and the L_H_OUT loop which contains the `shift_linebuf()` function, the `init_linebuf_win()` function, and the L_W_OUT loop. The L_W_OUT loop contains three functions with the dominating one being the `pixel_calc()` function.

The `pixel_calc()` function consists of the `calc_ch_out()` and `write_pix()` functions operating in dataflow; dataflow is a function-level pipeline operation mode. Function `calc_ch_out()` calculates one output-future-map pixel by assigning the computation to PAR_FACT parallel-working PEs, each of them calculating Q_CHOxKxKxCHI = CHOxKxKxCHI/PAR_FACT MAC operations, CHI_NUM operations at each cycle. The analytical description of the performance, in terms of cycle count, of the `calc_ch_out()` function is given by the following equation:

$$CCO_{CC} = CCO\_DSP\_LUT_{CC} =$$
$$(CHO{\cdot}K{\cdot}K{\cdot}CHI)/(PAR_{FACT}{\cdot}CHI_{NUM}) \qquad (1)$$
$$+PIPE\_CCO\_DSP\_LUT_{FILL} + CCO\_DSP\_LUT_{OVER}$$

where $CHO{\cdot}K{\cdot}K{\cdot}CHI$ is the total number of MACs required to calculate one output pixel (it is also the number of weight parameters; it is equal to output-channels by kernel-height by kernel-width by input-channels), $PIPE\_CCO\_DSP\_LUT_{FILL}$ is the pipeline fill overhead of the `calc_ch_out_dsp_lut()` function's loop; the `calc_ch_out_dsp_lut()` function call, which represents the calculation done by a PE, is called by the `calc_ch_out()` function, and $CCO\_DSP\_LUT_{OVER}$ is the overhead introduced with reading the arguments passed by a calling function. This overhead can be significant in the case where the function is called inside multiple nested loops as it is the case of the convolution operation. In general, for a pipelined loop the performance equation's form is:

$$LOOP_{CC} = (TRIPCOUNT{\cdot}INITIATION\_INTERVAL) + ITERATION\_LATENCY \qquad (2)$$

The accelerator is designed in such a way that forces the *INITIATION_INTERVAL* to be equal to 1 for all the pipelined loops. The *ITERATION_LATENCY* can be translated as the pipeline depth of the specific loop.

Using the above example as a guideline, we calculate the total performance of the SqueezeJet-2 accelerator.

6   Experiments and Results

Figure 1 presents results related to the analytical model of the SqueezeJet-2 dynamic fixed-point (SqJ-2-dfp) accelerator. L_TRACE represents the latency measurements of the accelerator layers using the hardware tracing feature of SDSoC when the network runs on the FPGA, L_COSIM represents the latency measurements of the accelerator layers using the C/RTL Co-Simulation feature of the SDSoC, L_PERFEST represents the worst case latency estimation of the accelerator layers using Vivado HLS synthesis; we explicitly set the min/max tripcounts for the loops of every layer, and L_MODEL represents the latency estimation of the accelerator layers using the analytical model. From Fig. 1 we conclude the following: (1) our analytical model is the closest to the L_TRACE results, (2) the L_PERFEST method is the most optimistic and shows up to 46.1 % error against the L_TRACE results; the L_COSIM presents the next max error which is 33.4 %, and finally our analytical model has a max error of 8.3 %, and (3) the average % error of the analytical model of the SqJ-2-dfp accelerator is bellow 5% (4.45%).

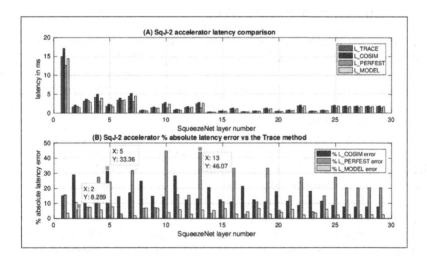

Fig. 1. (A) Latency of the accelerator measured with 3 methods and modeled analytically, and (B) the % absolute latency error of the L_COSIM, L_PERFEST, and the L_MODEL methods, against the L_TRACE method

Table 1(A) shows the resources usage of the SqJ-2-dfp, the SqueezeJet-2 floating point (SqJ-2-flp), and the ZynqNet [2] floating-point (ZqN-flp) design implementations. Table 1(B) shows the SqJ-2-dfp, the SqJ-2-flp, and the ZqN-flp accelerators' performance in terms of latency using SqueezeNet v1.1 and ZynqNet as test cases. Table 1(A) shows that, with the exception of the BRAMs, the SqJ-2-flp accelerator uses almost half the resources used by the ZqN-flp accelerator and Table 1(B) shows that the SqJ-2-flp accelerator is ten times faster than ZqN-flp when executing the ZynqNet CNN. Finally, Table 1(B) shows that the SqN-2-dfp accelerator achieves 13.34 fps for the execution of the SqueezeNet v1.1 and 11.54 fps for ZynqNet on the xc7z020clg484-1 FPGA SoC device.

Table 1. (A) Resources usage of the SqJ-2-dfp, SqJ-2-flp, and the ZqN-flp accelerators; the numbers in parentheses show the % device resource utilization, and (B) total CNN latency (ms) for the SqJ-2-dfp, SqJ-2-flp, and the ZqN-flp accelerators running at 100MHz; the ZynqNet ZqN-flp result (*) produced using HLS C/RTL Co-Simulation

(A) Resources Usage			
	SqJ-2-dfp xc7z020	SqJ-2-flp xc7z045	ZqN-flp xc7z045
LUT	36.2k *(68%)*	63k *(29%)*	154k *(70%)*
LUTRAM	3.1k *(18%)*	8.8k *(13%)*	?
FF	24.9 *(24%)*	75.6k *(17%)*	137k *(31%)*
BRAM	96.5 *(69%)*	324.5 *(60%)*	498 *(91%)*
DSP	172 *(78%)*	268 *(30%)*	739 *(82%)*
(B) Total CNN latency (ms)			
SqueezeNet v1.1	74.91	-	-
ZynqNet	86.62	*186.8	1955

7　Conclusion and Future Work

In this work we have demonstrated a workflow which eases the mapping of mobile-friendly CNNs onto low-cost low-power small FPGA SoC devices. We presented an improved version of the SqueezeJet accelerator which achieves 13.34 fps for the execution of the SqueezeNet v1.1 and 11.54 fps for the ZynqNet on the xc7z020clg484-1 FPGA SoC device. Using HLS performance estimation information, we formed an analytical performance estimation model which provides improved performance estimation when compared with the HLS build-in performance estimation and C/RTL Co-Simulation functionalities. Finally, we used C/RTL Co-Simulation and a floating-point version of our accelerator to estimate its performance for the execution of the floating-point version of ZynqNet. The results show that our accelerator is 10 times faster and, with the exception of the BRAMs, uses almost half the FPGA resources when compared against the ZqN-flp accelerator. Future work could use our analytical model for performing design space exploration and optimizing the design of our accelerator.

References

1. Ali, K.M.A., Ben Atitallah, R., Fakhfakh, N., Dekeyser, J.-L.: Exploring HLS optimizations for efficient stereo matching hardware implementation. In: Wong, S., Beck, A.C., Bertels, K., Carro, L. (eds.) ARC 2017. LNCS, vol. 10216, pp. 168–176. Springer, Cham (2017). https://doi.org/10.1007/978-3-319-56258-2_15

2. Gschwend, D.: ZynqNet: an FPGA-accelerated embedded convolutional neural network. Master ETH-Zurich: Swiss Federal Institute of Technology Zurich (2016)
3. Guo, K., et al.: Angel-Eye: a complete design flow for mapping CNN onto embedded FPGA. IEEE Trans. Comput.-Aided Des. Integr. Circ. Syst. **37**(1), 35–47 (2018)
4. Gysel, P., Pimentel, J., Motamedi, M., Ghiasi, S.: Ristretto: a framework for empirical study of resource-efficient inference in convolutional neural networks. IEEE Trans. Neural Netw. Learn. Syst. **99**, 1–6 (2018)
5. Iandola, F., Keutzer, K.: Small neural nets are beautiful: enabling embedded systems with small deep-neural-network architectures. In: Proceedings of the Twelfth IEEE/ACM/IFIP International Conference on Hardware/Software Codesign and System Synthesis Companion. ACM (2017). Article no. 1
6. Iandola, F.N., Han, S., Moskewicz, M.W., Ashraf, K., Dally, W.J., Keutzer, K.: SqueezeNet: AlexNet-level accuracy with 50x fewer parameters and <0.5 mb model size. arXiv preprint arXiv:1602.07360 (2016)
7. Jia, Y., et al.: Caffe: convolutional architecture for fast feature embedding. In: Proceedings of the 22nd ACM international conference on Multimedia, pp. 675–678. ACM (2014)
8. Kathail, V., Hwang, J., Sun, W., Chobe, Y., Shui, T., Carrillo, J.: SDSoC: a higher-level programming environment for Zynq SoC and Ultrascale+ MPSoC. In: Proceedings of the 2016 ACM/SIGDA International Symposium on Field-Programmable Gate Arrays, p. 4. ACM (2016)
9. Mousouliotis, P.G., Panayiotou, K.L., Tsardoulias, E.G., Petrou, L.P., Symeonidis, A.L.: Expanding a robot's life: low power object recognition via FPGA-based DCNN deployment. In: 2018 7th International Conference on Modern Circuits and Systems Technologies (MOCAST), pp. 1–4. IEEE (2018)
10. Mousouliotis, P.G., Petrou, L.P.: SqueezeJet: high-level synthesis accelerator design for deep convolutional neural networks. In: Voros, N., Huebner, M., Keramidas, G., Goehringer, D., Antonopoulos, C., Diniz, P.C. (eds.) ARC 2018. LNCS, vol. 10824, pp. 55–66. Springer, Cham (2018). https://doi.org/10.1007/978-3-319-78890-6_5
11. Nane, R., et al.: A survey and evaluation of FPGA high-level synthesis tools. IEEE Trans. Comput.-Aided Des. Integr. Circ. Syst. **35**(10), 1591–1604 (2016)
12. Springenberg, J.T., Dosovitskiy, A., Brox, T., Riedmiller, M.: Striving for simplicity: the all convolutional net. arXiv preprint arXiv:1412.6806 (2014)
13. Venieris, S.I., Bouganis, C.S.: fpgaConvNet: a framework for mapping convolutional neural networks on FPGAs. In: 2016 IEEE 24th Annual International Symposium on Field-Programmable Custom Computing Machines (FCCM), pp. 40–47. IEEE (2016)
14. Venieris, S.I., Bouganis, C.S.: Latency-driven design for FPGA-based convolutional neural networks. In: 2017 27th International Conference on Field Programmable Logic and Applications (FPL), pp. 1–8. IEEE (2017)

Partial Reconfiguration and Security

Probabilistic Performance Modelling when Using Partial Reconfiguration to Accelerate Streaming Applications with Non-deterministic Task Scheduling

Bruno da Silva[1,2]($\boxtimes$) (ID), An Braeken[2](ID), and Abdellah Touhafi[1,2](ID)

[1] ETRO Department, Vrije Universiteit Brussel (VUB), Brussels, Belgium
{bruno.da.silva,abdellah.touhafi}@vub.be
[2] INDI Department, Vrije Universiteit Brussel (VUB), Brussels, Belgium
an.braeken@vub.be

Abstract. Many streaming applications composed of multiple tasks self-adapt their tasks' execution at runtime as response to the processed data. This type of application promises a better solution to context switches at the cost of a non-deterministic task scheduling. Partial reconfiguration is a unique feature of FPGAs that not only offers a higher resource reuse but also performance improvements when properly applied. In this paper, a probabilistic approach is used to estimate the acceleration of streaming applications with unknown task schedule thanks to the application of partial reconfiguration. This novel approach provides insights in the feasible acceleration when partially reconfiguring regions of the FPGA are partially reconfigured in order to exploit the available resources by processing multiple tasks in parallel. Moreover, the impact of how different strategies or heuristics affect to the final performance is included in this analysis. As a result, not only an estimation of the achievable acceleration is obtained, but also a guide at the design stage when searching for the highest performance.

1 Introduction

Streaming applications are present in a wide range of domains such as digital signal processing, audio, and imaging, which require several compatible modes or configurations only active based on pre-defined contexts. Such dynamic streaming applications are able to adapt their response as reaction to an environmental change [2,5,9,13]. For instance, multifunction array radars based on a phased array need to execute multiple integrated functions such as tracking, surveillance, communication, calibration or counter measures in an unspecific order [12]. The multifunction radar has to search in multiple regions, which are sub-divided into beam positions with each position executing a task based on the previous monitoring operation. Hence, it is not possible to determine in advance what operations or tasks need to be computed at a certain moment [9]. However, such type of streaming applications can achieve high performance on FPGAs

© Springer Nature Switzerland AG 2019
C. Hochberger et al. (Eds.): ARC 2019, LNCS 11444, pp. 81–95, 2019.
https://doi.org/10.1007/978-3-030-17227-5_7

Table 1. Example of a cost table.

Task (T_i)	Probability (p_i)	Time cost (t_i)	Area cost (a_i)	Compatibility (RM_i)
T_A	1/3	t_A	1	RM_{T_A}
T_B	1/3	t_B	1/2	RM_{T_B}
T_C	1/3	t_C	1/4	RM_{T_C}

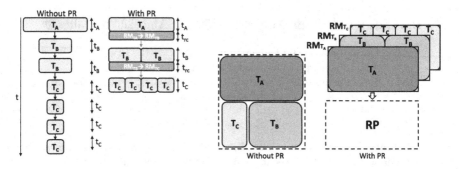

Fig. 1. Example of how PR can be used to increase performance (left) while maximizing the reuse of the reconfigurable resources (right). The dashed framed area represents the area consumption with and without PR.

when they are properly designed to exploit pipeline-level and instruction-level parallelism [8]. We believe that the use of Partial reconfiguration (PR) with the proper heuristics can further improve the performance. PR is a unique feature of FPGAs which allows the change of the functionality of reconfigurable partitions (RP) on the FPGA at runtime. The use of PR for such type of applications, where the order and the type of the tasks to be executed are not known in advance, might not justify the additional design effort to achieve residual performance acceleration.

In this paper, we not only present a general methodology to increment performance by using PR to maximize the area reuse but also a probabilistic approach to predict the achievable speedup. This probabilistic performance model provides performance insights at the design time, helping to decide parameters like the size of the RP or to evaluate the PR performance overhead. The principles of the methodology to exploit PR to accelerate a streaming application with unknown task scheduling are depicted in Fig. 1. The execution without PR requires $t_A + 2 \cdot t_B + 4 \cdot t_C$ units of time to complete one execution, where t_i corresponds to the computation time of a task i detailed in Table 1. By partially reconfiguring one RP with other configurations, called reconfigurable modules (RM), like for instance RM_{T_B} or RM_{T_C}, multiple tasks can be computed in parallel through the exploitation of the unused resources. The overall execution time is then reduced to $t_A + t_B + t_C + 2 \cdot t_{pr}$, where t_{pr} is the time overhead due to reconfiguring the RP. Moreover, this approach also leads to area savings as illustrated in Fig. 1. Instead of dedicating area to allocate each type of task, one RP can be properly dimensioned to not only allocate one instance of the most area demanding task, but also multiple instantiations of low-area demanding tasks (e.g. T_B or T_C in this example). This naive example, however, can become significantly more complex when considering multiple RPs computing hundreds of tasks that can be merged to share resources. As a result, the design effort that is required to fully exploit PR for performance acceleration is not negligible. The allocation of the tasks on the available RPs, the combination of multiple tasks to reuse resources or the schedule of the merged tasks on the reconfigurable RP are challenges that our approach helps to predict. The ultimate goal of our approach is to accurately predict the achievable acceleration when using the proposed methodology to exploit the benefits of PR.

The use of PR to support multiple configurations and to improve performance of streaming applications with unpredictable scheduling has been already used in [4] to accelerate a platform supporting PR through PCIe [3]. Although the approach used in [4] proposes heuristics to increase area reuse and performance, we present in this paper a general methodology to increase performance. For instance, our methodology introduces a parameter to reflect the reconfiguration cost which does not necessarily stands for PCIe-based reconfiguration like in [3,4] but it is also applicable for other reconfigurations interfaces like the Internal Configuration Access Port (ICAP) on Xilinx FPGAs. Moreover, a probabilistic approach to predict the achievable performance when using PR is here presented in order to reduce the design effort required to apply the proposed methodology. This probabilistic performance modelling can be used to evaluate different strategies or heuristics targeting either area savings or performance improvements without the need of implementing them on the FPGA. The main contributions of this work can be summarized as follows:

- We present a generalized heuristics-based methodology to exploit PR in order to accelerate streaming applications.
- Our approach represents the basis for probabilistic performance predictions when using PR to accelerate streaming applications.

This paper is organized as follows. Section 2 presents related work. The methodology to use PR for performance acceleration is described in Sect. 3. In Sect. 4 the problem formulation and the equations to predict performance based on the application's characteristics are introduced. An audio streaming application is used to validate the performance predictions when applying our methodology. The results are presented in Sect. 5. Finally, our conclusions are drawn in Sect. 6.

2   Related Work

Different performance prediction models when using PR have been proposed in the last decade. The authors in [6,7] present a theoretical analysis of the performance bounds of PR. The basis of their analysis is the full decomposition of the application in tasks. The tasks' timings and the operations involved in the PR are used to estimate performance bounds and speedups. Similarly, the authors in [10] propose a cost model to determine the performance impact of PR. Both approaches, however, are not directly applicable to applications with an unpredictable tasks' scheduling.

Different strategies using PR to maximize the area reuse or to increase performance have been proposed. The authors in [14,15] present a novel approach for the resource sharing of RPs by merging tasks of streaming applications with an unpredictable tasks' scheduling by identifying similarities between tasks. However, their approach targets the minimization of the FPGA reconfiguration time by optimizing the allocation of the applications on the FPGA rather than incrementing the area reuse per RP. The authors in [1] present solutions to reduce the PR cost. Their approach, consisting of an Integer-Linear Programming (ILP) and a heuristic to exploit PR techniques such as *module reuse*, does not consider the use of PR to increment the resource sharing of the RPs. Our methodology not only addresses similar types of applications, but also reduces the number of reconfigurations while prioritizing the area reuse of RPs by taking advantage of similarities between tasks to share logic resources of RPs. In addition, our probabilistic approach enables performance estimation at the design time, leading to a reduction of the overall design effort.

3   Proposed Methodology

Our generalized methodology exploits PR to accelerate streaming applications with non-deterministic task scheduling. This methodology consists of the three heuristics depicted in Fig. 2. An initial classification identifies the type of incoming tasks and tags them based on the Cost Table (CT). The merging heuristic groups tasks to be executed in parallel in the same RP based on their compatibility. The execution of all the tasks is split in iterations or time slots based on the number of tasks and RPs. Each RP has a dedicated task's queue which determines the time slot when the tasks are executed in the RP. However, scheduling strategies are needed in order to minimize the PR impact, leading to the desired performance [9]. A scheduling heuristic distributes the merged tasks between the available time slots of the RPs. As a result, the heuristics allow a performance acceleration by exploiting the area reuse.

Different heuristics can be applied on this methodology. For instance, the authors in [1] propose a scheduling heuristic targeting performance compatible with this methodology. A merging heuristic to exploit the compatibility of similar tasks, leading to a higher reuse of the available area by allocating different types of tasks in the same RM has been proposed in [4]. In any case, the proposed methodology increases the area reuse by computing compatible tasks in the same RP to accelerate the overall performance. Moreover, the proposed probabilistic approach can be adjusted to reflect the characteristics of the heuristics, like done in Sect. 4 for a merging and scheduling heuristics.

The usability of this general methodology is determined by the information available in the CT. The construction of such a table does not demand additional

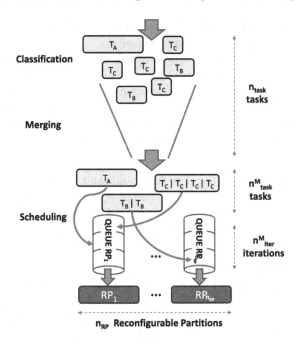

Fig. 2. Overview of the proposed methodology to exploit PR for performance accelerations.

effort than some profilings and measurements at the design stage. The probability of executing a specific task is defined by the application's characteristics and can be estimated in advance or obtained after multiple executions. The area cost of each task (a_i) is already known when implementing the task on the target FPGA. The number of tasks that can be allocated on the RP, which is hereby called the level of parallelism (LP), can be obtained based on the available resources in the RP. The parameter a_i represents the relative area demands of a task i in terms of one RP, which corresponds to the inverse of LP. The time cost (t_i) is obtained through simulations at high level or execution profiles on the FPGA once the task is implemented. The compatibility depends on the level of the desired area reuse, the available I/O and the task's characteristics. The area reuse can be increased when combining the execution of the same, or even different types of tasks on the same RM, like proposed in [4]. The available I/O bandwidth determines, together with the demanded area consumption, the value of LP. The task's characteristics determine if multiple tasks of different types can be executed in parallel. For instance, a high variance of t_i might lead to performance degradation when merging tasks with different t_i, since the merged tasks would have to wait for the most time demanding one. Finally, the size of PR must be adjusted to provide enough resources to allocate the most area demanding task. Nonetheless, its size can be enlarged to be able to allocate multiple instances of other tasks. Despite such enlargements would reduce the area savings, they might increase performance.

The cost of PR is reflected in t_{pr}, which is the time needed to reconfigure one RP. Moreover, t_{pr} increases with the amount of resources available in the RP, and must be considered when determining the size of the RP. The area overhead due to supporting PR is not considered in our approach and is assumed significantly lower than the area demanded by the streaming application's tasks.

The proposed methodology targets streaming applications with the following characteristics:

- *Non-deterministic scheduling:* The tasks and their schedule are not known in advance.
- *Non-priority tasks:* The tasks can be executed without a priority order.
- *Non-data dependencies between tasks:* The tasks in the same execution are not data dependent.

Notice that the non-data dependency between tasks enables the execution of tasks without any priority order. This is not a strong constraint for our approach since it can be overcome by considering data dependencies during scheduling. However, a priority order might reduce the achievable performance acceleration.

Applications like smart cameras adapt their response to the environmental context, demanding runtime decisions under unknown beforehand conditions [13]. The processing of SQL queries can also be accelerated by using PR when treating each type of SQL query as independent task. Each SQL query presents different query plan which can be implemented with a different architecture, like proposed in [11].

4   Problem Formulation

The following probabilistic approach intends to predict the achievable speedup obtained by using the described methodology. Let us consider a streaming application (Fig. 2) composed of a certain number of tasks (n_{tasks}) with a number of different types (n_{types}), which must be executed without following any particular schedule. At a certain instant, a number of independent tasks (n_{tasks}^{I}) must be scheduled to be executed on the FPGA. The probability of having a task i (T_i) is p_i. Each T_i demands a computational time (t_i) of the FPGA. Finally, t_{pr} is the time cost of the PR of one of the reconfigurable partitions (RPs) of the FPGA, which has a certain number of RPs (n_{RP}) available.

The tasks are grouped to be executed in parallel based on their area and I/O bandwidth demand as part of the design flow. The level of parallelism of each T_i is LP_i. As a result, several RMs compatible with the available RPs are generated to allocate all the tasks of the streaming application. A CT including the time cost of the tasks, their area cost and the compatible RMs is generated to be used by a set of heuristics designed to exploit the area reuse and to optimize the merged tasks' scheduling. The overall acceleration is determined by three properties: the number of available RPs (n_{RPs}), the average LP achieved by merging tasks, and finally, the scheduling of the tasks. The performance impact of the last two characteristics are firstly analysed from a probabilistic point of view.

4.1 Probabilistic Approach

Our methodology (Sect. 3) assumes that each execution on the FPGA is composed of mutually exclusive and independent n_{tasks}^I. The probability of a T_i in n_{tasks}^I follows a multinomial distribution. However, for a particular task it can be approximated to a binomial. Thus, the probability of having r tasks T_i in n_{tasks}^I is:

$$P(T_i = r) = \binom{n_{task}^I}{r} \cdot p_i^{\ r} \cdot (1 - p_i)^{(n_{tasks}^I - r)} \tag{1}$$

$$= \frac{n_{task}^I!}{r! \, (n_{tasks}^I - r)!} \cdot p_i^{\ r} \cdot (1 - p_i)^{(n_{tasks}^I - r)}$$

The average execution time needed (t_{exec}) is:

$$t_{exec}^I = \left\lceil \frac{n_{tasks}^I}{n_{RPs}} \right\rceil \cdot \sum^{n_{types}} p_i \cdot t_i \tag{2}$$

which is simplified to Eq. 3 when assuming only one RP:

$$t_{exec}^I = n_{tasks}^I \cdot \sum_i^{n_{types}} p_i \cdot t_i \tag{3}$$

The average area cost (A_{cost}) is defined based on the task's relative area cost (a_i) and their probability (p_i):

$$A_{cost} = \sum_i^{n_{types}} p_i \cdot a_i \tag{4}$$

4.2 Merging

As a consequence of the tasks' merging, n_{tasks}^I is reduced, the n_{types}^I becomes dependent of the number of RMs (n_{RMs}) and p_i is modified. The parameters involved in the tasks' merging have the following conditions:

$$n_{types}^M \leq n_{RMs} \tag{5}$$

$$n_{tasks}^M \leq n_{tasks}^I \leq n_{tasks} \tag{6}$$

where n_{types}^M is the different types of merged tasks and n_{tasks}^M is the number of merged tasks to be computed. Finally, p_i^M is the probability of having one particular type of merged task i. The value of these parameters depends on the CT and the type of the tasks' merging supported.

The example CT depicted in Table 1 shows how some of the tasks can be allocated in the same RP. The compatibility list reflects that only the same type of tasks can be merged, since an unique RM is exclusively dedicated to compute each type of task. As a result of the tasks' merging, the initial parameters of our approach are modified for a post-merging analysis. Hence, the probability p_i^M after merging tasks T_i becomes:

$$p_i^M = p_i \cdot \frac{a_i}{\sum_j^{n_{types}^I} a_j} \cdot \left(\sum_k^{n_{types}^M} \frac{a_k}{\sum_m^{n_{types}^I} a_m} \right)^{-1} = p_i \cdot a_i^M \tag{7}$$

where a_i^M represents the demanded area for the merged type of tasks i.

The computation time of T_i after merging tasks (t_i) is not modified by computing LP_i tasks in parallel (Eq. 8).

$$t_i^M = max(t_i) = t_i \tag{8}$$

Notice that t_i^M would be the maximum of t_i when merging different types of tasks.

The number of different types of tasks after merging (n_{types}^M) depends on the n_{types}^I (Table 1) and the probability of having a task of each type. This is only true when merging the same type of tasks. If two compatible types of tasks are merged, sharing the same RM, the value of n_{types}^M will be lower than n_{types}^I. The approach can be adjusted to merge compatible types of tasks by accumulating their probability. For the sake of simplicity, the following analysis only considers the merging of the same type of tasks.

$$n_{types}^M = n_{types}^I \cdot \sum_i^{n_{types}} p_i = n_{types}^I \tag{9}$$

Notice that n_{types}^I does not need to be equal to n_{types}. In fact, n_{types}^I is obtained by considering the tasks' probabilities and n_{task}^I since it follows a multinomial distribution. Finally, the number of tasks after merging (n_{tasks}^M) depends on LP and the probability of having a certain type of task (Eq. 10).

$$n_{tasks}^M = n_{tasks}^I \sum_i^{n_{types}^I} p_i \cdot a_i \tag{10}$$

The execution time after merging tasks, based on Eq. (10), is similarly defined like Eq. (3):

$$t_{exec}^M = \left(\sum_i^{n_{types}^I} p_i \cdot a_i \right) \cdot n_{tasks}^I \cdot \sum_i^{n_{types}^I} p_i \cdot t_i = \left(\sum_i^{n_{types}^I} p_i \cdot a_i \right) \cdot t_{exec}^I \tag{11}$$

where $\sum_{i}^{n_{types}^{I}} p_i \cdot a_i$ must be lower than 1 in order to have acceleration. Therefore, the theoretical acceleration by merging tasks ($Speedup_{th}$) is defined as:

$$Speedup_{th} = \frac{t_{exec}^{I}}{t_{exec}^{M}} = \frac{t_{exec}^{I}}{t_{exec}^{I} \cdot \left(\sum_{i}^{n_{types}^{I}} p_i \cdot a_i\right)} = \frac{1}{\sum_{i}^{n_{types}^{I}} p_i \cdot a_i} \tag{12}$$

Notice that the PR cost is not included yet in the theoretical acceleration. In fact, this acceleration is reduced when considering the PR cost. Let p_{pr} be the probability of PR and t_{pr} the time cost of such partial reconfiguration. Equation (11) is readjusted as follows:

$$t_{exec}^{M} = \left(\sum_{i}^{n_{types}^{I}} p_i \cdot a_i\right) \cdot \left(t_{exec}^{I} + n_{tasks}^{I} \cdot t_{pr} \cdot p_{pr}\right) \tag{13}$$

Therefore, the achievable acceleration thanks to merging tasks ($Speedup$) becomes:

$$Speedup = \frac{t_{exec}^{I}}{\left(\sum_{i}^{n_{types}^{I}} p_i \cdot a_i\right) \cdot \left(t_{exec}^{I} + n_{tasks}^{I} \cdot t_{pr} \cdot p_{pr}\right)}$$

$$= Speedup_{th} \cdot \frac{t_{exec}^{I}}{t_{exec}^{I} + n_{tasks}^{I} \cdot t_{pr} \cdot p_{pr}}$$

$$= Speedup_{th} \cdot PR_{cost} \tag{14}$$

where PR_{cost} represents the performance degradation due to PR and ranges from 0 to 1.

$$PR_{cost} = \frac{t_{exec}^{I}}{t_{exec}^{I} + n_{tasks}^{I} \cdot t_{pr} \cdot p_{pr}} \tag{15}$$

and, by applying Eq. 3, can be simplified to

$$PR_{cost} = \frac{\sum_{i}^{n_{types}} p_i \cdot t_i}{\sum_{i}^{n_{types}} p_i \cdot t_i + t_{pr} \cdot p_{pr}} \tag{16}$$

Due to the fact that PR_{cost} might be lower than 1, there is acceleration only if:

$$Speedup_{th} > \frac{1}{PR_{cost}} \tag{17}$$

4.3   Scheduling

A proper tasks' scheduling minimizes the impact of PR by reducing the number of PR (n_{pr}). The value of n_{pr} is directly related to p_{pr} and the merged n_{tasks}^{M}. Moreover, p_{pr} is determined by the supported RMs and the configuration of the RP at a certain instant.

No Scheduling. The number of iterations in one execution after merging (n_{iter}^M) is expressed as

$$n_{iter}^M = \left\lceil \frac{n_{tasks}^M}{n_{RP}} \right\rceil \tag{18}$$

which equals n_{tasks}^M when considering only one RP. Hereby, only one RP is assumed ($n_{RP} = 1$) for the sake of simplicity while introducing the probabilistic approach.

Let us consider $i \in <1, ..., n_{RPs}>$ and $j \in <1, ..., n_{RMs}>$. The probability to reconfigure a RP_i configured with a RM_j at a certain iteration $kj \in <1, ..., n_{iter}^M>$ can be expressed as:

$$p_{pr} = P(RP_i[k] \neq RP_i[k-1])$$
$$= P(RP_i[k] = RM_j \cap RP_i[k-1] \neq RM_j) \tag{19}$$

Notice that $RP_i[0]$ represents the initial configuration of the RP_i. Each iteration can be considered independent when there is no tasks' scheduling. Hence, p_{pr} can be expressed as:

$$p_{pr} = P(RP_i[k] = RM_j) \cdot P(RP_i[k-1] \neq RM_j) \tag{20}$$

which, based on Eq. 7, is reduced to:

$$p_{pr} = \sum_{idx=1}^{n_{types}^M} p_{idx}^M \cdot (1 - p_{idx}^M) \tag{21}$$

Without any tasks' scheduling the probability p_{pr} equally affects to each RP. Similarly, p_{pr} is independent between iterations. Hence, n_{pr} is expressed based on Eq. 18 as:

$$n_{pr} = n_{tasks}^M \cdot p_{pr} \tag{22}$$

Therefore, Eq. 16 can be expressed as:

$$PR_{cost} = \frac{t_{exec}^I}{t_{exec}^I + t_{pr} \cdot n_{pr}} \tag{23}$$

Iteration-Oriented Scheduling. The iteration-oriented scheduling heuristic proposed in [4] exploits the previous configuration of the available RPs to reduce n_{pr}. This strategy searches for those tasks in the available n_{tasks}^M compatible with the configuration of a RP at a certain iteration. The probability of having at least one task i in n_{tasks}^M is equivalent to

$$P(n_i > 0) = 1 - P(n_i = 0) \tag{24}$$

where n_i is the number of tasks i in n_{tasks}^M. This probability is calculated as a binomial distribution:

$$P(n_i = 0) = (1 - p_i^M)^{n_{tasks}^M} \tag{25}$$

Table 2. CT of the NE proposed in [4]. Each task emulates one node's configuration, which is determined by the number of active microphones. The compatibility shows that only the same types of tasks are merged. The t_i values are expressed in seconds.

Task (T_i)	Probability (p_i)	Time cost (t_i)	Area cost (a_i)	Compatibility (RM_i)
52 Mics	1/4	1.0834 ± 0.0029	1	RM_{52Mics}
28 Mics	1/4	1.0753 ± 0.0024	1/2	RM_{28Mics}
12 Mics	1/4	1.0679 ± 0.0023	1/4	RM_{12Mics}
4 Mics	1/4	1.0677 ± 0.0023	1/4	RM_{4Mics}

Therefore, the probability of reconfiguring when computing n_{tasks}^M is:

$$p_{pr} = \frac{\sum_{j=1}^{n_{tasks}^M} \sum_{i=1}^{n_{types}} p_i^M \cdot (1 - p_i^M)^j}{n_{tasks}^M} \tag{26}$$

The numerator is the value of n_{pr} since it considers all the possible n_{tasks}^M. Notice the difference with Eq. 21. The current strategy searches for a particular task in n_{tasks}^M to avoid reconfiguration while in Eq. 21 there is no search, and therefore, the incoming tasks are randomly selected.

5   Case Study

Our approach is evaluated on the audio streaming application detailed in [4]. This case study is a FPGA-based microphone array network emulator (NE) which has to combine the data received from multiple nodes processing streams of audio. A node of the network supports different configurations based on the number of active microphones, which directly determines the accuracy and the power consumption [3]. The response of the nodes is combined to estimate the location of sound sources, which is used to adapt the networks' topology and the node's configuration to balance the network's power consumption and its accuracy. The computation is repeated an undetermined number of times to evaluate different topologies, sound-sources profiles, node's configurations or data fusion techniques. As a result, tens to hundreds of nodes with different configurations must be evaluated before converging to a valid network configuration. This audio streaming application satisfies the constraints detailed in Sect. 3:

Non-deterministic scheduling: One execution of the NE demands an unpredictable number of nodes, each with a variable configuration.

Non-priority tasks: The NE needs to collect the node's results without any particular priority order.

Non-data dependencies between tasks: Each node can be considered like one independent task without data dependencies.

5.1 Validation

Our probabilistic approach is validated through experimental simulations using the heuristics proposed in [4]. The achievable speedup is estimated based on the heuristics and their combination, providing an early performance estimation and facilitating the generalized use of PR to accelerate similar applications.

The description of the application in [4] provides enough information to fetch our approach. The evaluation presented here goes, in fact, beyond the original evaluation and multiple t_{pr} and LPs are used to better understand the performance cost and acceleration when using PR. Table 2 is the CT obtained from the node's characteristics. The proposed probabilistic approach is used by considering a task as an emulation of one node of the NE. Therefore, the nodes of the NE are hereby called tasks.

Despite the evaluation of our approach uses the basis of the application, it presents some differences when compared to the experiments done in [4]:

- *Single RP*: The system analysed in [4] considered 4 RPs. For the sake of simplicity, our evaluation only considers one RP ($n_{RP} = 1$). Notice, however, that our equations are general enough to be applied for any n_{RP}.
- *Classification heuristic*: The tasks are not sorted per type during the classification heuristic performed before merging. This initial ordering already improves the followed heuristics and masks their performance contribution, justifying its absence in our approach. Furthermore, it provides a more general evaluation by respecting the original order of the task's execution. It can, nevertheless, be inserted in our equations as additional parameter, but its analysis is out of scope of this paper.
- *Merging heuristic*: The CT shown in Table 2 only considers the merging of the same type of tasks. Therefore, each RM only allocates the same type of task, which is not like in [4]. We consider that it is enough to evaluate the accuracy of our performance prediction.

The impact of the PR is evaluated beyond the configurations detailed in Table 2. The evaluation presented here explores the performance variance based on t_{pr} and A_{cost} to show how the acceleration changes based on the tasks' characteristics detailed in Table 2:

- t_{pr}: The original value of t_{pr} of the system in [4] slightly changes per RP. The average value of t_{pr} is used as reference and scaled by a factor to evaluate adverse situations where t_{pr} is significantly higher than any t_i. The considered scaling factor ranges from 0 to 2. Notice that there is no performance degradation when $t_{pr} = 0$.
- A_{cost}: The original a_i of the tasks is modified to cover a range of A_{cost} (Eq. 4). While originally $A_{cost} = 0.5$, the explored range of A_{cost} varies from 0.3 to 0.875.

Finally, notice that Table 2 provides information about p_i which is not originally available in [4]. Despite there are also 4 types of tasks, each type of task is assumed to be equally probable, since the authors in [4] do not specify this parameter.

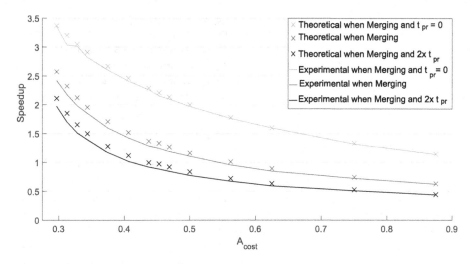

Fig. 3. Average speedup due to merging tasks. No task's scheduling is applied after merging. Notice the impact of t_{pr} in the performance degradation (Eq. 16). (Color figure online)

5.2   Results

The heuristics introduced in [4] have been implemented and simulated in Matlab 2016b. The tasks' occurrence is expressed through probabilities due to the non-deterministic scheduling. Therefore, the experimental results are average values obtained after 100 executions of 100 tasks. This relatively large number of executions guarantees that the tasks's occurrence is properly represented. Finally, our probabilistic approach is used to predict the theoretical speedup and compared to the experimental one. Notice that both speedups are averaged values due to the non-deterministic nature of the task's execution.

Figure 3 depicts the speedup based on A_{cost} when only merging the same type of tasks. The theoretical speedup is obtained through Eq. 12. The experimental speedup without PR cost is obtained when forcing t_{pr} to zero in Eq. 16, leading to no degradation in performance. A scaling factor of one (blue line) and two (black line) are applied to t_{pr}. The highest cost of PR occurs when $t_{pr} = 2 \times t_i$, as shown in the bottom line in Fig. 3. The difference between the theoretical speedup and the speedup including the PR cost represents the performance degradation due to PR without any scheduling strategy. Notice that A_{cost} decreases when more tasks can be merged, since their area demanding is lower, leading to an increment of achievable speedup.

Figure 4 shows how the performance increments when applying the iteration-oriented scheduling heuristic described in [4]. This heuristic schedules the tasks based on the RP's previous configuration to reduce the overall n_{pr}. The achievable acceleration is very close to the theoretical acceleration upper bound. The theoretical values, obtained by applying the equations described in Sect. 4 follow the experimental trend. Nevertheless, this heuristic does not perform as good

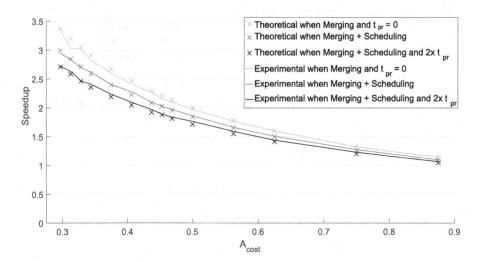

Fig. 4. Average speedup due to merging and scheduling tasks. The iteration-oriented scheduling is applied after merging.

when n_{RP} increases, as the results in [4] reflect. Their results show a lower performance besides 4 RPs are used. Further analysis on how n_{RP} affects to the achievable acceleration is needed to properly determine the reason of this performance degradation. Different heuristics should be proposed to target multiple RPs in order to achieve a closer performance to the theoretical acceleration upper bound.

The proposed probabilistic model needs to not only characterize the non-deterministic nature of the task's execution but also to reflect the behaviour of the merging and scheduling heuristics required by the general methodology. The comparison between the predicted acceleration and the experimental results depicted in Fig. 3 and in Fig. 4 demonstrate the accuracy of this model. Nevertheless, the proposed methodology and its probabilistic model are flexible enough to be adapted for different heuristics, like, for instance, the scheduling heuristics proposed in [1].

6   Conclusions

The proposed methodology enables the acceleration of streaming applications with non-deterministic task scheduling using PR. Moreover, the acceleration upper bounds can be predicted at the design time based on the application's characteristics. We believe that many streaming applications can benefit from our approach, specially the ones related to signal processing, to image processing or even to data stream management systems which present a high parallelism and multiple similar configurations. Future work includes the validation of our probabilistic approach for multiple RPs, more case studies and the development of optimized heuristics.

References

1. Cordone, R., et al.: Partitioning and scheduling of task graphs on partially dynamically reconfigurable FPGAs. IEEE Trans. Comput.-Aided Des. Integr. Circ. Syst. **28**, 662–675 (2009)
2. da Silva, B., et al.: Runtime reconfigurable beamforming architecture for realtime sound-source localization. In: 26th International Conference on Field Programmable Logic and Applications (FPL). IEEE (2016)
3. da Silva, B., et al.: A partial reconfiguration based microphone array network emulator. In: 27th International Conference on Field Programmable Logic and Applications (FPL). IEEE (2017)
4. da Silva, B., et al.: Exploiting Partial Reconfiguration through PCIe for a Microphone Array Network Emulator. Int. J. Reconfigurable Comput. **2018**, 16 p. (2018). Article no. 3214679. https://www.hindawi.com/journals/ijrc/2018/3214679/abs/
5. da Silva, B., et al.: A multimode SoC FPGA-based acoustic camera for wireless sensor networks. In: 13th International Symposium on Reconfigurable Communication-Centric Systems-on-Chip (ReCoSoC). IEEE (2018)
6. El-Araby, E., et al.: Performance bounds of partial run-time reconfiguration in high-performance reconfigurable computing. In: Proceedings of the 1st International Workshop on High-Performance Reconfigurable Computing Technology and Applications: Held in Conjunction with SC07. ACM (2007)
7. El-Araby, E., et al.: Exploiting partial runtime reconfiguration for high-performance reconfigurable computing. ACM Trans. Reconfigurable Technol. Syst. (TRETS) **1**, 21 (2009)
8. Gordon, M.I., et al.: Exploiting coarse-grained task, data, and pipeline parallelism in stream programs. ACM SIGARCH Comput. Archit. News **34**, 151–162 (2006)
9. Jimenez, M.I., et al.: Design of task scheduling process for a multifunction radar. Sonar & Navigation, IET Radar (2012)
10. Papadimitriou, K., et al.: Performance of partial reconfiguration in FPGA systems: a survey and a cost model. ACM Trans. Reconfigurable Technol. Syst. (TRETS) **4**, 36 (2011)
11. Malazgirt, G.A., et al.: High level synthesis based hardware accelerator design for processing SQL queries. In: Proceedings of the 12th FPGAworld Conference. ACM (2015)
12. Sabatini, S., et al.: Multifunction Array Radar-System Design and Analysis (Book). Artech House, Norwood (1994)
13. Wildermann, S., Oetken, A., Teich, J., Salcic, Z.: Self-organizing computer vision for robust object tracking in smart cameras. In: Xie, B., Branke, J., Sadjadi, S.M., Zhang, D., Zhou, X. (eds.) ATC 2010. LNCS, vol. 6407, pp. 1–16. Springer, Heidelberg (2010). https://doi.org/10.1007/978-3-642-16576-4_1
14. Wildermann, S., et al.: Placing multimode streaming applications on dynamically partially reconfigurable architectures. Int. J. Reconfigurable Comput. **2012**, 12 p. (2012). Article no. 608312. https://www.hindawi.com/journals/ijrc/2012/608312/abs/
15. Wildermann, S., et al.: Symbolic system-level design methodology for multi-mode reconfigurable systems. Des. Autom. Embedded Syst. **17**, 343–375 (2013)

Leveraging the Partial Reconfiguration Capability of FPGAs for Processor-Based Fail-Operational Systems

Tobias Dörr$^{(\boxtimes)}$ (ID), Timo Sandmann, Florian Schade, Falco K. Bapp, and Jürgen Becker

Karlsruhe Institute of Technology (KIT), Karlsruhe, Germany
{tobias.doerr,sandmann,florian.schade,becker}@kit.edu

Abstract. Processor-based digital systems are increasingly being used in safety-critical environments. To meet the associated safety requirements, these systems are usually characterized by a certain degree of redundancy. This paper proposes a concept to introduce a redundant processor on demand by using the partial reconfiguration capability of modern FPGAs. We describe a possible implementation of this concept and evaluate it experimentally. The evaluation focuses on the fault handling latency and the resource utilization of the design. It shows that an implementation with 32 KiB of local processor memory handles faults within 0.82 ms and, when no fault is present, consumes less than 46% of the resources that a comparable static design occupies.

Keywords: Fail-operational system · Graceful degradation ·
0 Partial reconfiguration · Dynamic redundancy · Simplex
architecture · Fallback processor · Multiprocessor system-on-chip ·
Soft-core processor

1 Introduction

Digital systems perform a large variety of tasks in a steadily increasing number of applications. Their advance into certain safety-critical realms, such as autonomous driving, imposes stringent dependability requirements on them. In order to meet these requirements, designers need to pay attention to the challenges that current state-of-the-art hardware brings along. At the same time, they often need to achieve their goals with as little redundancy as possible.

A *dependable system* has the property that reliance on its correct functioning is justified [1]. A system is *safe* if it does not endanger humans or the environment [18]. In practice, all electronic systems are at risk of experiencing *faults*. These anomalies or physical defects can lead to situations in which a system is unable to fulfill its desired function [12]. Such a condition is called a *failure* and might, in particular, impair the safety of the considered system.

Certain systems have a so-called *safe state*. It describes a state that can be entered in response to faults and ensures that the system continues to satisfy

© Springer Nature Switzerland AG 2019
C. Hochberger et al. (Eds.): ARC 2019, LNCS 11444, pp. 96–111, 2019.
https://doi.org/10.1007/978-3-030-17227-5_8

its safety requirements. At the same time, the actual function of the system becomes unavailable. Such systems are referred to as *fail-safe systems* [18].

A *fail-operational system* needs to maintain a certain minimum level of functionality, even when it is subject to a certain number of faults. Depending on the exact requirements, however, a degraded functionality might be sufficient [10].

Considerable research has been conducted in the field of *fault tolerance*. Fault tolerance techniques try to mitigate faults in a way that the emergence of failures is prevented [1]. They are usually based on some kind of redundancy [12] and play an important role in the design of fail-operational systems.

A known fault tolerance technique that aims at safety-critical systems with fail-operational requirements is the simplex architecture [2, 16]. Its general idea is to deal with the complexity of today's control systems by providing an additional controller. This controller is considerably simpler than the main one, able to deliver a functionality that meets all safety requirements of the system, and is disabled during normal operation. As soon as the main controller fails, however, the simple controller is activated and ensures safe but degraded operation.

Motivated by the need for efficient fail-operational systems in the automotive context, [4] builds upon the described concept and adapts it for use on modern and heterogeneous multiprocessor system-on-chips (MPSoCs).

Both the original and the adapted concept assume that some kind of fallback unit, i.e., a plant controller or a processor, is physically available during normal operation of the system. No attempts have yet been made to develop a processor-based simplex architecture in which the fallback processor is introduced on demand, i.e., in response to faults of the main controller.

In this work, we review the concept from [4], derive a motivation for the dynamic provision of the fallback processor, and extend the existing concept accordingly. In addition, we present an implementation of the concept on a commercially-available device, the Zynq UltraScale+ MPSoC from XILINX. To introduce the processor on demand, our implementation employs partial reconfiguration of the MPSoC's programmable logic. We optimize the design systematically and compare certain figures of merit to those of an equivalent design in which the fallback processor is present at all times.

2   Related Work

Extensive research has been conducted on the partial reconfiguration (PR) of field-programmable gate arrays (FPGAs). A survey that focuses on the performance of a PR process is given by Papadimitriou et al. in [13]. In a more recent work, Vipin and Fahmy [20] present the state of the art in this field and compare the PR performance values of several commercially-available architectures.

A survey of fault tolerance mechanisms for FPGAs is given in [6]. Some of the considered approaches, such as [9], make use of PR to tolerate faults at runtime. These mechanisms have in common that they deal with low-level details of the FPGA architecture to provide fine-grained fault tolerance. The fault tolerance approach described in [5] makes use of partial reconfiguration as well, but acts on coarse-grained logic blocks of an FPGA. All these techniques handle faults of the programmable logic itself. The approach that we present makes use of the programmable logic to increase the dependability of the overall system.

The techniques described in [14] and [19] employ PR to achieve fault tolerance of soft-core processors in FPGAs. As part of [15], the authors present a similar approach that does not require an external controller to handle the partial reconfiguration. This process is instead performed by a hardened part of the soft-core processor itself. Di Carlo et al. [7] propose a partial reconfiguration controller to perform the partial reconfiguration process in a safe way.

Shreejith et al. [17] react to faults of an electronic control unit's primary function, which is implemented on an FPGA, by performing a switch to a backup function. While the backup function is active and ensures that the safety requirements are met, the primary function is restored using partial reconfiguration.

Ellis [8] considers a network of processors and deals with the dynamic migration of software in response to failing nodes. [3] and [11] focus on processor-based systems and discuss certain aspects of fault-tolerant and fail-operational architectures in the automotive domain. However, neither of the three references deals with the utilization of FPGAs to achieve dependability or fault tolerance.

3   Background and Motivation

The problem that [4] considers can be described as follows: Assume that a given fail-operational system in a safety-critical environment has to perform a certain functionality. It is connected to its surroundings via dedicated interfacing components, such as sensors, actuators, or I/O controllers. Not all aspects of the normally delivered functionality are necessary from a safety perspective. The system comprises the interfacing components, an interconnection network, and a so-called *complex system*. The complex system consists of components that fulfill the actual system functionality. While both the interfacing components and the interconnect are assumed to be dependable, the complex system might be subject to faults that it cannot tolerate. As a result of the aforementioned fail-operational requirements, it must be ensured that such a fault does not lead to a failure of the overall system. Since at least a degraded functionality has to be maintained, suitable fault tolerance techniques must be applied.

To accomplish this in an efficient way, the authors propose a concept we will refer to as the *static simplex architecture*. Figure 1 shows a simplified block schematic of this concept from a logical perspective. A so-called *transaction* represents a communication channel from a transmission initiator (*master*) to a receiver or responder (*slave*). It is assumed that the complex system is able to detect all internal faults that the architecture needs to protect against. It could, for instance, comprise a lockstep processor (to protect against single faults of the CPU) or make use of a watchdog timer. The static simplex architecture defines the mechanism that is triggered after such a fault is detected. In this case, the control entity disables the complex system and enables the *fallback system*. The latter is considerably simpler than the complex system. However, it

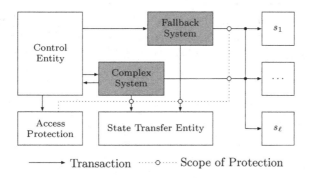

Fig. 1. Logical view of the static simplex architecture

focuses on and is able to meet the overall system's safety requirements. A set of *application-specific slave modules*, $S = \{s_1, \ldots, s_\ell\}$, is used to model slaves that both the complex and the fallback system need to interact with. One example of such an $s \in S$ is a dependable CAN controller that both the complex and the fallback system share. The overall system is always in one of two possible modes, which are given by $C = \{c_{complex}, c_{fallback}\}$ and referred to as *contexts*.

Depending on the active context, an access protection mechanism ensures that the disabled system is logically isolated from the slaves. During context switches, the state transfer entity can be used to transfer consistent snapshots of state variables (such as CPU register values) between the two systems.

It is important to understand that this concept makes use of dynamic redundancy to mitigate faults: If necessary, the essential functions of the complex system are dynamically moved to the fallback system. The reason we refer to this approach as the static simplex architecture is as follows: The fallback system needs to be present at all times, even when the complex system fulfills the functionality of the overall system. This implies a static resource overhead, which could be reduced by providing the fallback system on demand. It is the aim of this work to research and evaluate such an approach.

4   Extension of the Concept

We propose the concept of the *dynamic simplex architecture*. It addresses the same problem as the static simplex architecture and adopts the same general idea to achieve fail-operational behavior. The proposed concept, however, constitutes two distinguishing characteristics: First, it is assumed that the functionality of the fallback system can be implemented on a processor. Second, this processor must be partially reconfigurable on an FPGA that is part of the overall system. By partially reconfigurable we mean that a part of the FPGA can be reconfigured during runtime while the remaining logic continues to operate.

At any point in time, the overall system is in one of two contexts: either in $c_{complex}$ or in $c_{fallback}$. In the first case, the complex system is enabled and the fallback system is disabled. In the second case, it is vice versa. At any time, the currently enabled system has access to the application-specific slave modules and the state transfer entity. The disabled system is isolated from these components.

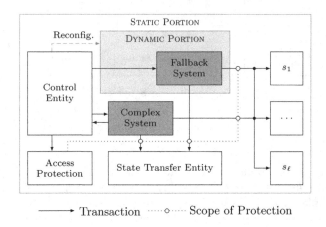

Fig. 2. Logical view of the dynamic simplex architecture

Figure 2 shows a block schematic of this concept from a logical perspective. The depicted *dynamic portion* represents a partially reconfigurable region of the FPGA. The complex system encapsulates a set of arbitrary components that deliver the full functionality of the overall system. It must be able to detect all relevant internal faults and notify the control entity about their occurrence. The fallback system consists of a soft-core processor and occupies the dynamic portion of the FPGA if and only if $c_{fallback}$ is active. If this is not the case, the dynamic portion can be utilized for other purposes. It could, for instance, be used to implement hardware accelerators that perform non-safety-relevant tasks.

$c_{complex}$ is the initially active system context. If faults of the complex system endanger safety, $c_{fallback}$ becomes active. A switch back to $c_{complex}$ is possible if the faults are no longer present. Context switches are orchestrated by the control entity. If a switch is pending, the entity initiates the partial reconfiguration of the FPGA and sets the access permissions in such a way that the disabled system is isolated from the slaves. Adherence to the access permissions is enforced by the visualized access protection mechanism. The state transfer entity provides a certain amount of buffered memory. Application developers can utilize this memory to transfer consistent snapshots of internal state variables.

It is important to note that the dynamic simplex architecture is a generic concept that focuses on the dynamic context switching mechanism. A valid implementation of the dynamic simplex architecture must behave according to the concept, but is nothing more than a framework that protects the overall system from faults of the complex system. An application developer who makes use of it needs to build upon the provided platform and supplement both the complex and the fallback system with their functions.

5   Implementation

As part of the previous work described in [4], the static simplex architecture
was implemented on a Zynq UltraScale+ MPSoC from XILINX. This device
combines a block of hard-wired components, such as a dual-core Cortex-R5 from
ARM, and an FPGA on a single chip. These portions are commonly referred to
as the processing system (PS) and the programmable logic (PL), respectively.
For brevity, we will abbreviate the Zynq UltraScale+ MPSoC as ZynqMP.

To allow for a quantitative comparison with the above-mentioned implementation, we will retain its structure wherever possible, but extend it by the
fault-triggered partial reconfiguration of the fallback system. Our implementation aims at processor-based fail-operational systems on the ZynqMP and can
be described as follows: The complex system is realized by the real-time processing unit (RPU), its generic interrupt controller (GIC), and its tightly-coupled
memory (TCM). In fact, the TCM contains software to fulfill the overall system's
complex functionality. This software is executed by the RPU's pair of Cortex-R5
cores operating in lockstep mode. As a proof of concept, we trigger a context
switch to $c_{fallback}$ whenever the RPU detects a lockstep error and assume that
no other faults can occur. Doing so allows us to focus on the context switching
mechanism, which is the focus of this work. If required by a particular use case,
more sophisticated fault detection techniques may be applied.

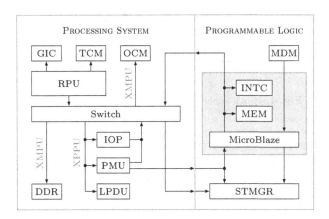

Fig. 3. ZynqMP-based implementation of the dynamic simplex architecture

Figure 3 shows the physical implementation of the system with the dynamic
portion highlighted in gray. The fallback system consists of a MicroBlaze processor, its local memory (MEM), and an interrupt controller (INTC). To simplify
the debug access to the MicroBlaze, we also include a MicroBlaze debug module (MDM). For technical reasons, the MDM cannot be partially reconfigured
and therefore needs to be moved outside of the dynamic portion. Strictly speak-
ing, this means that it is not part of the fallback system.

The platform management unit (PMU) contains a triple-redundant processor for various platform management tasks. We run a custom PMU firmware that implements the control entity. In response to lockstep error notifications from the RPU, it performs a context switch from $c_{complex}$ to $c_{fallback}$. Following this, the control entity resets the RPU and, in case of a transient fault, performs a controlled context switch back to $c_{complex}$, i.e., the initial context.

The access protection described in the concept is performed by the Xilinx peripheral protection unit (XPPU). This module is part of the PS and provides detailed control over accesses to the I/O peripherals (IOP), the low-power domain units (LPDU), and the PMU. In applications, IOPs and LPDUs are frequently used as application-specific slave modules. Developers who employ them in their designs have to define access permissions for each such module and context. During a context switch, the control entity uses the permission definitions to reconfigure the XPPU. Here, only the context-dependent part of the XPPU configuration (*context-sensitive apertures*) is written to save time. The state manager (STMGR) implements the state transfer entity from the concept.

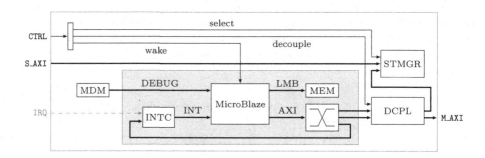

Fig. 4. Block schematic of the PL implementation

At design time, the developer creates two partial bitstreams for the dynamic portion: one containing the fallback system, including the software in MEM, and another one, for $c_{complex}$, describing its replacement logic. At runtime, both are stored in DDR memory and need to be accessible from the PMU. The partial reconfiguration of the dynamic portion is managed by the control entity. During a switch to $c_{fallback}$, it reads the partial bitstream from memory and configures the fallback system into the dynamic portion of the PL via the processor configuration access port (PCAP). During a switch to $c_{complex}$, it configures the custom replacement logic, such as a hardware accelerators, to this portion.

Figure 4 shows a more detailed block schematic of the PL implementation. The dynamic portion is again shown in gray, while the external ports connect to the PS. CTRL represents a control signal vector from the PMU. S_AXI refers to an AXI slave port from the low-power domain of the PS. IRQ represents an application-specific vector of PS-PL interrupt signals. M_AXI refers to an AXI master port to the low-power domain of the PS. The decoupling block (DCPL) is necessary to protect the outgoing AXI signals during the partial reconfiguration process. After this process, both the fallback system and its replacement may access the AXI connections. In particular, the MicroBlaze can use the M_AXI interface to communicate with application-specific slave modules. Note that the replacement block needs to have the same interface as the fallback system. The select, decouple, and wake lines are control signals that originate from the PMU. They are operated by the custom PMU firmware.

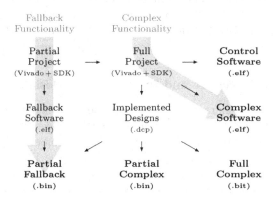

Fig. 5. Proposed development process

Figure 5 visualizes the development process through which application developers can make use of this implementation. Black arrows indicate precedence relations, while final items are shown in bold. The process is based on the Vivado Design Suite 2018.2 and employs the Xilinx SDK for the software portions. We developed a Tcl script that generates a partial Vivado project for the fallback system. The corresponding SDK workspace can be used to develop and build the fallback software. The partial project is then used by another script to generate a full Vivado project for the overall system. This project allows users to develop the logic that replaces the fallback system in $c_{complex}$. Its synthesis and implementation generates a full bitstream for $c_{complex}$ and partial bitstreams for both contexts. In the partial bitstream for $c_{fallback}$, the fallback system's local memory (MEM) is automatically initialized with the fallback software. Using the SDK workspace of the full project, the complex software for the RPU can be implemented. The control software for the PMU is automatically generated by our scripts. The shown final items are suitable for use on the ZynqMP.

6 Evaluation and Results

The proposed implementation of the dynamic simplex architecture is a generic framework that aims to protect a ZynqMP-based system from faults of its RPU. As described in Sect. 4, we see it as a platform that can be used by application developers when being faced with certain safety requirements. To compare it against an implementation of the static simplex architecture, we will now evaluate two particularly important characteristics of our implementation:

Fault handling latency. In comparison to the static simplex architecture, every context switch now comprises a partial reconfiguration of the PL. To evaluate how this affects the duration that the framework needs to react to faults, we will experimentally determine typical durations of context switches.

Utilization of PL resources. The primary motivation for the dynamic provision of the fallback system is to save PL resources during fault-free operation. To quantify the achieved resource savings, we will consider the PL resource utilization reports that Vivado creates after implementing a design.

6.1 Evaluation Procedure and the Reference Design

The implementation is characterized by many degrees of freedom. Designs can differ, for instance, by the configuration of the MicroBlaze, the size of its local memory, the capacity of the state transfer entity, the number of context-sensitive apertures, the PL clock frequency, and the region of the PL that the dynamic portion is constrained to. We therefore performed a semi-automated design space exploration by considering a fixed MicroBlaze configuration and a fixed state transfer capacity, while varying the other parameters. The automation was realized by a Tcl script that received the parameters, generated the final items from Fig. 5, and transferred them to the ZynqMP via JTAG. A dedicated PMU firmware module made it possible to inject a lockstep error into the RPU, measure the latencies of the initiated process, and output the results via UART.

To perform these experiments, we employed a ZCU102 evaluation board from XILINX. This board is based on the XCZU9EG variant of the ZynqMP. In all our designs, Vivado's routing expansion option was enabled.

As the *reference design*, we consider a design with a PL clock frequency of 100 MHz, a dynamic portion in the X2Y1 region, 32 KiB of local memory, 2 KiB of state manager capacity and $N_{CS} = 1$ context-sensitive apertures. Using this as our starting point, we varied certain parameters while keeping the others fixed.

6.2 Fault Handling Latency

We will now consider measurements of subsequent context switching intervals. D_i corresponds to the i-th interval of the fault handling process. The intervals that belong to a context switch to c_{fallback} can be described as follows:

- D_1 starts with the lockstep error injection and ends with the point in time at which the control entity is notified about the occurrence of the fault.
- At the end of D_2, the XPPU and STMGR reconfiguration is complete.
- During the third interval, D_3, the partial bitstream that describes the fallback system is read form the DDR and written to the PL.
- At the end of D_4, the fallback software that is part of MEM starts to execute on the MicroBlaze. This constitutes the end of a context switch to c_{fallback}.

D_5 and D_6 correspond to the initiation of an RPU reset, the actual reset of the RPU and the execution of its startup procedure. These intervals are not considered here. The remaining intervals belong to a context switch to c_{complex}:

- The following interval, D_7, corresponds to the time that the MicroBlaze needs to terminate the execution of the fallback software.
- D_8 comprises the partial reconfiguration of the PL as well as the XPPU and STMGR reconfigurations. It can be seen as the counterpart to D_2 and D_3.
- At the end of D_9, the RPU begins to execute the complex software again. This completes the context switch back to the initial context.

Table 1. Measured latencies for the reference design and a variation of N_{CS}

N_{CS}	Average interval duration and uncertainty (in µs)						
	D_1	D_2	D_3	D_4	D_7	D_8	D_9
1	2.340(4)	1.741(3)	1477.2(2)	19.76(5)	1.4(1)	1477.5(3)	5.8(2)
10	2.340(4)	4.82(1)	1477.2(2)	19.73(4)	1.4(1)	1480.5(4)	5.8(2)
100	2.340(5)	34.97(5)	1477.2(2)	19.74(4)	1.4(1)	1510.8(4)	5.8(1)

Table 1 shows the calculated means ($\hat{\mu}_i$) and standard deviations for the reference design in its first row ($N_{\text{CS}} = 1$). For this design, the average measured duration of a fault-induced context switch from c_{complex} to c_{fallback} sums up to $\tau_{\text{fallback}} \approx \sum_{i=1}^{4} \hat{\mu}_i = 1.5\,\text{ms}$. This is the average time between the injection of a fault and the point in time at which the fallback system begins to execute its program. The subsequent context switch back takes $\tau_{\text{complex}} \approx \sum_{i=7}^{9} \hat{\mu}_i = 1.5\,\text{ms}$. Note that the overall latency of a context switch is heavily dominated by the duration of the dynamic portion's partial reconfiguration process (D_3 and the largest part of D_8). The table also illustrates that a variation of N_{CS}, the number of context-sensitive apertures, has an effect on the duration of intervals D_2 and D_8. Each row of the table is based on 100 independent measurements.

Table 2. Measured latencies for a variation of different parameters

Variation of...	Average interval duration and uncertainty (in µs)						
	D_1	D_2	D_3	D_4	D_7	D_8	D_9
(a) Memory size	2.340(4)	1.741(3)	1477.2(2)	19.75(4)	1.4(1)	1477.5(3)	5.8(2)
(b) Clock region	2.340(5)	1.741(3)	(□)	19.8(1)	1.4(1)	(□)	5.8(2)
(c) PL frequency	2.340(5)	1.741(3)	1477.6(8)	(◇)	(◇)	1478.0(8)	5.8(1)

Using the reference design as a starting point, we then performed a variation of (a) the memory size, (b) the clock region of the dynamic portion, and (c) the

PL clock frequency to identify further parameters that have a significant influence on the latencies. Table 2 shows the average interval durations over these variations. Scenarios that are marked with (□) or (◇) exhibited a strong dependence on the performed variation. A detailed analysis of these cases will be given in the following. From the table, it can be seen that the interval durations are largely independent of the size of the local memory (a). Note that the reference design with 32 KiB of it leaves many BRAMs of the X2Y1 region unutilized. In our experiments, X2Y1 provided room for up to 128 KiB of local memory.

Table 3. Measured latencies for varying locations of the reconfigurable partition

Col.	Y0	Y1	Y2	Y3	Y4	Y5	Y6
			Average duration and uncertainty of D_3 (in µs)				
X0	–	–	–	1861.46(7)	1861.4(2)	–	1861.4(2)
X1	3520.6(6)	3520.6(5)	3524.4(2)	–	1717.3(2)	1717.3(3)	1717.3(2)
X2	1477.2(1)	1477.2(2)	1477.2(2)	1477.23(8)	1477.2(2)	1477.2(1)	1477.2(1)
X3	1378.9(1)	–	1378.9(1)	1378.9(2)	1370.23(5)	1370.25(8)	1370.2(1)
			Average duration and uncertainty of D_8 (in µs)				
X0	–	–	–	1861.6(5)	1861.6(5)	–	1861.7(4)
X1	3520.6(10)	3520.4(12)	3524.9(2)	–	1717.4(5)	1717.4(6)	1717.5(4)
X2	1477.5(3)	1477.5(3)	1477.5(4)	1477.4(4)	1477.4(4)	1477.5(3)	1477.5(4)
X3	1379.2(3)	–	1379.2(3)	1379.2(4)	1370.4(4)	1370.4(4)	1370.5(3)

Table 4. Size of the partial bitstream as a function of the clock region

Col.	Y0	Y1	Y2	Y3	Y4	Y5	Y6
			Size in KiB				
X0	–	–	–	1292.73	1292.73	–	1292.73
X1	2441.41	2441.41	2441.41	–	1192.91	1192.91	1192.91
X2	1026.78	1026.78	1026.78	1026.78	1026.78	1026.78	1026.78
X3	958.63	–	958.63	958.63	952.63	952.63	952.63

As indicated by the (□) symbols in Table 2, varying clock region constraints for the dynamic portion (b) lead to significant changes in D_3 and D_8. More detailed measurement results for this variation are shown in Table 3. No implementation was possible for the cases with omitted values. It is important to note that the clock regions differ not only in their location, but also in their size and resource composition. Table 4 gives the size of a partial bitstream for a design in which the dynamic portion is constrained to the specified clock region. Comparing the values from the two tables shows a strong correlation between the size of a partial bitstream and the average durations of D_3 and D_8. However, note that this observation alone does not prove a causal relation between minimizing the bitstream size and achieving a minimum fault handling latency.

The ($\diamond$) symbols in Table 2 indicate that a variation of f_{PL} (c) has a significant influence on D_4 and D_7. More detailed results for this variation are shown in Table 5. The achievable savings, however, are small compared to the overall fault handling latency. Since the latter is dominated by D_3 and D_8, we focused on the location constraint of the dynamic portion for further improvement.

Table 5. Measured latencies for varying frequencies of the PL clock (f_{PL})

f_{PL} in MHz	D_4 in µs	D_7 in µs
100	19.76(5)	1.4(1)
150	13.6(1)	1.24(1)
215	9.77(2)	1.24(1)
300	7.41(1)	1.24(1)

A more detailed analysis showed that within a certain clock region, lower reconfiguration times can be achieved by reducing the width of the reserved reconfigurable region. We did not consider reconfigurable regions spanning multiple clock regions or the influence of an enabled bitstream compression. Starting off with the reference design again, we reduced the width of the reconfigurable region as much as possible, ending up with what we refer to as the *optimized design*. 100 measurements of it resulted in $\hat{\mu}_3 = 800.85(9)$ µs and $\hat{\mu}_8 = 801.2(2)$ µs. Taking the region-independent durations from the reference design into account leads to overall latencies of $\tau_{\text{fallback}} \approx 0.82$ ms and $\tau_{\text{complex}} \approx 0.81$ ms.

To perform a quantitative comparison with a design in which the fallback system is always present, we created an implementation of the static simplex architecture that is—apart from the missing PR aspect—equivalent to the optimized design. Measurements of this version yielded overall latencies of $\tilde{\tau}_{\text{fallback}} \approx 5.31$ µs and $\tilde{\tau}_{\text{complex}} \approx 7.5$ µs. This means that with respect to the static case, a dynamic provision of the fallback system leads to a significant time overhead.

6.3 Resource Utilization

We now compare the resource utilization of the optimized design to that of its static equivalent. In particular, we focus on the following two aspects:

- The number of resources that can be saved during fault-free operation when employing the dynamic instead of the static simplex architecture.
- The resource overhead that goes along with the dynamic simplex architecture while the fallback system is active, i.e., while c_{fallback} is active.

Table 6. PL resource utilization of the optimized design and its static equivalent

Type	Static design	Dynamic design	
		c_{fallback}	c_{complex}
LUT (in CLB)	2932	2888	1209
Register (in CLB)	3171	3182	1459
Multiplexer (F7)	117	149	38
BRAM (36 Kb)	10	10	2

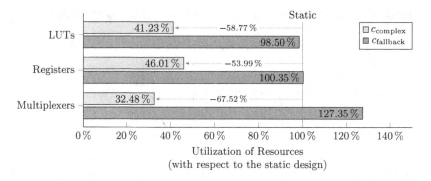

Fig. 6. Relative resource utilization of the optimized design in its two contexts

Table 6 shows that the relative utilization of PL resources in c_{complex} decreases considerably when employing our implementation of the dynamic simplex architecture instead of an equivalent static simplex architecture. This is also visualized in Fig. 6. From the figure, it can be seen that the optimized design in c_{complex} saves 59% of the LUTs, 54% of the registers, and 68% of the multiplexers that its static equivalent consumes. In c_{fallback}, its resource overhead is negligible for LUTs and registers, and amounts to 27% for multiplexers.

7   Discussion

From a qualitative perspective, the evaluation results show that the choice between a static and a dynamic simplex architecture involves a specific trade-off. The dynamic version exhibits prolonged context switching latencies and a slightly increased utilization of FPGA resources in c_{fallback}. At the same time, it consumes considerably fewer FPGA resources during fault-free operation of the system. The saved resources can, for instance, be used to implement hardware accelerators that are required for non-safety-relevant tasks in c_{complex} only.

It should be noted that context switching latencies are critical in the sense that during these intervals, no processor fulfills the desired functionality of the system. In general, we consider the dynamic simplex architecture a feasible solution for cases in which the context switching latencies are tolerable and the PL resources in $c_{complex}$ are too scarce to have the fallback system available at all times. We believe that the semi-automated design space exploration that we performed is a helpful procedure to map an implementation of the dynamic simplex architecture to arbitrary ZynqMP devices in an efficient manner.

The fault handling latencies that we achieved for our exemplary implementation with 32 KiB of MEM are lower than 1 ms. The results indicate that designs with up to 128 KiB of MEM have fault handling latencies of about 1.5 ms. In cases where these latencies are tolerable, we consider the implementation to be a suitable choice for systems that are subject to certain safety requirements.

8   Conclusion

Our goal was to develop a more resource efficient version of the static simplex architecture, a concept that aims at particular fail-operational systems.

The dynamic simplex architecture utilizes the partial reconfiguration capability of an FPGA to protect the overall system from hazardous failures. It does so by partially reconfiguring a fallback system to the FPGA in response to certain faults. We proposed an implementation of this concept and systematically optimized its fault handling latency. An exemplary design with 32 KiB of local MicroBlaze memory handles faults within 0.82 ms and, considering the nonfaulty case, consumes less than 46% of the resources that an equivalent design in which the fallback system is present at all times occupies.

Our future work will focus on an even more comprehensive design space exploration and an application to practical use cases. The latter will especially include an extensive analysis of the overall safety in such use cases.

Acknowledgements. This work was funded by the German Federal Ministry of Education and Research (BMBF) under grant number 01IS16025 (ARAMiS II). The responsibility for the content of this publication rests with the authors.

References

1. Avizienis, A., Laprie, J.C., Randell, B., Landwehr, C.: Basic concepts and taxonomy of dependable and secure computing. IEEE Trans. Dependable Secure Comput. **1**(1), 11–33 (2004). https://doi.org/10.1109/TDSC.2004.2
2. Bak, S., Chivukula, D.K., Adekunle, O., Sun, M., Caccamo, M., Sha, L.: The system-level simplex architecture for improved real-time embedded system safety. In: 2009 15th IEEE Real-Time and Embedded Technology and Applications Symposium, pp. 99–107, April 2009. https://doi.org/10.1109/RTAS.2009.20
3. Baleani, M., Ferrari, A., Mangeruca, L., Sangiovanni-Vincentelli, A., Peri, M., Pezzini, S.: Fault-tolerant platforms for automotive safety-critical applications. In: Proceedings of the 2003 International Conference on Compilers, Architecture and Synthesis for Embedded Systems, CASES 2003, pp. 170–177. ACM, New York (2003). https://doi.org/10.1145/951710.951734

4. Bapp, F.K., Dörr, T., Sandmann, T., Schade, F., Becker, J.: Towards fail-operational systems on controller level using heterogeneous multicore SoC architectures and hardware support. In: WCX World Congress Experience. SAE International, April 2018. https://doi.org/10.4271/2018-01-1072

5. Bolchini, C., Miele, A., Santambrogio, M.D.: TMR and partial dynamic reconfiguration to mitigate SEU faults in FPGAs. In: 22nd IEEE International Symposium on Defect and Fault-Tolerance in VLSI Systems (DFT 2007), pp. 87–95, September 2007. https://doi.org/10.1109/DFT.2007.25

6. Cheatham, J.A., Emmert, J.M., Baumgart, S.: A survey of fault tolerant methodologies for FPGAs. ACM Trans. Des. Autom. Electron. Syst. **11**(2), 501–533 (2006). https://doi.org/10.1145/1142155.1142167

7. Di Carlo, S., Prinetto, S., Trotta, P., Andersson, P.: A portable open-source controller for safe dynamic partial reconfiguration on Xilinx FPGAs. In: 2015 25th International Conference on Field Programmable Logic and Applications (FPL), pp. 1–4, September 2015. https://doi.org/10.1109/FPL.2015.7294002

8. Ellis, S.M.: Dynamic software reconfiguration for fault-tolerant real-time avionic systems. Microprocess. Microsyst. **21**(1), 29–39 (1997)

9. Emmert, J., Stroud, C., Skaggs, B., Abramovici, M.: Dynamic fault tolerance in FPGAs via partial reconfiguration. In: Proceedings 2000 IEEE Symposium on Field-Programmable Custom Computing Machines (Cat. No.PR00871), pp. 165–174, April 2000. https://doi.org/10.1109/FPGA.2000.903403

10. Isermann, R., Schwarz, R., Stölzl, S.: Fault-tolerant drive-by-wire systems. IEEE Control Syst. **22**(5), 64–81 (2002)

11. Kohn, A., Käßmeyer, M., Schneider, R., Roger, A., Stellwag, C., Herkersdorf, A.: Fail-operational in safety-related automotive multi-core systems. In: 10th IEEE International Symposium on Industrial Embedded Systems (SIES), pp. 1–4, June 2015. https://doi.org/10.1109/SIES.2015.7185051

12. Nelson, V.P.: Fault-tolerant computing: fundamental concepts. Computer **23**(7), 19–25 (1990). https://doi.org/10.1109/2.56849

13. Papadimitriou, K., Dollas, A., Hauck, S.: Performance of partial reconfiguration in FPGA systems: a survey and a cost model. ACM Trans. Reconfigurable Technol. Syst. **4**(4), 36:1–36:24 (2011). https://doi.org/10.1145/2068716.2068722

14. Pham, H.M., Pillement, S., Piestrak, S.J.: Low-overhead fault-tolerance technique for a dynamically reconfigurable softcore processor. IEEE Trans. Comput. **62**(6), 1179–1192 (2013). https://doi.org/10.1109/TC.2012.55

15. Psarakis, M., Vavousis, A., Bolchini, C., Miele, A.: Design and implementation of a self-healing processor on SRAM-based FPGAs. In: 2014 IEEE International Symposium on Defect and Fault Tolerance in VLSI and Nanotechnology Systems (DFT), pp. 165–170, October 2014. https://doi.org/10.1109/DFT.2014.6962076

16. Sha, L.: Using simplicity to control complexity. IEEE Softw. **18**(4), 20–28 (2001). https://doi.org/10.1109/MS.2001.936213

17. Shreejith, S., Vipin, K., Fahmy, S.A., Lukasiewycz, M.: An approach for redundancy in FlexRay networks using FPGA partial reconfiguration. In: 2013 Design, Automation Test in Europe Conference Exhibition (DATE), pp. 721–724, March 2013. https://doi.org/10.7873/DATE.2013.155

18. Storey, N.R.: Safety-Critical Computer Systems. Addison-Wesley Longman Publishing Co., Inc., Boston (1996)

19. Vavousis, A., Apostolakis, A., Psarakis, M.: A fault tolerant approach for FPGA embedded processors based on runtime partial reconfiguration. J. Electron. Testing **29**(6), 805–823 (2013). https://doi.org/10.1007/s10836-013-5420-x
20. Vipin, K., Fahmy, S.A.: FPGA dynamic and partial reconfiguration: a survey of architectures, methods, and applications. ACM Comput. Surv. **51**(4), 72:1–72:39 (2018). https://doi.org/10.1145/3193827

(ReCo)Fuse Your PRC or Lose Security: Finally Reliable Reconfiguration-Based Countermeasures on FPGAs

Kenneth Schmitz[1]([✉])(iD), Buse Ustaoglu[1](iD), Daniel Große[1,2](iD), and Rolf Drechsler[1,2](iD)

[1] Cyber -Physical Systems, DFKI GmbH, 28359 Bremen, Germany
{kenneth.schmitz,buse.ustaoglu}@dfki.de
[2] Institute of Computer Architecture, University of Bremen, 28359 Bremen, Germany
{grosse,drechsler}@uni-bremen.de

Abstract. Partial reconfiguration is a powerful technique to adapt the functionality of *Field Programmable Gate Arrays* (FPGAs) at run time. When performing partial reconfiguration a dedicated *Intellectual Property* (IP) component of the FPGA vendor, i.e. the *Partial Reconfiguration Controller* (PRC), among a wide range of IP components has to be used. While ensuring the functional safety of FPGA designs is well understood, ensuring hardware security is still very challenging. This applies in particular to reconfiguration-based countermeasures which are intensively used to form a moving target for the attacker. However, from the system security perspective a critical component is the above mentioned PRC as noticed by many papers implementing reconfiguration-based countermeasures against SCA/DPA attacks. In this work, we leverage a new proposed safety mechanism which creates a container around an IP, to encapsulate and thereby to protect and observe the PRC of an FPGA. The proposed encapsulation scheme results in an architecture consisting of so-called *ReCoFuses* (RCFs), each capturing a specific protective goal which have to be fulfilled at any time during PRC operation. The terminology follows the classical electric installation including a *fuse box*. In our scheme we employ formal verification to guarantee the correctness in detecting a security violation. Only after successful verification, the RCFs are integrated into the *ReCoFuse Container*. Experimental results demonstrate the advantage of our approach by preventing attacks on the PRC of a system secured by reconfiguration.

1 Introduction

Substantial progress for both, *Application Specific Integrated Circuits* (ASICs) and *Field Programmable Gate Arrays* (FPGAs) has been achieved over the last

This work was supported by the German Federal Ministry of Education and Research (BMBF) within the project SecRec under grant no. 16K1S0606K, the project SELFIE under grant no. 01IW16001 and by the University of Bremen's graduate school SyDe, funded by the German Excellence Initiative.

C. Hochberger et al. (Eds.): ARC 2019, LNCS 11444, pp. 112–126, 2019.
https://doi.org/10.1007/978-3-030-17227-5_9

decade. In particular, the programmable nature of FPGAs allows for great flexibility, and the strong feature of partial reconfiguration pays off in many application fields today. Practical examples include increasing fault tolerance [1], power-aware reconfiguration [2,3], and area reduction by time division multiplexing [4].

Although the realization of partial reconfiguration varies depending on the FPGA model, it commonly relies on vendor specific proprietary library cells and *Intellectual Property* (IP). Due to the black box characteristic of these IP blocks, the internal operation (i.e. source code) can not be *examined, tested or verified* by the user. As a consequence, integrating these components in a system requires *trust* in the test and verification methodologies of the respective IP vendor and – in worst case – jeopardizes the system's stability. Hence, several approaches to overcome this problem have been proposed. Unfortunately, many of these approaches require some knowledge of the design sources, which is impractical for the aforementioned scenario. For this reason, the encapsulation of an IP component has been thoroughly investigated in the past. The behavior of the encapsulated component is then monitored, controlled or even fixed by the surrounding logic at runtime. For example, in [5] a "shield" is synthesized which continuously monitors input/output of the design and corrects its erroneous outputs. A more general approach has been proposed in [6,7]. The paper presents the notion of a "container", in which the IP component is instantiated. The concept was applied in order to monitor and fix bus protocol glitches by automatic synthesis of correction logic from a property specification language. This way the container protects both, the IP and the surrounding system respectively. A similar principle was also applied on a hardware level by implementing a instruction replacement scheme for a modern RISC-V processor IP to circumvent errata and design flaws [8]. In [9] a similar technique has been proposed. Hardware sand boxes are employed for secure integration of non trusted IPs in modern *System-On-Chips* (SoCs). Only permissible interactions between the IP and the rest of the system are allowed by exposing the IP interface to isolated virtual resources and checking IP signals' correctness at run time.

Coming back to partial reconfiguration, the safe and secure operation of the overall system heavily depends on the *Partial Reconfiguration Controller* (PRC) of the FPGA which typically initiates the reconfiguration process in the design. In particular, reconfiguration-based countermeasures forming a *"moving target"* for the attacker may completely collapse, if the underlying IP-based reconfiguration fails or is attacked.

Contribution: In this work, we leverage the container principle – originally proposed as safety mechanism – to the security domain. We present a tailored encapsulation scheme for the PRC. The new architecture consists of individual *ReCo-Fuses*. Each **ReConfigurationFuse** (abbreviated as RCF) captures one specific protective property. During PRC operation (i.e. reconfiguration) all properties have to hold at any given time. To guarantee the correctness of each ReCoFuse, *we require* the formal verification of its behavior, i.e. to formally capture which PRC communication is "good" or "bad" and what will be the resulting action in the respective case. Overall, the ReCoFuses are integrated into the *ReCoFuse Container*.

For demonstrating the proposed scheme, we consider systems which use reconfiguration-based countermeasures and by this implementing the above mentioned moving target principle. Mentens et al. showed in [10] that introducing temporal jitter based on reconfiguration improves side channel attack resistance significantly. In their work, the importance for securing the reconfiguration control (i.e. the PRC) has already been recognized, but was not targeted there (as well as in many following papers). In the case study of this paper, we present two initial ReCoFuses to tackle two major vectors of attacks against the system via the PRC, i.e. to attack

1. the timing of the reconfiguration by keeping one single reconfiguration active for an extended period of time and
2. by disturbing the diversity of individual reconfigurations, such that (in the worst case) the same reconfiguration is used permanently.

In both cases, the moving target becomes a static one making reconfiguration-based countermeasures against physical attacks useless.

Related Work: The *Partial Reconfiguration Controller* (PRC) is an IP component of the respective FPGA vendor. Besides this black box realization, researchers have implemented their own PRC with the focus on higher performance [11], better timing wise predictability during reconfiguration [12] and even fault tolerance [13]. Dedicated protection of the PRC has not been considered in these works.

The authors of [14] proposed the secure reconfiguration controller (SeReCon). Semantically, it also provides an additional barrier to the partial reconfiguration infrastructure. This effectively forms an additional anchor of trust in terms of a gateway to the reconfiguration infrastructure in the design, granting more reliability in the case of IP core based reconfigurable FPGA systems. However, the aforementioned work primarily focuses on authentication of IP cores (in this context bit streams for partial reconfiguration).

Recently, Xilinx announced a security monitor based on a IP soft core which allows monitoring the partial reconfiguration process [15]. To the best of our knowledge, no non-IP-based protection of the PRC for reconfiguration-based countermeasures is offered.

Outline: The paper is structured as follows: First, Sect. 2 describes the adversary model we consider in this work. In Sect. 3 the preliminaries of partial reconfiguration and formal verification are reviewed. Our proposed encapsulation scheme for the PRC, implemented as ReCoFuse Container, is introduced in Sect. 4. Then, Sect. 5 presents a case study demonstrating the advantages of our scheme for a reconfiguration-based encryption system. The experimental evaluation, i.e. fault injection and resource utilization, is reported in Sect. 6. Finally, the paper is concluded in Sect. 7.

2   Adversary Model

The proposed architecture provides increased protection against attacks targeting reconfiguration-based countermeasures. Adversaries are derived from assumptions made in [10] and [16], allowing passive and semi invasive attacks. The malicious user desires to extract confidential information from the system by exploiting available attack measures to circumvent the security mechanisms.

Differential Power Analysis (DPA) represents a passive attack scenario where the malicious user can obtain – possibly a very large number – power consumption measurements of the attacked system over time. Since activity in the design's circuitry correlates to its power draw, DPA allows attacks based on statistical methods (e.g. Welch's t test [17]) to successfully extract cryptographic secrets. These attacks can be carried out with relatively small investments, since computer based oscilloscopes are readily available at decreasing price points.

For semi-invasive attacks, we assume an adversary, who can disturb (or deactivate) the reconfiguration procedure, thus leaving the system vulnerable to the aforementioned DPA-based passive attacks. Only on die attacks are assumed for this scenario. If mitigation against DPA is based on partial reconfiguration, directly attacking the PRC is most rewarding, since failing reconfiguration will leave the system unprotected. Where a single attack was sufficient in the past, the attacker must now attack at least two places at the same time to break the reconfiguration-based protection.

In practice, injecting faults into multiple wires or positions in the FPGA fabric increases the cost of an attack. Multiple instances of the proposed protection scheme allow mitigation (i.e. out scale) of attackers, by employing n modular redundancy in terms of ReCoFuses[1].

A second vector of attack is offered from black box IP cores in the design. As motivated in the introduction, malfunctions, flaws or malicious intents can jeopardize the system's stability. Even Trojans in cryptographic hardware blocks were reported in the literature [18]. If the IP core in the design is considered an adversary, it has direct access to signal lines inside the circuitry (e.g. stalling a shared bus). This scenario was reported to be realistic as demonstrated in [19]. The authors demonstrated an on chip power monitor based on ring oscillators to observe the power consumption of other modules on the FPGA. Furthermore, it allowed a DPA attack against an on chip (i.e. same FPGA) RSA crypto module, as well as side channel attacks against the CPU of the host system (PCIe based FPGA). The proposed RCFs must be capable to capture malformed communication with the surrounding system and reliably detect malicious behavior during operation (i.e. skipped reconfigurations in this particular use case).

---

[1] Please note that we advise to distribute (place) the ReCoFuses evenly in the FPGA, while attaching them to different clock buffers or PLLs.

3 Preliminaries

In this section we briefly review the basics of partial reconfiguration of FPGAs. Afterwards, an overview on formal verification as used later in order to verify the behavior of the ReCoFuses is provided.

3.1 Basics of Partial Reconfiguration

Partial reconfiguration is implemented with highly proprietary means inside the FPGA depending on the FPGA model. Different manufacturer achieve partial reconfiguration with different components. In the course of this work, we will focus on the specific implementation of partial reconfiguration from Xilinx [20], but our approach is also applicable for other FPGA vendors.

Figure 1 presents the essential components of the partial reconfiguration infrastructure:

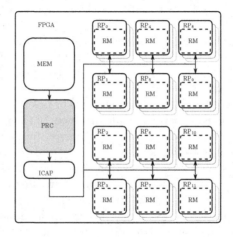

Fig. 1. Overview of partial reconfiguration infrastructure

- *Reconfigurable Partition* (RPs) describe the area and position in the FPGA, where *Reconfigurable Modules* (RMs) are placed (see $RP_{0...11}$ in Fig. 1).
- *Reconfigurable Modules* (RMs) represent the actual implementation which serves as replacement at runtime (see dashed squares in Fig. 1). For each additional RM a new partial bitfile is generated which is stored in the memory to be accessed by the PRC. (see MEM in Fig. 1)
- The partial bitfile represents the *actual* configuration data for the RM in the FPGA. This data is stored in on or off chip memory and it contains the configuration of the logic primitives (e.g. LUTs, DSPs, RAMs) and the connections in the RMs. For reconfiguration, such a bitfile is fed to the *Internal Configuration Access Port* (ICAP) by the PRC at runtime.

```
1   property check_req_ack;
2     // Assume part          Prove part
3     t ##0 req == 1 implies t ##3 ack == 1);
4   endproperty
```

Listing 1.1. Example property

- The ICAP implements the access to the partial reconfiguration infrastructure (see ICAP connecting the PRC to the RPs in Fig. 1). It is treated as a regular primitive in the tool flow during development, synthesis and place and route.
- The PRC is necessary to control the reconfiguration process in the FPGA. It is attached to the memory (e.g. via AXI4), holding the (partial) bitfiles, as well as to the aforementioned cell primitive. Depending on the manufacturers, different options are available, such as internal or external triggers to perform the reconfiguration.

3.2   Formal Verification

Formal verification as used in this work is the task of checking whether a circuit implementation satisfies its specification or not. The specification is thereby expressed with temporal properties. Several standardized property specification languages are available. In this work, we use *SystemVerilog Assertions* (SVA) in combination with *Timing Diagram Assertion Library* (TiDAL) for SVA which comes with the commercial property checking of OneSpin. TiDAL allows one to specify the temporal properties in a very intuitive way, i.e. (a) the time points when an expression is evaluated can be explicitly defined and (b) the properties follow a logic implication style.

A simple property example is presented in Listing 1.1. This property states that if request is 1 at timepoint $t + 0$ (assume part), then three clock cycles later, i.e. $t + 3$, the acknowledge should be 1 (prove part). Such properties can be verified on the circuit. If a property fails, a counter example is provided, i.e. a wave trace which can be simulated which shows the violation of the property.

In case of larger numbers of properties the time, spent for verification, will increase. However, due to impracticality of full re-verification, our proposed approach still provides a significant advantage.

4   ReCoFuse Container

This section presents our encapsulation-scheme for the *Partial Reconfiguration Controller* (PRC) of a FPGA which implements reconfiguration-based countermeasures against physical attacks. The scheme is based on two main components: (1) A "container" encapsulating the PRC, and (2) individual ReCoFuses to monitor and react on untrusted communication with the PRC which would compromise the security of the reconfiguration-based countermeasure.

In the following, we first introduce the overall architecture of the ReCo-Fuse Container. Then, we detail the interfacing of the PRC and the ReCoFuse Container which hosts the individual ReCoFuses. Finally, the required formal verification of ReCoFuse behavior is described.

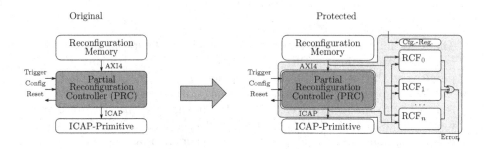

Fig. 2. Original PRC architecture vs proposed ReCoFuse container architecture

4.1 Architecture of ReCoFuse Container

The left part of Fig. 2 depicts the original unprotected PRC architecture. On the right of Fig. 2 the proposed architecture realizing our encapsulation-scheme for the PRC is shown. As can be seen the ReCoFuse Container has several "slots" for individual ReCoFuses (details see next section). The ReCoFuses are denoted as $RCF_{0...n}$ in Fig. 2. Moreover, all outgoing data connections between the main components, i.e. Reconfiguration Memory, PRC and ICAP, are now also fed into the ReCoFuses. Furthermore, a configuration register has been added which allows the user to dynamically enable or disable each RCF.

4.2 Interfaces and ReCoFuses

Listening on all reconfiguration interfaces allows to monitor the reconfiguration operations requested by the reconfiguration-based countermeasures. In Fig. 2, these are the AXI4 and ICAP interfaces. The ICAP protocol follows a valid/acknowledge scheme where the header of each partial bitfile can be analyzed during data communication. For more details, we refer to the Xilinx 7 Series partial reconfiguration user guide [21].

As can be seen in the architecture, the observed input data is sent to the ReCoFuses. A ReCoFuse essentially implements a *Finite State Machine* (FSM), and hence performs state transitions based on the observed data. Reaching a predefined "good" or "bad" state determines whether the usage of the PRC is considered as trusted or untrusted. The output signal of a ReCoFuse (e.g. in this work an error signal) allows each ReCoFuse to communicate untrusted behavior. As a consequence emergency actions can be executed, for instance to shut down the system. For simplicity, in Fig. 2 on the right we have just ORed all the error signals from each ReCoFuse.

```
1    property raise_error;
2      (t ##0 enter_bad_state()
3      implies
4        t ##1 raise_error_signal());
5    endproperty
```

Listing 1.2. ReCoFuse signal bad state property

4.3 Verification of ReCoFuses

To guarantee the correctness of each ReCoFuse, we require the formal verification of its behavior. Hence, temporal properties describing the state transitions of a ReCoFuse have to be specified by the user. In other words, these properties are used to prove which PRC communication with the control of the reconfiguration-based countermeasures is untrusted and what will be the resulting action in that case. Typically, a ReCoFuse observes the communication over several clock cycles and finally reaches a "bad" state. An example property for this last proof step basically states the following: If a ReCoFuse enters the bad state, the associated action must be taken in the next clock cycle. The corresponding property is shown in Listing 1.2.

In the next section we demonstrate our proposed scheme on a concrete case study.

5   Case Study

This section demonstrates the proposed encapsulation-scheme for the PRC. As a case study we selected an encryption system using AES. The system implements the moving target principle via reconfiguration by switching between different implementations of the AES. By this, the attacker is not faced with static logic in the FPGA, but permanently changing one and hence physical attacks become much harder.

In the following, we first describe two major attack vectors. Then, we present the ReCoFuse Container and the two ReCoFuses. Finally, we consider their verification.

5.1 Attack Vectors

Breaking the reconfiguration-based moving target characteristic of a cryptographic system, allows attackers to extract secret information via side channel leakage. In order to attack a specific area (e.g. the PRC) in a FPGA, electromagnetism and fault injection based attacks have both been reported to be effective [22] and are viable methods for disturbing the reconfiguration procedure. We identified two major attack vectors on the PRC – viable for both adversaries:

1. *Time-out attack:* Forcing the PRC to keep the same reconfiguration active for a too long time, would result in no protection. It removes the moving target characteristic of the design and makes it vulnerable to side channel attacks.

```
1    property advance_timer;
2       disable iff (rst) (
3          t ##0 (cnt!=TIMEOUT and RP_active)
4       implies
5          t ##1 (cnt==$past(cnt)+1)
6       );
7    endproperty
8
9    property detect_error;
10      disable iff (rst) (
11         t ##0 (cnt==TIMEOUT and RP_active)
12      implies
13         t ##1 (error)
14      );
15   endproperty
```

Listing 1.3. Example properties for timer

2. *Replay attack:* Forcing the PRC to chose a single reconfiguration continuously (or more often) removes the moving target characteristic as well.

This list, however, is not exhaustive and can must be extended by the respective adopters needs. The next section presents how the proposed ReCoFuse Container helps in protecting against the two attacks.

5.2 ReCoFuse Container

We encapsulated the PRC in a ReCoFuse Container. It instantiates the PRC and provides connection to the configuration memory via AXI and the ICAP primitive as described in Sect. 4. ReCoFuses are integrated inside the ReCoFuse Container to achieve countermeasures against the time out and replay attack. The concrete ReCoFuse are presented in the following two sections.

5.3 Timeout ReCoFuse

Functionality: The timeout ReCoFuse (RCF_0) basically keeps track of the time between two consecutive reconfigurations. Hence, after a successful reconfiguration, a timer is started. If this timer expires *before* a new reconfiguration procedure is initiated, the timeout ReCoFuse signals an error. Keeping a specific reconfiguration active for an extended period of time – rendering the moving target principle ineffective – can be detected reliably by this ReCoFuse.

Interface Events: The counter of the time-out ReCoFuse is started by a RP_active, which is derived from several signals, provided by the proprietary reconfiguration infrastructure. Alternatively, the sync word in combination with the bitfile length could serve for the same purpose.

Verification: In Listing 1.3, a subset of the properties for verifying the timeout ReCoFuse RCF_0 are shown. The first property advance_timer (Line 1–Line 7) states that the counter (which realizes the timer) advances with each time step after the previous reconfiguration is done. Here, `TIMEOUT` (Line 3) defines the allowed active duration of one Reconfiguration Module (RM), i.e. a concrete AES implementation. The `RP_active` (Line 3) signal is derived from multiple signals from the reconfiguration infrastructure and captures whether the Reconfigurable Partition (RP) is active, i.e. no reconfiguration is currently performed. In Line 5, the `$past()` statement is used to refer to the previous time point.

`detect_error` names the second verification property (Line 9–Line 15 in Listing 1.3). It ensures that RCF_0 enters the "bad" state (i.e. raising `error`), when the respective RM was not reconfigured in time (i.e. before `cnt` reaching `TIMEOUT`) (Line 11).

5.4   Replay ReCoFuse

Functionality: The replay ReCoFuse (RCF_1) contains an individual counter for each Reconfiguration Module (so, different AES implementations in our case study), i.e. functional alternative which is swapped in. Based on the individual counter values the distance of the *Least Frequently Used* (LFU) RM as well as the *Most Frequently Used* (MFU) RM is determined. This distance indicates whether the usage of the available RMs is uniform. Hence, this forms an effective measure to detect if a specific RM is preferred or used continuously, since the corresponding counter will advance *faster*. To illustrate the developed uniformity check, Fig. 3 shows a reconfiguration procedure over 13 reconfigurations (i.e. steps) in form of a bar chart, choosing from four different RMs. In Fig. 3, the y axis shows the four different RMs (i.e. different AES implementations). The x axis shows the frequency, how often the RMs were reconfigured. For example, after 2 time steps only RM_1 and RM_2 have been reconfigured both once; after 6 time steps this changes to respective frequencies of (1, 2, 2, 1) (for RM_1, RM_2, RM_3, RM_4).

A challenge when implementing this ReCoFuse in hardware, was that the logic (i.e. the counters) should not become too costly. The solution was the implementation of a shift window operation which essentially "cuts" all counters (similar to a histogram) at the *bottom*. As a consequence, the least frequently used counter is *zero aligned*. Figure 3 depicts this "cutting" in terms of the shift window operation in the left (highlighted gray), while preserving the distance between the LFU and MFU RM, i.e. shift window reduces the counters from (1, 2, 2, 1) to (0, 1, 1, 0) after $step_6$.

For the example at hand, we allow a distance of 6 between the least frequently used RM and the most frequently used RM. Assuming an attack (e.g. a replay attack) resulting in a more frequent reconfiguration of RM_1 is depicted in the figure: In $step_{13}$ we see a violation of our security condition of $MFU - LFU = 7 - 0 = 7^2$ and hence an error is signaled by the ReCoFuse.

Interface Events: The uniformity check of the replay ReCoFuse is applied between reconfiguration memory and PRC in the AXI communication. A unique

---

[2] The gray boxes have been removed by the shift window operation, so the counters are (7, 1, 1, 0).

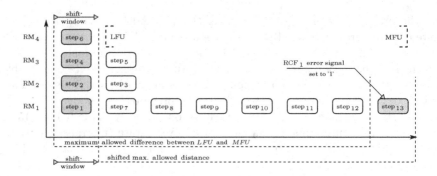

Fig. 3. Uniformity check and shift window operation

```
1    property decrease_counter;
2      disable iff(rst) (
3        t ##0 (state==SHIFT_WINDOW and RM_seen==ALL_RM)
4      implies
5        // omitted technicality
6        t ##1 (state==SYNQ and RM_seen==NO_RM
7          and cnt==$past(cnt)-1)
8      );
9    endproperty
10
11   property detect_error;
12     disable iff(rst) (
13       t ##0 (dist==MAX and state==CHECK_ERR)
14         and t ##1 (state==CHECK_ERR)
15     implies
16       t ##1 (error)
17     );
18   endproperty
```

Listing 1.4. Example properties for uniformity check

identifier of the individual RMs can be derived from the *Frame Address Register* (FAR) value together with its address in the configuration memory. To increment a specific counter, the replay ReCoFuse scans the transmissions on the AXI interface for its respective identifier which can be observed when the respective bitfile is loaded by the PRC.

Verification: In Listing 1.4, a subset of the properties to verify the behavior of the replay ReCoFuse are shown. Please note that the shown 2 properties are checked for each RM since the replay ReCoFuse has per RM an individual counter as explained above. The `decrease_counter` property is central to the shift window (`state==SHIFT_WINDOW`) operation in hardware. It is ensured that all counters are decreased (i.e. previously mentioned "cutting", `cnt==$past(cnt)-1`) when all RMs were active at least once (`RM_seen==ALL_RM`). In order to immediately capture new reconfigurations, the underlying FSM must transition to the `SYNQ` state, where it screens the AXI communication for the RM identifier. `RM_seen` is reset (`RM_seen==NO_RM`) in the next step to allow continuous counter cutting.

The second property in Listing 1.4 is called `detect_error` starting from Line 11. Following the idea from Listing 1.3, the ReCoFuse must raise its `error` signal, when the maximum allowed distance (`dist==MAX`) is exceeded. A dedicated error checking state (`CHECK_ERR`) in the FSM checks this violation (Line 13 + 14) and raises the error signal in the next cycle (Line 16). The FSM remains in this error state (i.e. the "bad" state).

In the following section, we present an experimental evaluation of our approach for our case study.

6   Results

All experiments have been conducted on a Xilinx Zync-7000 Series FPGA, more precisely our evaluation platform is a Zedboard featuring a XC7Z020-CLG484-1 FPGA component. More recent FPGA generations feature the same reconfiguration interface, thus our approach maintains applicability in the future. Enhanced capabilities, such as better encryption and authentication however can help to increase the difficulty of attacks further. Our encryption system implements the moving target principle by switching between different implementations of the AES core "tiny_AES" from https://opencores.org/project/tiny_aes via reconfiguration. A dedicated controller in the FPGA (called *SYSCTRL*) initiates the random (i.e. uniform) replacement of a *Reconfiguration Module* (RM), i.e. between the different AES implementations.

We have synthesized the encryption system using Vivado 16.04. The partial bitfiles are copied from the SD card to the on board DDR3 memory (serves as partial bitfile memory), using a bare metal executable which runs on the ARM core of the FPGA. To access from the programmable logic of the FPGA, we switched the DDR3 memory to AXI slave mode. The PRC is directly attached to the AXI slave DDR3 memory in the design and instantiates the ICAP primitive as well. A ReCoFuse Container encapsulates the PRC as presented in Sect. 4. The two ReCoFuses time out (RCF_0) and replay (RCF_1), as described in Sect. 5.2, are integrated in the ReCoFuse Container to protect against the two attacks as introduced in Sect. 5.1.

6.1   Injecting Faults

As mentioned above, the controller *SYSCTRL* for reconfiguring between the different AES implementations initiates the random (i.e. uniform) replacement of a RM and for this communicates with the PRC. During normal operation *SYSCTRL* replaces the current RM with a random successor before the timer of RCF_0 expires, such that no ReCoFuse raises an error. To run the experiments, we attacked the reconfiguration process by injecting faults in the encryption system in order to disturb the operation of the PRC. This was achieved by additional logic on the FPGA. Essentially, we disable the initiation of the replacement at runtime or alternatively remove the randomness from the RM selection. The following results have been obtained when using the Xilinx *Integrated Logic Analyzers* (ILAs):

Time-Out Attack. Figure 4 illustrates the functionality of RCF_0 for the time-out attack. The timer must expire, if a RM is kept active longer than acceptable; we set the TIMEOUT to 10 time steps. For demonstration we captured the activity for 960 ms (i.e. 15 time steps). After 64 ms, RM_1 is loaded, followed by, RM_2 and RM_3 (each active for 1 time step (64 ms)). RM_4 is kept active indefinitely (10 time steps), which exceeds the acceptable period (640 ms), such that the error signal is raised, when the counter value (`ctr`) reaches 640. The `error` signal indicates a violation of the time-out requirement.

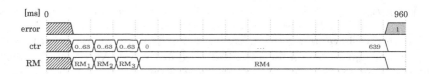

Fig. 4. Behavior of RCF_0 (time-out)

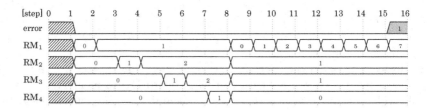

Fig. 5. Behavior of RCF_1 (replay)

Replay Attack. Figure 5 shows a sequence of the reconfigurations after 15 steps. We have for different RMs. The maximum allowed distance of the RMs is set to 6 as in Fig. 3. In step 7, the occurrence of RM_4 decreases all counters by the shift window operation, resulting in a *zero alignment* of all counters. At this point, the PRC is attacked (i.e. internally triggered faults are injected). In the 15th step, loading RM_1 will activate the error signal of the RCF_1. Since the difference between the most and least frequently used RM exceeds the allowed limit.

In summary, both experiments based on injecting faults demonstrated the effectiveness of our approach. In the next section, we report the resource utilization of our ReCoFuse Container for the encryption system.

6.2   Resource Utilization

Table 1 shows the utilization of the FPGA after implementation in Vivado. All synthesis runs and P&R runs were executed with the same settings. The first

Table 1. Hardware resource utilization

"Moving target AES"	Original	ReCoFuse protected	
Elements	Usage	Usage	Increase
Slices	2976	3036	2.02%
LUT as logic	10520	10620	0.95%
LUT as memory	203	203	0.00%
LUT FF pairs	4367	4409	0.96%

column *elements* of the table presents the respective resource. The second column *Original* shows the our encryption system employing reconfiguration based on different tiny_AES cores and the Xilinx reconfiguration infrastructure following the moving target principle. Three different AES cores and a blank module (Xilinx recommendation for system initialization) have been included and are randomly chosen for reconfiguration by the *SYSCTRL*. The third column *ReCo-Fuse protected: Usage* contains the resource utilization for the encryption system protected with the introduced ReCoFuse Container. Finally, the fourth column *ReCoFuse protected: Increase* shows the negligible overhead, caused by our solution.

7 Conclusion and Future Work

In this work, we leveraged an originally proposed safety mechanism which creates a container around an IP, to encapsulate and protect the PRC of an FPGA. We introduced ReCoFuses inside our encapsulation-scheme, each capturing a specific property of interest which has to be fulfilled at any time during PRC operation. Formal verification was employed to guarantee the correctness in detecting a security violation. For evaluation of our scheme, we have created a reference design, which we attacked by injecting faults. The experiments showed that the implemented measures – leveraging the proposed scheme – realize an effective and cost efficient protection for reconfiguration-based secured designs. Our flexible architecture allows adding more ReCoFuses (e.g. CRC, additional encryption, hash-based finger printing etc.) easily. The protective measures are dependent on the required degree of protection. Possibly, a full catalog of fuses can be maintained in the future. In summary, this work closes the gap of vulnerable reconfiguration infrastructure as identified in [10] by Mentens et al.

References

1. Emmert, J., Stroud, C., Skaggs, B., Abramovici, M.: Dynamic fault tolerance in FPGAs via partial reconfiguration. In: FCCM, pp. 165–174 (2000)
2. Paulsson, K., Hübner, M., Bayar, S., Becker, J.: Exploitation of run-time partial reconfiguration for dynamic power management in Xilinx spartan III-based systems. In: ReCoSoC, pp. 1–6 (2007)

3. Noguera, J., Kennedy, I.O.: Power reduction in network equipment through adaptive partial reconfiguration. In: FPL, pp. 240–245 (2007)
4. Trimberger, S., Carberry, D., Johnson, A., Wong, J.: A time-multiplexed FPGA. In: FCCM, pp. 22–28 (1997)
5. Bloem, R., Könighofer, B., Könighofer, R., Wang, C.: Shield synthesis: runtime enforcement for reactive systems. In: Baier, C., Tinelli, C. (eds.) TACAS 2015. LNCS, vol. 9035, pp. 533–548. Springer, Heidelberg (2015). https://doi.org/10.1007/978-3-662-46681-0_51
6. Drechsler, R., Kühne, U.: Safe IP integration using container modules. In: ISED, pp. 1–4 (2014)
7. Chandrasekharan, A., Schmitz, K., Kühne, U., Drechsler, R.: Ensuring safety and reliability of IP-based system design - a container approach. In: RSP, pp. 76–82 (2015)
8. Schmitz, K., Chandrasekharan, A., Filho, J.G., Große, D., Drechsler, R.: Trust is good, control is better: hardware-based instruction-replacement for reliable processor-IPs. In: ASP-DAC, pp. 57–62 (2017)
9. Hategekimana, F., Whitaker, T.J., Pantho, M.J.H., Bobda, C.: Secure integration of non-trusted IPs in SOCs. In: AsianHOST, pp. 103–108 (2017)
10. Mentens, N., Gierlichs, B., Verbauwhede, I.: Power and fault analysis resistance in hardware through dynamic reconfiguration. In: Oswald, E., Rohatgi, P. (eds.) CHES 2008. LNCS, vol. 5154, pp. 346–362. Springer, Heidelberg (2008). https://doi.org/10.1007/978-3-540-85053-3_22
11. Vipin, K., Fahmy, S.A.: ZyCAP: efficient partial reconfiguration management on the Xilinx Zynq. ESL 6(3), 41–44 (2014)
12. Pezzarossa, L., Schoeberl, M., Sparsø, J.: A controller for dynamic partial reconfiguration in FPGA-based real-time systems. In: ISORC, pp. 92–100 (2017)
13. Straka, M., Kastil, J., Kotasek, Z.: Generic partial dynamic reconfiguration controller for fault tolerant designs based on FPGA. In: NORCHIP, pp. 1–4 (2010)
14. Kepa, K., Morgan, F., Kosciuszkiewicz, K., Surmacz, T.: SeReCon: a secure reconfiguration controller for self-reconfigurable systems. IJCCBS 1(1–3), 86–103 (2010)
15. Xilinx: Monitor IP-core product brief (2015). https://www.xilinx.com/support/documentation/product-briefs/security-monitor-ip-core-product-brief.pdf
16. Lemke-Rust, K., Paar, C.: An adversarial model for fault analysis against low-cost cryptographic devices. In: Breveglieri, L., Koren, I., Naccache, D., Seifert, J.-P. (eds.) FDTC 2006. LNCS, vol. 4236, pp. 131–143. Springer, Heidelberg (2006). https://doi.org/10.1007/11889700_13
17. Schneider, T., Moradi, A.: Leakage assessment methodology. JCEN 6(2), 85–99 (2016)
18. Bhasin, S., Danger, J.-L., Guilley, S., Ngo, X., Sauvage, L.: Hardware Trojan horses in cryptographic IP cores. In: FDTC, pp. 15–29 (2013)
19. Zhao, M., Suh, G.E.: FPGA-based remote power side-channel attacks. In: S&P, pp. 229–244, May 2018
20. Xilinx: Xilinx official website - user guide - partial reconfiguration, January 2018. https://www.xilinx.com/support/documentation/sw_manuals/xilinx2018_1/ug909-vivado-partial-reconfiguration.pdf
21. Xilinx: User guide - 7 series FPGAs configuration, March 2018. https://www.xilinx.com/support/documentation/user_guides/ug470_7Series_Config.pdf
22. Li, H., Du, G., Shao, C., Dai, L., Xu, G., Guo, J.: Heavy-Ion microbeam fault injection into SRAM-based FPGA implementations of cryptographic circuits. IEEE Trans. Nuclear Sci. 62(3), 1341–1348 (2015)

Proof-Carrying Hardware Versus the Stealthy Malicious LUT Hardware Trojan

Qazi Arbab Ahmed$^{(\boxtimes)}$ (ID), Tobias Wiersema (ID), and Marco Platzner (ID)

Paderborn University, Paderborn, Germany
{qazi,wiersema,platzner}@mail.upb.de

Abstract. Reconfigurable hardware has received considerable attention as a platform that enables dynamic hardware updates and thus is able to adapt new configurations at runtime. However, due to their dynamic nature, e.g., field-programmable gate arrays (FPGA) are subject to a constant possibility of attacks, since each new configuration might be compromised. Trojans for reconfigurable hardware that evade state-of-the-art detection techniques and even formal verification, are thus a large threat to these devices. One such stealthy hardware Trojan, that is inserted and activated in two stages by compromised electronic design automation (EDA) tools, has recently been presented and shown to evade all forms of classical pre-configuration detection techniques. This paper presents a successful pre-configuration countermeasure against this "Malicious Look-up-table (LUT)"-hardware Trojan, by employing bitstream-level Proof-Carrying Hardware (PCH). We show that the method is able to alert innocent module creators to infected EDA tools, and to prohibit malicious ones to sell infected modules to unsuspecting customers.

1 Introduction

Hardware Trojans, i.e., malicious circuit inclusions, have grown into a mature research field over the last two decades, which has raised many questions regarding the integrity, security and trust in digital systems. Attack vectors are plentiful, especially since nowadays most integrated circuit (IC) designers rely on third-party Intellectual Property (IP) cores and closed-source Electronic Design Automation (EDA) tools, while the manufacturers outsource the actual fabrication step to third-party foundries that are often in different countries or even continents, to lower the cost and to speedup the development. As a consequence, attackers have the opportunity to manipulate a design at almost any stage of the

This work has been partially supported by the German Research Foundation (DFG) within the Collaborative Research Center 901 "On-The-Fly Computing" under the project number 160364472-SFB901.

The authors would like to thank the authors of [8] for the discussions and the release of their original material.

IC development life cycle [13]. Such an undesired modification of a circuit can alter its functionality, provide a covert channel to leak sensitive information, or even open a back door into the IC. A hardware Trojan is usually defined to comprise a trigger and a payload [2]. Typically, a trigger mechanism is implemented in a way that activates the payload mechanism either always, upon reception of some stimulus specified at design time, or at a some pre-determined time during the operation. Triggers of Trojans play an important role to conceal them throughout the development process of an IC. In order to hide the malicious circuitry, an adversary would design the trigger in a way that the Trojan does not affect the functionality of the original circuit under normal conditions. In literature, various trigger implementations have been published so far and most of them depend on rare events such as counters or a specific unlikely signal pattern to evade detection at the functional testing stage [2,13]. However, such Trojans can be caught by extensive functional simulation and testing during design time, as state-of-the-art detection techniques are exploiting the fact that malicious circuitry is more likely to reside in the rarely or unused portions of the circuit and thus investigate these areas with much more scrutiny.

Most of the work on hardware Trojans has been focused on static circuits, i.e., application-specific integrated circuits (ASICs), while very little effort has been shown towards dynamically reconfigurable hardware such as field-programmable gate arrays (FPGAs), where Trojans can affect not only the static (ASIC) part, but also the dynamic configuration. In this paper, we follow the attack presented in [8], in fact using the reference implementation provided by the authors, where compromised EDA tools add and activate a hardware Trojan into a design in two stages, making sure that it is dormant, and thus virtually undetectable, in every step of the design flow except the final bitstream. We propose to use a bitstream-level proof-carrying hardware (PCH) approach to detect the stealthy Trojan that is injected and activated in the compromised design flow. Replacing the consumer's need to trust in other parties with hard evidence is the core benefit of our approach, which places the computational burden of verification on the producer of a hardware module.

The novel contributions of this paper are as follows:

– We present a bitstream-level proof-carrying hardware method within the scenario defined in [8], which, to the best of our knowledge, is the first that is able to detect a stealthy Trojan before it runs on an FPGA.
– Using also tools from the IceStorm project [12], we present a complete open-source design-and-verification flow for iCE40 FPGAs that is able to protect bitstreams for these targets with the full power of PCH.

The rest of the paper is organized as follows. In Sect. 2, we look at the related work and background in hardware Trojans and their detection. Section 3 provides the overview about our proof-carrying hardware approach and the tool flow for iCE40 FPGAs. Section 4 elaborates our experimental setup and implementations. Finally, we conclude the paper and point to future work in Sect. 5.

2   Related Work and Background

In general, it is harder to attack a circuit on an FPGA in a foundry compared to an ASIC, as the actual functionality of the FPGA is only determined at runtime, when the static part and the dynamic configuration are combined to form the circuit. Attacks on the static part of the FPGA are closely related to ASIC attacks and out of the scope of this paper. Attacks on the FPGA configuration during the design step, can, e.g., be performed by compromising the EDA tools which are used to synthesize the design. This attack can be carried out either by actually modifying or replacing the tools themselves, as is described for instance in [9], or as a post-processing step, as demonstrated in [3], where the authors investigate the possibilities and limitations of direct bitstream modification attacks. For an attacker, compromising EDA tools can be very attractive, as potentially a higher number of designs can be compromised in one attack.

Recently, Krieg et al. [8] have published such an attack that basically adds a second trigger to the Trojan design, which is tied to specific steps in the FPGA design flow, as depicted in Fig. 1(a). Their stealthy Trojan relies on compromised design tools: First the front end synthesis tool injects the Trojan into a user design (Fig. 1(b)) and then the back end synthesis tool activates (triggers) it when writing the bitstream configuration file, and only then (Fig. 1(c)). The injected Trojan can still comprise a classical trigger-payload pair, which can then, e.g., be activated at operation time. The novelty of the approach lies in the fact that the infected circuit is functionally equivalent to the hardware specification during post-implementation simulation and testing, as the Trojan is dormant after insertion. This Trojan can thus circumvent all state-of-the-art detection techniques that rely on identifying unused, nearly unused or redundant inputs or portions of circuit, such as unused circuit identification (UCI) [6]. The only possibility to detect this stealthy Trojan pre-configuration, i.e., before the FPGA is configured with the design, is to analyze the configuration bitstream itself, as also the authors point out.

In this paper, we apply the idea of [4] to the tool flow from [8] to use PCH to detect the stealthy hardware Trojans for the lattice semiconductor iCE40 family of FPGA [1] using mainly tools from the open-source flow IceStorm [12]. Our approach differs from state-of-the-art Trojan detection techniques where comparison or equivalence checking is done at the *RT* level or *netlist* level to detect stealthy Trojans. While the attack we counter will not be caught by such techniques, as the activation is done at last stage, i.e., while writing the bitstream, our bitstream-level PCH scheme is able to detect Krieg et al.'s stealthy Trojans using an open-source tool chain.

3   Proof-Carrying Hardware Approach for ICE

The proof-carrying hardware concept was proposed by Drzevitzky et al. [4]. PCH considers third-party IPs that are integrated into FPGAs in a bitstream

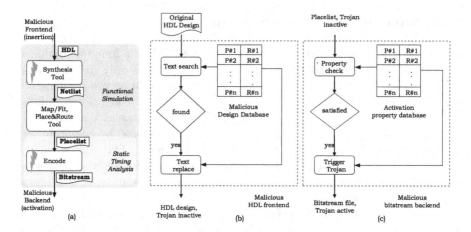

Fig. 1. (a) Depicts the function principle of the attack. In (b), a malicious front end injects malicious HDL code into an original design based on pattern matching. Whereas (c) shows a malicious back end which activates the attack by looking for the previously inserted cells and altering them. Figure from [8].

configuration format, as this is the lowest possible abstraction in reconfigurable hardware, which explicitly excludes the closed-source vendor EDA tools from the trusted base. To verify the third-party IPs, PCH uses automatic formal verification techniques that are easy to retrace, so as to enable the recipient of module and proof to perform a lightweight verification with the full power of the initial one. Principally, PCH has been evaluated using abstract and virtual FPGAs due to the unavailability of bitstream documentation to be used as a prototype for FPGA providing companies. Therefore, Wiersema et al. [11] evaluated and implemented PCH on a fine-grained virtual fabric, where they demonstrated and experimentally evaluated PCH at the bitstream level of virtual bitstreams for an overlay placed on a real FPGA. In this paper, we present a PCH prototype directly for the bitstream of a real FPGA by leveraging reverse engineering-based open-source design tools from the IceStorm project [12].

Figure 2 outlines the steps performed in our PCH scenario, derived from the steps described in [11]. The consumer specifies the functionality of the IP module as well as the security specification. As a simplifying assumption for our prototype, the design specification is provided as Verilog source code and the security specification is agreed upon in advance as demanding the full functional equivalence between the (golden) Verilog source and the circuit represented in the final bitstream, thereby detecting any Trojans that alter the functionality. The producer synthesizes the IP module for the target platform, in our case the iCE40 FPGA, resulting in a bitstream that will be sent to the consumer, as depicted in Fig. 3. The producer then re-extracts the Verilog from the bitstream to combine it with the original specification into a miter[1] function in CNF form.

---

[1] For details on miter functions in Proof-Carrying Hardware see, e.g., [4].

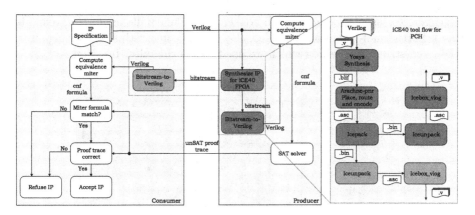

Fig. 2. PCH tool flow

This CNF formula is proven to be unsatisfiable by a SAT solver, which proves functional equivalence between specification and implementation. This works for combinational and time-bounded sequential circuits; for unbounded ones, or ones with no practical bounds like triggers using long running counters, more advanced proving techniques like induction are needed, which can also be found in related PCH work [7]. The resulting proof trace together with the bitstream is then sent to the consumer, who also formulates the miter with the reversed Verilog in order to compare this miter CNF with the one that is the basis of the proof trace. The consumer can only be sure that the provided proof trace is actually about the specified IP module, if the miters match. In case of a match, the consumer verifies the proof using the proof trace. If this step also is successful, the consumer configures the FPGA with the bitstream. If any of the two checks fail, the consumer indicates the failure through its user interface on the PC, about the rejection of an IP module.

3.1 Tool Flow for ICE

Project IceStorm is an open-source project by Wolf and Lasser that provides tools to create and manipulate or analyze bitstreams for Lattice iCE40 FPGAs [12]. The project aims at reverse engineering and documenting the iCE40's bitstream format, and together with other open-source tools they have defined a completely open-source tool flow for the iCE40 FPGAs. Lattice FPGAs, and especially the iCE family, can be used for smaller circuits for the verification of the design. Figure 3 shows the parts of the iCE40 tool flow that we used to implement the PCH approach. Here, *yosys* is used to synthesize the HDL description of the design. The output of yosys is a synthesized (and optimized) netlist in Berkeley logic interchange format (BLIF), that is then given to the place and route tool, *Arachne-pnr* [10], which after placement and routing, encodes the placed and routed design/netlist into a text file (ASCII). To generate the binary file, e.g., a bitstream configuration file, we use the *Icepack* tool. To reverse convert the bitstream, we use *Iceunpack*, which converts the binary file again to a text file (.asc). Furthermore, we use the *icebox_vlog* tool to convert this text file again to HDL, i.e., structural Verilog which we use to form the miter function.

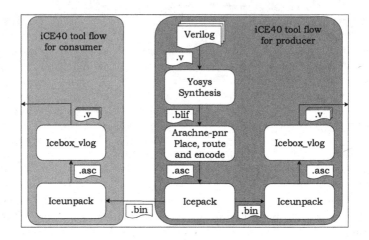

Fig. 3. Shows the iCE40 tool flow used for PCH

3.2   Threat Model

As explained in Sect. 2, IP modules obtained from third parties can be maliciously infected. We explain our threat model by discussing three different possible scenarios and show that in all three scenarios of attack, our bitstream-level PCH approach identifies the malicious intrusion and notifies that the implemented design is not functionally equivalent to the specified design. In the following subsections, we highlight the resiliency of the verification technique against attacks from various parties; Table 1 summarizes the details.

Scenario: 1. In this scenario, we assume that the adversary is either the vendor of an underlying IP Core used by the producer to make their own core, or an employee of the producer who deliberately inserts the stealthy Trojan into the original design specification received from the consumer, while the EDA tools and the transportation of IP modules in this case are not compromised. The Trojan would then remain dormant through all internal validation steps performed by the producer to be only activated upon writing the final bitstream. Since this bitstream forms the basis for the remaining PCH verification, the producer would subsequently compute the miter function using the compromised implementation with the active Trojan, as discussed in Sect. 3.1. There are two possibilities now:

1. The producer uses the consumer's original specification. This would lead to a satisfiable miter function, as the design extracted from the bitstream has

Table 1. Threat scenarios

Scenario	Malicious party	Attack vector	Detected at
1	Design house	Design specification	Producer
		Both specifications	Consumer
	IP vendor	Underlying IP core	Producer
2	EDA Tools	Bitstream [8]	Producer
3	Communication	→ Design specification	Producer
		→ Both specifications	Consumer
		← Bitstream	Consumer
		← Bitstream & proof	Consumer
Any	Any	Trojan infection with valid new proof	Undetected: Harmless

altered behavior, and hence the proof creation step would fail, meaning the producer would not be able to send a proof-carrying bitstream (PCB) to the consumer. Remark: Were the miter not satisfiable in this step, would the alteration of the Trojan be deemed harmless, since that would essentially mean that the inclusion of the Trojan does not violate the previously agreed upon property (functional equivalence in this case).

2. The producer uses a compromised specification with activated Trojan instance. With this specification, the producer would be able to create a proof of conformity of their core with the specification. The consumer, however, would compute the miter using their original copy of the specification, which cannot be compromised, which would lead them to a different miter compared to the producer. They would thus not accept the received proof, as the miter comparison step would fail.

Our proposed PCH approach would thus alert the consumer to the Trojan's presence in every possible case in this scenario, as long as the (activated) Trojan violates the property.

Scenario: 2. In this threat scenario, we assume that the producer and communication channel can be trusted, but the EDA tools used by the producer are compromised. One reasonable instance of this scenario would be a pre-compiled version of an open-source EDA tool that includes malicious code. This basically matches the attack from [8] shown in Fig. 1.

Since in this case no collaborator within the producer would replace the design received by the consumer, the verification miter would always be formed using the original specification and the infected bitstream with activated Trojan, which would lead to again either a satisfiable miter, which would alert the producer to the fact that their tools are compromised, or it would help to ensure that the Trojan is harmless, if its activation does not violate the property. In any case the producer again cannot, even by accident, create a malicious bitstream and matching proof that would fool the consumer into configuring an FPGA with it.

Scenario: 3. In this scenario, we assume that the design house and the EDA tools are trustworthy and the adversary has compromised the communication channel between producer and consumer, e.g., by performing a man-in-the-middle attack. There are several attack vectors, which would be detected in different steps of the flow:

1. The attacker replaces the design or security specification before it reaches the producer, inserting the Trojan in the specification or relaxing the properties that need to be proven. The producer would then go ahead and unknowingly (a) produce a wrong design, or (b) create an erroneous proof for the property afterwards. Since the consumer has an unmodified version of both specifications, however, and will use these to create their own version of the proof basis, both (a) and (b) would lead them to reject the module.
2. The attacker reverse engineers the proof-carrying bitstream and injects the Trojan into it. Since in this case the proof would not match the bitstream, the consumer would also be alerted when comparing the miter functions that the module is not trustworthy.
3. The attacker injects the Trojan into the PCB and modifies the proof. This leads to different outcomes, depending on the proof modification. If the new proof uses the correct miter, but consequently cannot actually prove its unsatisfiability, the consumer will reject the module. If the new proof is a correct proof of unsatisfiability using an alternative miter, the miter mismatch will be detected again. If the miter matches and the new proof indeed shows its unsatisfiability, then the attacker effectively has proven that their addition is not violating the property and is hence not considered to be malicious by the consumer. The last case would hence not be detected, but that would be considered a non-issue.

The consumer would thus be alerted of any malicious, i.e., property violating, alteration of the design in the PCB, no matter which communication direction the attacker compromises or what vector they choose, allowing the consumer to reject the module as untrustworthy.

4   Experimental Validation

In this section, we present experimental results obtained using an example module represented in Verilog description. In order to demonstrate the ability of the presented iCE40 PCH flow to counter the attack presented in [8], we have used the example Verilog provided by the authors and the tools that they described where applicable. We have infected the EDA tools with the patches provided by them, and thus to the best of our knowledge have a faithful recreation of one of their experiments at our disposal, which we embedded into the flow described in Sect. 3.

For our experiments, we have first used the example Verilog code with unmodified EDA tools, thus validating the overall flow depicted in Fig. 2. Using uninfected versions of yosys and arachne-pnr on the producer side allowed us to synthesize the design for an iCE40 1K FPGA, and icepack produced the corresponding bitstream (.bin in Fig. 3). Using the reverse tool iceunpack together with one of the icebox scripts allowed us, also on the consumer side, to obtain a Verilog representation of the implemented design. Using the original (behavioral) Verilog as specification counterpart, generically synthesized by a clean yosys, we formed a miter circuit and successfully proved its unsatisfiability using a SAT solver. On the consumer side, we then matched the miter functions and retraced the proof, leading us to an accepted proof-carrying bitstream. This confirmed that we had indeed successfully merged the iCE40 tool flow with the PCH tool flow to enable PCH-certified bitstreams for iCE40 1K FPGAs. We then replaced the synthesis tools with the infected versions and reran the experiment. After computing the bitstream on the producer side, we unpacked and reversed it again in order to form the miter function with the specification (the specification blif was still generated by a clean yosys). This miter, however, proved to be satisfiable, since the implementation now actually had been altered. We hence achieved the expected result from Table 1, where PCH allowed us to detect the malicious modification of the design at the producer. A malicious producer could now try to hide the infection from the user, but as detailed in Sect. 3.2 this would then definitely be detected by the consumer in a later phase.

5   Conclusion

As already concluded by Krieg et al. [8], bitstream formats have to be publicly available to enable users to reveal and protect themselves against malicious bitstream manipulations. Unfortunately, for commercial EDA tools this is usually not the case. In this paper, we have demonstrated that bitstream-level verification using proof-carrying hardware is indeed able to reveal the stealthy two-stage hardware Trojan attack presented in [8], which is undetectable using regular state-of-the-art pre-configuration detection approaches. The power of PCH ensures that even in a two-party contract work scenario, where the producer's tools are compromised, the consumer is protected against the modifications. We thus underline the claim by Krieg et al. that their attack is only possible because of the closed nature of commercial bitstream formats, and conclude that in a world with open bitstream formats the problem would not only be solvable but is indeed already solved. Not only for the one party version described in [8] (consumer + attacker), but also in the two party version defined by PCH (consumer, producer + attacker), which is a common case in today's market, where designers build their designs from a multitude of third party IP Cores. In our future work, we aim to implement our approach also for commercial FPGA tools like Xilinx Vivado, to bring the potential of PCH certified bitstreams demonstrated here directly to actual, modern devices. We are planning to compensate the absence of bitstream documentation in this world with the help of external tools like

RapidSmith2 [5], which will help us to at least remove most of the closed-source tools from the trusted base.

References

1. Lattice semiconductor. http://www.latticesemi.com/iCE40. Accessed 21 Nov 2018
2. Bhunia, S., Hsiao, M.S., Banga, M., Narasimhan, S.: Hardware trojan attacks: threat analysis and countermeasures. Proc. IEEE **102**(8), 1229–1247 (2014). https://doi.org/10.1109/JPROC.2014.2334493
3. Chakraborty, R.S., Saha, I., Palchaudhuri, A., Naik, G.K.: Hardware trojan insertion by direct modification of FPGA configuration bitstream. IEEE Des. Test **30**(2), 45–54 (2013). https://doi.org/10.1109/MDT.2013.2247460
4. Drzevitzky, S., Kastens, U., Platzner, M.: Proof-carrying hardware: towards runtime verification of reconfigurable modules. In: 2009 International Conference on Reconfigurable Computing and FPGAs, pp. 189–194. IEEE, December 2009. https://doi.org/10.1109/ReConFig.2009.31
5. Haroldsen, T., Nelson, B., Hutchings, B.: RapidSmith 2: a framework for BEL-level CAD exploration on xilinx FPGAs. In: Proceedings of the 2015 ACM/SIGDA International Symposium on Field-Programmable Gate Arrays, pp. 66–69. FPGA 2015, ACM (2015). https://doi.org/10.1145/2684746.2689085
6. Hicks, M., Finnicum, M., King, S.T., Martin, M.M.K., Smith, J.M.: Overcoming an untrusted computing base: detecting and removing malicious hardware automatically. In: 2010 IEEE Symposium on Security and Privacy, pp. 159–172. IEEE, May 2010. https://doi.org/10.1109/SP.2010.18
7. Isenberg, T., Platzner, M., Wehrheim, H., Wiersema, T.: Proof-carrying hardware via inductive invariants. ACM Trans. Des. Autom. Electron. Syst. **22**(4), 61:11–61:123 (2017). https://doi.org/10.1145/3054743
8. Krieg, C., Wolf, C., Jantsch, A.: Malicious LUT: a stealthy FPGA trojan injected and triggered by the design flow. In: 2016 IEEE/ACM International Conference on Computer-Aided Design (ICCAD), pp. 1–8. IEEE, November 2016. https://doi.org/10.1145/2966986.2967054
9. Peikari, C., Chuvakin, A.: Security Warrior. O'Reilly & Associates Inc., Sebastopol (2004)
10. Seed, C.: Arachne-pnr. https://github.com/YosysHQ/arachne-pnr. Accessed 15 Nov 2018
11. Wiersema, T., Drzevitzky, S., Platzner, M.: Memory security in reconfigurable computers: combining formal verification with monitoring. In: International Conference on Field-Programmable Technology (FPT 2014), pp. 167–174. IEEE (2014). https://doi.org/10.1109/FPT.2014.7082771
12. Wolf, C., Lasser, M.: Project icestorm. http://www.clifford.at/icestorm/
13. Xiao, K., Forte, D., Jin, Y., Karri, R., Bhunia, S., Tehranipoor, M.: Hardware trojans: lessons learned after one decade of research. ACM Trans. Des. Autom. Electron. Syst. **22**(1), 6:1–6:23 (2016). https://doi.org/10.1145/2906147

Secure Local Configuration of Intellectual Property Without a Trusted Third Party

Nadir Khan[1]([✉])[ID], Arthur Silitonga[2][ID], Brian Pachideh[1],
Sven Nitzsche[1], and Jürgen Becker[1,2][ID]

[1] FZI Research Center for Information Technology, Karlsruhe, Germany
khan@fzi.de
[2] Institute for Information Processing Technology (ITIV),
Karlsruhe Institute of Technology (KIT), Karlsruhe, Germany

Abstract. Trading intellectual property (IP) for FPGAs relies on configuring devices securely. This is achieved by using built-in security features of modern FPGAs, i.e. internal decryption engines. The disadvantage of using these features is that a trusted third party (TTP) needs to be involved for the preparation of the devices. Previously published schemes, in this area, are dependent on a TTP that mediates between core vendors (CVs) and system developers (SDs), which poses a major flaw in the chain of trust. In this paper, we propose a scheme where CV and SD can establish a licensing agreement without the participation of a TTP using off-the-shelf products. The IP is delivered in a secure format using state-of-the-art encryption methods. Decryption of the IP is handled by an application running on the FPGA that furthermore guarantees a secure configuration of the device. In order to prevent reverse engineering (RE) of the application, we rely on the progress made in hardware-assisted software (HAS) protection using a tamper and side channel attack (SCA) resistant hardware component. As a result, the application establishes a chain of trust between CVs and SDs without the need for a TTP.

Keywords: Intellectual property · FPGA · Trusted third party ·
Hardware-assisted software protection · IP licensing · Partial reconfiguration

1 Introduction

Since their beginning in the 1980s, Field Programmable Gate Arrays (FPGAs) have evolved from simple devices of a couple of thousand gates to fully programmable system on chips (SoCs) that are capable of implementing a multitude of diverse high-end digital systems. Today, industries that make use of FPGAs include consumer electronics, high performance computing, security, automobiles, aerospace, defense and telecommunication [1], reaching a market size of $63.05 billion in 2017 with an estimated growth to $117.97 billion by 2026 [2]. Their in-field reconfigurability makes FPGAs easily adaptable to changing requirements, eases prototyping and therefore reduces time-to-market as well as overall design cost. With the ever-increasing complexity in hardware design, reuse-based approaches that allow the use of hardware IP licensing have become commonplace. Here, third party CVs offer their designs as submodules to SDs. In the context of FPGAs, IP designs might be distributed as register transfer level (RTL) descriptions, netlists or as bitstreams. While RTL descriptions and netlists ensure compatibility with vendor tools, they also reveal the exact contents of the IP to the customer, which poses a major conflict with the CV's interest in preventing its IP from being duplicated, sold or used in other unauthorized manners. Using a bitstream for distribution increases the required effort to reverse engineer the IP [5], at the same time security against a sophisticated attacker cannot be guaranteed [6].

Several countermeasures against unauthorized IP use have been proposed in academia, and a common approach is to include a trusted third party (TTP) that mediates between CVs and SDs by managing secret keys or confidential data [7–12]. This way, an IP can be distributed as encrypted bitstream without giving customers access to any design data. The use of a TTP gives access of the devices, IPs and other confidential data to a third party that could be untrustworthy.

The main contributions of this paper is an IP licensing scheme that is secure, non-restrictive and convenient on existing devices without any modification. The scheme is based on a pay-per-device approach which gives CVs more flexibility to generate income, unlike one-time payment schemes, e.g. Xilinx' SignOnce IP Licensing [16].

2 Related Work

Zhang et al. proposed a pragmatic scheme in [11]. Steps of the scheme are depicted in Fig. 1, which is then followed by a summary. Since we consider this scheme to be the most feasible, we will use it as a reference going forward.

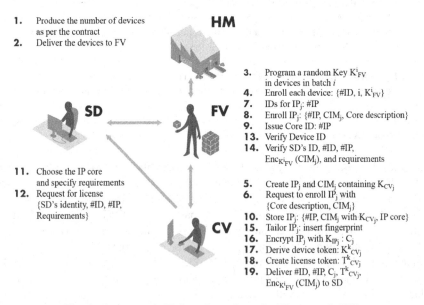

Fig. 1. A pragmatic IP licensing scheme by Zhang et al. [11]

In the 1st and 2nd step of the scheme, the Hardware Manufacturer (HM) produces a fixed amount of devices for the FPGA Vendor (FV). Afterwards, in 3rd and 4th steps, the FV stores secret keys onto the devices and registers them. Meanwhile, a CV that wishes to sell its IP needs to generate a Core Installation Module (CIM) including a key for IP decryption. Then, CV requests IP's registration into the FV's IP store by providing IP's ID along with the CIM where FV will encrypt CIM with the device specific key, as shown in Fig. 1 from steps 5 to 8. The 9th and 10th steps involve the delivery of encrypted CIM to the CV, which stores it in a database. Next come steps 11th and 12th in which SD provides its own identity, target device IDs and implementation requirements to the FV while requesting a license for a specific IP. If the device IDs are successfully verified against the FVs database of legal device IDs, the SD's request is granted and CV is notified to finalize the transaction that are the 13th and 14th steps. Now, the CV generates an encrypted authenticated IP according to the SD's requirements as well as device and license tokens. After invoicing the SD, the secured IP, CIM and tokens are delivered to the SD who can now configure its devices with the IP using the tokens and CIM. Altogether, the scheme exerts a very high complexity through many secured steps, which can be explained by the fact that some threats (like excess production by the HM) are considered, which are beyond the scope of this work. Nevertheless, even if these measures are ignored, complexity and overhead are substantial.

Before discussing other licensing schemes, we define four limitations that will help in the comparison of the schemes.

- Trusted Third Party Involvement (TTPI): Involvement of an external participant with access to devices, IPs or secret keys.
- High Execution Steps (HES): Excessive amount of steps in communication, logistics and execution among participants.
- Hardware Modification (HMO): Modification of FPGA devices [5, 10, 13, 14].
- Resource Overhead (RO): Induced overhead in execution time, area and power. Usually, the use of additional logic, e.g. by PUFs [20–22] or CIMs [5, 7, 10–12], leads to such overhead.

An early protection-based scheme was proposed by Kean et al. in [9]. There, tokens are used to securely communicate with the FPGA devices. These tokens are created by encrypting a user key with a secret key, whereas the secret key is stored in the FPGA itself, hence giving it the capability to decrypt tokens and extract user keys. Storing the secret key requires physical access to the device meaning a TTP is necessary. Guneysu et al. proposed another well-known scheme in [10], where multiple stages of protection are used. In this scheme, the HM acts as the TTP and programs a key into the non-volatile memory (NVM) of the device. A personalization module (PM) is encrypted with this key and delivered to the SD. The dedicated decryption engine (DDE) decrypts the PM and configures it onto the programmable logic (PL) of SD's device. The PM is used for public key establishment between the device and CV. The PM, by establishing the key, decrypts the IPs from CV and configures them on the PL. Both schemes [9, 10] involve a TTP which requires physical access to the device that makes them fall prey to multiple limitations like TTPI, RO and HES.

Drimer et al. [5] proposed an extension of [10] for protecting multiple IP cores. Similar to [10], their use of public key cryptography implies primitives that have large implementations with unique bitstreams for each device, resulting in a larger consumption of FPGA resources and increased communication between participating parties. Public key cryptography resulting in larger implementation can be seen in Table 2, which shows 10.60%, 14.44% and 33.40% of LUTs resource consumed, by Drimer et al. [5], Guneysu et al. [10] and Zhang et al. [12] respectively. A more practical scheme was proposed by Maes et al. in [7], which can easily be ported to current devices and does not require any hardware modification. However, it suffers from TTPI and HES limitations. Vliegen et al. published an improvement of the aforementioned scheme in [8]. Their improvements only focus on reducing overhead in the FPGA area by moving key storage from slice flip-flops to the configuration memory. Table 1 depicts an overview of the limitations in existing schemes. The proposed scheme, presented in the next section, improves upon all the defined limitations.

Table 1. Limitations in existing IP licensing schemes

	[9]	[13]	[10]	[5]	[14]	[22]	[7]	[8]	[11]	[12]	[15]	[21]	[28]
TTPI	*	*	*	*	*	*	*	*	*	*	*	*	*
HES	*	*	*	*	*	*	*	*	*	*	*	*	*
HM		*	*	*	*								
RO			*	*	*	*	*	*	*	*	*	*	*

The evaluation of TTPI and HMO is clear: either they exist or not. For HES, if a scheme has more steps than that in ours, it is considered to suffer from this limitation. For RO, we define a scheme to be suffering from this limitation if a resource is blocked permanently. The significance of this limitation depends on the amount of resources consumed. Table 3 depicts the related schemes' area consumption in # of LUTs as well as the utilization rate relative to the total amount of LUTs available on a Xilinx XC7Z020 device.

Table 2. Resource consumption in number of LUTs and utilization on a Xilinx XC7Z020

Schemes		# of LUTs	Utilization rate
Guneysu et al. [10]		7706	14.44%
Drimer et al. [5]		5674	10.60%
Gora et al. [22]		4563	8.50%
Maes et al. [7]		5656	10.60%
Vliegen et al. [8]		2636	4.95%
Zhang et al. [11]	Unprotected	2972	5.50%
	SCA resistant	8116	15.20%
	Fault attack resistant	5472	10.20%
	Physical attack resistant	15832	29.75%
Zhang et al. [12]		17772	33.40%
Sudeendra et al. [15]		Not reported	
Abtioglu et al. [21]		7379	13.87%
Kepa et al. [28]		4272	8.03%

3   Proposed Scheme

Common features of modern reconfigurable devices fulfill the technical requirements of our scheme. Thus, it is applicable to a wide range of FPGA products. Furthermore, the organizational effort is low compared to previous schemes [5, 7–9, 12–14, 22], as we do not require complex communication between system developer and core vendor. Nevertheless, some requirements are inevitable and are presented below:

- Partial Reconfiguration: Target device must support partial reconfiguration.
- Processor Core: A processor core is needed to run software applications.
- Software Protection Solution: Prevents unauthorized use of applications by encrypting or obfuscating the software binaries to prevent RE and tampering. They make use of hardware-based protection dongles that provide their own cryptographic algorithms and secure memory for storing keys and licenses.
- Secure Communication: The communication between SD and CV needs to be authenticated and confidential, but is otherwise not limited and it is up to the CV to choose a preferred way of communication.

3.1   Scheme Execution

At the planning phase, the SD can search a CV's IP Store for required IPs. Each IP has a detailed description about its functionality, supported interfaces, possible sizes, performance etc. Once an IP is chosen, the SD can initiate a license request for that IP. The request includes an identification number (ID) of the selected IP, implementation requirements, and identification information of the SD. This can be seen as steps 1 and 2 in Fig. 2. Based on this request, the CV generates a bitstream IP_j for the requested IP according to the requirements. An IP key K_{IP} is generated, which is used for authenticated encryption of the IP_j using a standard algorithm such as Advanced Encryption Standard [29] - Galois/Counter Mode [30] (AES-GCM). Afterwards, the CV updates an application $APP_{K_{IP}}$ with K_{IP}. This application uses the secret key K_{IP} to decrypt the encrypted bitstream $Enc_{K_{IP}}\{IP_j\}$ and configure it onto the FPGA. Since the key K_{IP} is in the application, it should be protected against SCA, RE and tampering; otherwise, such methods could be used to extract the key, which in turn will put the encrypted bitstream at risk. This is achieved using a HAS protection supported by an USB dongle. The CV uses this solution to make a protected application $Pro\{APP_{K_{IP}}\}$ and stores the corresponding license on the dongle. As a result, $Pro\{APP_{K_{IP}}\}$ will only work if it has access to this specific dongle, which contains a valid license. CV may choose between different license types that can, for example, be limited to a specific amount of usages or to a single device [26].

Now, the encrypted IP $Enc_{K_{IP}}\{IP_j\}$ and the protected application $Pro\{APP_{K_{IP}}\}$ can be delivered to the SD. This can be seen as step 7 in Fig. 2. SD then runs $Pro\{APP_{KIP}\}$ on a target device with the dongle attached and $Enc_{K_{IP}}\{IP_j\}$ accessible. At this stage the application is executed, which performs decryption and configuration of the IP. Note that the CV does not need to ship the dongle to its customers, but rather the SD may obtain them as an off-the-shelf product and CV can configure license on it remotely. Moreover, it is possible for the SD to reuse the dongle for multiple IPs and devices, making the acquisition of the dongle a one-time requirement. This results in a major simplification of logistics and required execution steps compared to previous schemes. Figure 2 depicts an overview of the execution steps needed in our scheme and there is a clear improvement over scheme [11], which is shown in Fig. 1.

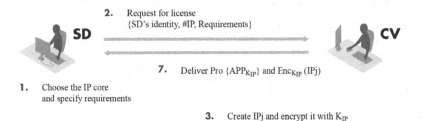

2. Request for license
{SD's identity, #IP, Requirements}

SD   **CV**

7.   Deliver Pro {APP$_{KIP}$} and Enc$_{KIP}$ (IPj)

1.   Choose the IP core
and specify requirements

3.   Create IPj and encrypt it with K$_{IP}$
4.   Create APP$_{KIP}$ which uses K$_{IP}$ to decrypt and
configure Enc$_{KIP}$ (IPj)
5.   Use software protection to APP$_{KIP}$
6.   Generate license and store license in USB-dongle

Fig. 2. Proposed IP licensing scheme

In case multiple IPs are requested from same CV, single application is enough. However, if IPs from several CVs are to be used, every CV has to provide its own application. The upside is one dongle can be used because it supports multiple licenses simultaneously. In addition, the proposed scheme can easily be used in a multi-device scenario by restricting the usage of license to a set of devices using their device IDs. Furthermore, the dongle is able to track license usage and can enforce a limit on the total amount of IP decryptions and configurations on a device. For further explanation, please refer to Sect. 3.2.

3.2   Implementation

This section shows a proof of concept of the proposed scheme, where available off-the-shelf products such as Xilinx' Zynq-7000 SoC device and Wibu's CodeMeter are used to demonstrate its execution. A tool command language (TCL) based flow for Xilinx's Vivado Design Suite is developed, which is used to generate bitstreams from a design that supports dynamic partial reconfiguration (DPR). Using this flow, a full bitstream (FB) (bitstream representation of static design) is generated from SD's design. Two partial bitstreams (bitstream representation of partial design) are generated that represents CV's design. An encryption application that implements AES-GCM is used to encrypt all the bitstreams with a key length of 256-bit. A Decryption-Configuration Application (DCA) is developed which implements AES-GCM decryption and authentication. Since DCA contains secret information, it is protected against RE using CodeMeter (a HAS protection solution from Wibu Systems). For protection, Code-Meter uses an AES-based algorithm in Cipher Block Chaining Mode (CBC) [26] backed by a crypto-controller and secure memory, both packaged in a single USB dongle. Licenses are generated and distributed to customers using the CodeMeter License Server solution [26]. The dongle is referred to as CmDongle, which is part of CodeMeter. This kind of approach is used in software IP licensing, but has not been used for protecting hardware IPs to the best of our knowledge.

As license type, we chose a pay-per-configure approach that allows a fixed number of FPGA configurations. Records of each consecutive FPGA configuration are kept on the USB dongle and the license turns invalid as soon as the usage limit is reached. Whenever a user runs the protected application, connectivity to a dongle containing a valid license must be provided. Failure to do so will prevent the application from running. For our test setup, we used Xilinx Zynq-7000 SoC, which combines software and hardware programmability by integrating an ARM-based Processing System (PS) and Programmable Logic (PL). Before the Linux image is built using Xilinx's PetaLinux tool flow, the protected DCA is added. The bootable image with the protected application and encrypted IPs are stored on an SD card, and used to boot the device. After booting, PS loads the Linux OS, and a user can execute the protected DCA to configure IPs from a CV. In order to allow the application to run, the required security dongle is connected via on-board USB ULPI.

Static and partial designs have been implemented using Xilinx Vivado, targeting ZYNQ ZC702 (XC7Z020-CLG484). A full bitstream of the static and two partial bitstreams (PBs) for the partial design are generated. One of the PB is the IP and the other one is a blank design. Since both PBs are of same size (149 KB), their decryption and configuration times are equal, which are 140 ms and 32 ms respectively. The total execution time of the protected DCA is 230 ms with HAS protection and 180 ms without. The 27.7% increase in time overhead is due to the HAS protection solution's license checking and unwrapping procedures. The time overhead is acceptable because the objective is configuring licensed IPs that will stay configured for a longer period. Execution time of the application and its sub-blocks is shown in Table 3.

Table 3. Execution times of the application and its sub-blocks

	Execution time (ms)	% of total the execution time
Protected DCA	230	100%
HAS protection overhead	50	21.7%
Copying bitstreams to RAM	4.2	1.8%
Decryption & Authentication	142	61.7%
Configuration	32	13.9%

4 Security Analysis

This section examines the complete chain of trust, starting with the CV and going all the way down to the point of configuration to SD's device, covering possible vulnerabilities. As stated in Sect. 1, it is common to distribute IPs either as a synthesized netlist or as a fully implemented bitstream. Netlists do not offer any kind of security and therefore are prone to all kinds of attacks [5]. While they might not be easily understandable, any design tool can analyze them and extract the functionality of the underlying circuit, as this is what they are made for. Bitstreams, on the other hand, add a simple security layer by obfuscation. Their format is not documented in detail and varies between devices and manufacturers, making attacks a time consuming and tedious task. Nevertheless, this kind of security is delusive as it is only based on the assumption that the format stays unknown. Consequently, additional reliable security measures are needed for bitstream based IP distribution. The major threats to IPs are Cloning, RE, Readback Attacks and SCA [6] as well as Trojan or Fault Insertion [11]. Except Readback and SCAs, which are only applicable during or after device configuration, all of them can be prohibited by using cryptographic primitives [6]. Therefore, we rely on state-of-the-art encryption of all IP bitstreams. We recommend symmetric AES-GCM encryption with a key length of 256-bit as suggested by the Intelligence Apparatus and governments [17, 25], but in general, any symmetric or asymmetric cryptographic algorithm is suitable.

In order to keep the bitstream's content secret from other parties including SD, it is encrypted with a secret key which is embedded inside a software application that handles decryption and configuration of the FPGA. It would be easy to extract the key from the application by RE or SCA. Therefore, we use HAS for the protection of the application. While purely software based protection against RE of the application typically relies on obfuscation [18, 19] and thus at most helps against semi-professional attackers, HAS approaches use strong cryptographic procedures and include countermeasures against SCAs [27]. Even though serious attempts by security experts have been made, those measures have not been breached [23]. The CmDongle used in our implementation provides AES encryption (in CBC mode) for the application and protects its execution [26]. Note that the CmDongle in our implementation is used as an example and the proposed scheme is not limited to a specific product.

The proposed scheme is secured against attacks from SD, but there are few areas where an uninvolved party can attack, specifically the transmission of IP and remote storage of licenses from CV to SD. These communications can be secured by cryptographic protocols used in network security such as Transport Layer Security (TLS) [6]. With secure communication, only the device is left as a target. Since an unencrypted bitstream is configured on the PL, the configuration process in the device is more prone to eavesdropping. The fact that the whole FPGA system is under full control of the SD makes this task even simpler and a well-designed protection utterly important. After decryption, the raw bitstream is passed to a driver, which then utilizes the kernel-managed configuration interface to program the device. At this point, either a modified driver or kernel could be used to redirect or copy any data sent to peripherals on the fly, i.e. the bitstream. We prevent driver modification by providing our own version of it within the application. Protection against kernel modification on the other hand cannot be fully guaranteed. However, we can increase the required effort for this kind of attack. In academia, sophisticated approaches on running trusted applications on untrusted OS have been proposed that could be used in this case [3, 4]. Alternatively, a custom operating system with restricted user access and a kernel module that provides kernel's authentication to the application can be provided. This flow provides security to the application against a tampered operating system, similar work in presented in [24]. However, for attackers with vast resources it would still be possible, though it would require effort beyond financial benefit.

5   Conclusion

In this work, an IP licensing scheme for FPGA IP cores is proposed, which to the best of our knowledge, is the first one that does not involve any TTP. In fact, it does not require any third party - CV and SD can get into a licensing agreement without sharing their devices' or IPs' confidential information with anyone. These features make the scheme a very secure and feasible one, unlike other publications who suffer from limitations that are shown in Sect. 2. The proposed scheme improves upon those limitations by providing e.g. independence from a trusted third party, lower resource overhead, and fewer execution steps. However, the scheme also has a noticeable drawback, which is the cost of using a hardware-assisted software protection solution. The upside is a single dongle is sufficient for the configuration of multiple devices.

Acknowledgements. This work was supported by the German Federal Ministry of Education and Research (BMBF) with funding number 16KIS0662.

References

1. Bhunia, S., Tehranipoor, M.: The Hardware Trojan War: Attacks, Myths, and Defenses. Springer, Heidelberg (2017). https://doi.org/10.1007/978-3-319-68511-3
2. Field Programmable Gate Array (FPGA) Market Size, Share, Report, Analysis, Trends & Forecast to 2026. https://reuters.com/brandfeatures/venture-capital/article?id=31516. Accessed 27 Nov 2018
3. Hofmann, O.S., Kim, S., Dunn, A.M., Lee, M.Z., Witchel, E.: Inktag: secure applications on an untrusted operating system. ACM SIGARCH Comput. Archit. News **41**, 265–278 (2013)
4. Chen, X., et al.: Overshadow: a virtualization-based approach to retrofitting protection in commodity operating systems. ACM SI-GOPS Oper. Syst. Rev. **42**(2), 2–13 (2008)
5. Drimer, S., Güneysu, T., Kuhn, M.G., Paar, C.: Protecting multiple cores in a single FPGA design. Unpublished
6. Wollinger, T., Guajardo, J., Paar, C.: Security on FPGAs: state-of-the-art implementations and attacks. ACM TECS **3**(3), 534–574 (2004)
7. Maes, R., Schellekens, D., Verbauwhede, I.: A pay-per-use licensing scheme for hardware IP cores in recent SRAM-Based FPGAs. IEEE Trans. Inf. Forensics Secur. **7**(1), 98–108 (2012)
8. Vliegen, J., Mentens, N., Koch, D., Schellekens, D., Verbauwhede, I.: Practical feasibility evaluation and improvement of a pay-per-use licensing scheme for hardware IP cores in Xilinx FPGAs. J. Cryptographic Eng. **5**, 113–122 (2015)
9. Kean, T.: Cryptographic rights management of FPGA intellectual property cores. In: Proceedings ACM Conference on FPGAs, pp. 113–118 (2002)
10. Guneysu, T., Moller, B., Paar, C.: Dynamic intellectual property protection for reconfigurable devices. In: 2007 International Conference on Field-Programmable Technology, pp. 169–176 (2007)
11. Zhang, L., Chang, C.H.: A pragmatic per-device licensing scheme for hardware IP cores on SRAM-based FPGAs. IEEE Trans. Inf. Forensics Secur. **9**(11), 1893–1905 (2014)

12. Zhang, L., Chang, C.H.: Public key protocol for usage-based licensing of FPGA IP cores. In: 2015 IEEE International Symposium on Circuits and Systems (ISCAS), pp. 25–28 (2015)
13. Simpson, E., Schaumont, P.: Offline Hardware/Software Authentication for Reconfigurable Platforms. In: Goubin, L., Matsui, M. (eds.) CHES 2006. LNCS, vol. 4249, pp. 311–323. Springer, Heidelberg (2006). https://doi.org/10.1007/11894063_25
14. Kumar, S.S., Guajardo, J., Maes, R., Schrijen, G.J., Tuyls, P.: Extended abstract: the butterfly PUF protecting IP on every FPGA. In: 2008 IEEE International Workshop on Hardware-Oriented Security and Trust, pp. 67–70 (2008)
15. Sudeendra K.K., Sahoo, S., Mahapatra, A., Swain, A.K., Mahapatra, K.K.: A flexible pay-per-device licensing scheme for FPGA IP cores. In: IEEE Computer Society Annual Symposium on VLSI (IS-VLSI), pp. 677–682 (2017)
16. SignOnce IP Licensing. https://www.xilinx.com/alliance/signonce.html. Accessed 17 Nov 2018
17. United States Central Intelligence Agency: Network Operations Division Cryptographic Requirements, Version: 1.1
18. Collberg, C.S., Thomborson, C.: Watermarking, tam-per-proofing, and obfuscation - tools for software protection. IEEE Trans. Softw. Eng. **28**(8), 735–746 (2002)
19. Barak, B., et al.: On the (Im)possibility of obfuscating programs. In: Kilian, J. (ed.) CRYPTO 2001. LNCS, vol. 2139, pp. 1–18. Springer, Heidelberg (2001). https://doi.org/10.1007/3-540-44647-8_1
20. Zhang, J., Lin, Y., Lyu, Y., Qu, G.: A PUF-FSM binding scheme for FPGA IP protection and pay-per-device licensing. IEEE Trans. Inf. Forensics Secur. **10**(6), 1137–1150 (2015)
21. Abtioglu, E., et al.: Partially reconfigurable IP protection system with ring oscillator based physically unclonable functions. In: 2017 New Generation of CAS (NGCAS), pp. 65–68 (2017)
22. Gora, M.A., Maiti, A., Schaumont, P.: A flexible design flow for software IP binding in commodity FPGA. In: 2009 IEEE International Symposium on Industrial Embedded Systems, pp. 211–218 (2009)
23. Wibu Systems: Hackers Contest. https://www.wibu.com/hacker-contest.html. Accessed 29 June 2018
24. Measuring Linux at Runtime. http://www.unixist.com/security/measuring-linux-at-runtime/index.html. Accessed 29 June 2018
25. German Federal Office for Information Security: TR-02102-1 Cryptographic mechanisms: Recommendations and key lengths, Version: 2018-02 (2018)
26. Wibu Systems: CodeMeter Developer Guide. https://www.wibu.com/manuals-guides/file/download/4881.html. Accessed 25 June 2018
27. Wibu Systems: CmDongle. https://www.wibu.com/de/codemeter/cmdongle.html. Accessed 27 June 2018
28. Kepa, K., et al.: SeReCon: a secure reconfiguration controller for self-reconfigurable systems. Int. J. Crit. Comput.-Based Syst. **1**, 86–103 (2010)
29. U.S. DoC/NIST: FIPS Publications 197: The Advanced Encryption Standard (AES) (2001)
30. NIST/U.S. Department of Commerce: Recommendation for block cipher modes of operations: Galois/Counter Mode (GCM) and GMAC, NIST Special Publication 800-38D (2007)

Image/Video Processing

HiFlipVX: An Open Source High-Level Synthesis FPGA Library for Image Processing

Lester Kalms$^{(\boxtimes)}$ [ID], Ariel Podlubne [ID], and Diana Göhringer [ID]

Technische Universität Dresden, Dresden, Germany
{lester.kalms,ariel.podlubne,diana.goehringer}@tu-dresden.de

Abstract. The field of computer vision has been increasing over the past years as it is applied to many different applications nowadays. Additionally, they have become more complex and power demanding. On one hand, standards and libraries such as OpenCV and OpenVX have been proposed to ease development. On the other hand, FPGAs have proven to be energy efficient on image processing. The tendency over the last years has turned into using High-Level Synthesis (HLS), to ease their programmability. We present a highly optimized, parametrizable and streaming capable HLS open-source library for FPGAs called HiFlipVX. Due to its structure, it is straightforward to use and simple to add new functions. Furthermore, it is easily portable as it is based on the OpenVX standard. HiFlipVX also adds different features such as autovectorization. The library achieves an efficient resource utilization and a significant scalability, also in comparison to the reference (xfOpenCV), as shown in the evaluation.

Keywords: OpenVX · FPGA · SoC · High-Level Synthesis ·
Computer vision · Image processing

1 Introduction

The complexity and applications for image processing and computer vision are growing continuously [1]. To ease the development process, standards and libraries such as OpenCV and OpenVX have been proposed. The first one is an open source computer vision software library, which is built to provide a common infrastructure for computer vision applications [2]. The second one is an open, royalty-free standard for cross platform acceleration of computer vision applications [3]. Field Programmable Gate Arrays (FPGAs) have proven to be energy efficient on image processing tasks [4] in comparison to other architectures like CPUs or GPUs. Using High-Level Synthesis (HLS) for FPGA has several benefits, like an easier and faster way of testing functional correctness, portability of code and shortened design cycles. Tools, such as Vivado HLS [5] from Xilinx, use pragmas to improve code for FPGAs. Intel's OpenCL SDK and Xilinx's

© Springer Nature Switzerland AG 2019
C. Hochberger et al. (Eds.): ARC 2019, LNCS 11444, pp. 149–164, 2019.
https://doi.org/10.1007/978-3-030-17227-5_12

SDAccel tool further abstract the underlying hardware using OpenCL and Xilinx's SDSoC [6] for System-on-Chips (SoCs) using C/C++. C++ has advantages to OpenCL (version 2.0 and older) for the implementation of a parametrizable library, e.g. due to templates.

In this work, we introduce an Open Source **High**-Level Synthesis **FPGA Library** for **Image Processing** (HiFlipVX), available at [7]. It is highly optimized, parametrizable and includes, in its current form, 28 image processing functions based on the OpenVX specification including some extension. For example, an auto-vectorization of the functions is included to increase throughput and decrease latency. Most functions support additional data-types to increase the usability. HiFlipVX uses SDSoC for HLS, which can easily be changed for other HLS tools. SDSoC uses the same directives as Vivado HLS except for the interface. SDSoC additionally creates the software layer and hardware needed for memory access and control, for an easy HW/SW Co-Design. Furthermore, HiFlipVX implements all functions for streaming, which makes it easy to connect them, since it creates a simple stream interface. Different vendors like AMD (AMDOVX) or NVIDIA (VisionWorks) already follow the standard. Using C++ for HLS with OpenVX eases the cross-platform development. Furthermore, no new programming language has to be learned, as if a Domain-Specific Language (DSL) is used. HiFlipVX does not require additional libraries, which eases the integration to an existing project. In the following, Sect. 2 provides information about the related work, Sect. 3 describes the implementation of HiFlipVX, Sect. 4 compares the achieved results with related work and Sect. 5 contains conclusion and outlook.

2   Related Work

Several approaches have been done to decrease the complexity of developing image-processing applications targeting FPGAs. Özkan et al. [8] propose a highly efficient and parametrizable C++ library for image processing applications. It targets HLS to produce optimized algorithms for FPGAs. The motivation behind their work is the implementation of image processing applications that can be expressed as (DFGs). They also provide designers multiple Pareto-optimal architectures for the same library instances to tailor their implementation. The new programming language for image processing and computational photography Halide [9] is designed to ease high-performance image processing code writing. It supports several CPU architectures, Operating Systems and GPU's APIs. Pu et al. extend Halide so a portion of the software can explicitly become a hardware accelerator [10]. They also provide a compiler for such task and a complementary code for the user to access the hardware created to accelerate the specified portion of the software. Membarth et al. proposed a framework for automatic code generation image processing algorithms based on DSL. They showed that domain knowledge can be captured in the proposed language and that this knowledge enables to generate tailored implementations for a given target architecture [11]. Reiche et al. extend the work by proposing a code generation technique for C-based HLS from a common high-level DSL description

```
 1 template<typename T, vx_uint8 vector_size>
 2 struct img { T data[vector_size]; };
 3
 4 void Example(img<vx_uint8, 1> *in, img<vx_int8, 1> *out){
 5    static img<vx_int8, 1> lx[PIXELS_FHD];
 6 #pragma hls stream variable = lx depth = 512
 7    static img<vx_int8, 1> ly[PIXELS_FHD];
 8 #pragma hls stream variable = ly depth = 512
 9 #pragma hls dataflow
10    Scharr3x3<...>(in, lx, ly);
11    Magnitude<...>(lx, ly, out);
12 }
```

Listing 1.1. Example application showing how to connect a HiFlipVX function and a template based data type for auto-vectorization.

targeting FPGAs. This is done to circumvent the issue that designers still need to tailor their HLS coding techniques to obtain efficient implementations based on the used target [12]. Xilinx released their own FPGA-oriented OpenCV implementation called xfOpenCV. It includes a large number of functions and it is based on OpenCV. Using a library over a DSL does not force the developer to a restricted language. Besides, HiFlipVX follows OpenVX to provide designers the flexibility to add new functions easily, as long as they comply with the proposed standard. Furthermore, it maximizes functional and performance portability, e.g. between CPU and FPGA. In this work, we targeted embedded applications and the hardware-software co-design optimizations were carried out using SDSoC. The library provides an optimized base structure for different function types, like windowed and pixel-wise functions. Therefore, it is easy and straightforward to implement new efficient image processing functions.

3   Implementation

This section describes the implementation of HiFlipVX and its 28 vision functions. They follow the OpenVX standards [3,13], but include additional parameters to make the library more flexible. HiFlipVX is written in C++, template-based, optimized for FPGAs and in our case for Xilinx's products. To make the library easier to use, it uses static assertions to throw an error if parameter values or data types with undefined behavior are used. For arbitrary data types not given by C++ we use bit masks and for bit-widths above 64-bit we use template based data types. We did not use the *Arbitrary Precision Fixed-Point Data Types* from Xilinx, to be more vendor independent. Listing 1.1 shows the template based data type used for auto-vectorization. Since all functions are streaming capable, it is easy to connect different functions with each other (Listing 1.1). The static arrays are converted to FIFOs at synthesis time, to stream data between functions. HiFlipVX provides functions to allocate global memory and the pragmas in Listing 1.1 are the only ones needed.

3.1   Pixel-Wise Functions

Table 1 shows the implemented pixel-wise functions, which have several characteristics in common. They carry out their operations on the input image(s)

Table 1. Image pixel-wise functions.

Bitwise AND	$out(x,y) = in_1(x,y) \wedge in_2(x,y)$
Bitwise XOR	$out(x,y) = in_1(x,y) \oplus in_2(x,y)$
Bitwise OR	$out(x,y) = in_1(x,y) \vee in_2(x,y)$
Bitwise NOT	$out(x,y) = \overline{in_1(x,y)}$
Arithmetic Addition	$out(x,y) = in_1(x,y) + in_2(x,y)$
Arithmetic Subtraction	$out(x,y) = in_1(x,y) - in_2(x,y)$
Min	$out(x,y) = [(in_1(x,y) < in_2(x,y)) \rightarrow (in_1(x,y))] \wedge$ $[(in_1(x,y) \geq in_2(x,y)) \rightarrow (in_2(x,y))]$
Max	$out(x,y) = [(in_1(x,y) > in_2(x,y)) \rightarrow (in_1(x,y))] \wedge$ $[(in_1(x,y) \leq in_2(x,y)) \rightarrow (in_2(x,y))]$
Data Object Copy	$out(x,y) = in_1(x,y)$
Absolute Difference	$out(x,y) = |in_1(x,y) - in_2(x,y)|$
Pixel-wise Multiplication	$out(x,y) = in_1(x,y) \cdot in_2(x,y) \cdot scale$
Magnitude	$out(x,y) = \sqrt{in_1(x,y)^2 + in_2(x,y)^2}$

pixel by pixel. Input and output data types are the same and can be signed or unsigned integer values with a bit-width of 8, 16 or 32-bit. Independent of the bit-width, 1, 2, 4 or 8 pixels can be computed in parallel in a vector. Due to the template-based implementation, higher vector widths would also be possible. A shared, template-based function is used to implement all pixel-wise operations for an easy expandability of new functions. It includes the verification of data types and template parameters, reading the input vector(s) and writing back the result. The function is pipelined to exploit temporal parallelism and the operation is executed on each element of the vector in parallel. In general, to reduce resource consumption while maintaining precision, we internally perform fixed-point integer operations.

To illustrate the pixel-wise function implementation in HiFlipVX we use the Multiplication and Magnitude functions as examples. The first one performs element-wise multiplication between two images and a scalar value (see Table 1). The scalar value can be fixed at synthesis time, and we use this to optimize the implementation. In particular, we use a shift operation instead of a multiplication if the scalar is a multiple of two. This saves a significant amount of FPGA resources because fixed shifts can be performed with re-routing wires. The only difference can occur while rounding, if a negative value is shifted to the right (e.g. $(-3 >> 1 = -2)$ and $(-3/2 = -1)$). Therefore, we have added a shift operation that gives equal results to the division. To reduce the resource consumption of the Magnitude function, we implemented our own HLS integer square root function (see Listing 1.2). Here, N is the output bit-width that is half of the input bit-width. For each output bit, two additions and one comparison is performed. The shift values are signal connections, computed at synthesis time and the OR-operation simply concatenates the result bits. Only for the computation of a

```
 1 A1 = 0;  // Intermediate result
 2 A2 = 0;  // Square of intermediate result
 3 for (n = N - 1; n < N; n--) {
 4 #pragma HLS unroll
 5      // (A1 + B1)^2 and add new bit at position n
 6      B1 = 1 << n;   B2 = B1 << n;   AB = A1 << n;
 7      A2_next = A2 + B2 + (AB << 1);
 8      // Store if A2_next does not exceed value
 9      if (A2_next <= input) {
10          A1 |= B1;
11          A2 = A2_next;}}
```

Listing 1.2. Integer square root function. Each stage computes 1 bit of the resulting vector.

Table 2. Image filter functions.

Gaussian Filter	Median Filter	Box Filter	Sobel Filter
Custom Convolution	Dilate Image	Erode Image	Schar Filter

square root that computes on data with a width of 64-bit, we use the double precision floating point unit from Xilinx. This is done, since we do not need a higher precision to comply with OpenVX and it reduces the resource utilization for this bit-width. If the result of an arithmetic operation cannot be represented with the chosen bit-width, overflow or underflow occurs. Therefore, we implement different policies. On the one hand, overflow can be ignored (Wrap) or the min-max representable number is used (Saturate). On the other hand, underflow can be ignored (Truncated) or rounded to the nearest integer value. The needed operations (min-max) for saturation are chosen depending on the function (e.g. add, sub) and data type (unsigned/signed).

3.2   Filter Functions

Table 2 shows the implemented HiFlipVX filter functions, which have several characteristics in common. HiFlipVX determines the kernel of a specific filter at synthesis time, since it will not change during run-time. Kernel sizes (K_S) of 3, 5, 7, 9 and 11 are supported for all filters, except for the Scharr filter, which is fixed at 3 due to its characteristics. Further, they support the same data bit-widths and vector sizes as the pixel-wise operations (see Sect. 3.1). Every filter supports three different border behaviors: Values beyond borders can be undefined, constant zero, or replicated. In some feature detection and description algorithms, we experienced better results using replicated border handling.

Filter Structure: HiFlipVX uses a common pipelined structure for all filters, which is inspired by [4], containing several stages (see Fig. 1). A base function for filters contains all of these stages and depending on a parameter, only the *Kernel* function is exchanged at synthesis time. To add a new function only a new case needs to be added that implements the new *Kernel* function. An image filter needs parallel access to a window of pixels, to compute one output pixel

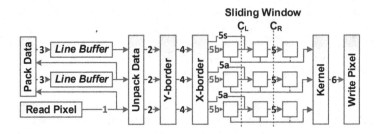

Fig. 1. The common structure used for all filters shown for a 3×3 kernel. Numbers mark the different stages in the pipeline.

in each clock cycle. These observed pixels are stored in a sliding window built of registers. In this window, pixels are shifted from left to right in every clock cycle. The number of rows of this sliding window is equal to the kernel size (K_S). The number of columns W_C in the sliding window depends on the kernel radius ($K_R = \lfloor \frac{K_S}{2} \rfloor$) and vector size V_S, which determines the amount of pixels computed in parallel.

$$W_C = 2 \cdot K_R + V_S + [V_S - (K_R \bmod V_S)] \bmod V_S \tag{1}$$

These window columns are divided into three parts, separated by a left border ($C_L = W_C - V_S - K_R$) and a right border ($C_R = W_C - V_S$). The input source of the left and middle parts, depend on the proximity of the kernel to the image boundary. To be able to stream data and read each pixel only once from memory, complete image rows are buffered in line buffers. Line buffers and the sliding window need to be filled, before the first output value can be generated. The overhead to fill the line buffer is equal to the kernel radius K_R. The overhead to fill the sliding window can be computed as follows: ($O_C = (W_C - K_R) \div V_S - 1$). The filter gets image rows (I_R) times image columns (I_C) pixels as input. The amount of image columns is reduced to vector columns ($V_C = I_C/V_S$), due to the vectorization. To compute the total latency of the filter, the line buffer overhead, the sliding window overhead, and the pipeline stages (P) need to be accounted for:

$$\text{Latency} = (I_R + K_R) \cdot (V_C + O_C) + P \tag{2}$$

To achieve an optimum usage of Block Random-Access Memory (BRAM), which is needed for the line buffers, we pack the data into new data types, before writing them to the line buffers. The maximum usable bit-width of the used 18 Kb BRAM from Xilinx in C++ is 32-bit. Depending on the bit-width of 1 pixel (D_W), our complete bit-width of data to store is: $V_S \cdot (K_S - 1) \cdot D_W$. Therefore, the data is evenly packed into new data types with a maximum width of 32-bit. Data that needs to be accessed in parallel cannot be packed in consecutive memory addresses in BRAMs. This is because we would lose latency, since the BRAM is only dual port and we need one port to read and one port to write in each clock cycle. In Fig. 1 we use numbers to mark the different stages of the

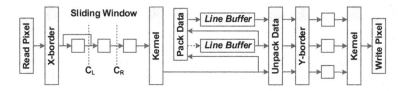

Fig. 2. The common structure used for all separable filters shown for a 3 × 3 kernel.

pipeline. Depending on the x- and y-coordinate of the image the key operation in each stage is:

1. If $(y < I_R)$ and $(x < V_C)$ read the next input pixel-vector.
2. Read and unpack data from line buffers at x coordinate.
3. Pack and write data to line buffers at x coordinate for next output row.
4. If parts of the kernel go outside the border, the border handling method is invoked (e.g. replicated or constant zero).
5. The sliding window shifts pixels from left to right. The source changes if the pixel is beyond the image border:
   (a) If $x = 0$, *border* data is written into middle columns $(C_L \le C < C_R)$.
   (b) If $x \ge V_C$, *border* data is written into left columns $(CR \le C)$.
6. Compute the kernel function for each vector element (pixel) in parallel.
7. If $(y \ge K_R)$ and $(x \ge O_C)$ write the next output pixel-vector.

Separable Kernels: Some 2-dimensional filters have the advantage that they can be computed by using two 1-dimensional filters in sequence [14]. Such filters are called *separable*, and we exploit this property to reduce resource consumption. The effect is most significant for larger compute kernels. For example, the window elements for a 7 × 7 kernel would be reduced to a 1 × 7 and a 7 × 1 kernel. Equation 3 exemplifies this optimization using a 3 × 3 Gaussian filter:

$$Gauss_{kernel} = \frac{1}{4}\begin{bmatrix}1 & 2 & 1\end{bmatrix} \cdot \frac{1}{4}\begin{bmatrix}1\\2\\1\end{bmatrix} = \frac{1}{16}\begin{bmatrix}1 & 2 & 1\\2 & 4 & 2\\1 & 2 & 1\end{bmatrix} \tag{3}$$

Figure 2 shows the compute pipeline used for separable filters. It is similar to the non-separable pipeline. The separable filter pipeline first reads the input pixel and writes it into a horizontal sliding window with a size of $1 \times W_C$. This sliding window only needs to check the image boundaries on the x-axis. The next stage computes the horizontal compute kernel and stores its intermediate results in the line buffers. As mentioned for the non-separable filter, data is packed before it is written to the line buffers. Then, data is read from the line buffers and written to a vertical sliding window with a size of $(K_S \times V_S)$. This sliding window only checks the image boundaries on the y-axis. The final stage computes the vertical compute kernel and writes the result back to memory. HiFlipVX provides separable filter implementations of the Gaussian, Box, Dilate and Erode filters.

There is a non-separable implementation of the Box and Gaussian filter, because the values of the results in comparison to the separable filter differ by a maximum of one. The deviation results due to the fact that normalization is done in both filter steps of the separable filter, to not increase the data bit-width of the line buffers. The Median filter cannot be expressed using a separable filter, since it needs the complete input window at once. Bigger Sobel or Scharr kernels would benefit for the consumption of Lookup Tables (LUTs) and FlipFlops (FFs) when using a separable filter. Since these filters compute the x and y derivatives, different parts after the vertical kernel (e.g. line buffer) are needed for each derivative separately and therefor more BRAM is used.

Filter Kernels: HiFlipVX optimizes the operations of its filters depending on the pattern of the kernel coefficients. This can be done, because the coefficients are fix at synthesis time. For example, the coefficients of the Gaussian kernel are symmetrical on the x and y axes independent of the kernel size, as shown in Eq. 3. This symmetry gives us the possibility to optimize the amount of multiplications for different functions, such as the Gaussian, the Sobel and the Scharr filter. Equation 4 shows the optimized computation of 1 pixel ($I_{x,y}$) for symmetric 1d kernels, like the Gaussian kernel (B), for an input window (A).

$$I_{(x,y)} = B_{(K_R)} + \sum_{n=0}^{K_R-1} \left(B_{(n)} \cdot \left(A_{(n)} + A_{(K_S-n-1)} \right) \right) \tag{4}$$

We use shift operations to implement normalization, if the normalization value is a multiple of two (e.g. Gaussian and Scharr filter). Otherwise, we approximate the normalization by multiplying ($mult$) and shifting ($shift$), to avoid a costly division operation (e.g. Box filter). The type of normalization and the normalization values are computed at synthesis time using a provided function (e.g. Custom Convolution and Sobel filter). To compute the $mult$ and $shift$ values for a 16-bit accurate normalization, first all kernel coefficients are summed up (sum). Then, the normalization value is computed as floating point value. Afterwards, this values is shifted to the maximum value, which can be represented by a 16-bit unsigned integer number: $mult = \lfloor (1/sum) << shift \rfloor$. Higher Gaussian and Sobel kernel coefficients are computed using discrete convolution of the 1d kernels with the standard smoothing kernel [1 2 1] as shown in Eq. 5 for the Gaussian kernel. We also supply a function that computes a more accurate Gaussian kernel based on standard deviation input using floating point numbers. The function returns a fixed-point kernel and the bit-width of its fraction part.

$$B = \begin{bmatrix} 1 & 2 & 1 \end{bmatrix} * \begin{bmatrix} 1 & 2 & 1 \end{bmatrix} = \begin{bmatrix} 1 & 4 & 6 & 4 & 1 \end{bmatrix} \tag{5}$$

The Median filter implementation differs from the other filters because it requires searching for the median value within the input window. A common algorithm for computing the median is to sort the pixels of the input window and select the middle value of the sorted array as output. Several sorting networks exist, such as odd-even merge-sort, bitonic-sort and shell-sort. These networks are a good fit for FPGAs, since they can be implemented with simple

Table 3. Image conversion and analysis functions.

Convert Bit Depth	Integral Image	Scale Image	Color Convert
Channel Combine	Channel Extract	Histogram	TableLookup

comparator networks. We have chosen the odd-even merge-sort algorithm, since it requires fewer comparators than the others [15]. Since the array size is not a multiple of two, we use a generic sorting algorithm [16]. Furthermore, specific sorting networks have been proposed for specific array sizes. Since 3 × 3 filters are common, we use the sorting network proposed by [17] for these filters.

3.3   Conversion and Analysis Functions

This Subsection describes the implemented conversion and analysis functions shown in Table 3. The Channel Combine function takes multiple unsigned 8-bit planes and combines them to a multi-planar or interleaved image format. Whereas the Channel Extract function extracts a single plane (channel) from a multi-planar or interleaved image format. The main supported image formats are RGB, RGBX and gray-scale (8-bit unsigned). For gray-scale conversion, we approximate to the BT.601 recommendation: $(gray = R \cdot 306 + G \cdot 601 + B \cdot 117 + 512) >> 10$. The Color Convert function can convert between these image formats. Additionally, the Channel Combine and Channel Extract functions support interleaving two or four 8-bit pixels in an unspecified 16- or 32-bit image format. Since C++ does not define 24-bit variables, we use 32-bit variables to store RGB values in memory (e.g. [RGBR][GBRG][BRGB]). The Convert Bit Depth function, can convert between any signed/unsigned 8, 16 or 32-bit format and also supports vectorization.

The Scale Image function re-sizes an image to a smaller resolution. It supports nearest neighbor or bi-linear interpolation for an unsigned 8-bit data type. The bi-linear interpolation needs to buffer pixels of two consecutive rows in BRAM for streaming capability. In the Integral Image function, an output pixel is the sum of the corresponding input pixel and all other pixels above and to its left. Equation 6 shows the hardware optimization for the Integral Image function. The integral result $(area)$ is the sum of the current row (sum_{row}) added to the integral value at position $I(x, y-1)$. Therefore, the function buffers the integral results of one row (buf) in BRAM. The bit-width is 8-bit for the input image and 32-bit for the output image.

$$sum = sum + src_{x,y}$$
$$dst_{x,y} = area = [(y > 0) \rightarrow (sum + buf_x)] \wedge [(y \leq 0) \rightarrow (sum)] \qquad (6)$$
$$buf_x = area$$

The Histogram function counts the number of occurrences of each pixel value for each image region dependent of the number of bins. A pixel with its intensity value I will result in incrementing Histogram bin i as shown in Eq. 7 [13].

Table 4. Standard configuration of functions in evaluation.

Kernel Size	3	Frequency	100 MHz
Vector Size	1	Border Type	Constant
Output Type	8-bit	Conversion Type	Wrap
Input Type	8-bit	Scale	0.25

The function supports 8-bit and 16-bit unsigned data types, and sets the *Range*, *Offset* and *Bins* values as template parameters. It is separated in three stages. The first stage resets the Histogram entries to zero. The second one reads one input pixel in each clock cycle and increments the Histogram. It increments two independent Histogram buffers alternately since incrementing a BRAM entry cannot be done in one clock cycle. The last stage sums the Histogram bin of both buffers at positions (i) and writes them pixel by pixel to the output.

$$i = (I - Offset) \cdot \frac{Bins}{Range}, \quad Offset \leq I < Offset + Range \tag{7}$$

The TableLookup function takes the image input pixels to index into a LUT and stores the indexed value in the output image. The function supports 8-bit unsigned and 16-bit signed data types, which are equal for input, LUT and output, and sets the LUT size and offset as template parameters. The implementation consists of two stages. The first one adds the LUT contents to a table. The second stage computes the output pixel ($output[i] = table[input[i] + offset]$). The implementation outputs a zero value when the index is out of range because the output expects an image stream.

4   Evaluation

In this section, we evaluate resource utilization and latency of the synthesis results of HiFlipVX. Table 4 shows the standard configuration of the tested functions. The input and output data type are 8-bit unsigned, filter functions have a kernel size of 3, no vectorization is applied, the frequency is set to 100 MHz. Data is truncated (Wrap) for overflow handling, the pixel-wise multiplication is scaled with a factor of 0.25 and a constant border of zero is considered for filter functions. From this configuration, additional settings have been tested, where only one parameter changes from the standard one. Furthermore, we compare HiFlipVX with the xfOpenCV library from Xilinx. The evaluation has been carried out on the Zynq UltraScale+ MPSoC ZCU102 Evaluation Kit from Xilinx using SDSoC 2017.4 for 1080p images. A part of the library has been verified in hardware [18] for dynamic voltage scaling and dynamic partial reconfiguration.

4.1   HiFlipVX Resource Utilization and Latency Results

Table 5 shows the resource utilization of the HiFlipVX functions for the standard configuration (see Table 4). The filters consume one BRAM for each line buffer

Table 5. Resource utilization of the HiFlipVX functions on the Zynq UltraScale+ MPSoC ZCU102 for the standard configuration, shown in Table 4.

Function	FF	LUT	DSP	BRAM
Dilate Image, Erode Image	257	580	0	2
Box Filter	257	536	2	2
Gaussian Filter	257	624	0	2
Sobel Filter	292	758	0	2
Scharr Filter	292	822	0	2
Custom Convolution	393	760	6	2
Median Filter	490	1180	0	2
Data Object Copy	27	147	0	0
NOT	27	162	0	0
AND, XOR, OR, Addition, Subtraction	27	171	0	0
Min, Max	27	175	0	0
Absolute Difference	27	195	0	0
Pixel-wise Multiplication	27	156	1	0
Magnitude	345	1106	0	0
Convert Bit Depth (signed 16-bit to unsigned 8-bit)	27	154	0	0
Channel Extract (1×8-bit from RGBX image)	27	147	0	0
Channel Combine (4×8-bit to RGBX image)	27	195	0	0
Color Convert (RGBX to Grayscale)	50	258	2	0
Integral Image	82	389	0	4
Table Lookup	52	293	0	1
Histogram	113	593	0	2
Scale Image (Bilinear, from 1080p to 720p)	617	1282	8	2

and the Box filter needs one DSP for each normalization (horizontal and vertical filters). The DSP consumption of the Custom Convolution is not 10 (one for each kernel coefficient and one for normalization) as expected, because we let the compiler decide to use LUT or Digital Signal Processor (DSP) for multiplications. Testing different fixed solutions for the usage of LUT vs. DSP has shown that this is the most flexible solution, independent from the FPGA. The Data Object Copy function, which is a memory copy function, indicates the overhead of the interfaces and the logic needed to read and write data. When combining two functions for streaming in one accelerator as shown in Listing 1.1, only 75 FFs, 150 LUTs and 2 BRAMs are consumed additionally. The latency of most of the functions can be computed with Eq. 2. For the pixel-wise functions, the kernel radius K_R and the columns overhead O_C are zero. The pipeline stages P of the different functions are between two and six (Magnitude). Only the Histogram and TableLookup functions adds two or one loops respectively with a latency of $BINS + P$ each, needed for the histograms.

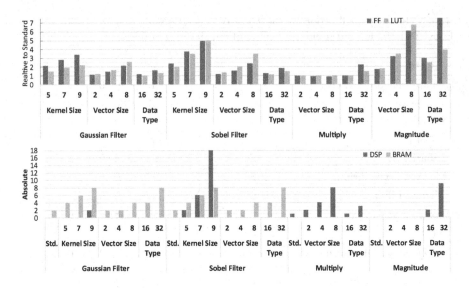

Fig. 3. Compares relative LUT & FF utilization (Top) and absolute DSP & BRAM utilization (Bottom) in comparison to standard (std.) configuration for scalability.

4.2   HiFlipVX Scalability Results

Figure 3 shows the scalability results of the resource consumption in relation to the standard configuration. We compare one separable filter (Gaussian) and one non-separable filter (Sobel). Furthermore, the Sobel filter computes two kernels. The graph on the top shows relative values for better readability and the graph on the bottom shows absolute values to avoid division by zero because some functions do not consume DSPs or BRAMs. From the pixel-wise operations, we evaluate the two functions, which have the highest resource consumption. The BRAM consumption is equal for both filters and scales with the amount of line buffers, which depends on the kernel size. Only for a vector-size of 8, double the amount of BRAM is consumed, since it was not possible to further pack data without increasing the latency. Increasing the bit-width of the data type also increases the overall BRAM usage, since the 1920 image columns consume almost all available 2048 BRAM entries. Many multiplications have been eliminated, by making use of the kernel coefficient patterns. For example, this reduces the multiplications for coefficients of a 9×9 Sobel kernel (without the zero line in the middle) from $(2 \cdot (K_S-1) \cdot K_S = 144)$ to $(2 \cdot K_R \cdot (K_R+1) = 40)$. Additionally, DSPs are replaced by LUTs for small multiplications by the compiler. Furthermore, HiFlipVX replaces multiplications by shift operations if the normalization is a multiple of two. The FF and LUT usage scales well, since increasing the bit-width or vector size does not increase by the same factor. Increasing the vector size decreases the total amount of clock cycles, which also gives the opportunity to decrease the frequency and do Dynamic Voltage and Frequency Scaling (DVFS). Only 5 times more FF and LUT are consumed for a Sobel filter with a kernel size

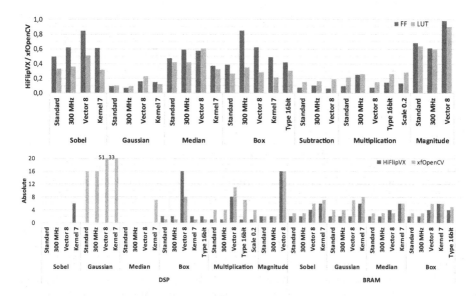

Fig. 4. Compares relative LUT & FF utilization (Top) and absolute DSP & BRAM utilization (Bottom) between HiFlipVX and xfOpenCV.

of 9, although the sliding window is 9 times bigger and contains 12 times more coefficients. For the separable filters, such as the Gaussian filter, the scalability is even better. The vector size has no effect on the FF and LUT usage for the Multiply function, since most computation is done by the DSP. The Magnitude function shows a different behavior for the 32-bit data type, since we use floating point numbers for the needed 64-bit square root function.

4.3   HiFlipVX Comparison to Related Work

Figure 4 compares the resource utilization between HiFlipVX and xfOpenCV for some selected functions. Results for BRAMs or DSPs are only shown if one of the libraries utilizes resources. We obtained the results for xfOpenCV by creating the bitstream. In most cases, xfOpenCV complies with our standard configuration and also allows a vectorization of 8 or kernel sizes of 5 and 7. For most functions, we allow additional kernel sizes (9 & 11), data types (16-bit & 32-bit signed/unsigned), border types (replicated & undefined) or vectorization sizes (2 & 4), which makes HiFlipVX much more flexible. For some functions, xfOpenCV implements one 16-bit data type. We have changed the border type of the Median filter (replicated) and the data type of the Magnitude function (16-bit signed), due to the fact that xfOpenCV supports only that border and data type respectively. A small difference relies in the input/output data types of the Sobel and Scharr filters. In xfOpenCV they are u8/s16 (unsigned 8-bit/signed 16-bit) or u8/u8 and for HiFlipVX they always are from unsigned to signed. In general, all filter and pixel-wise functions consume less FFs and LUTs in the different configurations. Other filter and pixel-wise functions show similar behavior than the selected ones. HiFlipVX consumes 0.39 of FFs and 0.32 of LUTs in average for the selected functions in comparison to xfOpenCV.

The libraries perform more similar when vectorization is enabled and the difference is more significant for the larger kernel sizes. The main reason is that HiFlipVX uses separable filters or exploits the kernel coefficients. For the Gaussian kernel, xfOpenCV computes the kernel based on a standard deviation while HiFlipVX uses the OpenVX Gaussian kernel. Supporting arbitrary standard deviations require using more bits to represent the kernel and therefore require more FPGA resources. If a specific standard deviation is required, HiFlipVX provides a function that can pre-compute a Gaussian kernel for an arbitrary standard deviation. The highest total resource usage is observed for higher kernel sizes of the Median filter, due to the high amount of comparisons in the sorting network. The most significant difference for the DSP usage can be seen for the Gaussian and Box filter. The xfOpenCV Gaussian filter consumes up to 51 DSPs for the 8-bit data types while HiFlipVX consumes none, due to the simplified Gaussian kernel. Conversely, the HiFlipVX Box filter consumes two DSPs for each vector element, because it uses separable filters, while xfOpenCV only uses one DSP. Therefore, HiFlipVX implements the Gaussian and Box filter using separable and non-separable kernels. In average, HiFlipVX consumes 1.42 less BRAMs for the shown filter functions than xfOpenCV.

Comparing the relative results for FFs and LUTs of the multiplication for a scale that is not a power of two ($scale = 0.2$) to the standard ($scale = 0.25$), shows the advantage of detecting the power of two. For the Subtraction and Multiplication functions, HiFlipVX highly decreases the consumption of all resources. The results for other arithmetic (Addition, Absolute Difference) and bit-wise (AND, OR, XOR, NOT) are similar to the result of the subtraction function. The Magnitude function, which has the highest resource consumption, reduces the FF and LUT utilization, the advantage decreases for a higher vectorization.

5   Conclusion

In this work, we have introduced HiFlipVX, an OpenVX based, open-source, image-processing library for FPGA-SoCs. It is implemented and highly optimized for streaming capable functions using HLS. Due to its modular structure, it is easy to add new optimized functions. They are template-based, to enable several compile time optimizations and a variety of options for a high flexibility. On one hand, the described compile time optimizations lead to an efficient resource utilization. On the other hand, we have also shown that a high flexibility was achieved due to the template based structure of the functions. In comparison to xfOpenCV, HiFlipVX consumes less LUTs and FFs for all functions and, in average, less BRAMs and DSPs. Additionally, HiFlipVX achieves a remarkable scalability in terms of resource utilization. Using a standardization like OpenVX with its graph-based representation gives several possibilities for the future. HiFlipVX can easily be combined with other available libraries, which consider GPUs or CPUs. Additionally, HiFlipVX will be combined with an application distribution tool, which also considers hardware-software co-design.

Acknowledgment. This work has been partially supported by European Unions Horizon 2020 research and innovation programme as part of the TULIPP project under grant agreement No. 688403 and partially by the German Federal Ministry of Education and Research BMBF as part of the PARIS project under grant agreement number 16ES0657.

References

1. Kalb, T., Kalms, L., Göhringer, D., et al.: Tulipp: towards ubiquitous low-power image processing platforms. In: International Conference on Embedded Computer Systems: Architectures, Modeling and Simulation, pp. 306–311, July 2016
2. Bradski, G.: The openCV library. Dr. Dobb's J. Softw. Tools **25**, 120–125 (2000)
3. Giduthuri, R., Pulli, K.: OpenVX: a framework for accelerating computer vision. In: SIGGRAPH ASIA 2016 Courses, pp. 14:1–14:50 (2016)
4. Kalms, L., Göhringer, D.: Exploration of OpenCL for FPGAs using SDAccel and comparison to GPUs and multicore CPUs. In: 27th International Conference on Field Programmable Logic and Applications (FPL), pp. 1–4, September 2017
5. Winterstein, F., Bayliss, S., Constantinides, G.A.: High-level synthesis of dynamic data structures: a case study using vivado HLS. In: International Conference on Field-Programmable Technology (FPT), pp. 362–365, December 2013
6. Sekar, C., Hemasunder: Tutorial T7: Designing with Xilinx SDSoC. In: 30th International Conference on VLSI Design and 16th International Conference on Embedded Systems (VLSID), pp. xl–xli, January 2017
7. Kalms, L., Podlubne, A., Göhringer, D.: Hiflipvx, February 2019. https://github.com/TUD-ADS/HiFlipVX
8. Oezkan, M.A., Reiche, O., Hannig, F., Teich, J.: A highly efficient and comprehensive image processing library for C++-based high-level synthesis. In: International Workshop on FPGAs for Software Programmers, pp. 1–10, September 2017
9. Ragan-Kelley, J., Barnes, C., Adams, A., Paris, S., Durand, F., Amarasinghe, S.: Halide: a language and compiler for optimizing parallelism, locality, and recomputation in image processing pipelines. SIGPLAN Not. **48**(6), 519–530 (2013)
10. Pu, J., et al.: Programming heterogeneous systems from an image processing DSL. ACM Trans. Archit. Code Optim. **14**(3), 26:1–26:25 (2017)
11. Membarth, R., Reiche, O., Hannig, F., Teich, J., Krner, M., Eckert, W.: HIPAcc: a domain-specific language and compiler for image processing. IEEE Trans. Parallel Distrib. Syst. **27**(1), 210–224 (2016)
12. Reiche, O., Schmid, M., Hannig, F., et al.: Code generation from a domain-specific language for C-based HLS of hardware accelerators. In: International Conference on Hardware/Software Codesign and System Synthesis, pp. 1–10, October 2014
13. Giduthuri, R., The Khronos OpenVX Working Group: The OpenVX Specification 1.2.1. Khronos Group, August 2018
14. Palomares, J.M., Gonzalez, J., Ros, E., Prieto, A.: General logarithmic image processing convolution. IEEE Trans. Image Process. **15**(11), 3602–3608 (2006)
15. Hematian, A., Chuprat, S., Manaf, A.A., Parsazadeh, N.: Zero-delay FPGA-based odd-even sorting network. In: IEEE Symposium on Computers Informatics (ISCI), pp. 128–131, April 2013

16. Knuth, D.E.: The Art of Computer Programming, Volume 3: (2nd Ed.) Sorting and Searching. Addison Wesley Longman Publishing Co., Inc, Boston (1998)
17. Aranda, L.A., Reviriego, P., Maestro, J.A.: A fault-tolerant implementation of the median filter. In: 16th European Conference on Radiation and Its Effects on Components and Systems (RADECS), pp. 1–4, September 2016
18. Podlubne, A., et al.: Low power image processing applications on FPGAs using dynamic voltage scaling and partial reconfiguration. In: Conference on Design and Architectures for Signal and Image Processing (DASIP), pp. 64–69, October 2018

Real-Time FPGA Implementation of Connected Component Labelling for a 4K Video Stream

Piotr Ciarach, Marcin Kowalczyk⬭, Dominika Przewlocka⬭,
and Tomasz Kryjak$^{(\boxtimes)}$⬭

AGH University of Science and Technology,
Al. Mickiewicza 30, 30-059 Krakow, Poland
piotrciarach@gmail.com, {kowalczyk,dprze,tomasz.kryjak}@agh.edu.pl

Abstract. We present a hardware implementation in reconfigurable logic of a single-pass connected component labelling (CCL) and connected component analysis (CCA) module. The design supports a video stream in 4 pixel per clock format (4 ppc) and allows real-time processing of 4K/UHD video stream (3840×2160 pixels) at 60 frames per second. We discuss the applied modification and simplifications and their impact on the algorithm's performance. We verified the proposed module in an exemplary application – skin colour areas segmentation – on the ZCU 102 evaluation board with Xilinx Zynq UltraScale+ MPSoC device.

Keywords: FPGA · Zynq UltraScale+ MPSoC · 4K · UHD ·
Real-time video processing · Connected Component Labelling (CCL) ·
Connected Component Analysis (CCA)

1 Introduction

Connected component labelling (CCL) and connected component analysis (CCA) are operations often used in vision systems. The first one will assign an unique label to each connected group of pixels. Pixels belong to the same group if there is a path of adjacent pixels between them. Usually an 8-pixel, less frequent a 4-pixel neighbourhood is used. The second operation allows to calculate selected parameters of detected objects. Most often these are: bounding box, area and centroid. Others are: number of pixels on the perimeter, major axis length, minor axis length and orientation (obtained using ellipse fitting) and other so-called shape coefficients. However, not all of them can be computed efficiently in a pipeline pixel processing system.

CCL and CCA are an intermediate step between image analysis and recognition. Their input is a binary image obtained after binarization (thresholding) or segmentation (e.g. of moving or foreground objects). The output is a list of detected objects (i.e. groups of connected pixels) and their features. The described approach is widely used in advanced video surveillance systems (AVSS), e.g. for abandoned luggage or prohibited zone violation detection. On

© Springer Nature Switzerland AG 2019
C. Hochberger et al. (Eds.): ARC 2019, LNCS 11444, pp. 165–180, 2019.
https://doi.org/10.1007/978-3-030-17227-5_13

this basis simple classification can be implemented – for example, rejection of objects that are too small or of incorrect shape. In addition, using the bounding box to select a ROI (Region of Interest) can significantly reduce the computational complexity of the algorithm.

In recent years, we observe a dynamic development of vision sensors. The analysis of a high definition images or video stream allows to improve the efficiency of the considered vision system – e.g. to detect objects further away from the camera, which is important in the case of advanced driver assistance systems (ADAS), advanced video surveillance systems (AVSS), as well as autonomous vehicles (cars, drones). Higher resolution also results in a larger field of view of a single camera, which allows to limit their number within the considered surveillance system. Currently, the most common are three resolutions: High Definition (HD – 1280 × 720), Full High Definition (FHD – 1920 × 1280) and recently Ultra High Definition (UHD, or 4K – 3840 × 2160). There are also 8K (7680 × 4320) and 16K (15360 × 8640) solutions, but due to the high cost they are currently not widely used. It should be noted that the resolution directly affects the amount of data to be processed or stored.

An uncompressed 4K video stream i.e. 3840 × 2160 at 60 frames per second (fps) results in a data flow of 1424 MB/s. Its processing in real-time is quite a challenge and requires the use of a proper computing platform. The designer can choose from the following solutions:

- general purpose processors (GPP),
- general purpose graphical processing units (GPGPU),
- application specific integrated circuits (ASICs),
- field programmable gate arrays (FPGAs),
- heterogeneous multi-processor system on chips (MPSoC) – which are composed of an ARM processor system, reprogrammable logic and GPU (e.g. Zynq UltraScale+ from Xilinx).

It is worth emphasizing that energy efficiency and the ability to update the applied algorithm are very important in applications such as: ADAS, AVSS or autonomous vehicle perception systems. We claim, that the best solution in these cases is the use of state-of-the-art FPGA or reconfigurable heterogeneous MPSoC devices – they allow 4K video stream processing in real-time, are relatively energy-efficient and can be reprogrammed many times.

The main contributions of this paper are:

- according to the authors knowledge this is the first FPGA implementation of CCL and CCA modules capable of processing a 4K @ 60 fps video stream in real-time,
- verification of the proposed module in a skin colour detection vision system on a development board with Zynq UltraScale+ device.

The remainder of this paper is organized as follows. In Sect. 2 research related to CCL and CCA algorithms and their FPGA implementation is presented. In Sect. 3 the properties of a 4K video stream are discussed. The proposed CCL and

CCA module is described in Sect. 4. Its evaluation in the skin colour detection system is presented in Sect. 5. The paper ends with conclusion and possible further research directions.

2   Previous Work

2.1   CCL Algorithms Overview

There are two approaches to connected component labelling. The first one can be described as region growing [3]. The binary input image is analysed line by line. When a pixel belonging to an object without a label is encountered, a new label is assigned and a neighbourhood search procedure is executed. Then connected pixels are labelled recursively. It should be noted that this solution in not suitable for implementation in a pipeline vision system, where pixels are processed "one-by-one" and practically there is no possibility of random access to image data.

The second solution assumes linear/sequential image processing. These are so-called two-pass and single-pass algorithms. The two-pass solution by Rosenfeld and Platz [9] should be considered as "classic". It consists of two scans of the image and three stages. During the first scan, pixels are given temporary labels and possible conflicts (mergers), i.e. situations in which the same object has received two or more labels, are written to the equivalence table, which has a graph structure. For example, a conflict occurs for an U-shaped object. Within the first scan, two separate labels are given to pixels and information about the connection appears when both arms are converging (Fig. 1). In the second stage, the equivalence table is analysed – the transitive closure of the graph is calculated. As a result, the final labels are determined and assigned to particular pixels during the second image scan.

In the context of hardware implementation, this solution requires buffering of the pre-labelled image. Due to the limited internal memory resources of FPGA devices, it is necessary to use external modules. These increases the complexity of the system and impacts energy efficiency.

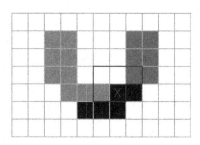

Fig. 1. A "U" shaped object. The place where a conflict (merger) occurs is marked with a red cross (8-pixel neighbourhood). (Color figure online)

There are also single-pass algorithms that do not require buffering of a pre-labelled frame. Emerging conflicts are resolved "on-line" during the first scan. The implementation is more complex than in the two-pass case – this will be shown in detail in Sect. 4. It should also be noted that the result of this operation is not an image with labels, but only a set of parameters of the detected objects. However, in the vast majority of applications, this information is sufficient.

2.2   CCL/CCA Implemented in FPGA

Due to the large practical significance of CCL and CCA in vision systems, a number of articles about the hardware implementation of these operations in FPGA have been published. In the further part of this sub-section we briefly discuss the most representative ones.

A classic two-pass approach implementation has been described in the work [8] from 1995. The proposed system used 9 Xilinx XC4010 FPGA devices and processed up to 30 images with a resolution of 512 × 512 per second.

A two-pass approach was also proposed in the paper [1] from 2010. It is distinguished by the analysis of a series of pixels appearing in a single row (so-called run). The algorithm works in four steps:

- Conversion of pixels into series in the form (ID, EQ, s, e, r), where: ID - series identifier, EQ - assigned label, s - series start in the given line, e - end of the series in the given line, r - number of the image line.
- The first run over series and creation of the equivalence table.
- Solving mergers/conflicts.
- Second pass over the image – assigning appropriate labels.

The solution has been implemented on the RC340 platform with a Xilinx Virtex 4 device. Real-time processing of a 640 × 480 @ 35 fps video stream was obtained.

In the case of hardware implementation in FPGAs, however, the single-pass approach seems to be the most attractive solution. It was first proposed by the team Ma, Bailey and Johnston in 2008 [2]. In this approach to CCL, only the last line of the image that has already received its labels is required during analysis thus reducing the amount of buffered data (single delay line vs. frame). An equivalence table is also used to correctly handle any mergers of labels. In addition, the authors proposed a mechanism that protects against so-called merge chains, i.e. the occurrence of several mergers within the same object, in one line. For this purpose, a special stack was created, in which both labels involved in such merger were stored. Then, during the horizontal blanking time in each line (the period in the video signal during which no pixels are transmitted), the equivalence table was updated with the stored mergers. The only disadvantage of this solution is the limitation of the maximum number of mergers present in the chain. The worst case requires the length of blanking time to be about 50% of the length of the actual image line. Meanwhile, this value usually does not exceed 30%. In real applications, however, the chance of the "worst case scenario" is very low, as usually some pre-processing operations like morphological or median filtering are applied. In addition, the authors proposed a mechanism for recovering labels between successive image lines. The module has been implemented in the Handel-C language and verified on the RC300 card with the Xilinx Virtex II FPGA device. For 640 × 480 resolution, 100 frames per second were processed.

A development of the above presented idea is described in the work [5] from 2016. A module was added that protects against incorrect labelling in very specific cases when using the label re-use approach. The possibility of implementing the module on various FPGA devices: Virtex 6, Spartan 6 and Kintex 7 for different resolutions – also 4K and 8K was analysed. However, the obtained maximum operating frequency of the module does not allow real-time (i.e. 60 fps) operation for such large resolutions. For Virtex 6 and Kintex 7 real-time processing was obtained for 1920 × 1080 (pixel clock about 150 MHz).

A non-standard implementation of a CCL module was described in the work [4] from 2016. The equivalence table was omitted and a shift register of length equal to the entire image line was applied. This register kept $n + 1$ last assigned labels, where n – width of the image. To implement the required functionality, DRAM (Distributed RAM) memory resources are required. In consequence, in case of a merger event, all labels could be updated in the shift register at the same time. However, the solution has significant limitations. The maximum number of labels is 63 or 127. The rather complicated logic results in a small maximum clock frequency which translates into the number of frames that can be processed in one second. For example, for 1920 × 1080 resolution and 127 labels: 37 fps (calculating only bounding box) or 28 fps (calculating bounding box and centroid) were obtained. The Altera Cyclone IV device was used in the experiments.

Summarizing this short survey, it should be noted that the single-pass solution proposed in the work [2] is the most popular one. In addition, according to the authors' knowledge, no module capable of processing a 4K video stream with a frequency of 60 fps has been presented so far.

3   4K Video Stream

A video stream in RGB format with a resolution of 3840 × 2160 and 60 frames per second sent in 1 pixel (24 bits) per clock format (the so-called pixel clock) requires a pixel frequency of approx. 500 MHz. The so-called vertical and horizontal blanking fields present in the video signal increase these value to 600 MHz. This is the "limit" value for currently available reconfigurable systems (FPGA and reconfigurable SoC). Admittedly, selected components, such as block memories (BRAMs), hardware multipliers (DSPs) are, according to the Xilinx manufacturer's declaration, able to work with even higher frequencies (this depends, among others, on the version of the device (speed grade), supply voltage, type of operations). However, in practice, for more complex logic, achieving such frequencies can be very difficult, since the delay associated with the connection resources has also to be considered.

Due to the above described 4K signal parameters and the limitations of the currently available reconfigurable devices, it is not possible to use the 1 pixel per clock scheme (1 ppc), which was the basis of the modules described in Sect. 2 and most of the works related to real-time vision systems implemented in this technology. Therefore, for a 4K signal, 2 ppc or 4 ppc format is used. This allows to reduce the pixel clock frequency to 300 MHz and 150 MHz respectively. However, its use has quite significant implications for the way the CCL/CCA operation is implemented in a pipelined vision system – this will be discussed in detail in Sect. 4. It is also worth mentioning that for the 2 or 4 ppc format it is necessary to multiply the used computing resources. In addition, contextual operations such as filtering or median require modification of a typical context generation scheme [7].

4   The Proposed CCL/CCA Module

The starting point for the design of the proposed module were: literature analysis presented in the Sect. 2, previous work on a CCL module by the first author and the characteristic of a 4K video signal. Firstly, we decided to work with the 4 ppc format, as obtaining a frequency over 300 MHz for a quite complex labelling logic could be very difficult (thus the 2 ppc format will be part of future work). Then, we considered how the extended context (4 pixels simultaneously) affects the CCL algorithm itself. It turned out that this configuration may have pixels arrangements that were not present in the 1 ppc approach. The most complex is the case of merging three labels. Its handling in one clock cycle is impossible, as it requires two memory operations.

Therefore, we proposed a solution to eliminate the above-described case. It is based on connecting two adjacent (binary) pixels using the "OR" operator, which eliminates the possibility of three mergers event. This is shown in Fig. 2. The applied approach also reduces the necessary hardware resources required to implement the module.

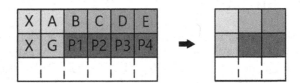

Fig. 2. Illustration of the proposed concept. Pixels joined by the OR operator are marked with colours, P1–P4 - pixels to be labelled.

We compared the presented approach with popular morphological operations with a 3×3 mask: erosion, dilation, opening and closing, as their use also eliminates the possibility of triple merging. Experiments carried out in the MAT-LAB environment showed that all simplifications/filtrations affect the three key objects parameters: area, bounding box and centroid. The biggest changes were observed for small objects, but these are usually discarded from analysis. The use of the proposed method for medium and large objects results in an area change of 4% and 2%, respectively. However, the error for the bounding box and centroid was in the range of ±1 pixel. Considering the obtained benefits, such deterioration is fully acceptable.

An overview of the proposed algorithm is presented in Fig. 3. First, the context is extracted from the incoming video stream. Then, if at least one of the considered pixels (P1–P4) belongs to an object a label is assigned. Details of

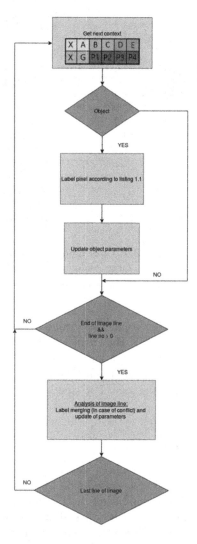

Fig. 3. Overview of the implemented algorithm.

this process are depicted in Listing 1.1. Moreover, object parameters like area, bounding box or centroid are updated. Additionally, at the end of a line, if some labels were merged the used look-up-tables are updated, as well as object parameters.

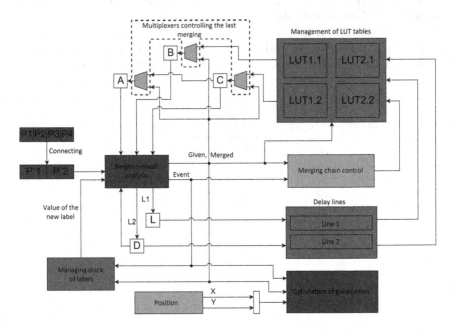

Fig. 4. Scheme of the proposed 4K CCL/CCA module. Colours indicate the difference to a standard 1 ppc version: orange – large, yellow – medium, green – slight modifications. (Color figure online)

The scheme of the proposed connected components labelling and analysis module for the 4K video stream is shown in Fig. 4. The used colours indicate the differences to a typical 1 ppc single-pass approach – like in [2]. In the next subsections, we will discuss each sub-module separately. All were described in Verilog hardware description language. For simulation and implementation the Vivado 2017.4 tool was used.

4.1 Neighbourhood Analysis

The module assigns labels to subsequent groups of two pixels – two labels in parallel for four pixels previously integrated with OR operation. The information about the neighbourhood is obtained from A, B, C and D registers (c.f. Fig. 5a). If the group belongs to a new object, the stack of labels is used (see Subsect. 4.5). Because of the 4 ppc format, the context generation scheme is different than e.g. in the work [2]. The value from register C is transferred to A, whereas B and C get values from the delay line (the values read from the delay lines are updated according the equivalence table in the LUT module). Register D stores the value that has been assigned to the two connected pixels P3 and P4 in the previous clock cycle and register L the value assigned to connected pixels P1 and P2. Multiplexers in front of registers A, B and C are used in the case of merging – the correct (merged) label is passed directly to all registers. Their usage eliminates the latency introduced by the equivalence table implemented as a BRAM memory (its update takes at least one clock cycle). In result, the module informs about the given label and a possible merger event.

The label assignment pseudocode is depicted in Listing 1.1. It is worth to emphasize the separation of operations into two cases – when P1 belongs to the background or object. In the first one, a separate sub-case is additionally handled when P2 also belongs to the background. Then a specific situation may occur, in which, despite the fact that both considered elements are equal to 0, a merger operation should be performed.

Listing 1.1. Label assignment procedure – pseudocode. ct. – conflict.

```
if  P1 == 0  (background)  then
  if  P2 == 1  (objects)  then
    if  B == 0  and  C == 0  then
      set  new  label  (Case  1)
    else
      if  B == 0  and  C != 0  then
        set  label  C  (Case  2)
      else
        set  label  B  (Case  3)
  else
    if  B != 0  and  D != 0  and  B != D  then
      no  label  --  ct.  B,  D  (Case  4)
else
  if  B != 0  then
    if  D == 0  or  D == B  then
      set  label  B  (Case  5)
    else
      set  label  min(B,  D)  --  ct.  B,  D  (Case  6)
  if  C == 0  then
    if  A != 0  then
      set  label  A  (Case  7)
    else
      if  D != 0  then
        set  label  D  (Case  8)
      else
        set  new  label  (Case  9)
  else
    if  A == 0  and  D == 0  then
      set  label  C  (Case  10)
    else
```

```
if A != 0 then
  if A != C then
    set label min(A, C) -- ct. A, C (Case 11)
  else
    set label A (Case 12)
else
  if D != C then
    set label min(C, D) -- ct. C, D (Case 13)
  else
    set label C (Case 14)
```

The listed cases are shown in Fig. 5. The sub-image in Fig. 5a contains a reminder of used symbols, and each next corresponds to the cases from Listing 1.1. White boxes are background, blacks are the analysed groups of objects, labels are marked with orange and blue colours. In case when two values of one register are possible, the respective colours are placed in two halves of a given block – as it can be seen in Fig. 5d. The C register may have the same value as the B register or it may belong to the background and it will not change the result of the analysis. In addition, pixels coloured in grey are not taken into account in the analysis or are not yet known at this stage of the processing.

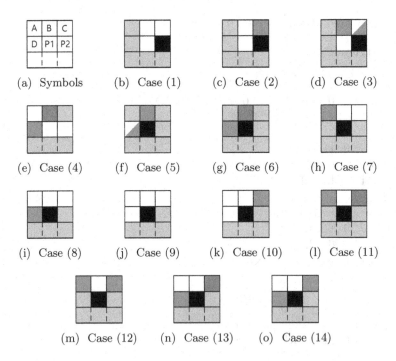

(a) Symbols   (b) Case (1)   (c) Case (2)   (d) Case (3)

(e) Case (4)   (f) Case (5)   (g) Case (6)   (h) Case (7)

(i) Case (8)   (j) Case (9)   (k) Case (10)   (l) Case (11)

(m) Case (12)   (n) Case (13)   (o) Case (14)

Fig. 5. All the possible cases from Listing 1.1. (Color figure online)

4.2 Delay Lines

We used block memory resources (BRAM) to implement delay lines, as in the work [7]. The use of two module instances results from the processing of two elements in parallel.

4.3 LUT Tables

To allow the reuse of previously merged labels we decided to assign two LUT tables for each group of two pixels. The applied solution is based on the work [2]. The first table contains equivalences of labels that have occurred at least once during the scan of the previous image line. Those are used for resolving correct value of labels coming from delay lines. On the other hand, all assigned (new and already existing) labels during analysis are stored in the second LUT. Every merger imposes the update of this table in order to preserve the correctness of equivalents during the next line scan. At the end of each image row, the roles of the mentioned tables are swapped.

4.4 Merger Chain Control

The merger chain is a situation in which several mergers occur in one line for the same object. In the software version of the algorithm, the correct handling of this event is guaranteed by the used graph structure. In a pipelined hardware version, where a new label must be determined during one clock cycle, it is necessary to use an additional mechanism. This module uses a solution derived from work [2].

Its basis is a stack storing the merged and the given labels (only in case when the label with greater value is located to the left of the analysed group of pixels). Then, during the horizontal blanking period, three operations are performed: (1) retrieving from the stack, (2) reading the equivalent of the given label from the corresponding LUT table, (3) writing this value into the LUT table at the address of the merged label. In addition, in the second step, it is necessary to check whether the currently considered label is equal to the merged one from the previous stage (which protects against access conflict to the BRAM memory). Finally, it is worth noting that the use of an appropriate pre-processing (morphological operation, median filtering) allows to significantly reduce the occurrence probability of this type of pixel configurations.

4.5 Label Stack

In the described module, we applied a mechanism for recovering unused (i.e. merged) labels – we used a stack-based approach. The value of a new label (that could be used) is present on the top of the stack. Labels "recovered" during merging are placed on the stack at the end of the image line.

An important stage of the module's operation is restoring the stack to its initial state between consecutive frames. It is filled with successive numbers in the opposite order (the maximum number of labels is a parameter of the module). Due to the specificity of the 4K signal and the data transfer in the AXI Stream format (bus used on ZCU 102 hardware platform), it was not possible to reset the entire stack (BRAM memory) during the vertical blanking period, as it was too short[1]. We therefore decided, to implement a stack restoring mechanism that starts operation during the blanking period and when necessary also continues to work in parallel with the processing of the next frame.

4.6 Calculation of Parameters

The single-pass connected components labelling module would be practically useless if it was not integrated with the functionality allowing to compute object parameters. The calculation of bounding box coordinates, area (m_{00}) and the first order moments (m_{01}, m_{10}) has been implemented. Based on the last two, objects' centroids can be calculated.

The implementation uses a double buffering mechanism. In one data structure, the parameters of the objects from the previous frame are stored and available for further processing. In the second one, the current calculations are carried out. The switch is performed at the beginning of a new frame.

The key element of the module is merger handling. In the case of a 1 ppc stream, the single-pixel gap between two objects is used. It allows, after merger, to read the feature vector of the second object and save the integrated results to the data structure.

For the 4 ppc format, the application of the above described approach would require a gap of at least 4 pixels. Therefore, a solution based on a FIFO queue is used, where values of merged labels are stored. The data integration itself takes place during the horizontal blanking period.

It should be noted that in the considered system, the blanking period lasts about 60 clock cycles. For this value, the maximum number of "handled" mergers is 30. During analysis of the test sequences, we established that there are usually no more than 10 such events in a single line, which justifies the use of the described solution.

5   Evaluation and Analysis

5.1 Sample Application

One of the applications of the created CCL/CCA module is the segmentation of areas with a given colour, e.g. skin. It is a component of face detection and recognition systems that enables pre-selection of candidates and speeds-up further image analysis.

---

[1] It should be noted that the blanking periods in the native format are much longer and the conversion to AXI Stream format "shortens" them. This is a result of the assumption that in AXI Stream only valid data is transferred.

Fig. 6. Working system. Right screen – input image. Left screen – CCA/CCL result.

The vision system consists of the so-called video pass-through, colour space conversions and segmentation module, CCL/CCA and visualization of its results. The source of the image is a computer graphics card or a 4K camera with HDMI output. Image processing is performed on the Xilinx ZCU 102 evaluation board with the Xilinx Zynq UltraScale+ MPSoC device. The results are displayed on a 4K monitor.

The input image in RGB format is subjected to a series of operations, which result in segmentation of skin colour areas – finally a binary image is obtained. In order to minimize the impact of variable lighting, different skin colour, occlusion and shadows, the frame is analysed in three colour spaces: RGB, YCbCr and HSV. Thus, the necessary conversions are carried out first.

Then, based on the algorithm described in the paper [6], the image is binarized by thresholding channels R, G, B, Y, Cb, Cr, H, and The obtained binary map is subjected to median filtration and morphological operations (erosion and dilatation) in order to remove minor disturbances. The next step is the CCL/CCA described in the Sect. 4. Its result is a description of the detected objects in the form of bounding box coordinates and geometric moments m_{00}, m_{01} and m_{10}.

In the final stage visualization is carried out. First, it is checked whether the object has an area larger than a pre-defined threshold. If so, its parameters are saved to one of the K registers (K = 10 – it is also the maximum number of objects that can be displayed). Then, for each pixel from the video stream, it is checked whether it belongs to one of the pre-designated bounding boxes. This is performed in K modules in parallel. In the last step, the OR operation is applied on the outputs from the modules – if a pixel belongs to at least one bounding box, its colour is changed (to red). The working system is shown in Fig. 6 and the use of hardware resources is summarized in Table 1. Power consumption estimation by the Vivado tool of the Zynq UltraScale+ device

Table 1. Resource utilization – 4 ppc format.

Resource	Video pass-through	CCL/CCA	System
LUT	32025 (11.68%)	1724 (0.63%)	50272 (18.34%)
FF	39037 (7.12%)	796 (0.15%)	65632 (11.97%)
BRAM	6 (0.66%)	11 (1.21%)	23 (2.52%)
DSP	3 (0.12%)	0 (0.00%)	3 (0.12%)

Table 2. Comparison of the proposed solution with state of the art

Paper	Alg.	Features	Device/Clk. freq.	Real-time processing
[8] (1995)	2-pass	—	9 x Xilinx XC4010 10 MHz	512 × 512 @ 30 fps
[2] (2008)	1-pass	Label re-use	Xilinx Virtex II Pro —	640 × 480 @ 100 fps
[1] (2010)	2-pass	Pixel runs analysis	Xilinx Virtex 4 65 Mhz	640 × 480 @ 35 fps
[5] (2016)	1-pass	Label re-use	Xilinx Virtex 6, Kintex 7 180 MHz, 150 MHz	1920 × 1080 @ 60 fps
[4] (2016)	1-pass	Shift register	Altera Cyclone IV 58–90 MHz	1920 × 1080 @ 37 fps
Proposed (2018)	1-pass	4 ppc support	Xilinx Zynq UltraScale+ 150 MHz	**3840 × 2160** **@ 60 fps**

equals 4.973 W (2.151 W for programmable logic and 2.822 W for processing system). It should be noted that the proposed CCL/CCA module does not use much logic resources. Significant is only the BRAM utilization (11 modules), as they are used for context generation and at different steps of the algorithm. Therefore, the module could be also used on a lower grade FPGA device. The only limiting factor is the possibility to receive a 4K video stream, which requires high-speed serial differential transceivers.

5.2   Comparison with Other Solutions

In Table 2 the modules discussed in Sect. 2, as well as the proposed one are summarized. The used "pixel merging" and other algorithmic advances allowed to obtain real-time processing for 4K @ 60 fps video stream in 4 ppc format. It should be emphasized that this performance is not a simple derivative of using a rather new device. To process this type of video stream, the well known modules had to be significantly re-designed. Moreover, the module could also be implemented in e.g. Virtex 7 series – here the main limitation is HDMI 2.0 format support (high-frequency differential input and output (for visualisation)). We did not compared the used logic resources for two main reasons. First, not all papers provide this information [1,2,8]. Second, in all other cases the utilization is rather low (one exception [4]). In our opinion, the main issue with real-time implementation of CCL/CCA modules is the design of a rather complicated control logic (label assignment, label merging, label re-use and parameters computation) and not resource optimization (like for example in advanced image filtering – Vector Median Filter or Non-Local Means filter).

6   Summary

The combining of two neighbouring pixels allowed to obtain real-time processing for a 4K @ 60 fps stream. At the same time, the conducted experiments showed that this modification does not have a significant impact on the determined object parameters (bounding box, centroid, area). The proposed module has been verified on the ZCU 102 development board with a Xilinx Zynq UltraScale+ device as a component of a skin-colour area segmentation application. For the currently available programmable logic it is not possible to process a 4K stream in 1 ppc format, as it would require designing all modules to work with 600 MHz clock. In the 4 ppc format some complex merge operations need to be handled in one clock cycle, which is very difficult or almost impossible – this is why the neighbouring pixels were merged in the presented module. Therefore, the most promising solution to run connected component labelling in 4K without any simplifications is the 2 ppc format. This requires very careful design to support 300 MHz clock frequency and will be the first step in our further work. We also plan to analyse the reasonableness of pixel series analysis (like in [1]). In addition, we considered to describe the presented algorithm in C/C++, use a HLS (High Level Synthesis) tool like Vivado HLS to generate the module and then to compare the results with the implementation in Verilog hardware description language.

Acknowledgements. The work presented in this paper was supported by the National Science Centre project no. 2016/23/D/ST6/01389 entitled "The development of computing resources organization in latest generation of heterogeneous reconfigurable devices enabling real-time processing of UHD/4K video stream".

References

1. Appiah, K., Hunter, A., Dickinson, P., Meng, H.: Accelerated hardware video object segmentation: from foreground detection to connected components labelling. Comput. Vis. Image Underst. **114**(2), 1282–1291 (2010)
2. Ma, N., Bailey, D.G., Johnston, C.T.: Optimised single pass connected components analysis. In: 2008 International Conference on Field-Programmable Technology, pp. 185–192 (2008)
3. Haralick, R.M.: Some neighborhood operations. In: Onoe, M., Preston, K., Rosenfeld, A. (eds.) Real Time Parallel Computing, pp. 11–35. Springer, Heidelberg (1981). https://doi.org/10.1007/978-1-4684-3893-2_2
4. Jeong, J., Lee, G., Lee, M., Kim, J.-G.: A single-pass connected component labeler without label merging period. J. Sig. Process. Syst. **84**(2), 211–223 (2016)

5. Klaiber, M.J., Bailey, D.G., Baroud, Y.O., Simon, S.: A resource-efficient hardware architecture for connected component analysis. IEEE Trans. Circ. Syst. Video Technol. **26**(7), 1334–1349 (2016)

6. Kolkur, S., Kalbande, D., Shimpi, P., Bapat, C., Jatakia, J.: Human skin detection using RGB, HSV and YCbCr color models. In: International Conference on Communication and Signal Processing (2016)

7. Kowalczyk, M., Przewlocka, D., Kryjak, T.: Real-time implementation of context image processing operations for 4K video stream in Zynq UltraScale+ MPSoC. In: 2018 Conference on Design and Architectures for Signal and Image Processing (2018)

8. Rachakonda, R.V., Athanas, P.M., Abbott, A.L.: High-speed region detection and labeling using an FPGA-based custom computing platform. In: Moore, W., Luk, W. (eds.) FPL 1995. LNCS, vol. 975, pp. 86–93. Springer, Heidelberg (1995). https://doi.org/10.1007/3-540-60294-1_101

9. Rosenfeld, A., Pfaltz, J.L.: Sequential operations in digital picture processing. J. ACM **13**(4), 471–494 (1966)

A Scalable FPGA-Based Architecture for Depth Estimation in SLAM

Konstantinos Boikos$^{(\boxtimes)}$ⓘ and Christos-Savvas Bouganis

Department of Electrical and Electronic Engineering,
Imperial College London, London, UK
k.boikos14@imperial.ac.uk

Abstract. The current state of the art of Simultaneous Localisation and Mapping, or SLAM, on low power embedded systems is about sparse localisation and mapping with low resolution results in the name of efficiency. Meanwhile, research in this field has provided many advances for information rich processing and semantic understanding, combined with high computational requirements for real-time processing. This work provides a solution to bridging this gap, in the form of a scalable SLAM-specific architecture for depth estimation for direct semi-dense SLAM. Targeting an off-the-shelf FPGA-SoC this accelerator architecture achieves a rate of more than 60 mapped frames/sec at a resolution of 640×480 achieving performance on par to a highly-optimised parallel implementation on a high-end desktop CPU with an order of magnitude improved power consumption. Furthermore, the developed architecture is combined with our previous work for the task of tracking, to form the first complete accelerator for semi-dense SLAM on FPGAs, establishing the state of the art in the area of embedded low-power systems.

Keywords: Simultaneous Localisation and Mapping · FPGAs ·
Embedded systems · Custom computing · Computer vision

1 Introduction

In recent years, there has been a lot of interest and research effort surrounding intelligent machines and systems. One area of particular interest is the push towards fully autonomous machines that can move and interact in an unknown environment. This includes emerging applications such as household robots, environment-aware industrial robots, autonomous drones that can operate indoors and self-driving cars among others. One of the core elements in this effort is a family of algorithms and systems called Simultaneous localisation and Mapping (SLAM), which aims to provide a solution to the problem of exploring an unknown environment while keeping tracking of one's own position in it.

From this point, the paper focuses on real-time SLAM, which refers to performing all processing at the camera's rate of operation. The exact rate necessary can vary per application. Focusing on robotics which is one of the central

© Springer Nature Switzerland AG 2019
C. Hochberger et al. (Eds.): ARC 2019, LNCS 11444, pp. 181–196, 2019.
https://doi.org/10.1007/978-3-030-17227-5_14

motivations for this work, research has shown that effective localisation needs a performance of at least 30 frames/sec for most moving robotic platforms. Moving to faster platforms, such as self-driving cars and quadcopters, higher framerates are required for SLAM not to fail under agile movement [5]. Meanwhile, the resolutions used are normally in the region of 640 × 480. It was found that increasing the resolution provides a small benefit to some algorithms [3], while the runtime usually increases at least linearly with the number of pixels. However, the state of the art in algorithms has focused on resolutions in this region and research results indicate that the camera resolution is not currently the limiting factor.

SLAM in the literature is usually comprised of two main tasks [2,8]. Localisation, often referred to as tracking, is the act of continuously estimating the position and orientation, or pose, of the camera. Mapping is the task of generating and continuously updating a coherent model of the environment based on the sensor observations. These two tasks are very closely interconnected and strongly dependent on each other. Tracking compares the incoming data from the sensor with the map that has been generated to estimate a current pose. Then, the accuracy of that estimation will determine the quality of the updated map, and how close it will be to reality.

In the past, different sensors have been used including Lidar, sonar and recently RGB-D cameras. The first two generate a map in two dimensions around a moving platform, and are used for their simplicity and effectiveness. However they are usually heavy, require high power consumption and are mostly constrained in two dimensions, making them unsuitable for many applications. Active RGB-D cameras recover depth directly by projecting a light pattern in infrared or using time-of-flight. They have enabled high-quality dense 3D reconstruction in indoor spaces [13] but are constrained in their area of operation because of their design. They are also more expensive and power-hungry than a simple visual sensor, making them less attractive for embedded low-power robotics and outdoor spaces. As such, this work focuses on enabling high quality embedded SLAM using visual information from RGB or greyscale cameras.

Towards addressing the challenges of real-time visual SLAM, the field has gradually split in different approaches, each with their own advantages and disadvantages. A main categorisation is in terms of Sparse to Dense SLAM. Representative examples of these are [2,8,13], demonstrated in a continuum in Fig. 1. Sparse SLAM uses a smaller set of observations for tracking and maintains a sparse map of the environment consisting of a few points of interest. These approaches exhibit relatively lower computational requirements, but are mainly limited to accurate localisation.

SLAM algorithms categorised as Dense are able to construct a complete model of the environment as interconnected surfaces, but are very computationally intensive. In published works usually they require GPU acceleration, as for example in the work of Whelan et al. [13], to process all of the available information in real time. To address this drawback a family of works described as semi-dense SLAM have emerged, e.g. [2]. These aim to provide a more dense and information-rich representation compared to sparse methods, while achieving better computational efficiency from processing a subset of high quality observations. However, they are still computationally complex and target desktop-grade multicore CPUs for real-time processing.

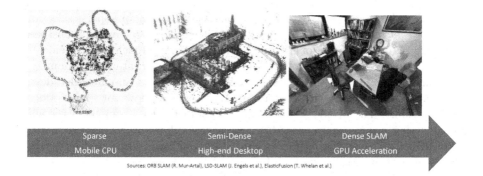

Sources: ORB SLAM (R. Mur-Artal), LSD-SLAM (J. Engels et al.), ElasticFusion (T. Whelan et al.)

Fig. 1. SLAM continuum from sparse to dense

Another important distinction is the difference between a full SLAM system and a visual odometry algorithm. Visual odometry focuses on maintaining an accurate position estimate and uses the most efficient form of map possible. On the other hand, full SLAM methods attempt to recover as much of their environment as possible, as well as keep a globally consistent map and enabling loop-closing. Recent solutions, such as SVO [4], can achieve high accuracy tracking using a small set of high-quality observations. However, much of their efficiency stems from their generation of sparse and local maps which encode significantly less information about the environment.

There are many examples of emerging applications that require a high level of understanding of their environment that sparse SLAM or visual odometry inherently cannot provide. At the same time, due to safety and robustness requirements, there is often a need for a low processing latency, while most embedded platforms have significant power and weight constraints. These specifications rule out most of the conventional hardware that can perform cutting-edge SLAM in real time. In this context, to close this gap we propose a novel architecture, based on an FPGA-SoC to accelerate semi-dense mapping, targeting state-of-the-art semi-dense SLAM. This accelerator design combines dynamic iteration pipelines and traditional streaming elements to achieve high performance and power efficiency, with a combination of dataflow processing and local on-chip caching to match the unique demands of these algorithms. Our contributions are twofold. First the design of a scalable and high performance, power efficient specialised accelerator architecture, that can process and update a map in less than 20 ms. Second, a system which, when combined with our previous work in [1], forms the first, to the best of our knowledge, complete SLAM accelerator on FPGAs, pushing the state of the art in performance and quality for SLAM on low-power embedded devices.

2   Related Work

Since platforms in the embedded space have significant constraints in power and performance, most embedded visual SLAM implementations focus on sparse SLAM that is adapted towards reducing computational requirements further such as [11]. The downside to these approaches is that they map a sparse selection of features that reduces the quality of the reconstruction as well as the robustness of tracking in different types of environments. Another approach towards embedding SLAM has been to design a lightweight, sparse but accurate visual odometry algorithm that can achieve real-time performance on-board an embedded devic [4]. This, however, comes with the limitations discussed above for sparse odometry algorithms. The option of offloading computation to a remote server and reconstructing a dense map there has also been explored [9]. This comes with increased power consumption for wireless communication, increased latency, a reduced area of operation and high bandwidth requirements.

Dense SLAM has been advancing rapidly but its requirements in sensors, energy and computation are infeasible for an embedded platform. Works in semi-dense methods such as LSD-SLAM, are more applicable to the embedded space thanks to lower computational complexity and reliance on simpler cameras. LSD-SLAM [2] for example, provides a tracking accuracy comparable to other state of the art sparse methods but generates a much denser map that provides more information about the environment. As such, it was selected as the target for the custom accelerator presented in this work.

Recently, there have been attempts in designing custom hardware for SLAM in the embedded space. Suleiman et al. [10] demonstrated a custom ASIC design for visual-inertial odometry targeting nano-drones. It belongs in the category of sparse odometry and achieves high performance together with power efficiency, realised as a chip printed at 65 nm CMOS technology. It enables environment awareness for very lightweight robots, but because of its specialisation it only performs the version of sparse visual-inertial odometry it was designed and cannot be extended to semi-dense or dense SLAM. This is a typical example of an optimised ASIC implementation of an algorithm, which trades flexibility and cost to achieve the highest performance and power efficiency for a specific task.

Most related work on FPGAs in the past has been limited in scope to accelerating selected computation kernels for sparse SLAM such as [12]. In contrast, our work targets a more complete implementation of a semi-dense mapping task. Honegger et al. [6] proposed a custom board combining an FPGA and a mobile CPU for robotic vision, evaluated by offloading a disparity estimation algorithm (SGM stereo) to the FPGA. Disparity matching with a fixed stereo camera is well-known on FPGAs but is only a pre-processing step needing further processing to be utilized for SLAM. Additionally, their work is focused on a fixed system architecture, providing a one way link with the FPGA between the camera and off-chip memory. In contrast, we target a more flexible system architecture that can allow more fine-grained cooperation between hardware and software.

In our previous work [1] we presented an architecture for high-performance tracking for semi-dense SLAM on embedded platforms. However, that work did not provide a solution for mapping, still performed on an embedded CPU at a relatively low performance. This work addresses this so that both of these demanding, interdependent tasks can be offloaded in an efficient way to a reconfigurable platform. The two accelerators are combined to provide higher system performance and release the mobile CPU to be used for other tasks.

3 Mapping Algorithm

LSD-SLAM [2], a state-of-the-art semi-dense SLAM algorithm, is the target of acceleration. For tracking, LSD-SLAM uses the most recent depth observations projected on the current camera frame to optimise directly on the pixel intensity residual. This is expressed as a weighted least squares optimisation, using only the information-rich points in the camera's view. These points are selected based on the intensity gradient in their immediate area. It is then the aim of the mapping algorithm to use the camera pose, estimated from the tracking task, to triangulate points from two views; the current camera frame and the Keyframe, a previous frame in the camera's trajectory stored with its world-to-camera pose along with depth information in a data structure with the same name. That set of depth observations and the selected camera frame on which they project constitutes the current depth map.

All points with a sufficient gradient successfully matched from Keyframe to camera frame will have a depth value stored in this data structure. Using this information, the mapping algorithm adds a new observation for the points observed for the first time, and performs a filtering update to improve the estimate for points seen in the past. At the end of this process, successfully observed points in space will have an estimated depth and depth variance value stored in the Keyframe. For a more detailed description of the algorithms that constitute LSD-SLAM and the theory behind them one can refer to Engel et al.'s work [2]. From this point on, for reasons of brevity the paper will focus on just the information necessary to discuss the proposed custom hardware architecture.

The aim of Depth Estimation is to perform an exhaustive search for each high quality point in the Keyframe using its pixel intensity, along a line on the current frame to then be able to estimate its depth. This line is the epipolar line. Geometrically, if the relative position and orientation of the camera for two captured frames is known, it is proven that a point observed on one camera frame will always project to a line on the plane of the other camera's frame. Two camera frames will not always observe the same point. The line may lie completely outside the frame that a sensor will capture. As such the search is restricted on the intersection of the line and the image frame.

In LSD-SLAM a maximum amount of steps is used to define the search distance. Also, if there is a prior estimation with sufficient confidence, the estimated variance is used to limit the search interval to $d \pm 2\sigma_d$, where d and σ_d denote the mean and standard deviation of the prior hypothesis. At the end of the search for a good match, a sub-pixel accurate localisation is performed for the matching disparity. In [2], instead of scanning to match a single pixel, a squared error function comparing 5 equidistant points is used to improve accuracy. This approach significantly increases robustness with a small increase in complexity.

In this work, the tasks involved in SLAM were profiled, running as software on an Intel i7-4770 CPU. The results showed that the mapping task was one of the most demanding tasks happening during LSD-SLAM. It consumed 44% of the computation time spent on SLAM and together with tracking constitutes 85% of the CPU cycles spent on the SLAM algorithm with the rest spent on pose-graph optimisation and other background tasks. Further testing on the ARM-Cortex A9 of our FPGA board verified the conclusions of the profiling results, with timing tests measuring the mapping task at an average of 530 ms per map update.

4   Architecture

The architecture targets an FPGA-SoC that contains an FPGA fabric and a mobile CPU. The CPU and FPGA can function independently and can operate on the same memory space and both have direct access to a common physical DRAM. There are master memory controllers on the custom hardware for Direct Memory Access (DMA), designed to operate at full-speed bursts for updating the caches before operation or to provide a constant stream of map points for the execution of the algorithm. In addition to the high-speed memory connections, there is a direct slave-to-master connection to the CPU, where the CPU acts as a master. In this manner, the CPU has the high-level control of the coprocessor on the FPGA, and can change its operating parameters and coordinate its operation with the software back end. This part of the system architecture is in a similar philosophy to our work in [1]. The way both accelerators were implemented on the FPGA is that they each have exclusive access through an AXI-interconnect to a pair of high performance DMA ports. They share a dedicated DRAM region and the software calls the accelerators to replace the functionality of the software functions. As mentioned in [1], that accelerator has a more fine-grained sharing of computation with the software threads, owing to the iterative, multi-level nature of tracking. In this work, all tasks included in a map update are completely moved to the FPGA and the software only handles the synchronisation of data and tasks.

In general, the co-processor architecture is designed to perform most of the heuristic processing of LSD-SLAM in a streaming fashion. This was chosen to keep compatibility with this state-of-the-art method and maintain the same accuracy and robustness. Nevertheless, in order to increase the performance that is attainable by the proposed custom hardware design, the actual hardware implementation is modified with respect to the original software implementation. For instance, a number of values, such as the maximum gradient in a neighbourhood were more efficiently calculated on the fly than pre-computed as done in software. Additionally, most of the functions in the algorithm are combined in one streaming pipeline utilizing buffers to overlap computation, as this avoids redundant memory traffic and significantly improves performance

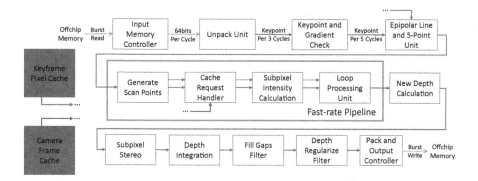

Fig. 2. Block diagram of the coprocessor architecture

and power efficiency. Finally, to remain faithful to the algorithm, most of the computation happens on floating-point as in the original implementation. There are variables where high-dynamic range or multiple divisions make the floating-point implementation necessary for accuracy or performance reasons. For the rest of the units the conversion to fixed-point arithmetic was not straightforward but requires careful analysis. However the principles behind choosing the most suitable arithmetic representation are well known in the field of custom and reconfigurable computing. As such, we chose first to focus on developing the most suitable architecture, presented in this work, leaving custom-precision representation as future work after the system and the microarchitecture were fixed.

4.1   High-Level Functionality and Algorithm Mapping

Figure 2 contains a high level view of this architecture omitting some connections for clarity. The first step is the update of the caches if necessary. Then as input the architecture receives all the points of the Keyframe sequentially as described in Sect. 3, and its output is the final state of the updated Keyframe data structure, again output sequentially. The first two units ensure a fast and consistent stream of Keyframe points. The 'Input Memory Controller' performs full-speed burst reads from the off-chip memory, that are then buffered and streamed as Keypoints from the 'Unpack Unit' to the rest of the pipeline.

As the Keypoints stream in, the 'Keypoint and Gradient Check' unit is responsible for calculating on the fly the max gradient in a neighbourhood of the pixel. Based on the gradient threshold for the area and the pixel's confidence rating, the Keypoint's fitness is calculated as a candidate to try to map. It is then forwarded to the 'Epipolar Line and 5-Point Unit' that is responsible for calculating the scan range, center and steps. Next, a check of the robustness of the search is performed, including if it is inside the frame's limits. If all the checks are valid, this information is forwarded to the fast-rate pipeline. If it fails, the map point is still forwarded to be used for later processing such as filtering, followed with flags to mark this decision and the reason for failure.

In the fast-rate pipeline, as shown in Fig. 2, the thinner lines correspond to the map point together with its metadata being forwarded. The main operation of these units has to do with the scan and best match selection on the epipolar line. The information pertaining to this scan is passed between them at a faster rate as long as the scan is going on for one single point, indicated by the thicker lines in the center of the units. In this faster rate pipeline, the 'Generate Scan Points' unit supplies a steady stream of pixel locations to be fetched from the cache unit, according to the calculations in the Epipolar line unit. The 'Cache Request Handler' fetches these pixels from the caches and forwards them to the 'Subpixel Intensity Calculation' unit where linear interpolation is performed in a neighbourhood of 4 pixels around the floating point coordinates.

All these streams are passed on to the 'Loop Processing Unit' (LPU) that performs the core of the scanning algorithm. It reconstructs the pattern of 5 pixels we are looking for and performs the scan steps to find the position with the minimum sum of squared errors. It keeps the best match and second best match and additional information regarding the search. This includes the steps performed, the distance of the search and the match error. After a scan is completed, this is forwarded to the 'New depth Calculation' unit. This calculates a new depth and depth variance value based on the results of the LPU, which the next unit 'Subpixel Stereo' can further refine if the conditions are right.

Finally, the 'Depth Integration' and the Filter units. The first is responsible for putting all the information together for each map point, and the filter units perform regularization operations. The first one, if it finds sufficient confidence in a window around a pixel without an observation, fills it with a weighted average of its valid neighbours. The second filter calculates a smoothed value for the depth and variance of valid map points, stored separately to the actual depth, again operating on a sliding window around a center pixel. Here row buffers allowed region of interest processing, without breaking the streaming interface of the filter units. After the processing and filtering finishes, we reverse the operations at the input in a pack-and-output unit that streams it out to the off-chip DRAM with burst write transactions.

4.2   Multi-rate Dataflow Operation

Semi-dense SLAM is characterised by a large amount of data that needs to be processed. For a map of size 640×480 there are 7.37 MBytes for the depth map representation. That is in addition to the actual frame size of 307 kBytes. To put that into perspective, in order to process 60 frames/sec as they come from a camera, and extract depth information for all of them the total time between captured frames would be less than 17 ms, but that amount of data requires approximately 8–10 ms just to be read from memory with the typical memory bandwidth available on off-the-shelf FPGA-SoCs. To keep up with that time it would be necessary to process one map point every 6 cycles on average. A straightforward implementation trying to perform all necessary epipolar line scan steps inside this time would provide a large, underutilized design, with a high power consumption.

Alternatively certain properties of semi-dense SLAM can be leveraged to design a much more efficient solution. An epipolar line scan often is not required when the point does not currently contain a valid observation or is not visible in the current frame. Moreover, in confident observations, it can be safely reduced to the region $d \pm 2\sigma_d$, as described in the Sect. 3. The designed coprocessor takes advantage of the pattern and frequency of the aforementioned cases by utilizing fully pipelined units, each designed to efficiently execute a part of the computation of the entire algorithm, as discussed in Sect. 4.1.

We found the most efficient design to be self-contained, deeply-pipelined hardware blocks that perform different types of operations by re-using math units, clocked at a synchronous rate, while logic changes the operation path. This way we overlapped different parts of the algorithm in the same hardware units, and designed everything with the principle of data always moving forward. The pipelines contain multiple math units for multiplication, addition and division, and logic and multiplexers shift the structure of the unit as necessary. This way they can change from an initialization phase, to operating on points, to scanning across the frame cache, depending on the unit, or skipping a scan and forwarding metadata to the next unit in the pipeline.

The units were also designed to operate at different rates, with fast-rate processing units in the middle to perform epipolar scans, find the best match and perform the depth estimation, and more relaxed processing at most of the input and output stages. The cache accessing was normalised to one access window per cycle, with buffering and control allowing a very simple and high efficient cache controller to serve different kinds of requests from other units. The units are connected to each other through large streaming FIFO buffers that allow communication to happen asynchronously, and hide a lot of the latency that would arise from the variable processing rate design. In this way we offer a much higher performance level, but use a fraction of the resources of a pipelined statically allocated for the worst processing load.

As shown in Fig. 2, the units in the fast-rate pipeline operate at a faster rate. When an epipolar line scan and depth update is necessary, they perform some initialisation steps at a rate of one step per cycle. Otherwise, if there is a point that does not require a depth update, they directly forward that point's metadata to the next unit in a single cycle. Finally they use most of their resources in a normal operation to perform one scan step per cycle. Their accesses to cache are pre-computed and pre-fetched at the 'generate scan points unit' so they perform the necessary operations directly on incoming data.

By reducing the amount of multiplier, divider and accumulation units built in each block and time sharing them for a larger amount of operations, we can increase the amount of cycles necessary for a scan but with an almost linear decrease in resources for that unit. The most efficient designs must have units in the fast-rate pipeline match with each other, as otherwise the slowest one would dictate the rate of processing, leaving unused resources in the rest. In a similar fashion the rate of processing outside the fast-rate pipeline should be tuned as one number, and the same or slightly slower processing rate should be targeted for the units after the fast-rate pipeline. The resulting architecture is tunable in terms of its performance and resources, allowing it to scale to different FPGA devices and resource budgets. In Sect. 5 we show different example design points achieved by changing the target processing rates as described previously.

4.3   Performance Analysis

To explore the optimal hardware rates described in Sect. 4.2, and verify that our design assumptions hold when running with real-world datasets, monitoring instrumentation was added in the software version of LSD-SLAM and it was executed for the entire duration of real datasets. Firstly, we collected statistics regarding the average processing load that is expected for each iteration of a map update, and then studied the distribution and extrema of these samples. The results showed that the frequency that any Keyframe point will contain a valid map point requiring an epipolar line scan is consistently lower than the 30% mark. Further testing for peak loads across a dataset revealed that the average amount of points per line that require scanning peaks around the center of the image at a frequency averaging 18%. By looking for extrema we discovered some outlier cases, which however were usually less than 1–2% of the frames processed. Those have to do with special cases consisting of initialisation steps or very sharp motions. However, the worst case scenario will always have an upper bound, and have a linear relationship with the fast-rate pipeline processing rate and the processing load per frame. Thus, it can be predicted and designed against.

In the implemented accelerator, a processing rate of one scan/interpolation per cycle was chosen for the fast-rate pipeline and a processing rate of one target point per 5 cycles for the others. For the datasets tested, this relationship of 5-to-1 was a good ratio for the processing rates, with the majority of frames not filling the buffers completely. The average case for one epipolar line scan was calculated at 11 steps for the presented design. Given the results from the instrumented code, if 25% of the points in a line require an epipolar scan, and the 75% are skipped, one per cycle, the total latency per row would be 2240 cycles, or 3.5 cycles per point on average, which leaves a good margin of safety.

In datasets tested, 98% of frames were within one millisecond of the target processing time and more than 99% were within two. There were some outlier cases with a performance drop of up to 30%, from 16.3 ms to 21 ms. For example in the Machine hall dataset, one of the two depicted in the Evaluation Section, out of 3268 map updates only 19 were around the 20 ms mark, with a maximum recorded value of 20.9 ms. However that is considered acceptable in this application for two reasons. Firstly, the application can dismiss more than 1% dropped updates and can handle a lower mapping rate than the one we targeted. Moreover, in actual tests the software version had a worse behaviour with outliers, with an increase of almost 200% in the processing time for some cases.

Secondly, the proposed architecture is tunable and can be changed to adapt to different application requirements. One can increase the capabilities of the fast-rate pipeline to have the system guarantee a very small performance degradation even in outlier cases at the cost of some underutilized resources. Alternatively, if the application allows, one can go the other way and under-provision the fast-rate pipeline to target a more resource-and-power efficient system, by allowing some degradation of a few percentage points in more cluttered scenes. In Fig. 3, we can see the scaling to target different performance points. The 32.5 fps and 42.5 fps are examples of a design point where an extra cost in resources guarantees a lower maximum latency, and therefore a higher target performance.

5   Implementation and Evaluation

Figure 3 demonstrates scaling from a smaller device (Zynq-7020), to a 60fps design point, selected to allow a second accelerator to fit in the larger ZC706 board (Zynq-7045). We can see that some resources such as the DSPs, ubiquitous in most math units, scale almost linearly with the target performance, followed by the LUTs, while Flip-Flops have a relatively stable cost owing to their extensive use in I/O and memory access units which were not part of the tuning process. The architecture is designed to be platform agnostic and optimised on resource usage. Nevertheless, the use of Vivado HLS tools drove a number of implementation decisions in order to develop and test the IP on the target FPGA-SoC, leading to certain overheads[1].

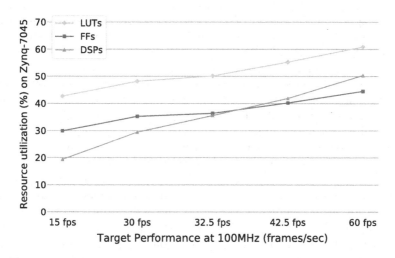

Fig. 3. Resource scaling with architectural tuning targeting 100 MHz

For evaluation, the design was synthesized and placed-and-routed with Vivado and Vivado HLS (v[2018.2]), targeting a Xilinx Zynq ZC706 board and

---

[1] For example, the tool always rounds up memory size to the next power of two for BRAM utilization. To reduce that overhead we partitioned memory cyclically by a factor of 5, saving BRAMs at the cost of increased DSPs and LUTs.

ran on the same board. For the parameters described in Sect. 4, timing was met for the coprocessor at 125 MHz. The resource usage for that result, post-implementation, is described on Table 1. Combined with our design from [1] executing on the same reconfigurable fabric, the accelerators were successfully tested working side-by-side, setting the target frequency to 100 MHz, replacing key functions in the software implementation running on the mobile CPU.

Table 1. Resources post-implementation

Resource	This work	With [1]	Available on Z-7045
LUT	151,674	184,993	218,600
LUTRAM	12,242	15,317	70,400
FF	213,761	256,665	437,200
BRAM	958	1089	1090
DSP	594	718	900

On Fig. 4, we can see the mapping performance (total processing time for a map update step) on three high-end platforms across two separate datasets[2]. The colour corresponds to the platforms, an Intel i7-4770, our accelerator implemented on a Zynq-7045 and the Cortex-A57 on a Tegra TX1. The width of the shape corresponds to the density of observations around a particular value of milliseconds, similar to a sideways kernel density plot. The white line in the middle corresponds to the mean value of the observations, while the thinner orange one to the median. Finally, the lines at the top and bottom are the minimum and maximum values observed. The figure demonstrates the variability of this processing load on general purpose hardware, and how robust this accelerator is to these delays, appearing almost flat since most observations were very close to the ideal value of approximately 16.2 ms at 100 MHz.

In addition to performance, power consumption was measured for each platform at the wall, including board and power supply losses. Static and dynamic power are separated to demonstrate the chip power contribution at full load. The measurement is accurate to ± 0.5 W, an accuracy sufficient to reach some conclusions for these different platforms. In the case of our accelerator we can estimate approximately 1–2 W of the static power draw to be due to the FPGA. Testing power draw with an empty bitstream on the FPGA showed a decrease in static power of approximately 2 W adding merit to this. We achieve a performance on par with the high-end desktop CPU, but for an order of magnitude less power consumed at the FPGA fabric.

We can see that the FGPA development board is at a similar power level at full load with the Tegra TX1, but with more than a 4x increase in performance on average for our accelerator design. We estimate the total power of mobile

---

[2] These were the Room and Machine Hall trajectory from TUM's website: https:// vision.in.tum.de/research/vslam/lsdslam.

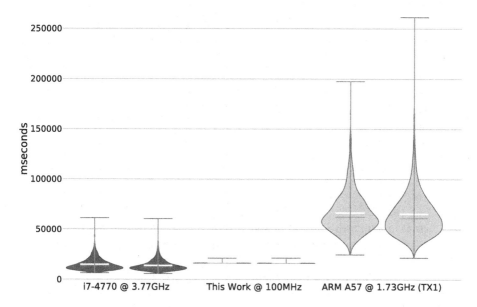

Fig. 4. Mapping latency in ms - different platforms on two datasets

CPU + FPGA fabric on the Zynq-7045 at 6.5 W, using the estimator on Vivado post-implementation, combined with the results shown on Fig. 5. Static is high since it includes several unnecessary peripheral devices on the FPGA board such as a second DDR memory. On the Tegra, the GPU was set to run at the lowest clock setting so that the power measurements would reflect mainly the CPU's behaviour.

The aim of the accelerator, together with our previous work [1], was to provide a complete acceleration solution for LSD-SLAM, a state-of-the-art semi-dense SLAM method. The two designed architectures both achieve real-time performance, evaluated running LSD-SLAM with a pre-recorded dataset utilizing the two accelerators, with a board power draw at the wall of 15 W. So far we have compared the performance of the accelerator to that of the software implementation executing in an embedded and a desktop-grade CPU. In Table 2 we collect some representative examples of the current state of the art both in SLAM algorithms as well as typical embedded solutions.

The table is not meant to be exhaustive or rank the works. Instead, it was compiled to focus on the characteristics of different solutions and provide an overview of different software and hardware approaches to SLAM and their power characteristics[3]. The key takeaway is the gap between fast but sparse

---

[3] The power figures were often not mentioned in works, or measured with varying methods. Thus, in the interest of providing a qualitative view, we include a typical expected power for the chip/platform mentioned in the publications (e.g. nVidia 680GTX, Jetson TX1, Intel i7-4700MQ etc.). For our work, we report the estimated chip power instead of the board power to be in line with other papers.

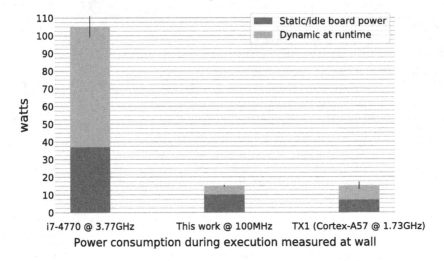

Fig. 5. Power consumption of the devices tested.

odometry with no large-scale capabilities or loop-closure on embedded systems and accurate, complex and dense solutions occupying different positions on the algorithmic landscape but requiring high-end hardware for real-time operation.

Table 2. State-of-the-art SLAM examples. Compiled with a focus on features and characteristics of different solutions to demonstrate the breadth of the field

Work	Type	Hardware plat	Density	Close-loop	Inertial	Typical power
[8]	SLAM	Laptop CPU	Sparse	✓		38–47 W
[2]	SLAM	Laptop CPU	Semi-dense	✓		40–50 W
[13]	SLAM	GPU accelerated	Dense	✓		170–250 W
Ours	SLAM	FPGA SoC	Semi-dense	✓		6–7 W
[7]	SLAM	Laptop CPU	Sparse	✓	✓	30–50 W
[4]	Odometry	Laptop/Jetson-Tx1	Sparse			40 W/15 W
[12]	Kernel Acc	FPGA	Sparse			5.3 W
[10]	Odometry	ASIC-65nm CMOS	Sparse		✓	2–24 mW

6   Conclusions

Our findings were that the most efficient designs for the target application combine features that include a high-bandwidth streaming interface to common memory and local caching of the region of interest or if possible the entire image frame processed. Dealing with the complex control-flow of these algorithms we found the most efficient choice to be multi-rate, multi-modal units, separated by buffers. We also found the most efficient and high performance choice to be a pipeline design that follows the dataflow paradigm, trying to move every data point through once. To have the most efficient design we separated the memory accesses from the actual computation, and carried unit control parameters as metadata along the processing path leading to more efficient designs.

In conclusion, this work proposes an FPGA-based architecture that achieves the required performance to run high quality state-of-the-art semi-dense SLAM with high-end desktop performance at the power level of an embedded device. It has good scalability and is parametrised to address various SLAM specifications and target different FPGA-SoC devices, demonstrated by successfully running alongside the accelerator from [1] to provide cutting-edge performance.

Acknowledgments. The support of the EPSRC Centre for Doctoral Training in High Performance Embedded and Distributed Systems (HiPEDS, Grant Reference EP/L016796/1) is gratefully acknowledged.

References

1. Boikos, K., Bouganis, C.S.: A high-performance system-on-chip architecture for direct tracking for SLAM. In: 27th International Conference on Field Programmable Logic and Applications (FPL). IEEE (2017)
2. Engel, J., Schöps, T., Cremers, D.: LSD-SLAM: large-scale direct monocular SLAM. In: Fleet, D., Pajdla, T., Schiele, B., Tuytelaars, T. (eds.) ECCV 2014. LNCS, vol. 8690, pp. 834–849. Springer, Cham (2014). https://doi.org/10.1007/978-3-319-10605-2_54
3. Engel, J., Usenko, V., Cremers, D.: A photometrically calibrated benchmark for monocular visual odometry. arXiv:1607.02555 (2016)
4. Forster, C., Pizzoli, M., Scaramuzza, D.: SVO: fast semi-direct monocular visual odometry. In: International Conference on Robotics and Automation (ICRA). IEEE (2014)
5. Handa, A., Newcombe, R.A., Angeli, A., Davison, A.J.: Real-time camera tracking: when is high frame-rate best? In: Fitzgibbon, A., Lazebnik, S., Perona, P., Sato, Y., Schmid, C. (eds.) ECCV 2012. LNCS, vol. 7578, pp. 222–235. Springer, Heidelberg (2012). https://doi.org/10.1007/978-3-642-33786-4_17
6. Honegger, D., Oleynikova, H., Pollefeys, M.: Real-time and low latency embedded computer vision hardware based on a combination of FPGA and mobile CPU. In: International Conference on Intelligent Robots and Systems (IROS), IEEE/RSJ (2014)
7. Leutenegger, S., Lynen, S., Bosse, M., Siegwart, R., Furgale, P.: Keyframe-based visual-inertial odometry using nonlinear optimization. Int. J. Robot. Res. **34**(3), 314–334 (2015)
8. Mur-Artal, R., Montiel, J.M.M., Tardos, J.D.: ORB-SLAM: a versatile and accurate monocular slam system. IEEE Trans. Robot. **31**(5), 1147–1163 (2015)
9. Sturm, J., Bylow, E., Kerl, C., Kahl, F., Cremer, D.: Dense tracking and mapping with a quadrocopter. Unmanned Aerial Vehicle in Geomatics (UAV-g) (2013)
10. Suleiman, A., et al.: Navion: a fully integrated energy-efficient visual-inertial odometry accelerator for autonomous navigation of nano drones. In: IEEE Symposium on VLSI Circuits (2018)

11. Vincke, B., Elouardi, A., Lambert, A., Merigot, A.: Efficient implementation of EKF-SLAM on a multi-core embedded system. In: IECON 2012–38th Annual Conference on IEEE Industrial Electronics Society, pp. 3049–3054. IEEE (2012)
12. Weberruss, J., Kleeman, L., Boland, D., Drummond, T.: FPGA acceleration of multilevel ORB feature extraction for computer vision. In: 27th International Conference on Field Programmable Logic and Applications (FPL). IEEE (2017)
13. Whelan, T., et al.: Real-time large-scale dense RGB-D SLAM with volumetric fusion. Int. J. Robot. Res. 34(4–5), 598–626 (2015)

High-Level Synthesis

Evaluating LULESH Kernels on OpenCL FPGA

Zheming Jin[✉] and Hal Finkel

Leadership Computing Facility,
Argonne National Laboratory, Argonne, IL 60439, USA
zjin@anl.gov

Abstract. FPGAs are becoming promising heterogeneous computing components for high-performance computing. In this paper, we evaluate the resource utilizations, performance, and performance per watt of our implementations of the LULESH kernels in OpenCL on an Arria10-based FPGA platform. LULESH is a complex proxy application in the CORAL benchmark suite. We choose two representative kernels "CalcFBHourglassForceForElems" and "EvalEOSForElems" from the application in our study. Compared with the baseline implementations, our optimizations improve the performance by a factor of 1.65X and 2.96X for the two kernels on the FPGA, respectively. Using directives for accelerator programming, we also evaluate the performance of the kernels on an Intel Xeon 16-core CPU and an Nvidia K80 GPU. We find that the FPGA, constrained by the memory bandwidth, can perform 1.05X to 3.4X better than the CPU and GPU for small problem sizes. For the first kernel, the performance per watt on the FPGA is 1.59X and 7.1X higher than that on an Intel Xeon 16-core CPU and an Nvidia K80 GPU, respectively. For the second kernel, the performance per watt on the GPU is 1.82X higher than that on the FPGA. However, the performance per watt on the FPGA is 1.77X higher than that on the CPU.

Keywords: FPGA · OpenCL · LULESH · Kernel optimizations

1 Introduction

Heterogeneous reconfigurable computing systems are becoming competitive hardware accelerators for scientific applications [1–6]. A standard central processing unit (CPU) with an attached hardware accelerator such as a field-programmable gate array (FPGA), allows users to evaluate the benefits of offloading computationally intensive tasks of an application to the accelerator. With FPGA-based reconfigurable computing systems, programming standards have facilitated the transformation of algorithms from standard systems to heterogeneous systems.

Open Computing Language (OpenCL) is an open-source, royalty-free framework for writing parallel and portable programs on CPUs, graphics processing units (GPUs), FPGAs, and other hardware accelerators [7]. Several FPGA vendors have been constantly improving the OpenCL conformant compilers [8–11]. The maturing compilers enable developers and researchers, who have little experience in hardware development, to express algorithms in a high-level language, and then instruct the compiler to realize the hardware implementations on an FPGA.

© Springer Nature Switzerland AG 2019
C. Hochberger et al. (Eds.): ARC 2019, LNCS 11444, pp. 199–213, 2019.
https://doi.org/10.1007/978-3-030-17227-5_15

In this paper, we use LULESH, a complex proxy application, to evaluate the potential of using an OpenCL-based FPGA platform for developing high-performance computing applications. We choose the representative kernels from the application, and explore the kernel optimizations and their resource and performance implications on a heterogeneous computing platform that features an Intel Arria 10 FPGA. Taking the directive-based accelerator programming approach, we also evaluate the performance of the kernels on an Intel Xeon 16-core CPU with OpenMP and an Nvidia K80 GPU with OpenACC. This paper makes the following contributions:

- We transform the OpenMP C kernels into the OpenCL kernels for an FPGA
- We evaluate the resource and performance implications of our optimizations of the OpenCL kernels on the Intel Arria 10 FPGA
- We compare the performance of the kernel implementations on the CPU, GPU and FPGA platforms.

2   Porting of LULESH Kernels to OpenCL FPGA

2.1   LULESH Kernels

Livermore Unstructured Lagrangian Explicit Shock Hydrodynamics (LULESH) has been widely studied and ported to different programming models, such as OpenMP, CUDA C/C++, OpenACC [12]. LULESH is also one of the large-scale scientific applications in the set of benchmarks of the CORAL collaborative exascale effort [13]. Data parallelism in LULESH is exploited through a hexahedral mesh at both vertex (kinematic values) and element (thermodynamic variables) levels. Generally, each element can be processed independently of the other. The number of elements in the cube mesh along each dimension is set at runtime.

There are 45 statically scheduled OpenMP parallel loops over elements and vertices in the LULESH 2.0 OpenMP implementation and 10 kernels in the CUDA C/C++ implementation [14]. In this paper, we focus on the two kernels "CalcFBHour-glassForceForElems" and "EvalEOSForElems". Both kernels are interesting as they are floating-point intensive with various floating-point operations. The first kernel has no control flow while the second kernel contains data-dependent control flow and a large number of intermediate values. There are seven inner loops in the first kernel, and the trip counts of the inner loops are static, which allows the compiler to perform the optimization of loop unrolling. The trip count of the inner loop in the second kernel is determined at runtime from a set of values, which prevents the compiler from performing loop optimizations. Overall, the two kernels are representative of the range of kernels found in the application.

2.2   OpenCL Implementation of CalcFBHourglassForceForElems

The baseline OpenCL implementation of the kernel is shown in Listing 1. The function "CalcElemFBHourglassForce()", which is called in the OpenMP C kernel, is flattened as the loops from L2 to L7. The "__global" qualifier indicates that the data pointed to by a pointer are stored in global memory. The "restrict" keyword is added for each global address space. Inserting the keyword in pointer argument prevents the compiler from creating unnecessary memory dependencies between non-conflict memory load and store operations. The "gamma" array is stored in a constant memory. In each iteration of loop L1, each work-item, identified by the OpenCL API function "get_-global_id(0)", loads eight consecutive elements from the arrays "x8n", "y8n", and "z8n" for the dot product operations with eight consecutive elements in the gamma array. The results are then used to compute each column in the 2D array "hourgam". Due to the space constraints, calculating the coefficient and loading eight elements from the arrays "xd", "yd", and "zd" at the indices specified by the eight consecutive elements in the array "elemToNode" are omitted. It should be pointed out that the indices are not necessarily consecutive, so memory access orders to "xd", "yd", and "zd" are random. After the coefficient is computed, an 8×8 dot product is performed on each column of "hourgam" and "xd", "yd", and "zd" in loops L2, L4, and L6, respectively. The results, stored in the 1D arrays "hxx", "hyy", and "hzz", are then accessed to compute the values of the 1D arrays "hgfx", "hgfy", "hgfz" in loops L3, L5, and L7. Finally, the values of "hgfx", "hgfy", "hgfz" are written back to the global memory at the locations "fx_elem", "fy_elem", and "fz_elem".

```
__kernel void fb (
    __global const Real_t*   restrict dvdx,
    __global const Real_t*   restrict dvdy,
    __global const Real_t*   restrict dvdz,
    __global const Real_t*   restrict x8n,
    __global const Real_t*   restrict y8n,
    __global const Real_t*   restrict z8n,
    __global const Real_t*   restrict determ,
    __global const Real_t*   restrict xd,
    __global const Real_t*   restrict yd,
    __global const Real_t*   restrict zd,
    __global const Real_t*   restrict ss,
    __global const Real_t*   restrict elemMass,
    __global const Index_t*  restrict nodelist,
    __constant     Real_t*   restrict gamma,
              const Real_t            hourg,
    __global       Real_t*   restrict fx_elem,
    __global       Real_t*   restrict fy_elem,
    __global       Real_t*   restrict fz_elem )
{
    int i2 = get_global_id(0);
    Index_t i3 = 8 * i2;
    __global const Index_t* elemToNode = &nodelist[i3];
    __global Real_t *fx_local, *fy_local, *fz_local;

L1: for(Index_t i1 = 0; i1 < 4; ++i1) {
    Real_t hourmodx =
        x8n[i3]*gamma[i1*8] + … + x8n[i3+7]*gamma[i1*8+7];
    Real_t hourmody =
        y8n[i3]*gamma[i1*8] + … + y8n[i3+7]*gamma[i1*8+7];
    Real_t hourmodz =
        z8n[i3]*gamma[i1*8] + … + z8n[i3+7]*gamma[i1*8+7];

    hourgam[0][i1] = gamma[i1*8+0] - volinv*(
        dvdx[i3]*hourmodx + dvdy[i3]*hourmody + dvdz[i3]*hourmodz);
```

```
hourgam[1][i1] = gamma[i1*8+1] - volinv*(
    dvdx[i3+1]*hourmodx+dvdy[i3+1]*hourmody+dvdz[i3+1]*hourmodz );
... ...
hourgam[7][i1] = gamma[i1*8+7] - volinv*(
    dvdx[i3+7]*hourmodx+dvdy[i3+7]*hourmody+dvdz[i3+7]*hourmodz );
}

// we omit the retrieval of data from xd, yd, and zd using the indi-
ces
// computed by eight consecutive elements of the array "elemToNode"
Index_t n0si2 = elemToNode[0];
xd1[0] = xd[n0si2];
yd1[0] = yd[n0si2];
zd1[0] = zd[n0si2];
... ...

L2: for (Index_t i = 0; i < 4; i++)
    hxx[i] = hourgam[0][i]*xd1[0] + ... + hourgam[7][i]*xd1[7];
L3: for (Index_t i = 0; i < 8; i++)
    hgfx[i] = coefficient *
            (hourgam[i][0]*hxx[0] + ... + hourgam[i][3]*hxx[3]);
L4: for (Index_t i = 0; i < 4; i++)
    hyy[i] = hourgam[0][i]*yd1[0] + ... + hourgam[7][i]*yd1[7];
L5: for (Index_t i = 0; i < 8; i++)
    hgfy[i] = coefficient *
            (hourgam[i][0]*hyy[0] + ... + hourgam[i][3]*hyy[3]);
L6: for (Index_t i = 0; i < 4; i++)
    hzz[i] = hourgam[0][i]*zd1[0] + ... + hourgam[7][i]*zd1[7];
L7: for (Index_t i = 0; i < 8; i++)
    hgfz[i] = coefficient *
            (hourgam[i][0]*hzz[0] + ... + hourgam[i][3]*hzz[3]);

fx_local = &fx_elem[i3];
fx_local[0] = hgfx[0]; ... fx_local[7] = hgfx[7];
fy_local[0] = hgfy[0]; ... fy_local[7] = hgfy[7];
fz_local[0] = hgfz[0]; ... fz_local[7] = hgfz[7];
}
```

Listing. 1. The kernel "CalcFBHourglassForceForElems" in OpenCL

2.3   Optimizations of the OpenCL Kernel

Memory Access Optimization. To efficiently utilize the bandwidth of the data bus on the target FPGA system, we can use the OpenCL vector data types and operators to access data as a vector for each memory transaction to improve the memory access efficiency. Listing 2 shows the relevant modifications. The OpenCL function "vload8 ()" eliminates the indirect scaled access to "nodelist". For clarity, the "dot8" function is defined for the dot product operation of two 8-element vectors. Vector elements are accessed using a numeric index to refer to the appropriate elements in a vector. For example, "elelemToNode.s7" refers to the eighth element of the vector "elemToNode". We also call the OpenCL function "vstore8()" to write the final results as an 8-element vector to the global memory at locations "fx_elem", "fy_elem", and "fz_elem". These optimizations improve not only the readability of the kernel but the efficiency of global memory accesses.

```
__kernel void fb ( ... ... ) {
  int i2 = get_global_id(0);
  Index8_t elemToNode = vload8(i2, nodelist);
  Real8_t x8n_vec  = vload8(i2, x8n);
  Real8_t y8n_vec  = vload8(i2, y8n);
  Real8_t z8n_vec  = vload8(i2, z8n);
  Real8_t dvdx_vec = vload8(i2, dvdx);
  Real8_t dvdy_vec = vload8(i2, dvdy);
  Real8_t dvdz_vec = vload8(i2, dvdz);

  L1: for(Index_t i1 = 0; i1 < 4; ++i1) {
    Real8_t gamma_vec = vload8(i1, gamma);
    Real_t hourmodx = dot8(x8n_vec, gamma_vec);
    Real_t hourmody = dot8(y8n_vec, gamma_vec);
    Real_t hourmodz = dot8(z8n_vec, gamma_vec);
    hourgam[0][i1]  = gamma_vec.s0 - volinv * (dvdx_vec.s0*hourmodx +
                      dvdy_vec.s0*hourmody + dvdz_vec.s0*hourmodz);
    ...
    hourgam[7][i1]  = gamma_vec.s7 - volinv * (dvdx_vec.s7*hourmodx +
                      dvdy_vec.s7*hourmody + dvdz_vec.s7*hourmodz);
  }
  ... ...
  Index_t n0si2 = elemToNode.s0;
  ... ...
  Index_t n7si2 = elemToNode.s7;
  ... ...
  vstore8(hgfx_vec, i2, fx_elem);
  vstore8(hgfy_vec, i2, fy_elem);
  vstore8(hgfz_vec, i2, fz_elem);
}
```

Listing. 2. Memory access optimizations of the kernel "CalcFBHourglassForceForElems"

Loop Unrolling. Loop unrolling can improve the kernel performance by creating a feed-forward structure to increase the number of operations per clock cycle that a kernel can perform in hardware. Loop unrolling is most effective when computations involving the loop control variable can be determined at compile time. For this kernel, we unroll the inner loops using "#pragma unroll N", where "N" is the loop unrolling factor. We will evaluate the impact of loop unrolling on the performance and resource usage of the kernel implementation on the FPGA.

Kernel Vectorization. Vectorization generates a memory interface that can coalesce multiple memory loads/stores into a single wide load/store to improve memory access efficiency. In addition, the datapath of the kernel is duplicated to parallelize the kernel computation without generating additional memory interfaces for each duplicated datapath. A kernel can be vectorized by annotating the kernel function with the vendor-specific attribute "__attribute__((num_simd_work_items(SIMD_LANE_WIDTH)))". Besides the attribute-based kernel vectorization supported by the compiler, kernel vectorization can be realized by the OpenCL vector operations.

Listing 3 shows our vectorized kernel using the OpenCL vector operations. For this kernel, the number of SIMD lanes is at most two due to the FPGA resource constraints that will be shown in the next section. Each work-item is assigned the workload for two work-items in the kernel shown in Listing 2. Hence, the global work size of the vectorized kernel is reduced by half.

```
__kernel void fb ( … … )
{
  Real_t hgfx[16], hgfy[16], hgfz[16];
  Real_t hourgam[16][4];
  Real_t xd1[16], yd1[16],zd1[16];
  Real2_t coefficient, ss1, mass1, volume13;
  Real2_t det = vload2(i2, determ);
  Real2_t volinv = c1 / det;

  int i2 = get_global_id(0);
  Index16_t elemToNode = vload16 (i2,nodelist);
  Real16_t x16n_vec = vload16(i2, x8n);
  Real16_t y16n_vec = vload16(i2, y8n);
  Real16_t z16n_vec = vload16(i2, z8n);
  Real16_t dvdx_vec = vload16(i2, dvdx);
  Real16_t dvdy_vec = vload16(i2, dvdy);
  Real16_t dvdz_vec = vload16(i2, dvdz);

L1: for (Index_t i1 = 0; i1 < 4; ++i1) {
  Real8_t gamma_vec = vload8(i1, gamma);
  Real_t hourmodx  = dot8(x16n_vec.lo, gamma_vec);
  Real_t hourmody  = dot8(y16n_vec.lo, gamma_vec);
  Real_t hourmodz  = dot8(z16n_vec.lo, gamma_vec);
  Real_t hourmodx2 = dot8(x16n_vec.hi, gamma_vec);
  Real_t hourmody2 = dot8(y16n_vec.hi, gamma_vec);
  Real_t hourmodz2 = dot8(z16n_vec.hi, gamma_vec);

  hourgam[0][i1] = gamma_vec.s0 - volinv.s0*(dvdx_vec.s0*hourmodx +
                    dvdy_vec.s0*hourmody + dvdz_vec.s0*hourmodz);

  … …
  hourgam[15][i1]= gamma_vec.s7 - volinv.s1*(dvdx_vec.s15*hourmodx2 +
                    dvdy_vec.s15*hourmody2 + dvdz_vec.s15*hourmodz2);
}
  … …
Index_t n0si2 = elemToNode.s0;
  … …
Index_t nfsi2 = elemToNode.s15;
xd1[0]  = xd[n0si2];
  … …
xd1[15] = xd[nfsi2];
  … …
L2: for (Index_t i = 0; i < 4; i++)
  hxx[i] = hourgam[0][i] * xd1[0] + … + hourgam[7][i] * xd1[7];
L3: for (Index_t i = 0; i < 4; i++)
  hxx2[i] = hourgam[0][i] * xd1[8] + … + hourgam[7][i] * xd1[15];
L4: for (Index_t i = 0; i < 8; i++)
  hgfx[i] = coefficient.s0 *
            (hourgam[i][0]*hxx[0] + … + hourgam[i][3] * hxx[3]);
L5: for (Index_t i = 8; i < 16; i++)
  hgfx[i] = coefficient.s1 *
            (hourgam[i][0]*hxx2[0] + … + hourgam[i][3] * hxx2[3]);

Real16_t hgfx_vec = to_Real16(hgfx)
  … …
vstore16(hgfx_vec, i2, fx_elem);
vstore16(hgfy_vec, i2, fy_elem);
vstore16(hgfz_vec, i2, fz_elem);
}
```

Listing. 3. SIMD2 vectorization of the kernel "CalcFBHourglassForceForElems"

2.4   OpenCL Implementations of EvalEOSForElems

The baseline OpenCL implementation of the kernel "EvalEOSForElems" is converted directly from the OpenMP C kernel. To facilitate the optimization of the kernel which will be described next, the inner loop of the kernel is wrapped in an "update" function as shown in Listing 4.

```
void update(Real_t e_cut, Real_t p_cut, Real_t q_cut,
            Real_t eosvmin, Real_t eosvmax, Real_t pmin,
            Real_t emin, Real_t rho0, Index_t rep,
            Real_t e_temp, Real_t delv_temp, Real_t p_temp,
            Real_t q_temp, Real_t qq_temp, Real_t ql_temp,
            Real_t vnewc_t, Real_t *p_new_out, Real_t *e_new_out,
            Real_t *q_new_out, Real_t *pbvc_out, Real_t *bvc_out)
{
    ...
    for (Index_t j = 0; j < rep; j++) {
        // the content of the loop body is omitted to save space
    }
    *p_new_out = p_new;
    *e_new_out = e_new;
    *q_new_out = q_new;
    *bvc_out   = bvc;
    *pbvc_out  = pbvc;
}
```

Listing. 4. The function "update" wraps the loop with data-dependent trip count "rep"

Because the trip count of the loop is computed at runtime, kernel vectorization using the vendor-specific OpenCL attribute fails to vectorize the kernel. To improve the kernel performance, we vectorize the kernel using the OpenCL vector operations. Listing 5 shows the kernel vectorized with two SIMD lanes as an example. Each lane performs the same operations as in the un-vectorized kernel. However, the vectorization can improve memory access efficiency, and allows both lanes to execute in a parallel fashion to improve the computing throughput. The number of times the "update" function is called is equal to the number of SIMD lanes. Each lane performs the inner loop iterations independently of the other lanes. The "update" function helps improve the readability of the kernel. In addition, it makes kernel vectorization that involves loops less error-prone because any variables accessed in the loop body are not modified.

```
__kernel void eos ( ... ... ) {
    Index_t  elem      = get_global_id(0);
    Index2_t rep       = vload2(elem, elemRep);
    Real2_t  vnewc_t   = vload2(elem, vnewc);
    Real2_t  e_temp    = vload2(elem, e);
    Real2_t  delv_temp = vload2(elem, delv);
    Real2_t  p_temp    = vload2(elem, p);
    Real2_t  q_temp    = vload2(elem, q);
    Real2_t  qq_temp   = vload2(elem, qq);
    Real2_t  ql_temp   = vload2(elem, ql);
    Real2_t  vc        = vload2(elem, v);
    ... ...
```

```
if (eosvmin != ZERO) {
    if (vnewc_t.s0 < eosvmin)
        vnewc_t.s0 = eosvmin;
    if (vnewc_t.s1 < eosvmin)
        vnewc_t.s1 = eosvmin;
}
... ...
update(e_cut, p_cut, q_cut, eosvmin, eosvmax, pmin, emin, rho0,
rep.s0,
        e_temp.s0, delv_temp.s0, p_temp.s0, q_temp.s0, qq_temp.s0,
        ql_temp.s0, vnewc_t.s0, &p_new_out[0], &e_new_out[0],
        &q_new_out[0], &pbvc_out[0], &bvc_out[0]);

update(e_cut, p_cut, q_cut, eosvmin, eosvmax, pmin, emin, rho0,
rep.s1,
        ... ...
        &q_new_out[1], &pbvc_out[1], &bvc_out[1]);

p_new = (Real2_t)(p_new_out[0], p_new_out[1]);
... ...
bvc = (Real2_t)(bvc_out[0], bvc_out[1]);
... ...
if ( FABS(vnewc_t.s0 - ONE) < v_cut ) vnewc_t.s0 = ONE;
...
vstore2(p_new, elem, p);
vstore2(e_new, elem, e);
vstore2(q_new, elem, q);
vstore2(ssTmp, elem, ss);
vstore2(vnewc_t, elem, v);
}
```

Listing. 5. SIMD2 vectorization of the kernel EvalEOSForElems

3   Evaluation

In this section, we describe our experimental setup and results. We are interested in the resource utilizations of the kernel implementations, kernel execution time, and performance per watt. In our experiments we focus on the runtime of the kernels. We do not take into consideration the time spent moving data between the host and the device.

3.1   Experimental Setup

We use Intel FPGA SDK for OpenCL version 16.0.2 Pro Prime, and a heterogeneous computing system, which consists of a dual-socket Intel Xeon E5-2687W host and a Nallatech 385A FPGA card, for our experiment. The card features an Intel Arria 10 1150 GX FPGA chip and two channels 4 GB DDR3L-2133 memory (8 GB in total). The FPGA chip contains 427,200 adaptive logic modules, 67,244 Kb of internal memory, and 1,518 variable-precision DSP blocks. The card is installed on a host machine using a PCIe x8 3.0 interface. The theoretical DDR3 memory bandwidth limit of the card is approximately 34 GB/s. The data width between DDR3 and PHY is 64-bit and the data width between the memory controller and the user FPGA design is 512-bit.

For the resource overhead of the OpenCL runtime infrastructure on the FPGA, both the logic utilization and RAM block utilization are 12% of the total FPGA resources, and DSP is not utilized. The kernel execution time is measured with the OpenCL API function "clGetEventProfilingInfo()" that returns the time in nano-seconds consumed by the kernel execution on the FPGA.

A kernel application consists of host and kernel programs. To eliminate the warnings of unaligned memory accesses at runtime, we allocate the host side buffers to be at least 64-byte aligned, which enables direct memory access transfers to and from the FPGA. Previous research shows that current FPGAs are not suitable for a double-precision floating-point intensive kernel in terms of resource usage, performance, and power consumption [15]. Hence, each kernel performs single-precision floating-point operations (i.e., "Real_t" equals "float") in our experiment. The type of array index ("Index_t") is integer. We compile the kernels with the OpenCL floating-point optimizations enabled. The optimizations remove floating-point rounding options and conversions whenever possible, and may lead to more efficient hardware resource usage by relaxing the order of arithmetic floating-point operations. The FPGA results are verified on the host.

3.2   Resource Utilizations of the Kernel Implementations on the FPGA

Table 1 shows the resource utilizations of the kernel "CalcFBHourglassForce ForElems" on the FPGA. K0 is the baseline OpenCL kernel presented in Listing 1. We find that the toolchain fails to implement the optimized kernel in Listing 2 due to routing congestion. The congestion is caused by the overhead of realizing the inner loops in the kernel on the FPGA. K1 is the optimized kernel with the loops from L2 to L7 fully unrolled. Compared to K1, K2 fully unrolls all the loops. K3 is the vectorized kernel shown in Listing 3. K4 is the kernel vectorized with the vendor-specific attribute, and the number of SIMD lanes is two. Both kernels fully unroll the inner loops. K5 is a single work-item that iterates over the outermost loop as shown in the OpenMP C kernel. The loops from L2 to L7 are fully unrolled. Compared to K5, K6 is a single work-item kernel which fully unrolls all the inner loops. The toolchain also fails to implement a single work-item kernel with two SIMD lanes and inner loops unrolled due to FPGA routing congestion.

Table 1. Resource utilizations of the kernel implementations on the FPGA

Kernel	Logic utilization (%)	RAM blocks utilization (%)	DSP count
K0	33	60	192
K1	23	61	297
K2	20	56	489
K3	27	95	977
K4	27	95	977
K5	23	58	297
K6	21	55	489

While fully unrolling the inner loops increases the number of DSPs from 192 to 489, it eliminates the looping overhead by decreasing the logic utilization from 33% to 20%, and the utilization of RAM blocks from 60% to 56%. The manual and attribute-based vectorizations (K3 and K4) require the same resource utilizations, but 95% utilization of RAM blocks indicates that the number of SIMD lanes, constrained by the memory resources, is at most two on the target FPGA. On the other hand, the differences in resource utilizations between the NDRange kernels (K1, K2) and single work-item kernels (K5, K6) are insignificant.

Table 2 shows the resource utilizations of the kernel "EvalEOSForElems" on the FPGA. K0 is a single work-item kernel which iterates over the set of elements as in the OpenMP C kernel. K1 is an NDRange kernel whose global work size equals the number of elements. K2, K3, and K4 represent the vectorized kernels with two, four, and eight SIMD lanes, respectively. The toolchain fails to implement a kernel with 16 SIMD lanes due to the resource constraint of RAM blocks.

Table 2. Resource utilizations of the kernel implementations on the FPGA

Kernel	Logic utilization (%)	RAM blocks utilization (%)	DSP count
K0	17	18	80
K1	16	21	80
K2	17	23	160
K3	22	27	320
K4	35	45	640

3.3   Performance and Power of the Kernel Implementations on the FPGA

The problem size is given by the number of elements in the mesh. We run our experiments with the following mesh sizes: 16^3, 32^3, 64^3, 128^3, and 256^3. There is insufficient memory for buffer allocation in the OpenCL host application when the mesh size is 512^3. Each kernel is called once for one LULESH timestep. By default, the number of distinct regions, load balance, and extra cost are 11, 1, and 1, respectively. When verifying the FPGA results of the kernel "CalcFBHourglassForceForElems" by comparing them with the CPU results, we initialize the data arrays "dvdx", "dvdy", "dvdz", "x8n", "y8n", "z8n", "ss", "elemMass", "xd", "yd", "zd" using the C function "rand()" to generate random values divided by the maximum value (RAND_MAX). The seed for the random number generation is two. Randomization facilitates the validation process as the kernel outputs contain non-zero distinct values. The random data are also used for measuring the kernel performance.

Table 3. Execution time (ms) of the kernel "CalcFBHourglassForceForElems" on the FPGA

Kernel	Size = 16^3	Size = 32^3	Size = 64^3	Size = 128^3	Size = 256^3
K0	0.198	1.41	11.114	89.24	713.243
K1	0.132	0.914	7.146	56.898	454.368
K2	0.127	0.903	7.079	56.271	449.384
K3	0.19	1.377	10.796	85.874	685.545
K4	0.179	1.294	10.137	80.639	643.591
K5	0.134	0.92	7.164	57.025	457.691
K6	0.122	0.857	6.682	53.228	426.482

Table 3 shows the execution time of the implementations of the kernel "CalcFBHourglassForceForElems" for each problem size. For each kernel implementation, the execution time increases approximately by a factor of eight when the problem size increases by a factor of eight. With memory access optimizations and fully unrolling the loops L2 to L7, K1 reduces the execution time of K0 by approximately 35%. However, fully unrolling all the loops in K2 reduces the execution time of K1 by approximately 1%. Kernel vectorizations are not effective in improving the kernel performance. For example, K4 increases the execution time of K2 by approximately 43%. We consider that the performance hit is caused by the increasing number of parallel random accesses to the arrays "xd", "yd", and "zd" in the global memory for a vectorized kernel. While the performance differences between K1 and K5 are insignificant, the single work-item, which fully unrolls all the loops, can achieve approximately 5% better performance than the NDRange kernel K2.

Table 4. Execution time (ms) of the kernel "EvalEOSForElems" on the FPGA

Kernel	Size = 16^3	Size = 32^3	Size = 64^3	Size = 128^3	Size = 256^3
K0	0.178	1.066	6.593	45.658	381.763
K1	0.159	0.952	5.655	38.544	324.214
K2	0.102	0.713	4.499	31.593	261.454
K3	0.08	0.499	3.211	23.311	189.942
K4	0.072	0.293	2.145	16.478	132.048

Table 4 shows the execution time of the kernel "EvalEOSForElems" for the problem sizes. For each kernel implementation, the execution time increases approximately by a factor of eight when the problem size increases by a factor of eight. The NDRange kernel K1 reduces the execution time of the single work-item kernel K0 by 13% on average. Compared to K1, vectorization with eight lanes reduces the kernel time by a factor of 2.6.

For measuring the FPGA board power consumption, the vendor's board support package provides memory-mapped device library functions for monitoring the board power consumption in real time. The idle power of the FPGA board ranges from 27 W to 28 W. The FPGA power data includes other components, such as fan power and PCIe bus power, in addition to the FPGA chip and DRAM. The maximum power consumptions of the two kernel implementations are 35.8 W and 34.5 W, respectively.

3.4   Comparison with the CPU and GPU

The host has two CPU sockets, each with an Intel Xeon E5-2687W v2 processor (16 total cores, each 2-way hyper-threaded), clocking at 3.4 GHz, and a total of 64 GB of DDR3 RAM. The theoretical memory bandwidth is 119.4 GB/s. The CPU program using the single-precision floating-point type is compiled with an Intel C++ compiler, version 2018. The kernel optimization options are "-qopenmp -O3 -ffast-math". The outermost loop of both OpenMP C kernels are annotated with the OpenMP directive "#pragma omp parallel for simd". The inner loops of the first kernel are unrolled fully. The kernel execution time is measured using the OpenMP function "omp_get_wtime()".

We choose an Nvidia Tesla K80 with 2,496 cores as the target GPU. The theoretical memory bandwidth is 240 GB/s. The GPU's power limit is 149 W with persistence mode enabled. The idle power is approximately 26 W. The OpenACC program, based on the OpenMP C program, is compiled with a PGI compiler, version 18.3. The compiler optimization options are "-acc -ta=tesla:cc35,fastmath -O3 -Minline". The GPU power is measured with the Nvidia Management Library. For the kernel "CalcFBHourglassForceForElems", each inner loop is annotated with the OpenACC directive "#pragma acc loop independent". We observe that CUDA shared memory is used for the arrays "hgfy", "hyy", "hgfx", "hxx", "hzz", "hgfz", "hourgam, "zd1, "yd1, "xd1".

We evaluate the kernel execution time with respect to the number of OpenMP threads on the CPU and the number of vector lanes on the GPU. Table 5 shows the lowest execution time of Kernel1 (CalcFBHourglassForceForElems) and Kernel2 (EvalEOSForElems) for each problem size on the CPU, GPU, and FPGA in our experiment. The execution time of Kernel1 on the FPGA is 2.5X to 3.1X faster than that on the GPU for all problem sizes. However, the CPU is faster than the FPGA for large problem sizes (e.g., 256^3). The execution time of Kernel2 on the FPGA is slower than that on the CPU when the problem sizes are larger than 64^3. The GPU is slower than the FPGA for the smallest problem size, but the execution time on the GPU is 2X to 3.75X faster than that on the FPGA for the large problem sizes. The performance trends show that the FPGA can perform 1.05X to 3.4X better than the CPU and/or GPU for small problem sizes. As the problem sizes become larger, the limited memory bandwidth on the FPGA becomes a performance bottleneck.

Table 5. Lowest execution time (ms) of the two kernels on the CPU, GPU, and FPGA

Kernel1	Size = 16^3	Size = 32^3	Size = 64^3	Size = 128^3	Size = 256^3
CPU	0.42	1.26	7.14	51	268.1
GPU	0.307	2.365	18.86	151.53	1333.2
FPGA	0.122	0.857	6.68	53.23	426.48
Kernel2	Size = 16^3	Size = 32^3	Size = 64^3	Size = 128^3	Size = 256^3
CPU	0.11	0.625	2.64	12.96	99.97
GPU	0.076	0.147	0.656	4.42	35.13
FPGA	0.072	0.293	2.145	16.478	132.05

We define *performance per watt* as the number of elements processed per second per watt. We compute the performance per watt using the lowest kernel execution time and the maximum power consumption for the problem size of 256^3. The power consumption of Kernel1 is 91 W and 81.4 W on the CPU and GPU, respectively. The power consumption of Kernel2 is 81 W and 71 W on the CPU and GPU, respectively.

Table 6. Performance per watt of the two kernels on the CPU, GPU, and FPGA

	CPU	GPU	FPGA
Kernel1	687,672	154,596	1,098,849
Kernel2	2,071,883	6,726,411	3,682,667

Table 6 shows the performance per watt for the kernel implementations on the CPU, GPU, and FPGA. For Kernel1, the performance per watt on the FPGA is 1.59X and 7.1X higher than that on the CPU and GPU, respectively. For Kernel2, the performance per watt on the GPU is 1.82X higher than that on the FPGA. However, the performance per watt on the FPGA is 1.77X higher than that on the CPU.

4 Related Work

Previous studies explored the optimizations of LULESH for performance, power, and energy on the CPUs [16–18] and the GPUs [19–21]. In our experiment, we evaluate the performance of kernel implementations with a wide range of problem sizes, and the impacts of thread size and vector length on the kernel performance. As far as we know, the performance of the LULESH kernels on an OpenCL-based FPGA platform is not explored. On the other hand, emerging frameworks can convert a C program annotated with the OpenMP or OpenACC directives to FPGA implementations based on the vendors' OpenCL-to-FPGA design flows [22–24]. Our research work will provide useful feedback to the developers of the frameworks and compilers, enhancing the capabilities of these toolchains. Previous studies investigated the OpenCL kernel optimizations on FPGAs [25–29]. Compare to their findings, our work shows that loop unrolling can not only improve the performance but reduce the utilizations of logics and memory blocks on an FPGA. In addition, we present in details our optimizations of the LULESH kernels in OpenCL. Our vectorization method can be applied to a kernel in which data-dependent backward branching in a loop prevents a compiler from performing the attribute-based vectorization.

5 Conclusion

For floating-point intensive kernels with deep pipeline depth and many branching controls, FPGAs can achieve higher performance than the CPU and GPU when the problem size does not cause memory bandwidth constraint. While we should exploit memory access optimizations to improve memory access efficiency, expanding the limited memory bandwidth between an FPGA and an external memory will allow more scientific kernels to benefit from data parallelism and energy efficiency offered by FPGAs. Due to the resource constraints, current FPGAs are not perfectly suitable for the acceleration of double-precision floating-point intensive applications. However, the experimental results show that FPGAs are becoming energy-efficient heterogeneous computing component for supercomputing applications in research and laboratories facilities. As future work, we are interested in exploring the performance of the kernel implementations on Stratix 10 FPGAs.

Acknowledgments. The research was supported by the U.S. Department of Energy, Office of Science, under contract DE-AC02-06CH11357 and made use of the Argonne Leadership Computing Facility, a DOE Office of Science User Facility.

References

1. Huang, S., Manikandan, G.J., Ramachandran, A., Rupnow, K., Hwu, W.M.W., Chen, D.: Hardware acceleration of the pair-HMM algorithm for DNA variant calling. In: Proceedings of the 2017 ACM/SIGDA International Symposium on Field-Programmable Gate Arrays, pp. 275–284. ACM, February 2017
2. Casper, J., Olukotun, K.: Hardware acceleration of database operations. In: Proceedings of the 2014 ACM/SIGDA International Symposium on Field-Programmable Gate Arrays, pp. 151–160. ACM, February 2014
3. Inggs, G., Thomas, D., Luk, W.: A heterogeneous computing framework for computational finance. In: 2013 42nd International Conference on Parallel Processing (ICPP), pp. 688–697. IEEE, October 2013
4. Chen, D., Singh, D.: Fractal video compression in OpenCL: an evaluation of CPUs, GPUs, and FPGAs as acceleration platforms. In: 2013 18th Asia and South Pacific Design Automation Conference (ASP-DAC), pp. 297–304. IEEE, January 2013
5. Sharma, H., et al.: From high-level deep neural models to FPGAs. In: 2016 49th Annual IEEE/ACM International Symposium on Microarchitecture (MICRO), pp. 1–12. IEEE, October 2016
6. Kirsch, S., Rettig, F., Hutter, D., de Cuveland, J., Angelov, V., Lin-denstruth, V.: An FPGA-based high-speed, low-latency processing system for high-energy physics. In: 2010 International Conference on Field Programmable Logic and Applications (FPL), pp. 562–567. IEEE, August 2010
7. Stone, J.E., Gohara, D., Shi, G.: OpenCL: a parallel programming standard for heterogeneous computing systems. Comput. Sci. Eng. **12**(3), 66–73 (2010)
8. Intel FPGA SDK for OpenCL Cyclone V SoC Getting Started Guide. Intel (2017)
9. Intel FPGA SDK for OpenCL Stratix V Network Reference Platform Porting Guide. Intel (2017)
10. Intel FPGA SDK for OpenCL Arria 10 GX FPGA Development Kit Reference Platform Porting Guide. Intel (2017)
11. Loring Wirbel: Xilinx SDAccel Whitepaper. Xilinx (2014)
12. Karlin, I.: LULESH programming model and performance ports over-view (No. LLNL-TR-608824). Lawrence Livermore National Laboratory (LLNL), Livermore, CA (2012)
13. CORAL Benchmark Codes. https://asc.llnl.gov/CORAL-benchmarks/

14. Bercea, G.T., et al.: Performance analysis of OpenMP on a GPU using a CORAL proxy application. In: Proceedings of the 6th International Workshop on Performance Modeling, Benchmarking, and Simulation of High Performance Computing Systems, p. 2. ACM, November 2015

15. Jin, Z., Finkel, H., Yoshii, K., Cappello, F.: Evaluation of a floating-point intensive kernel on FPGA. In: Heras, D.B., Bougé, L. (eds.) Euro-Par 2017. LNCS, vol. 10659, pp. 664–675. Springer, Cham (2018). https://doi.org/10.1007/978-3-319-75178-8_53

16. León, E.A., Karlin, I.: Characterizing the impact of program optimizations on power and energy for explicit hydrodynamics. In: 2014 IEEE International Parallel and Distributed Processing Symposium Workshops (IPDPSW), pp. 773–781. IEEE, May 2014

17. León, E.A., Karlin, I., Grant, R.E.: Optimizing explicit hydrodynamics for power, energy, and performance. In: 2015 IEEE International Conference on Cluster Computing (CLUSTER), pp. 11–21. IEEE, September 2015

18. Wu, X., Taylor, V., Cook, J. Juedeman, T.: Performance and power characteristics and optimizations of hybrid MPI/OpenMP LULESH miniapps under various workloads. In: Proceedings of the 5th International Workshop on Energy Efficient Supercomputing, p. 4. ACM, November 2017

19. Lim, R., Malony, A., Norris, B., Chaimov, N.: Identifying optimization opportunities within kernel execution in GPU codes. In: Hunold, S., et al. (eds.) Euro-Par 2015. LNCS, vol. 9523, pp. 185–196. Springer, Cham (2015). https://doi.org/10.1007/978-3-319-27308-2_16

20. Sulyok, A.A., Balogh, G.D., Reguly, I.Z., Mudalige, G.R.: Improving locality of unstructured mesh algorithms on GPUs. arXiv preprint arXiv:1802.03749 (2018)

21. Karlin, I., McGraw, J., Gallardo, E., Keasler, J., Leon, E.A., Still, B.: Memory and parallelism exploration using the LULESH proxy application. In: 2012 SC Companion: High Performance Computing, Networking, Storage and Analysis (SCC), pp. 1427–1428. IEEE, November 2012

22. Lee, S., Vetter, J.S.: OpenARC: open accelerator research compiler for directive-based, efficient heterogeneous computing. In: Proceedings of the 23rd International Symposium on High-performance Parallel and Distributed Computing, pp. 115–120. ACM, June 2014

23. Lee, S., Kim, J., Vetter, J.S.: OpenACC to FPGA: a framework for directive-based high-performance reconfigurable computing. In: 2016 IEEE International Parallel and Distributed Processing Symposium, pp. 544–554. IEEE, May 2016

24. Sommer, L., Korinth, J., Koch, A.: OpenMP device offloading to FPGA accelerators. In: 2017 IEEE 28th International Conference on Application-specific Systems, Architectures and Processors (ASAP), pp. 201–205. IEEE, July 2017

25. Gautier, Q., Althoff, A., Meng, P., Kastner, R.: Spector: an OpenCL FPGA benchmark suite. In: 2016 International Conference on Field-Programmable Technology (FPT), pp. 141–148. IEEE, December 2016

26. Wang, Z., He, B., Zhang, W., Jiang, S.: A performance analysis framework for optimizing OpenCL applications on FPGAs. In: 2016 IEEE International Symposium on High Performance Computer Architecture (HPCA), pp. 114–125. IEEE, March 2016

27. Wang, Z., Zhang, S., He, B., Zhang, W.: Melia: a map reduce framework on OpenCL-based FPGAs. IEEE Trans. Parallel Distrib. Syst. **27**(12), 3547–3560 (2016)

28. Settle, S.O.: High-performance dynamic programming on FPGAs with OpenCL. In: Proceedings of the IEEE High Perform Extreme Computing Conference (HPEC), pp. 1–6, September 2013

29. Chen, D., Singh, D.: Fractal video compression in OpenCL: an evaluation of CPUs, GPUs, and FPGAs as acceleration platforms. In: 2013 18th Asia and South Pacific Design Automation Conference (ASP-DAC), pp. 297–304. IEEE, January 2013

The TaPaSCo Open-Source Toolflow
for the Automated Composition
of Task-Based Parallel Reconfigurable
Computing Systems

Jens Korinth⬤, Jaco Hofmann⬤, Carsten Heinz⬤, and Andreas Koch$^{(\boxtimes)}$⬤

Technical University of Darmstadt, Darmstadt, Germany
{korinth,hofmann,heinz,koch}@esa.tu-darmstadt.de

Abstract. In this paper we present *TaPaSCo – the Task Parallel Systems Composer*, an open-source, toolflow and software framework for automated construction of System-on-Chip FPGA designs for task parallel computation. TaPaSCo aims to increase the *scalability* and *portability* of FPGA designs by performing the construction of heterogeneous many-core architectures from custom processing elements, and providing a simple, uniform programming interface to utilize spatially parallel computation on FPGAs. A key feature of TaPaSCo's is automated *design space exploration*, which can be performed in parallel on a computing cluster. This greatly simplifies scaling hardware designs, facilitating iterative growth and portability across FPGA devices and families.

Keywords: FPGA · Reconfigurable computing ·
Design space exploration · System-on-Chip design ·
Design automation · High-level synthesis · Scalability · Portability ·
TaPaSCo · Heterogeneous computing · Parallel computing

1 Introduction

Compared to modern software development methods it has been and still is very hard to achieve **scalability** and **portability** for FPGA-based solutions.

In this paper we present *TaPaSCo, the Task Parallel Systems Composer*, an open source toolchain addressing these challenges. TaPaSCo consists of a scriptable toolflow for the automated construction of heterogeneous, many-core System-on-Chip hardware architectures, and a set of APIs to facilitate task parallel computing on TaPaSCo FPGA accelerator designs. TaPaSCo aims to harness and exponentiate the power of existing tools and approaches by providing the missing *glue* between state of the art HLS tools and modern parallel computing paradigms and languages: It allows the designer of FPGA accelerators to raise their level of abstraction and disregard many specific features of the target FPGA by delegation of optimizing these choices to TaPaSCo's automated *design space exploration*. Using TaPaSCo, existing designs can be more easily

© Springer Nature Switzerland AG 2019
C. Hochberger et al. (Eds.): ARC 2019, LNCS 11444, pp. 214–229, 2019.
https://doi.org/10.1007/978-3-030-17227-5_16

re-targeted to new FPGAs and boards without requiring changes to the accelerators themselves. Furthermore, this allows to postpone the decision for the target technology until much later in the design process. TaPaSCo's APIs complete the picture by providing the necessary foundations to implement higher-level runtimes (e.g., OpenCL, OpenMP) for platform-agnostic application software.

The rest of this paper is organized as follows: Sect. 2 contains a brief survey of related work, in Sect. 3 we give a general overview of TaPaSCo and its primary design abstractions. Specifically, we aim to show how TaPaSCo addresses portability, scalability and extensibility of FPGA hardware designs for systems-on-chip. A practical usage example, including the actual commands for using the tool, is discussed in Sect. 4. The simple use-case is the creation of a many-core design using MicroBlaze CPUs as processing elements, demonstrating the usage and advantages of TaPaSCo. However, the tool easily allows intermixing of arbitrary kinds of PEs (software-programmable processors, IP blocks, HLS-generated functions etc.) to create truly heterogeneous systems, as well.

2   Related Work

The work presented here is not focused on actual high level synthesis tools such as Vivado HLS [20], Nymble [9], or LegUp [3]. Instead, it was initiated to address common problems occurring when employing these tools: When trying to assess the performance of HLS tools, one can either stop in *simulation* at the cycle count level (using far from realistic assumptions about the behavior of memory in a real system), or perform the experiments on *real hardware*. The latter, however, requires one to implement the entire hardware and software design required to run the experiments. Not only is this approach tedious and error-prone, but most importantly the impact of the system design on overall performance and characteristics greatly reduces the comparability of different implementations. This problem is precisely what motivated the work on Thread-PoolComposer [12], our prior research effort in this area. TaPaSCo is based on ThreadPoolComposer, which is in turn is closely related to previous work on ReconOS [14], hthreads [15], or FUSE [11]. ThreadPoolComposer aimed to provide both programming and hardware abstractions to increase FPGA developer productivity. But unlike the other approaches, ThreadPoolComposer focused on typical high-performance computing systems using a mainstream, non-modified Linux kernel, and catering for commercial (OpenCL, OpenMP) and academic (X10 [4,5], FastFlow [2]) parallel programming frameworks. Redsharc [17] is an academic hardware/software system design framework with a similar approach as TaPaSCo; it shares concepts such as the grouping of heterogeneous PEs into clusters, and uniform, scriptable construction of cluster groups into architectures. However, the Redsharc source is not publicly available, is not portable and does not support current hardware. Furthermore, Redsharc is focused on hardware architectures processing regular data streams, whereas TaPaSCo explicitly supports more general hardware that also allows random-memory accesses. Similar commercial tools, such as Xilinx SDSoC and SDAccel became publicly available later in late 2015/2016; the former works only on select boards of the Zynq family of FPGAs, the latter only on select PCIe-based boards for OpenCL computing and does not provide support for job dispatches or custom infrastructure cores. In contrast, TaPaSCo allows much deeper customization, e.g., black-box extension of existing cores with caches, using infrastructure cores to change the interconnection (e.g., by buses, networks-on-chip) of processing elements and interface adapters. TaPaSCo's customizability is key to enable performance for very different computing approaches by not imposing too many restrictions on the design. In [7], ThreadPoolComposer was extended with automated design space exploration capabilities to increase scalability of the designs even further. TaPaSCo extends this significantly by providing a fully asynchronous job launch interface, support for a memory hierarchy of device-local and PE-local memories, a unified kernel module interface, and offering support for a wide range of FPGA families from small embedded to high performance segments with PCIe Gen3/4-based data transfers (currently supported boards: Digilent ZedBoard, Digilent PyNQ, Xilinx ZC706, Xilinx ZCU102 UltraScale+ MPSoC, Xilinx VC709, Xilinx VCU118 and NetFPGA SUME).

3   TaPaSCo

TaPaSCo consists of two main parts: An automated toolflow to generate System-on-Chip (SoC) designs based on custom processing elements (PEs, e.g., as Verilog/VHDL, Bluespec, Chisel, or generated using HLS), and a general application programming interface (API) and accompanying libraries to facilitate platform-agnostic software development. In the following, Sect. 3.1 will focus on the former, Sect. 3.2 on the latter. In Sects. 3.3, 3.4 and 3.5, we will argue how TaPaSCo addresses the central issues of portability, scalability and extensibility for future proofing FPGA designs.

3.1   Hardware Design Abstractions

TaPaSCo hardware designs as shown in Fig. 2 consist of a configurable number of *processing elements (PEs)*; PEs of the same *kind* are grouped into PE *clusters*, which are in turn grouped into the *Architecture* of the design. Finally, the *Platform* instantiates board- or FPGA-specific resources to implement data and control accesses, and signaling, leading to the complete system shown in Fig. 3. TaPaSCo hardware designs are based on three fundamental abstractions (ordered by scope): **A1:** T-model of processing elements, **A2:** Architecture, and **A3:** Platform. Each of the abstractions is implemented as a set of *scripts* in TaPaSCo: **A1** consists of scripts to configure the interface generation of supported HLS compilers. **A2** is implemented in a modular Tcl script to perform the wiring of *PEs* into *clusters*, and *clusters* into an *Architecture*, using suitable bus topologies. The fundamental idea is to keep the *Architecture* independent of the target FPGA, making it reusable across targets. **A3** finally connects the *Architecture* to the hardware components of the target FPGA board. The scripts

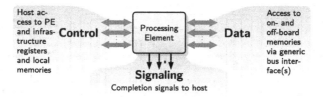

Fig. 1. Basic *T-shape* of processing elements: each processing element has a *control channel*, a *data channel* and a *signaling* channel, all of which can be implemented by arbitrary means, e.g., AXI4, or Avalon.

currently utilize the Vivado Tcl APIs to automate the wiring of high pin count interfaces (e.g., AXI4). The *T-model*, named for its T-shape shown in Fig. 1, defines the interface requirements for a TaPaSCo PE module and abstracts from implementation details. Each PE in the T-model requires three basic channels: 1. a control channel to communicate with the host, 2. a signaling channel to indicate completion, and 3. a data channel to access data. The exact nature of the channels (e.g., AXI4, Avalon, Wishbone, NoC, . . .) is determined by **A2**, the *Architecture*: TaPaSCo supports heterogeneous PE architectures, i.e., groups of different PE kinds scaling linearly. To achieve this, PEs are grouped into PE *clusters*, each *cluster* containing all PEs of a kind and abstracting away the concrete number of contained individual PEs. The T-shape is repeated here: Each *cluster* itself is T-shaped and can be wired like the PEs themselves (see Fig. 2).

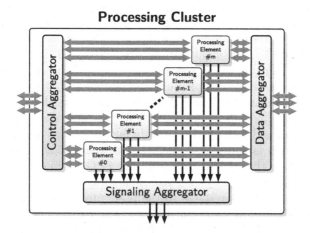

Fig. 2. Processing elements of same kind are grouped into *clusters* using channel aggregators for the three basic channels, e.g., AXI4 Interconnects and interrupt controllers.

On the outermost platform-independent level, this process is repeated across *clusters*. The collective term we use to describe the automated wiring of all three

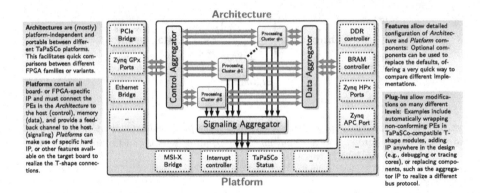

Fig. 3. Using the T-model to hierarchically repeat the automated wiring process to connect the individual clusters into a heterogeneous pool architecture. The availability and presence of components in the *Platform* layer depends on the target FPGA and board; the *Architecture* does not depend on their presence or availability, making the essential design portable.

levels is *Architecture*, i.e., the organization and wiring of PEs into a heterogeneous pool as shown in Fig. 3. In TaPaSCo, *Architectures* are designed to be platform-agnostic: Whatever protocol or technique is used to actually perform the wiring, this part of the design should remain portable. TaPaSCo currently uses an *Architecture* based on AMBA AXI4: All control interfaces are AXI4Lite slaves, all memory interfaces are AXI4 masters, signaling is done via a single wire interrupt line. AXI4 Interconnects are used for both slave and master interfaces at the *cluster* and *Architecture* levels to wire the connections. Note that TaPaSCo's blackbox approach regarding the PE internals is suitable to support many different compute architectures: The AXI-based architecture has been used both in the random-access architecture discussed in Sect. 4 for near-data processing, as well as for a complex high-performance Stereovision accelerator based on a systolic array [7]. It would also be entirely possible to use TaPaSCo to connect only a single PE (containing a full architecture inside). TaPaSCo does not impose a model on the PE, it only facilitates easy spatial replication. The last abstraction is called the *Platform*: All parts of the hardware design which are specific to the target board (e.g., the FPGA, pin constraints, peripherals, memory) are generated by the *Platform* abstraction. Minimally, a *Platform* must connect the control interfaces to the host, provide some memory shared between PEs and the host, and an interface toward the host for PE signals. Furthermore, all peripherals and other infrastructure are instantiated here (e.g., memory controllers, interrupt controllers). *Platform* scripts can be seen as *smart base designs*: They instantiate target-specific infrastructure, but retain a significant amount of configurability without requiring manual intervention by the user. Originally, both ThreadPoolComposer and TaPaSCo used a fixed address map scheme to facilitate communication between host and PEs. Now TaPaSCo solves this more elegantly by storing the on-chip address map in a custom hardware module generated on the fly during composition. This address map is then queried at runtime by the software layers. This approach yields great flexibility: E.g., every kind of PE may have a different number and/or differently sized control interfaces. It is also possible to integrate custom, user-defined infrastructure modules and use the TaPaSCo software layers to communicate with them: The TaPaSCo scripts for *Architecture* and *Platform* are skeletons with numerous injection points for extensions, where *plug-ins* can be inserted to modify the design in flight.

Example 1. If a PE does not have a TaPaSCo-compatible register interface (see [16] for a more detailed description of the register conventions used by TaPaSCo), a plug-in can automatically instantiate a suitable wrapper and TaPaSCo continue with the automated wiring. A different example can be found in the zedboard *Platform*: The Digilent ZedBoard [6] has an on-board OLED display that can be used to show the number of completion signals at each slot; this is achieved by a plug-in that instantiates the corresponding display controller and wires it to the design. Such modifications are common, especially when exploring different variations of a design, e.g., using different DMA engines. To simplify the use of such plug-ins, TaPaSCo provides support for so called *features*: Features can be defined using a simple, but consistent key-value syntax and can be queried by plug-ins during composition. This allows the user to easily pass configuration values, and enable or disable specific plug-ins.

3.2   Software Design Abstractions

Key to providing a productive environment for FPGA developers is to eliminate as many manual tasks as possible that are not directly related to the problem at hand. This specifically includes handling low-level communications with the hardware. Using an automated process as described in Sect. 3.1 to construct hardware designs has the benefit of yielding very regular designs, which can be used in software without requiring repetitive manual protocol implementations. The core abstraction for the *application programming interface (API)* of TaPaSCo is the *task-parallel model*: Every computation is broken into *tasks*, which can execute in parallel. Each work item of a task is split into a number of individual *jobs*, each of which can be computed independently. This model is widely used in heterogeneous computing, because it accommodates different computing architectures by abstracting computation from concrete algorithm: The user submits jobs to the abstract machine, which are then processed by any of its available PEs, regardless of their internals. Even the original interface defined by TaPaSCo s predecessor ThreadPoolComposer was already sufficiently portable to also support execution on *digital signal processors*, without having to change the host code (cf. [16]). In TaPaSCo's software framework, a task corresponds to a *cluster* and job corresponds to one execution of a single PE. At this granularity, a domain expert can develop the core application by defining tasks and splitting work items into jobs; this is the top-most, user-facing

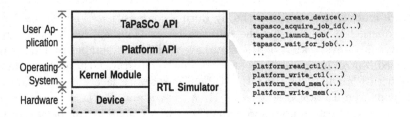

Fig. 4. Software layer hierarchy in TaPaSCo: the top-level API provides task-parallel abstraction, the *Platform API* provides a thin user-space layer above either (a) the operating system primitives implemented in the *TaPaSCo Loadable Kernel Module (TLKM)*, which in turn interacts directly with the device(s), or, alternatively, (b) interfaces with a RTL simulator of the hardware design.

API that TaPaSCo defines (for a concrete usage example see Sect. 4). To implement this rather abstract API, TaPaSCo internally mirrors the abstractions of the hardware design (see Fig. 4): The *TaPaSCo library* is concerned with the *Architecture*. It manages PEs and the address map, performs the communication required to transfer data and arguments, launch a job, and wait for the result(s). In order to implement the interactions in a platform-agnostic manner, the TaPaSCo library is implemented on top of the *platform library*, which encodes primitive operations, such as accessing a PE's registers, or allocate/free and read/write device-accessible memory. This allows any *Architecture* to be used on any *Platform* with the same user application code. The platform library operations are themselves realized using an operating system layer implemented in the *TaPaSCo loadable kernel module (TLKM)*: Without going into unnecessary details, TaPaSCo uses a fixed set of `ioctl` commands, which need only be implemented at most once for each *Platform* (often code can even be shared among families of devices). They are sufficiently generic to accommodate a wide variety of transport mechanisms, from shared memory (e.g., Zynq, MPSoC) to PCIe Gen3 (e.g., VC709). Please see our documentation [13] for more details on the internal APIs.

3.3   Portability

The overall approach outlined in Sects. 3.1 and 3.2 has proven to be very useful to isolate the domain expert (i.e., the application developer) from the details of the chosen target platform: A TaPaSCo application's code does not need to be changed when executing on a different TaPaSCo platform.

This also applies to the hardware level: If a hardware module conforms to the TaPaSCo interface requirements, it can be used on any supported platform. Furthermore, TaPaSCo was designed to be easily extensible to new platforms: At the time of writing, TaPaSCo supports seven different platforms, ranging from small embedded boards using Zynq devices, up to high-performance PCIe-based expansion cards with large FPGA devices.

3.4   Scalability

Scaling a TaPaSCo design, e.g., from using five PEs of a certain kind to 30 PEs, requires only automated rebuilding of the hardware design via TaPaSCo. Everything else, including the application code, does not need to be changed and will adapt automatically to the new design. Furthermore, additional support for *design space exploration* in TaPaSCo simplifies a crucial task in optimization: When designing an SoC with a large number of PEs, there will always be a trade-off between the number of PEs in the design and its operating frequency. More PEs means more potential for spatial parallelism and better area utilization; however, with increasing area, path lengths in the design also increase, making timing closure increasingly more difficult to achieve. Finding a good trade-off for any given application can be a very tedious and slow trial-and-error process. TaPaSCo supports the user by providing an *automated design space exploration (DSE)* along three axes of operating frequency, area utilization, and use of design variants. Each axis can be separately activated or deactivated in a DSE run, e.g., to determine only the highest operating frequency for a fixed number of PEs, or find the maximal number of PEs that will fit on a given device at a fixed operating frequency. The algorithm first computes upper and lower bounds for each activated axis. For the operating frequency, TaPaSCo uses an *out-of-context synthesis run* (abbreviated as OOC here) to perform a full place-and-route on an otherwise empty target FPGA. Since this design is almost unconstrained, this yields an overly optimistic approximation of the achievable operating frequency. The lower bound is usually determined by the target FPGA; by default, TaPaSCo cuts off at 50 MHz, discarding compositions with a lower operating frequency. The remaining interval is then divided evenly in 5 MHz steps by default, each step being the frequency component of a coordinate in the design space. Bounds for area utilization are also based on out-of-context synthesis: OOC yields an estimate of the area used by each kind of PE. The area utilization for the entire design is then estimated using a linear extrapolation based on the number of PEs of each kind and an estimation for the architectural overhead. By default, TaPaSCo assumes zero overhead, making a very optimistic approximation. This is justified, as modern place-and-route tools perform very extensive optimizations and can compact similar circuits very aggressively, sometimes yielding lower values for area utilization than the linear extrapolation would suggest. Since these optimization efforts are very hard to estimate a-priori for any given design, TaPaSCo compensates by using an optimistic approximation of the design overhead instead, to avoid cutting off viable designs. To increase or decrease the area utilization, the initial composition is scaled linearly in the number of PEs. This yields the area component of the design space coordinates. Design *variants* represent different implementations of the same PE kind, e.g., using more Block RAM, or more pipeline stages, or different sizes of FIFOs. For each *cluster*, a single variant is chosen; the design variants are then generated combinatorially by combining with every variant of every other PE kind in the composition. This yields the choice of a design variant as the third coordinate component within the design space. Due to combinatorial explosion, the size of the design space quickly exceeds the limits for brute force exploration. Therefore TaPaSCo supports different heuristic functions to score each element in the design space and then explore batches of elements ordered by their score; at each step, the design space is pruned, e.g., of the elements which have a lesser score than the best element found so far. Since such explorations still require a lot of computing power, TaPaSCo supports the use of the Slurm Workload Manager [1] to parallelize the DSE across entire high-performance computing clusters.

Example 2. Assume the user specifies an initial composition consisting of three different PE kinds, called A, B and C, with two PEs in the A *cluster*, four PEs in the B *cluster*, and six PEs in the C *cluster*. In TaPaSCo syntax this would be expressed as $[A \times 2, B \times 4, C \times 6]$; in the following, we will call such a configuration a *composition*. When scaling linearly, the smallest composition with the same ratios containing all PEs is thus $[A \times 1, B \times 2, C \times 3]$. Also assume that TaPaSCo has determined via OOC that the largest composition fitting on the target FPGA is $[A \times 3, B \times 6, C \times 9]$. This would yield three viable compositions in the design space. Furthermore assume that the OOC for A has given us an f_{max} of 100 MHz, 75 MHz for B and 150 MHz for C. Since all PEs are clocked at the same frequency, B provides the upper bound on frequency at 75 MHz. Leaving the lower cut-off at the 50 MHz default yields six frequency coordinates: 50 MHz, 55 MHz, 60 MHz, 65 MHz, 70 MHz and 75 MHz. Finally, assume that only A has variants, called A0 and A1. Thus, the design space TaPaSCo will explore will contain a total of 36 elements (listed in Table 1). Details of the actual DSE algorithm, including the heuristics used for pruning the search space, have been presented in [8].

Table 1. Initial design space for TaPaSCo DSE run. F = Target design frequency, R = Replication factor.

F \ R	1	2	3
50	$[A0 \times 1, B \times 2, C \times 3]$	$[A0 \times 2, B \times 4, C \times 6]$	$[A0 \times 3, B \times 6, C \times 9]$
	$[A1 \times 1, B \times 2, C \times 3]$	$[A1 \times 2, B \times 4, C \times 6]$	$[A1 \times 3, B \times 6, C \times 9]$
55	$[A0 \times 1, B \times 2, C \times 3]$	$[A0 \times 2, B \times 4, C \times 6]$	$[A0 \times 3, B \times 6, C \times 9]$
	$[A1 \times 1, B \times 2, C \times 3]$	$[A1 \times 2, B \times 4, C \times 6]$	$[A1 \times 3, B \times 6, C \times 9]$
60	$[A0 \times 1, B \times 2, C \times 3]$	$[A0 \times 2, B \times 4, C \times 6]$	$[A0 \times 3, B \times 6, C \times 9]$
	$[A1 \times 1, B \times 2, C \times 3]$	$[A1 \times 2, B \times 4, C \times 6]$	$[A1 \times 3, B \times 6, C \times 9]$
65	$[A0 \times 1, B \times 2, C \times 3]$	$[A0 \times 2, B \times 4, C \times 6]$	$[A0 \times 3, B \times 6, C \times 9]$
	$[A1 \times 1, B \times 2, C \times 3]$	$[A1 \times 2, B \times 4, C \times 6]$	$[A1 \times 3, B \times 6, C \times 9]$
70	$[A0 \times 1, B \times 2, C \times 3]$	$[A0 \times 2, B \times 4, C \times 6]$	$[A0 \times 3, B \times 6, C \times 9]$
	$[A1 \times 1, B \times 2, C \times 3]$	$[A1 \times 2, B \times 4, C \times 6]$	$[A1 \times 3, B \times 6, C \times 9]$
75	$[A0 \times 1, B \times 2, C \times 3]$	$[A0 \times 2, B \times 4, C \times 6]$	$[A0 \times 3, B \times 6, C \times 9]$
	$[A1 \times 1, B \times 2, C \times 3]$	$[A1 \times 2, B \times 4, C \times 6]$	$[A1 \times 3, B \times 6, C \times 9]$

3.5   Extensibility

Given the vast variety of scenarios in which FPGAs are often used, it is impossible for a generic toolchain like TaPaSCo to anticipate and support every use

case out of the box. Instead of a one-size-fits-all approach we opted for a high
degree of modularity and extensibility in all parts and aspects of TaPaSCo. Using
plug-ins and features to modify the hardware design generated by TaPaSCo has
already been discussed in Sect. 3.1. Adding new *Platforms* or *Architectures* is
very easy, too. But one of the core goals of TaPaSCo is to provide a re-usable
foundation for further work and to eliminate some of the tedious work for every
prototyping engineer or scientist. We therefore also aimed at making most parts
of TaPaSCo modular and allow for their standalone usage.

Example 3. Some people may not be interested in using the task-parallel abstractions provided by the TaPaSCo API, but would still like to use the rest of the
toolchain to iterate their designs more quickly; in this case, the *Platform* API
can be used on its own to directly interact with the hardware. For others, the
TaPaSCo API may not be sufficiently abstract yet; in this case, TaPaSCo can be
used as a *foundation* for implementing more complex environments and frameworks, such as OpenMP (cf. [18]), or OpenCL.

4   Case Study: MicroBlaze-Based Many-Core Architecture

TaPaSCo was recently used in a study of *near data processing (NDP)*, where
an FPGA is inserted in between storage elements and the host, and simple
data processing tasks (which require no inter-task synchronization facilities) are
offloaded to be performed by the FPGA instead of the host. This approach can
free the main CPU from trivial, but data-intensive tasks, such as summing or
calculating averages, and avoid expensive data transfers. To simplify the programming of the system, the first prototype of the NDP system, called *Shishito*,
consists of MicroBlaze soft-core processors [19] with small local BRAM storage
and direct access to the memory controller. Each core runs independently of
and asynchronously to the others without synchronization across tasks. The following sections will discuss the design of the Shishito processing elements and
the overall architecture, then proceed to illustrate how TaPaSCo accelerated
the whole design and implementation process, showing the actual commands
required to assemble the SoC. The NDP use-case also employs capabilities just
recently added to TaPaSCo to describe and manage more complex memory systems (e.g., distinguishing between PE-global and PE-local memories).

4.1   Shishito Processing Elements

To allow TaPaSCo to automatically construct the SoC design for us, the first
step was to design a TaPaSCo-compatible MicroBlaze PE. The MicroBlaze processor has a multitude of configuration options, from minor changes such as
enabled/disabled exception support, over support for optional instructions, up to
different instruction pipeline architectures. In the NDP scenario, the programs
running in the MicroBlazes are relatively simple. We thus deactivated most

instruction set extensions in favor of larger data caches. A common headache in this scenario is to find a good size for the caches, so we decided to explore different sizes, where both data and instruction cache share the same BRAM-backed storage. To make this design work well with TaPaSCo, we needed to wrap it into the T-shape, previously discussed in Sect. 3.1, as follows:

While the AXI4 memory interface can simply be turned on using a configuration parameter for the MicroBlaze, the signaling and control interfaces require additional modules. The control interface is implemented as an AXI4Lite register file module written in Chisel, called MBCtrl. This module uses the direct wire interface of the MicroBlaze to hold the processor in reset until the start register is written. The processor will then start to execute its program, which should end with triggering an interrupt at a local interrupt controller (see Fig. 5). MBCtrl receives and acknowledges the interrupt immediately, then puts the MicroBlaze back in reset. Finally, it raises the interrupt on the external line to signal completion to the host.

MicroBlaze Processing Element for TaPaSCo

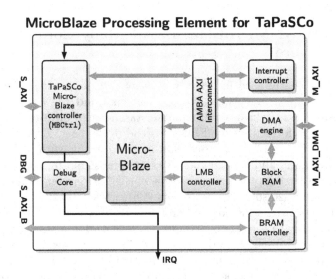

Fig. 5. Shishito processing element: MBCtrl provides an AXI4Lite slave interface for TaPaSCo; BRAM is accessible via LMB from the MicroBlaze, as well as via an AXI4 controller. An optional DMA engine can transfer data between local and device memory.

In order to be able to communicate with the host via BRAM, we attached an AXI4 controller to the local BRAM. This allows us to directly transfer the MicroBlaze programs using the standard mechanisms of TaPaSCo (see Sect. 4.3). The diagram in Fig. 5 shows the final PE design for the prototype; this design is assembled by a Tcl script for Vivado Design Suite. It could have been generated by BlueSpec, or Chisel, or directly from Verilog/VHDL, just as well, but since we are using several components from the Xilinx IP catalog, this approach was the fastest. Note, however, that any of these approaches to define the PE would have worked with TaPaSCo.

TaPaSCo only requires an IP-XACT [10] description of the module and the T-shape of interfaces to perform the wiring of any PE automatically. In our case, we used the Vivado Design Suite to generate an IP-XACT description of the PE and packaged it into a .zip file, which can be directly imported into TaPaSCo:

```
tapasco import shishito.zip as 1337
```

The import command performs several actions: In general, it makes the PE contained in shishito.zip available to TaPaSCo using the *kind ID* 1337. This kind ID will later be used in the application to identify the kind of PE a job requires. Note that this only identifies the abstract algorithm; different implementations or algorithms performing the same computation will usually share the same kind ID, since this knowledge should be hidden from the user. Unless given with the --skipEvaluation command argument, the import command will perform OOC synthesis and place-and-route for all targeted Platforms, in this case all known Platforms (this could be restricted, e.g., to the ZedBoard Platform using -p zedboard). OOC will yield estimations for both area utilization A per instance and maximal operating frequency F_{max}.

4.2 Shishito Architecture

The core goal of TaPaSCo is to free the engineer from having to focus on anything not directly related to the acceleration problem at hand. In our case this means that we will let TaPaSCo construct the entire on-chip architecture for us, leaving us free to concentrate on the MicroBlaze PEs and their application code. To get the software engineers up and running, we can generate a fully working bitstream with two MicroBlazes for them with a single command:

```
tapasco -v compose [shishito x 2] @ 100MHz -p zedboard
```

The compose command can be used to construct a specific composition, without using any design space exploration; in this case, the composition will include two instances of our MicroBlaze PE running at 100 MHz and a bitstream will be generated for the ZedBoard. The low operating frequency and number of PEs ensures that the synthesis time will be reasonably short, so we can use frequent iterations while working in tandem with the software engineers on the application side. For the final evaluation of the prototype, we will use the design space exploration feature of TaPaSCo to find a good trade-off between number of instances and operating frequency. By default, TaPaSCo will optimize job throughput, i.e., the number of computation jobs per second. However, to estimate job throughput, we need a good approximation of the average computation time required for each job. Luckily, this is very simple: Once the MicroBlaze program is assembled, the number of clock cycles for any given input can be determined by offline simulation. A number of ways can be used to provide this data to TaPaSCo's DSE, the simplest being re-importing the PE with the additional data:

```
tapasco import shishito.zip as 1337 --averageClockCycles 1250000
```

Now we're ready to harness the power of TaPaSCo's automated design space exploration:

`tapasco explore [shishito x 2] in area, freq -p zedboard`

The `explore` command will take an *initial composition* and a list of design space dimensions; the initial composition determines the ratio of PE kinds to each other, e.g., for an initial composition $[A \times 1, B \times 2]$, TaPaSCo will only use compositions where there are twice as many instances of B as of A when varying the area utilization. The design space dimensions `area` and `freq` activate the exploration along the area utilization and operating frequency axes, respectively. Note that we used a `-p zedboard` Platform filter this time, to restrict the exploration to a single Platform. By default, `explore` will spawn one thread for each active CPU core on the executing machine performing a single composition run in parallel, taking the top elements of the ordered design space (in this case ordered by their estimated job throughput). The DSE will repeat this until it finds a design that achieves timing closure automatically (see [7] for a more thorough discussion of the algorithm itself). This will usually take a lot of time and computing resources, but does not require any interaction. After a few hours, or days, depending on the complexity of the design, TaPaSCo will generate a working bitstream with close to ideal operating frequency and number of PEs.

```
1    #include<vector>
2    #include<tapasco.hpp>
3
4    /* Perform automatic initialization of first device: */
5    Tapasco tapasco;
6    auto prog { /* MicroBlaze program */ };
7    std::vector<JobData> data { /* data for each job */ };
8    std::vector<JobFuture> threads;
9    /* Launch jobs asynchronously. */
10   for(JobData& jd : data)
11     threads.push_back(
12       tapasco.launch(1337, Local(InOnly(prog)), jd);
13     );
14   /* Wait for all jobs to finish. */
15   for(auto& t : threads)
16     t.wait();
17   /* do something with the result */
```

Listing 1: Excerpt of the main loop of the Shishito host program (C++17).

4.3   Application Development with TaPaSCo

The last missing piece for our prototype is the application software: To be precise, we need the MicroBlaze programs to execute on our PEs and a host program that offloads the computations to the FPGA. Discussing the former is out-of-scope for this paper, but the latter will be examined briefly to give an idea of software development with TaPaSCo. Listing 1 contains excerpts from the host program focusing on the main offloading loop. Assume that the executable binary code of the target MicroBlaze program has been inserted as the array `prog` into the source code, and the actual input data has already been split into a number of `JobData` segments suitable for parallel processing, stored as `data`. Note that this assumption is not unrealistic. In many simple cases, such as summing up an array of numbers, an `array_view` data structure can be used on a raw data block to perform a useful split very easily and at practically no runtime cost. In Line 14, we launch a TaPaSCo job for each data element. This line looks intentionally, but deceptively, simple. In fact, there is an enormous amount of work being performed under the hood, which we can only briefly gloss over: In the `launch` call, the kind ID 1337 is used to identify the target PE kind, as expected; the program `prog` is wrapped in class constructors called `Local` and `InOnly`, which simply serve as a type annotation for C++ template expansion in `tapasco.hpp`. Seeing a `Local` argument, TaPaSCo will allocate PE-local memory for the data block (as opposed to device-global memory) at the PE where the execution will take place. It will then copy the executable code `prog` to the PE memory and pass the handle returned by the allocation to the MicroBlaze program. For `jd`, TaPaSCo performs much the same procedure, only that allocation takes place on the device-global memory shared by all PEs. `launch` then proceeds to perform the setup for the launch, starts the PE and returns a closure to the bottom half of the launch to be executed asynchronously. The bottom half consists of 1. waiting for the corresponding completion signal, then 2. copying back data from the device-global memory for `jd` to the CPU's memory location for `jd`, 3. releasing of the allocated memory for `prog` and `jd`, and 4. finally releasing the PE. Note that the bottom half does not launch a separate thread, but is instead executed only at the call to its `wait` method in the loop below; each bottom half thus executes on the main thread of the application. This approach allows us to hide the fact, that a PE for the kind 1337 may not be available when calling `launch`; in this case the job will be queued and executed as soon as a PE is available. Since `prog` is marked `InOnly`, it will only be copied *to* the device, but not *back* after execution. On the other hand, since `jd` is not marked `InOnly`, it will both be copied to the device prior to the execution, as well as back to main memory afterwards. There exists another type annotation called `OutOnly`, which allows to specify the third case of elements, which need to be allocated on the device, but not copied to the device *before* execution, only *from* the device afterwards (e.g., data generated on the device).

4.4   Scaling Out with TaPaSCo

Assuming our initial prototype on the ZedBoard was satisfactory, we can now easily scale up to larger boards using TaPaSCo: E.g., we can simply target a much larger ZC706 by running our DSE again with `-p zc706`, which will generate a new bitstream, likely with significantly more PEs than on the ZedBoard, likely even running at a higher frequency. The application code shown in Listing 1 does *not* need to be changed at all to make use of the new PEs. In fact, since the CPU architecture on ZC706 and ZedBoard is the same, it does not even need to be recompiled!

5 Conclusion

We have shown how TaPaSCo can reduce the development effort required to implement *scalable, portable FPGA-based computing architectures* by providing both hardware and software abstractions for embedding custom accelerators in FPGA designs. Furthermore, we argue that TaPaSCo's *design space exploration* facilities can remove guesswork and manual design iterations, while improving upon the final result (cf. [8]). Last but not least, TaPaSCo is freely available as open-source. It provides a reproducible baseline and is easy to extend, simplifying benchmarking and performance evaluation for the academic FPGA community. TaPaSCo is licensed under the GNU LGPLv3 and available on our public GitLab website [13].

References

1. Slurm Workload Manager. https://slurm.schedmd.com/overview.html. Accessed 03 Aug 2018
2. Aldinucci, M., et al.: Fastflow: high-level and efficient streaming on multi-core. In: Programming Multi-Core and Many-Core Computing Systems (2017)
3. Canis, A., et al.: Legup: high-level synthesis for FPGA-based processor/accelerator systems. In: Proceedings of the 19th ACM/SIGDA International Symposium on Field Programmable Gate Arrays. ACM (2011)
4. Charles, P., et al.: X10: an object-oriented approach to non-uniform cluster computing. In: ACM Sigplan Notices, vol. 40. ACM (2005)
5. de La Chevallerie, D., Korinth, J., Koch, A.: Integrating FPGA-based processing elements into a runtime for parallel heterogeneous computing. In: 2014 International Conference on Field-Programmable Technology (FPT). IEEE (2014)
6. Digilent Inc.: ZedBoard. http://zedboard.org/product/zedboard (2015). Accessed 16 May 2018
7. Hofmann, J., Korinth, J., Koch, A.: A scalable high-performance hardware architecture for real-time stereo vision by semi-global matching. In: Proceedings of the IEEE Conference on Computer Vision and Pattern Recognition Workshops (2016)
8. Hofmann, J., Korinth, J., Koch, A.: A scalable latency-insensitive architecture for FPGA-accelerated semi-global matching in stereo vision applications. In: Proceedings of International Conference on ReConFigurable Computing and FPGAs (ReConFig) (2016)
9. Huthmann, J., Liebig, B., Oppermann, J., Koch, A.: Hardware, software co-compilation with the nymble system. In: 2013 8th International Workshop on Reconfigurable and Communication-Centric Systems-on-Chip (ReCoSoC). IEEE (2013)
10. IEEE Standards Association. IEEE 1685–2014 - IEEE Standard for IP-XACT, Standard Structure for Packaging, Integrating, and Reusing IP within Tool Flows (2014). Accessed 16 May 2018
11. Ismail, A., Shannon, L.: FUSE: front-end user framework for O/S abstraction of hardware accelerators. In: 2011 IEEE 19th Annual International Symposium on Field-Programmable Custom Computing Machines (FCCM). IEEE (2011)

12. Korinth, J., de la Chevallerie, D., Koch, A.: An open-source tool flow for the composition of reconfigurable hardware thread pool architectures. In: IEEE 23rd Annual International Symposium on Field-Programmable Custom Computing Machines (FCCM). IEEE (2015)
13. Korinth, J., Koch, A.: TaPaSCo (2017). https://git.esa.informatik.tu-darmstadt.de/tapasco/tapasco. Accessed 16 May 2018
14. Lübbers, E., Platzner, M.: ReconOS: multithreaded programming for reconfigurable computers. ACM Trans. Embedded Comput. Syst. (TECS) 9(1), 8 (2009)
15. Peck, W., et al.: Hthreads: a computational model for reconfigurable devices. In: International Conference on Field Programmable Logic and Applications (FPL 2006). IEEE (2006)
16. REPARA Project Consortium. Work Package 5 Deliverables (2016). Accessed 16 May 2018
17. Skalicky, S., Schmidt, A.G., French, M.: High level hardware/software embedded system design with redsharc. CoRR, abs/1408.4725 (2014)
18. Sommer, L., Korinth, J., Koch, A.: OpenMP device offloading to FPGA accelerators. In: 2017 IEEE 28th International Conference on Application-Specific Systems, Architectures and Processors (ASAP). IEEE (2017)
19. Xilinx Inc.: UG984 - MicroBlaze Processor Reference Guide (2018). Accessed 16 May 2018
20. Xilinx Inc.: Vivado High Level Synthesis (2018). https://www.xilinx.com/products/design-tools/vivado/integration/esl-design.html. Accessed 16 May 2018

Graph-Based Code Restructuring Targeting HLS for FPGAs

Afonso Canas Ferreira[1,2]([⊠]) [iD] and João M. P. Cardoso[1,2] [iD]

[1] Faculty of Engineering, University of Porto, Porto, Portugal
ascferreira@gmail.com, jmpc@acm.org
[2] The Institute for Systems and Computer Engineering, Technology and Science,
INESC TEC, Porto, Portugal

Abstract. High-level synthesis (HLS) is of paramount importance to enable software developers to map critical computations to FPGA-based hardware accelerators. However, in order to generate efficient hardware accelerators one needs to apply significant code transformations and adequately use the directive-driven approach, part of most HLS tools. The code restructuring and directives needed are dependent not only of the characteristics of the input code but also of the HLS tools and target FPGAs. These aspects require a deep knowledge about the subjects involved and tend to exclude software developers. This paper presents our recent approach for automatic code restructuring targeting HLS tools. Our approach uses an unfolded graph representation, which can be generated from program execution traces, and graph-based optimizations, such as folding, to generate suitable HLS C code. In this paper, we describe the approach and the new optimizations proposed. We evaluate the approach with a number of representative kernels and the results show its capability to generating efficient hardware implementations only achievable using manual restructuring of the input software code and manual insertion of adequate HLS directives.

Keywords: Software code restructuring · HLS ·
Graph transformations · FPGA · Hardware accelerators

1 Introduction

Field-programmable gate arrays (FPGAs) can provide efficient hardware accelerators. Their use can contribute to the performance improvements and energy efficiency needed in many computing systems (see e.g., [1]), from embedded to high-performance computing systems. Custom hardware implementations provide concurrent execution of many independent operations, thereby improving the execution of algorithms with high operation-, data- and task-level parallelism. In order to design efficient hardware accelerators, one must have specific

This work was partially supported by the TEC4Growth project.

skills and understand very distinct programming languages and tools than a typical software developer. Additionally, hardware design is still a very error-prone and time-consuming task. As these aspects impose substantial barriers to use FPGAs as accelerators, many efforts in high-level synthesis (HLS) focus on improvements in terms of the use of FPGAs by developers (including software programmers) by providing higher abstraction levels and the use of typical software programming languages.

The high-level of abstraction provided by HLS tools thus intends to allow developers to program FPGAs more easily and be able to handle more complex applications, without the long time efforts needed by typical hardware design. Even thought most HLS tools start from software programming languages, they still require hardware expertise to generate efficient hardware. For example, the C programming language is a common input for many HLS tools [1]. However, the C programming model is tailored to CPUs and does not consider the concurrent nature of hardware and the possible customization. HLS tools circumvent these limitations by allowing programmers to guide the synthesis through directives. Nonetheless, the structure of the code has a large impact on the performance of the generated hardware via HLS [2]. Complex code restructuring is usually required and HLS tools and compilers may neither provide such optimizations nor ensure their automatic application. As it is well known that current HLS tools still have a barrier of entry for software programmers, by lowering this barrier more developers will be able to use the computing power of FPGAs, e.g., to accelerate applications. In order to make C-based HLS more accessible, we need a way to easily restructure the input software code.

This paper presents an approach to automatically restructure C code targeting HLS for FPGAs. Our approach is based on a dataflow graph (DFG), currently generated from execution traces of the input critical function, and on graph transformations, such as folding and unfolding, before generating C code added with HLS directives. Although a DFG could be generated by compilers, the current trace-based approach is taken, so that in future work we can also specialize the hardware generation with the use of runtime information. The global approach was firstly introduced in [3] and here we describe in more detail important aspects of the approach and provide useful extensions with significant impact in the results achieved. The main contributions of this paper are:

- an automatic code restructuring approach based on dataflow graph transformations and on a framework, partially implementing the approach, tuned to code restructuring and insertion of HLS directives for FPGA-based accelerators;
- graph-based optimizations allowing the generation of C code and considering different aspects such as folding/unfolding, loop pipelining, arithmetic optimizations and array partitioning;
- an evaluation of the approach using a number of kernels and results that show some advantages of the approach. This includes a comparison to the optimized code for an SVM implementation provided in [4] and evidence

of the capability of the approach and current framework to automatically achieve comparable code restructuring.

This paper is organized as follows. Section 2 presents a motivating example regarding code restructuring and HLS directives. Section 3 presents our approach and describes the framework developed to implement and evaluate the approach and the main optimizations already implemented. In Sect. 4, we show the results obtained by applying our framework to a number of benchmarks. We present in Sect. 5 some of the most relevant related work, and we finalize in Sect. 6 with some concluding remarks and planned future work.

2 Motivating Example

In order to show the possible code restructuring and HLS directives needed to achieve an efficient hardware accelerator, we show here the C code of the *filter subband* function (see Fig. 1), a function present in an MPEG audio encoder [5]. This function consists of a nested loop that calculates y values that are then used in a second nested loop to calculate the output array s.

```
void filter_subband(double z[Nz],
    double s[Ns], double m[Nm]){
    double y[Ny];
    int i,j;
    for (i=0;i<Ny;i++){
        y[i] = 0.0;
        for (j=0; j<(int)Nz/Ny;j++)
            y[i] += z[i+Ny*j];
    }
    for (i=0;i<Ns;i++){
        s[i]=0.0;
        for (j=0; j<Ny;j++)
            s[i] += m[Ns*i+j] * y[j];
    }
}
```

(a) Original *Filter subband* source code

```
void filter_subband_pipe(double z[512],
    double s[32], double m[1024]){
    #pragma HLS array_partition
    variable=s cyclic factor=16 dim= 1
    #pragma HLS array_partition
    variable=z cyclic factor=16 dim= 1
    #pragma HLS array_partition
    variable=m cyclic factor=64 dim= 1
    s[0]=0;
    ...
    s[31]=0;
    for( int i =0; i < 64; i=i+4){
    #pragma HLS pipeline
        part11=z[i+320] + z[i+256];
        part12=z[i+321] + z[i+257];
        part13=z[i+322] + z[i+258];
        part14=z[i+323] + z[i+259];
        ...
        y0=final_part1;
        y0_a10=final_part2;
        y0_a20=final_part3;
        y0_a30=final_part4;
        for( int j =0; j < 32; j=j+1){
            temp1=m[(32)*j+i] * y0;
            temp2=m[(32)*j+i] * y0_a10;
            temp3=m[(32)*j+i] * y0_a20;
            temp4=m[(32)*j+i] * y0_a30;
            partial_in1=temp1+temp2;
            ...
            final_partin=part_in3 + part_in4;
            s[j]=s[j] + final_partin;
        }
    }
}
```

(b) *Filter subband* restructured source code, added with Vivado HLS directives

Fig. 1. *Filter subband* source code considering Nz, Ns, Nm and Ny equal to 512, 32, 1024 and 64, respectively

Figure 1b shows the C code after code restructuring and insertion of Vivado HLS directives. This new C code of the *filter subband* provides an efficient FPGA implementation. Although this code implements the same algorithm, it has been restructured substantially and to the best of our knowledge none HLS tool is able to automatically apply the code restructuring stages needed to achieve the code presented. The code in Fig. 1b consists of a single nested loop instead of two nested loop structures. In each iteration of the new outermost loop, four y values are calculated and then used to calculate values for the output array s. The array y is promoted to scalar variables. The outermost loop is then pipelined in hardware due the use of the Vivado HLS pipeline directive. This representation of the algorithm leads to more efficient implementation than the original (Fig. 1a). When using the original code, the hardware resultant implementation calculates all the y values in the first nested loop, stores them in BRAMs, and use them in the next nested loop.

In the restructured code version, presented in Fig. 1b, the calculated y values are being used for the calculation of the output array. They can also be concurrently calculated in the pipeline, which would not be possible with the previous representation. Additionally, the calculated y values are used immediately to calculate the outputs, so they do not need to be stored in memory. Furthermore, the accumulations are implemented using partial sums that allow for more concurrent summations. Also, array partitioning directives are used to increase the memory throughput, so that the resultant loop pipelining has a lower initiation interval (II).

Although both codes implement the same algorithm, the restructured version generates a more efficient FPGA hardware. In the following section we show how our framework can automatically generate the C code in Fig. 1b from the C code in Fig. 1a.

3   Our Approach

Our approach to automatically restructure C code targeting HLS tools is based on graph transformations. The current implementation of our approach (see Fig. 2a) consists of two main components: a frontend and a backend. The frontend transforms a given execution trace in a dataflow graph (DFG). Each DFG is then processed and optimized in a backend that, as final step, generates C code for a HLS tool.

We chose DFGs for our graph-based approach, as DFGs are tailored to represent the flow of data and naturally express parallelism, both essential for hardware implementations. Additionally, we focused on a flexible frontend to make possible the generation of DFGs from multiple input languages as this may allow programmers of different languages to use C-based HLS tools.

3.1   Frontend

As already mentioned, the frontend of our framework generates a DFG from an execution trace of the input code. Figure 3 shows a simplified DFG for the *Filter*

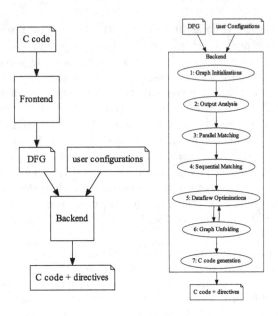

(a) framework main stages   (b) backend main stages

Fig. 2. Compilation flow of our framework

subband function in Fig. 1. The DFG represents in nodes the operations from the original execution and in edges the data dependencies between operations. We kept the frontend as simple and generic as possible in order to address different input languages. Although our initial frontend was implemented for C code input, it can be easily ported to other software programming languages.

Our current approach to generate the DFG representing the execution of a kernel is to write the dot (GraphViz) description to a file at runtime. By injecting instrumentation code into the original C code (before each statement), compiling and executing, the input DFG is generated.

3.2 Backend

Currently, the backend consists of seven stages (see Fig. 2b) focused on analysis and optimizations of the DFG. It implements all the code restructuring, optimizations and insertion of directives for the target HLS tool. The exact optimizations applied depend on the input DFG and on the configurations provided by users. In a configuration file, users can define the number of simultaneous load/stores supported by the hardware - important for the tool to explicitly generate code with a number of load/store statements -, inputs and outputs of the kernel and optimization options.

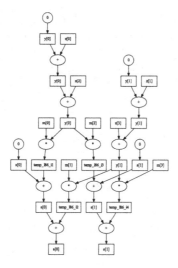

Fig. 3. DFG for the *filter subband* considering an execution with Nz, Ns, Nm and Ny equal to 4, 2, 1024, and 2, respectively

The first stage of the backend compacts the graph by pruning unnecessary nodes and prepares it for the following stages. Afterwards, the tool tries to obtain improved dataflow representations. Since currently the input DFG is fully unfolded, it is important to identify repeating patterns that can be folded. As these patterns may occur multiple times, the tool can optimize a large part of some applications by improving these patterns. Stage 2 separates the dataflows that generate each individual output and Stage 3 tries to find matches among these dataflows. If a repeating pattern is identified, this stage folds them into a loop that is represented by a dataflow of a single iteration. Stage 4 attempts to optimize the dataflow by identifying loop pipelining opportunities. Stage 5 applies various optimizations to the DFG and Stage 6 unrolls some of the generated loops based on the users' configurations. Finally, Stage 7 generates the C output code plus the appropriate HLS directives.

3.3   Backend Optimizations

In this subsection we describe in more detail the main backend stages (see Fig. 2b) that optimize the DFG. We describe Stage 6 before Stage 5 as graph unfolding has an impact on the graph optimizations.

Sequential Matching (Stage 4). Although the first three stages compact the DFG, it can still be very large and contain properties to be further explored. In Stage 4, the tool identifies a potential variable and pipelines the graph along this variable. This variable is selected by traversing the DFG and identifying which variable is written more often (an heuristic that attempts to build the longest pipeline).

The backend then proceeds to match all the dataflows that generate all the separate writes of the selected variable. After the tool has obtained the pipelining structure, it handles dataflows without matches. The tool moves the subgraphs that represent the dataflow of the pipelining into a "hyper" node (represents a loop) and all the nodes that do not fit in the pipelining are maintained outside of this "hyper" node.

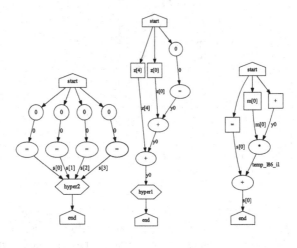

(a) DFG of the high-   (b) outer loop   (c) inner loop
est hierarchy level

Fig. 4. DFG for *filter subband* after Stage 4 of the tool and considering an execution with Nz, Ns, Nm and Ny equal to 8, 4, 1024, and 4, respectively

By applying the Stage 4 pipelining to *filter subband*, the tool obtains the DFG shown in Fig. 4. The graph is pipelined along the array s. The subgraphs in Figs. 4b and c represent single iterations of the outer and inner loops of the pipelining. In each iteration, the outer loop calculates a y value, which is then used in the inner loop. In the inner loop, each y is used to calculate all the outputs of the s array. The subgraph in Fig. 4a shows the dataflows that do not match the pipelining. In this case, they represent the initialization of the s array.

It is through Stage 4 that the tool obtains the improved code structure depicted in the example in Fig. 1b. By transforming the DFG according to pipelining, the tool identifies a better structure for the algorithm. By comparing this DFG to the input DFG seen in Fig. 3, and although the input sizes are different, we can still recognize the patterns that are compacted into the pipelining in the smaller version of the input DFG.

Graph Unfolding (Stage 6). Stage 6 is dedicated to unfolding loops that were generated in stages 3 and 4. Unfolding loops opens new avenues for optimizations in Stage 5. As mentioned before, compacting the DFG is very efficient for optimizations, but to take further advantage of Instruction Level Parallelism the tool needs to unfold some of the loops. Due to the DFG-based approach, the tool can unfold a loop simply by copying the dataflow multiple times and updating the indexes of array accesses and appending a label to the new variables.

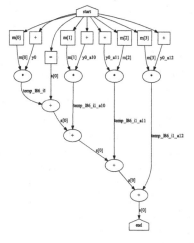

The unfolding process starts at the innermost loops. After a loop is unrolled the resulting dataflow is checked for Stage 5 optimizations, and after these the resulting DFG returns to Stage 6. The unfolding process needs to be ordered from innermost to outermost loops, because unfolding an inner loop does not affect the outer loop, but unfolding an outer loop affects its nested loops. In case the outer loop is pipelined, the inner loop is not unrolled as Vivado HLS automatically unrolls it.

When dealing with inner loops, it is essential to distinguish which loop to unfold. Therefore, the tool starts the unrolling transformation with the name, unfolding factor and loop type of the initial loop. If that loop has a nested loop, the tool unrolls it and propagates the name of the outer loop, the unfolding factor and type. The inner loop is unrolled based on that inherited information. Thus, if a memory access depends

Fig. 5. Unrolled dataflow of the inner loop of the pipelined *filter subband* of Fig. 4c by a factor of four .

on the iteration of the inner and outer loop, the tool can correctly identify how to calculate the index of the new access.

Figure 5 shows the result of unfolding the inner loop of *filter subband* pipeline loop shown in Fig. 4. The backend replicates the dataflow, in this case a sum and a multiplication, and then connects them to maintain the correct dependencies between iterations, resulting in the accumulation chain. It is through this unfolding the tool obtains the unfolded iterations seen in the code in Fig. 1b.

Dataflow Optimizations (Stage 5). Stage 5 is dedicated to various dataflow optimizations. Currently, it involves two types of optimizations. One focuses on arithmetic optimization, such as the accumulation optimization, which restructures an accumulation as partial sums. The backend substitutes accumulation chains with the same calculations through balanced trees. The result of the balanced tree is then summed with the starting value of the accumulation. In case the optimized chain consists of floats or doubles the user would need to verify if the result is within acceptable accuracy.

As illustrated in Fig. 5, the first addition depends on the result of the last sum. Therefore, the next stage of the pipelining can only initiate after the clock cycles necessary to execute that chain. However, by balancing the chain, the value calculated in the previous iteration is used only once at the final sum. Therefore, the pipeline only needs to be delayed for the duration of a single sum instead of an entire accumulation chain. It is through balancing that we obtain the partial sums in the motivating example (see Fig. 1b). Vivado HLS is able to automatically balance operations, but it does not balance floats or doubles without changing the settings, which would require the knowledge of an experienced user.

Another arithmetic optimization is applied to divisions. In this case, if at least one operand is unique to multiple divisions, the tool extends the DFG with the calculation of its inverse, and substitutes the divisions by multiplications with the inverse.

The user can also choose to optimize memory accesses. One of the optimizations is data reuse. The tool analyzes the current loops to identify if there are redundant memory accesses between two consecutive iterations of a loop. If the same memory location is also accessed in the next iteration of a loop, the tool uses buffers to store values between iterations, reducing the number of memory reads. This can greatly minimize the memory bottlenecks of certain applications.

Another optimization the user can choose to diminish memory bottlenecks is the full partitioning of arrays. This optimization can be applied through array partitioning directives provided by HLS tools. If the user chooses to fully partitioning the arrays, the tool makes a final pass through the whole DFG. Based on the number of separate concurrent accesses, the tool sets the appropriate array partitioning factor so that the maximum number of concurrent accesses detected can be scheduled in a single cycle. This optimization can significantly increase the resource usage. First by using more BRAMs. Second by lowering the memory bottleneck more operations can be executed in parallel. This optimization does not change the structure of the graph, it only leads to different directives. When applied to the *filter subband* function, this optimization injects the array partitioning directives included in the motivating example (see Fig. 1b).

4   Experimental Results

This section presents some experimental results achieved by our framework. The benchmarks used represent DSP algorithms and are either from the DSPLIB from Texas Instruments [5], the UTDSP Benchmark Suite [6] or from an MPEG audio encoder [7]. *dotproduct* and *Autocorrelation* are from DSPLIB. *1D fir* is a typical code implementing a FIR filter with N taps. *filter subband* is from an MPEG audio encoder. *2D Convolution* is the largest benchmark and is a kernel that performs a 2D convolution, which is part of the Sobel edge detection benchmark provided in UTDSP. The source code used for the *SVM* kernel is from [4].

Table 1. Framework optimization levels

Optimization level	Brief description
01	None of the optimizations
02	DFG is folded as much as possible, and unfolded according to user configurations
03	Adds array partitioning to level 02 to complement the unfolded DFG
04	Adds data reuse to level 03
05	Adds arithmetic optimizations to level 03
06	Adds arithmetic optimizations to level 04
07	Adds full array partitioning optimization from Stage 5 to level 05
08	Adds full array partitioning optimization from Stage 5 to level 06

Table 2. Versions of input code used for comparisons

Comparison code	Brief description
C	Original code without any modifications
C-inter	Input code optimized with basic directives such as the pipeline directive
C-high	Improve the C-inter implementation with unroll and memory partitioning directives

We analyze the effectiveness of our tool for multiple optimization levels as depicted in Table 1. The C code baselines are briefly summarized in Table 2. It is a fair assumption that a typical software programmer could use a number of very basic directives, but is not proficient with all types of directives. This approach to the evaluation allows us to study the effectiveness of our tool when comparing to different levels of hardware design knowledge.

Table 3. Resource usage for fastest optimization levels up to level 04 and Level 08

Benchmark	LUT	FF	DSP	BRAM	LUT	FF	DSP	BRAM
filter subband	12605	18849	59	0	47537	42589	118	0
Autocorrelation	9083	7277	160	0	8025	7114	160	0
dotproduct	294	581	8	0	294	581	8	0
1D fir	4587	6579	192	0	4297	5641	192	0
2D Convulution	5354	6575	54	0	6376	3408	57	0
SVM	9228	9068	56	68	14203	12506	91	76

Table 4. Speedups for fastest optimization levels up to level 04 and Level 08

Benchmark	Latency	Period (ns)	Speedup C	Speedup C-inter	Speedup C-high	Latency	Period (ns)	Speedup C	Speedup C-inter	Speedup C-high
filter subband	563	18.34	39.60	2.81	2.81	293	17.09	81.66	5.79	5.79
Autocorrelation	96	8.6	49.6	16.4	7.91	16	8.6	297.7	98.6	47.5
dotproduct	255	8.93	16.81	5.61	1.00	255	8.93	16.81	5.61	1.00
1D fir	135	8.74	211	26.7	14.4	120	8.74	237.3	30	16.2
2D Convulution	8563	8.74	34.5	2.25	1.36	3886	8.74	76.1	5	3
SVM	11365	9.38	31	0.9	0.9	3208	8.4	123.4	3.5	3.5

Speedups and FPGA resource values are obtained through synthesizing the C code with Vivado HLS 2017.4 [8], in a PC with an Intel Core i7-7700 with 32 GB RAM, and targeting a Xilinx Artix™-7 FPGA (xc7z020clg484-1). All of the benchmarks had a time constraint of 10 ns except *filter subband*, which has a constraint of 20 ns. The total time of each hardware implementation is calculated by multiplying the minimum clock period reported and the latency. The speedups are the result of dividing the total time of the implementations from Table 2 by the total time of the implementations from code generated with different framework optimizations levels.

Tables 3 and 4 show the results presented in [3], which considered 04 as the highest level. Level 03 achieves the fastest implementations for the *filter subband* and *dotproduct*. The remaining benchmarks achieve the fastest implementations at Level 04. The results showed that it was essential to reduce the memory bottleneck to increase the throughput of the implementations. Those results also show that just through folding and unfolding the input DFG, the resulting implementation was already faster for *Autocorrelation* and *filter subband*. Overall, the results show the benefits of our approach in terms of speedups and the enhancements when adding the optimizations (arithmetic optimizations and array partitioning) proposed in this paper.

Tables 3 and 4 also present the results from the synthesis reports of Vivado HLS for the benchmarks, considering the manually improved C versions and the C code automatically generated using our tool, with optimization levels between 05 and 08. With more optimizations it is possible to achieve higher speedups for every benchmark with the exception of *dotprod*. For *filter subband*, the highest speedup was achieved at Level 07 with 5.8× and 81.7× compared with C-high and C, respectively. This is due to improving the Level 03 pipeline with arithmetic optimizations and array partitioning, thereby improving the Latency and II of the pipelining. Level 08 would possibly achieve an even higher speedup, but would require a larger FPGA.

The *Autocorrelation* achieves the best speedup at Level 08, which is considerably higher than the previous best result. This is due to the fact that through data reuse the main loop of the kernel is highly optimized to the point that considerable clock cycles are dedicated to filling the buffers, thus partitioning the memory has a large impact. The same applies to the *1D fir*, but the increase is not as large due to less buffers being used. There is also a large improvement for the *2D Convolution* benchmark whose best speedup went from 1.4× to 3× compared to C-high at Level 07. Compared to C and C-inter, the best speedups for this benchmark are 76× and 5×, respectively. As with the previous cases, the arithmetic and memory optimizations lead to a pipelined loop with both lower latency and an initiation interval value. Initially, Level 08 was expected to achieve the fastest implementation and it in fact achieves a lower latency than Level 07. However, the way Vivado HLS schedules the code, Level 08 results in a higher minimum clock period leading to a slower implementation when considering executions operating at the maximum clock frequencies.

In addition to the above benchmarks, we also applied our framework to the machine-learning *SVM* (Support Vector Machine) kernel presented in [4]. The results achieved by the framework are presented in Tables 3 and 4. Compared with previous benchmarks, Levels 02 to 06 have lower performances than C-high. The loop generated by the backend contains 36 accesses to the matrix that contains the support vectors. There is no redundancy between memory accesses and thus Level 04 has little impact. Level 05 shows that the arithmetic optimizations alone have little impact, merely an insignificant reduction of the latency compared to Level 03. In order to lower the bottleneck caused by the memory accesses, it is necessary to use array partitioning. By partitioning the support vectors, the speedup compared to C-high is only 1.22×. However, when array partitioning is combined with arithmetic optimizations as in levels 07 and 08 the speedups are 123× and 3.47× relative to C and C-high, respectively.

In [4] the authors optimize an FPGA implementation of the *SVM* kernel by manually restructuring the code, and then use design space exploration (DSE) for selecting parameter values and HLS directives. When comparing the code proposed by them with the one generated using our tool, there are many similarities. The main difference is that our tool does not partition the *SVM* kernel itself to increase concurrency. Our tool attempts to obtain a similar result through unfolding the outer loop and applying array partitioning directives. The rest of the optimizations proposed in [4] are very similar, such as balancing the accumulations in a tree, unrolling loops and applying pipeline and array partitioning directives. Thus, our tool automatically obtains a similar code compared to the optimized one shown in [4], depending on the users given configurations. These results show once again the capability of our framework to achieve efficient code restructuring plus HLS directives.

4.1 Limitations

The current version of the framework imposes restrictions on the input code to handle. Some limitations are due to the framework being at an initial stage, others are due to inherent characteristics of the approach. One limitation is related to the information loss through the execution tracing. As described, our approach simply represents the dataflow and executed operations and does explicitly represent constructs such as *for*, *while* or conditional statements at the frontend. The DFG at the frontend only represents the execution for the given inputs. Conditional statements or loops branching into different dataflow paths depending on the inputs will conduct to different DFGs for the same input code. Currently, the existence of control-flow that may make a certain DFG invalid would require exit points or a decision about the execution on the accelerator. Our future plans consider the merging of DFGs representing different execution traces and the representation in the DFG of ternary conditional operators.

One of the major bottlenecks of the current implementation of our approach is related to scalability. The DFGs generated by the frontend are fully unfolded and represent each operation executed with a distinct DFG node. This results in large DFGs, even when input datasets and/or loop iterations are not so big. One possibility is to generate condensed DFGs by using expressions and parameters that represent the repetition of certain patterns. We recognize the importance to solve this problem and our future work plans include R&D of techniques to improve the scalability of our approach.

5   Related Work

Source to source transformations have been the subject of study in the field of HLS. For example, Cong et al. [9] presents a framework to facilitate code restructuring for software developers. Cardoso et al. [10] present an approach to allow users to program strategies to apply code transformations and insertion of directives. The LegUP HLS tool [11] also accepts C as an input and implements code restructuring through a modified LLVM compiler [12] to implement HLS optimizations.

Although the previous work efforts on code restructuring for HLS, it is well known that the problem is complex and difficult to make automatic as in many cases to achieve the required code a sequence of specific optimizations is needed [10]. Furthermore, in this sequence of optimizations there might be needed compiler optimizations that *per se* do not justify their inclusion in a typical compiler, and the selection of the optimizations (and associated parameter values) and the way to devise their sequence of application require exploration of a large design space.

Also relevant are the approaches dealing specifically with data streaming based computations. For example, Mencer et al. [13] present an approach that uses a C-based language called ASC to implement data-streaming based computations in hardware. With some similarities, the Max-Compiler [14] is a HLS tool to implement streaming computations described as dataflow graphs in a programming language based on Java and named as MaxJ. In [15] the authors discuss DFG optimizations for generating better FPGA implementations in the context of the MaxJ compiler. Most of these optimizations are also suitable for our approach.

A pertinent approach to source to source code optimizations is the inclusion of loop transformations based on polyhedral models [16] as presented, e.g., by Cong et al. [9]. For example, the polyhedral models focused on nested loops transformations can be used to optimize code, so that HLS tools can implement improved pipelines in hardware [17,18]. Although polyhedral models can only be successfully applied to nested loops with specific structure, memory accesses and predetermined upper and lower bounded loops, a future analysis and comparison with the approach presented in this paper is required.

Our approach addresses code restructuring as a graph transformation problem and can automatically achieve more aggressive code restructuring. Although in the current work we consider C code as input, our approach has the potential to address different input programming languages via the inclusion of adequate instrumentation code. We also believe that our approach can target programming models such as the one used by MaxJ and in this case our approach could possibly act as an optimizer for the MaxCompiler.

6   Conclusion

This paper presented an automatic code restructuring approach to output software code more suitable to high-level synthesis (HLS) tools. Our approach starts with a dataflow graph (DFG) representation of the computations, currently obtained by executing the critical functions of the application previously added with instrumentation code, followed by graph optimizations and folding/unfolding graph operations. The proposed approach has been implemented in a framework able to automatically optimize DFGs to fully generate HLS-friendly C code added with HLS directives. The experimental results show that the C code automatically generated by our tool outperforms the original code (including the insertion of HLS directives) by achieving significant speedups. The restructured C code is even comparable to, and in most cases better than, manually optimized C code added with directives. Although the C code plus directives generated by the tool can be always replicated by manual code transformations applied by experts, our approach can enable software developers to target efficient hardware accelerators using HLS tools as backend and without requiring support of HLS experts.

We note however that our framework is at the moment a proof of concept for our approach and further work needs to be done to improve it. Ongoing work is focused on the generation of DFGs and on additional DFG optimizations. Future work will focus on more complex memory optimizations through analyses of the DFG, and on parameterized schemes to make possible to represent large execution traces in a more compact DFG.

Acknowledgments. This work was partially funded by the project "NORTE-01-0145-FEDER-000020", financed by the North Portugal Regional Operational Programme under the PORTUGAL 2020 Partnership Agreement, and through the European Regional Development Fund (ERDF) through the Operational Programme for Competitiveness and Internationalisation - COMPETE 2020 Programme, and by National Funds through the Portuguese funding agency, FCT - Fundação para a Ciência e a Tecnologia within project POCI-01-0145-FEDER-016883.

References

1. Nane, R., et al.: A survey and evaluation of FPGA high-level synthesis tools. IEEE Trans. Comput.-Aided Des. Integr. Circ. Syst. **35**(10), 1591–1604 (2016)
2. Cardoso, J.M.P., Weinhardt, M.: High-level synthesis. In: Koch, D., Hannig, F., Ziener, D. (eds.) FPGAs for Software Programmers, pp. 23–47. Springer, Cham (2016). https://doi.org/10.1007/978-3-319-26408-0_2
3. Ferreira, A.C., Cardoso, J.M.P.: Unfolding and folding: a new approach for code restructuring targeting HLS for FPGAs. In: FSP Workshop 2018: Fifth International Workshop on FPGAs for Software Programmers, Dublin, Ireland, pp. 1–10 (2018)
4. Tsoutsouras, V., et al.: An exploration framework for efficient high-level synthesis of support vector machines: case study on ECG arrhythmia detection for Xilinx Zynq SoC. J. Sig. Process. Syst. **88**(2), 127–147 (2017)
5. Texas Instrument, TMS320C6000 DSP Library (DSPLIB). Accessed 16 June 2018. http://www.ti.com/tool/sprc265
6. Lee, C.G.: 15 August 2002. http://www.eecg.toronto.edu/~corinna/. Accessed 16 June 2018
7. Cardoso, J.M.P., et al.: REFLECT: rendering FPGAs to multi-core embedded computing. In: Cardoso, J., Hübner, M. (eds.) Reconfigurable Computing, pp. 261–289. Springer, New York (2011). https://doi.org/10.1007/978-1-4614-0061-5_11
8. Xilinx. Vivado design suite user guide: high level synthesis, 20 December 2017
9. Cong, J., Huang, M., Pan, P., Wang, Y., Zhang, P.: Source-to-source optimization for HLS. In: Koch, D., Hannig, F., Ziener, D. (eds.) FPGAs for Software Programmers, pp. 137–163. Springer, Cham (2016). https://doi.org/10.1007/978-3-319-26408-0_8
10. Cardoso, J.M.P., et al.: Specifying compiler strategies for FPGA-based systems. In: 2012 IEEE 20th International Symposium on Field-Programmable Custom Computing Machines, pp. 192–199, April 2012
11. Canis, A., et al.: LegUP: an open-source high-level synthesis tool for FPGA-based processor/accelerator systems. ACM Trans. Embed. Comput. Syst. **13**(2), 24:1–24:27 (2013)
12. LLVM. The LLVM compiler infrastructure project (2018). https://llvm.org
13. Mencer, O.: ASC: a stream compiler for computing with FPGAs. IEEE Trans. Comput.-Aided Des. Integr. Circ. Syst. **25**(9), 1603–1617 (2006)
14. Maxeler Technologies. Maxcompiler white paper (2017)
15. Voss, N., et al.: Automated dataflow graph merging. In: International Conference on Embedded Computer Systems: Architectures, Modeling and Simulation (SAMOS 2016), pp. 219–226, July 2016
16. Bondhugula, U., Hartono, A., Ramanujam, J., Sadayappan, P.: A practical automatic polyhedral parallelizer and locality optimizer. In: Proceedings of the 29th ACM SIGPLAN Conference on Programming Language Design and Implementation (PLDI 2008), pp. 101–113. ACM, New York (2008)
17. Zuo, W., Liang, Y., Li, P., Rupnow, K., Chen, D., Cong, J.: Improving high level synthesis optimization opportunity through polyhedral transformations. In: Proceedings of the ACM/SIGDA International Symposium on Field Programmable Gate Arrays (FPGA 2013). ACM, New York, pp. 9–18 (2013)
18. Morvan, A., Derrien, S., Quinton, P.: Polyhedral bubble insertion: a method to improve nested loop pipelining for high-level synthesis. Trans. Comput.-Aided Des. Integr. Circ. Syst. **32**(3), 339–352 (2013)

CGRAs and Vector Processing

Ultrasynth: Integration of a CGRA into a Control Engineering Environment

Dennis Wolf[1(✉)], Tajas Ruschke[1], Christian Hochberger[1], Andreas Engel[2], and Andreas Koch[2]

[1] Computer Systems Group (RS), TU Darmstadt, Darmstadt, Germany
{wolf,ruschke,hochberger}@rs.tu-darmstadt.de
[2] Embedded Systems and Applications Group (ESA), TU Darmstadt, Darmstadt, Germany
{engel,koch}@esa.tu-darmstadt.de

Abstract. Coarse Grained Reconfigurable Arrays (CGRAs) can exploit parallelism of compute-intense applications by distributing their workload across a set of Processing Elements (PEs). They are highly efficient in computation and flexible due to their reconfigurability. While these attributes make CGRAs highly interesting as general purpose hardware accelerators, their incorporation into a complete computing system raises severe challenges at the hardware and software level. To overcome the stage of a simulated concept, CGRAs need to be applied to the real-world in order to demonstrate the practicability of the overall system. This paper presents the integration of a CGRA into a control engineering environment targeting a Xilinx Zynq System on Chip (SoC). It focuses on the fully automated tool-chain mapping abstract engineering models to CGRA configurations, and on the SoC-internal runtime communication on hardware level.

1 Introduction

There are many requirements to a computing system in the field of control engineering. Hard real time, low jitter, computational power and the ability to incorporate sensors and actuators are the major demands. When control cycles below $10\,\mu s$ are required, Field Programmable Gate Arrays (FPGAs) are often suggested. However, engineers would like to test and evaluate different choices of parametrization or varying control algorithms with virtually no delay and preferably with a real test rig. For a continuous engineering work flow, the compilation or synthesis of an application should ideally not take longer than several seconds. Thus, custom designs or High-Level Synthesis (HLS) on FPGA are impractical due to their long synthesis runtime. In contrast, CGRAs promise efficiency and high performance without long reconfiguration delays. While most CGRA publications focus on runtime performance, only a few consider the important step of integrating the CGRA into a test rig and its development environment.

Within the research project Ultrasynth, a CGRA-based hardware accelerator was integrated into a Realtime (RT) target for control engineering purposes.

© Springer Nature Switzerland AG 2019
C. Hochberger et al. (Eds.): ARC 2019, LNCS 11444, pp. 247–261, 2019.
https://doi.org/10.1007/978-3-030-17227-5_18

All targeted applications are modeled with CAMeL-View, which is a design environment for mechatronic systems [6]. This paper describes the integration of a CGRA architecture and its toolflow into the hardware and software system of CAMeL-View. Therefore, the requirements of the engineering environment to a hardware accelerator are described in Sect. 3. The communication between the CGRA and its surroundings is detailed in Sect. 4. The integration of the configuration toolflow into CAMeL-View is presented in Sect. 5. Afterwards, Sect. 6 evaluates the run- and compile-time performance of the CGRA and its toolflow.

2   Related Work

There are a few commercial solutions integrating a hardware-accelerator in a general purpose design or an environment for engineering control applications. For example, the Mathworks MATLAB and National Instruments Labview environments can be extended by FPGA-based front-ends like the dSpace DS5203 [2]. However, those accelerators either come along with a fixed set of predefined functionality (e.g. for signal conditioning), or they are limited to a small synthesizable block-set. In the latter case, changing the accelerated kernel requires a significant amount of time and the licenses for the FPGA vendor tools.

Aside commercial products, numerous CGRA architectures have been proposed in literature. Most of them are evaluated in a stand-alone fashion or based on simulation.

In [5], an array of functional units (DySER) is integrated in the execution stage of an OpenSPARC processor. A compiler detects compute-intense code regions and maps those onto the array. Except for simple control flow structures, most of the control flow is handled by the OpenSPARC processor. Memory access has to be handled by the processor as well, and in every loop iteration each local variable has to be written to and read from the computation slices. The CGRA is completely integrated, but not suitable for real-time applications.

[4] presents an automated toolflow that utilizes a CGRA as an overlay architecture on an FPGA. The project is in a promising stage of development, but misses a verified realization on a chip. It appears that the architecture does not support control flow.

A CGRA that is primarily constructed for mobile phones with the capability to process floating-point operands is contributed in [7]. The design is implemented with 130 nm CMOS technology and tested with JPEG and physics engine kernels. While achieving a significant higher performance than an ARM9 for the given benchmark, the architecture is neither coupled with an actual host processor nor an automated tool for software integration is provided.

[1] presents a fully pipelined CGRA. It is capable of high performance and shows that incorporating pipelined operations can lead to significant increase in performance. However, the system lacks of applicability as a general purpose accelerator, since only innermost loops can be executed and control flow heavy applications cannot be mapped.

3   Requirements and System Outline

In CAMeL-View, mechatronic systems are modeled as a hierarchy of interconnected subsystems with inputs, outputs, parameters, and internal states. Instead of explicitly resolving differential equations describing complex physical behavior, the engineers formulate how the outputs and the first derivative of internal states are computed from the inputs, parameters, and the internal states. When generating code for executing these models either as simulation or on an embedded processor as part of the test rig, numerical integrators are required to derive the values of internal states after a certain time step from their current value and derivative, e.g. $x(t + \Delta t) = x(t) + \dot{x}(t) \cdot \Delta t$. Those integrators are not explicitly represented in the CAMeL-View models.

When executing control models on a test rig, CAMeL-View runs on a control terminal (e.g. an industrial PC), which is connected to a RT target over a wired network link as shown in Fig. 1. An embedded system is used as RT target to fulfill the system requirements on jitter and fast peripheral I/O in the microsecond range. It consists of a host processor for the network communication stack and other basic computations, as well as an accelerator for compute-intense application kernels and communication with peripheral devices (i.e. sensors and actuators). In this scenario, CAMeL-View is also the user interface of the test rig capturing change requests for runtime parameters and visualizing data received from the RT target as charts or animations.

CAMeL-View control algorithms are processed in a loop with a fixed frequency. In each period, sensor inputs and/or data from the host processor is loaded, processed according to the control algorithm and the resulting values are sent to the actuators or back to the host processor. The accelerator can either execute the whole CAMeL-View model, such that the host processor is just used as a communication gateway. Alternatively, a control algorithm can also be distributed over the CGRA and the host processor, where the control cycle of the host processor can be an integer-multiple of the accelerator control cycle. This requires an efficient and well synchronized exchange of runtime data. More specifically, the accelerator has to distinguish between high priority inputs produced by the host in every control cycle and low priority parameter updates sporadically generated by the control terminal. In the reverse direction, accelerator results directly processed by the host have a high priority but typically

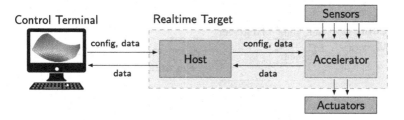

Fig. 1. Application scenario

a low volume, while computed results to be displayed at the control terminal have a lower priority but require a higher bandwidth, when lots of intermediate signals are to be observed.

During the development of a test rig, structural modifications of the control models require the regeneration and redeployment of the configuration for the host processor and the accelerator. Besides the runtime data, the host processor thus has to be able to send application-specific configurations to the accelerator. The round trip time of such modification and reconfiguration cycles has to be in the orders of seconds to ensure an acceptable and efficient workflow for the control engineers. Thus, instead of using a HLS toolflow to translate and synthesize CAMeL-View models into bitstreams for FPGA-based hardware accelerators, a CGRA-based accelerator is exploited. Besides its fast mapping from abstract application descriptions to corresponding CGRA configurations, this approach is independent from any FPGA or ASIC synthesis tools and their required licenses, which was another main requirement within the UltraSynth project.

Finally, a CGRA Application Programming Interface (API) is required for the host processor to encapsulate all data and configuration transfers as well as the execution synchronization. Besides improving the portability to other target devices, this API hides CGRA-specific optimizations such as the rearrangement or duplication of data transfers (see Sect. 4.2) from the CAMeL-View backend developer.

4   Hardware Integration

The micro-architecture of the proposed CGRA decouples the core computation (i.e. interconnected PEs and control flow modules) from the hardware interface to the host processor. As this paper focuses on the CGRA integration into the RT target, the core architecture is described only briefly. More details can be found in [8].

4.1   Core Architecture

A PE consists of an Arithmetic Logic Unit (ALU), a Register File (RegFile), and a Context Memory (CMem), as shown in Fig. 2. The context indexed by the

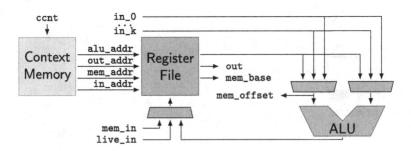

Fig. 2. PE with access to external memory

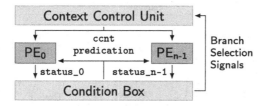

Fig. 3. CGRA core overview

current context counter (i.e. ccnt) is loaded from the CMem. Besides multiplexer settings and ALU operand selections, a context defines the addresses for the read and write ports of the RegFile.

The ALU has a modular structure. Operands are selected by multiplexers in front of the ALU. They select either data from the RegFile or from inputs (i.e. in) driven by the out-port of neighboring PEs. The multiplexer in front of the RegFiles selects either results from the ALU, data from an external memory or setup parameters (i.e. live_in). The setup mechanism is detailed in Sect. 4.2.

The CGRA is able to process kernels with heavy control flow and nested loops by using speculative computing and predicated stores in the PEs. The Condition Box (C-Box) combines status signals from comparison operations and drives the store predication signals, as shown in Fig. 3. Furthermore, branch selection signals drive the Context Control Unit (CCU), which performs branching. Consequently, all CMems of the PEs are controlled by the CCU with a common ccnt signal.

4.2 Peripheral Communication

To utilize the CGRA core as a hardware accelerator, it has to be properly integrated into a processing system. In this section, the integration of the CGRA core into a Xilinx Zynq SoC is described. An alternative system integration of the same CGRA core can be found in [10].

As described in Sect. 3, the accelerator has to pull sensor samples, push actuator samples, receive configurations and runtime data from the host processor, and push back different kinds of computed results to the host processor. To support these data transfers within the Zynq SoC, additional hardware modules have to be arranged around the CGRA core, as shown in Fig. 4. Just like the PEs inside the CGRA, those modules include CMems to be configurable for a specific application. An Advanced eXtensible Interface Bus (AXI) interconnect is used to transfer configuration and runtime data from the host processor to the CGRA. Therefore, all CMems are memory mapped into the AXI address space by an appropriate *AXI slave* module.

To ensure the accurate timing of the periodic control loops, a configurable hardware *cycle counter* provides a heart beat for the overall system in terms of periodic sync_in pulses. Upon this trigger, the *sensor controller* captures new values from its attached peripherals and writes those samples into the

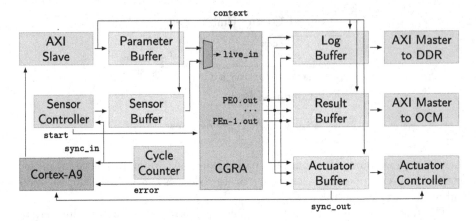

Fig. 4. Communication between the CGRA and its peripherals (sensors, actuators, and host processor) on the Zynq SoC

BRAM-based *sensor buffer*. The sensor controller then signals the CGRA to start executing a control cycle. During this execution, the CGRA can read values from the sensor buffer. The required read address is provided by the CMem within the sensor buffer. The sensor data is transferred into the RegFile of one (or more) PEs via the live_in path (see Fig. 2). The sensor sampling cannot be interleaved with a control cycle, as the scheduler has no information about the time required to capture specific samples. This sensor sample delay may even vary between successive control cycles.

Besides the sensor samples, runtime parameters sent from the host processor via AXI are used as inputs for the CGRA processing. Those parameters can be categorized into *constants* (loaded once for each application), *initial values* of internal states (loaded after each application reset), *runtime parameters* (updated sporadically upon user interaction at the control terminal), and *inputs from the host processor* (updated before every control cycle). In any case, those parameters must not be updated while a control cycle is executed, as the computed results would depend on the scheduled operator ordering and the exact time of the parameter update. The latter cannot be predicted accurately enough due to latency variations on the host processor and the AXI interconnect. Thus, a BRAM-based *parameter buffer* is memory mapped into the AXI address space to delay all parameter updates until the end of the current control cycle. Besides this delay mechanism, the parameter buffer also contains a configurable table to map parameter indices (derived from the AXI write address) to the targeted PE index and the targeted address within the corresponding RegFile. As soon as the current control cycle is done, the buffered parameters are written to the RegFiles via the live_in path (see Fig. 2). If a certain parameter has to be written to multiple RegFiles within the CGRA to reduce data copy operations at runtime, multiple AXI writes to the parameter buffer are generated by the host processor, as detailed in Sect. 5.3.

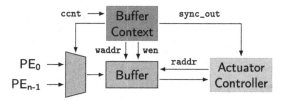

Fig. 5. Actuator buffer

The parameter buffer can be configured such that the execution of the next control cycle is delayed until the expected number of inputs from the host processor have been received and transferred into the RegFiles. This mechanism is exploited to synchronize the execution of CGRA and the host processor when a control algorithm is distributed over both of them. However, the dynamic delay until all required inputs are received adds up to the possible uncertainty from the sensor sampling stage, which might cause the overall application period to be exceeded. To detect such timing violations at runtime, an error is signaled to the host processor if the CGRA receives another sync_in pulse while still executing the current control cycle.

The out signal of the PEs (see Fig. 2) are not only used to drive the in signals of their neighboring PEs, but also to push calculated results to the *actuator controller* and the host processor, as shown in Fig. 4. Within the *actuator buffer*, the *buffer context* loaded for the current ccnt selects the correct PE output to be buffered (see Fig. 5). For the last actuator sample generated within a control cycle, a sync_out pulse is derived from the actuator buffer context to let the *actuator controller* transfer the buffered values to the attached peripheral devices.

To transfer CGRA outputs to the host processor, two different kinds of outputs are distinguished, as described in Sect. 3. *Result* outputs have to be available at the host processor before the next control cycle is started. Those results are typically intermediate values of a control loop distributed over CGRA and the host processor. As shown in Fig. 6, one PE output per clock cycle can be pushed into the *result buffer*. To reduce the scheduling constraints, the results can be buffered out of order. The *output context* then forwards the results in order to the On-Chip Memory (OCM) within the Zynq processing system via a high priority *AXI master*, from where they can be accessed by the host processor. The output

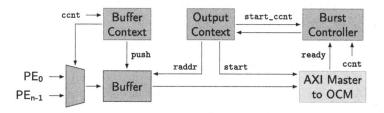

Fig. 6. Result buffer

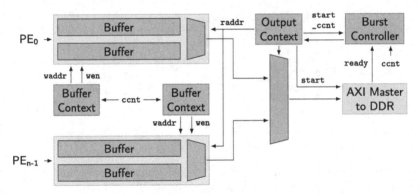

Fig. 7. Log buffer

context cannot be indexed by the continuously incremented ccnt, as the AXI master must be able to stall the transfer as long as the AXI slave is not ready to receive more data. Thus, a *burst controller* drives the output context such that an AXI burst is generated, as soon as the slave is ready and all burst data is available in the result buffer.

The other type of PE outputs to be transferred to the host processor is referred to as *log data*. These are typically values to be monitored by the user at the control terminal or to be captured over a long run to retrace the overall calculation. Compared to the result data discussed before, the *log data* transfer is not time critical, as the host processor does not have to respond immediately. On the other hand, the amount of *log data* is typically much larger than the amount of result data. Using the same approach of the result buffer for the *log data* would result in a bottleneck, as only one log datum could be buffered in every cycle. As most *log data* is generated near the end of a control cycle, this output generation could not be interleaved completely with other computations, and thus would increase the overall schedule length. To overcome this bottleneck, the input stage of the *log buffer* consists of a double buffer for each PE, as shown in Fig. 7. The buffers for write (PE to buffer) and read (buffer to AXI) access are switched after each control cycle. This allows to buffer more *log data* at once and furthermore, an entire control cycle can be used to transfer the log buffer content to the host processor. This is actually done by writing the *log data* and the index of the current control cycle into a circular buffer in the SoC-external Double Data Rate (DDR) memory via a low priority *AXI master* to not interfere with the transmission of the result data. The host processor is thus relieved from immediately processing the received *log data*.

5   Toolflow Integration

The CGRA-specific toolflow partially integrated into CAMeL-View is shown in Fig. 8. The main toolflow is implemented in Java, as portability and reusability are considered more important than the tool runtime at the moment. It is divided

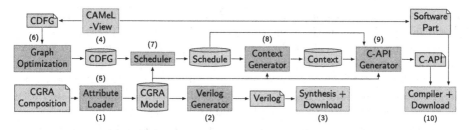

Fig. 8. Toolflow for generating a Verilog bitstream from a CGRA composition (1 to 3) and CGRA contexts for a specific CAMeL-View application (4 to 10). Third-party tools (red) are interconnected by the CGRA-specific tools (blue) implemented in Java. (Color figure online)

into two interconnected tool-chains for generating the CGRA composition bit-stream (i.e. Steps 1 to 3, described in Sect. 5.1) and the application-specific CGRA configuration (i.e. Steps 4 to 10, described in Sect. 5.2). The latter one can be executed on the control terminal from within CAMeL-View. The final download of the configuration is part of the API used by the host processor and described in Sect. 5.3.

5.1   CGRA Composition and Bitstream Generation

At some point the question arises, how a CGRA should be composed. This composition defines the number of PEs, their interconnection topology, the selection of operations in each PE, and the size of the IO buffers. Each application has its own configuration (i.e. CMem entries), but many applications can use the same composition. The actual mapping between application and composition is done by a scheduler. To research and exploit heterogeneous CGRA compositions, a static Verilog description is impractical. Instead, a generator framework was implemented.

Arbitrary CGRA instances can be modeled either manually by providing a corresponding JavaScript Object Notation (JSON) description, or automatically optimized for a set of applications, which is however beyond the scope of this paper. After parsing the composition into a Java object model by the *attribute loader* (Step 1), corresponding Verilog code is generated (Step 2). The resulting hardware description and constraints also include all required modules for inter-facing the CGRA to the host processor and to peripheral sensors and actuators, as described in Sect. 4.2. Finally, the bitstream is generated and downloaded to the Zynq device using the Xilinx Vivado tool-chain (Step 3).

5.2   CGRA Configuration

The second tool-chain starts with the application modeled in CAMeL-View (Step 4). Within this environment, the submodules of the control algorithm to be accelerated by the CGRA can be selected. These computational kernels are then exported as Control and Data Flow Graph (CDFG), which is represented in JSON along with other settings like the numerical integrator details. All remaining parts of the application are exported as C-functions to be executed on the host processor. Furthermore, the user selects a specific RT target (i.e. Zynq device), which is already programmed with the synthesis result from the bitstream tool-chain. The corresponding CGRA composition associated with the selected RT target is then loaded, again as Java object model (Step 5).

Afterwards, the application CDFG is parsed and optimized into a Java object model (Step 6). Those optimizations comprise typical compiler passes (e.g. common subexpression elimination, constant propagation, dead code elimination, and bitwidth optimization) and other steps required to adjust the CAMeL-View execution model to the CGRA execution model. For instance, selection operations (e.g. a = b ? c : d) have to be transformed into predicated store operations (e.g. if (b) a = c; if (!b) a = d). Furthermore, update operations for the CDFG state variables have to be inserted depending on the user-selected integration type. Currently, first and second order integrators (i.e. Euler and Heun [3]) are supported. All integrator steps rely on the calculation of the time derivative for the internal states, which is already part of the CDFG generated by CAMeL-View.

The optimized CDFG and the CGRA model are then fed into the *scheduler* (Step 7), which is based on list scheduling with additional constraints to cope with routing resources and inter-PE data transfers [9]. This approach produces very good results in short time [8]. Since the CAMeL-View models are based on reading and writing physical inputs and outputs, additional input and output operations need to be scheduled. The input operation allows a PE to read a value from the sensor buffer, as shown in Fig. 4. Output operations write the actuator, result, or log buffer, or even to multiple of them at once. As the result and actuator buffer may only be written by one PE at a time, the scheduler has to avoid write conflicts on these buffers. Furthermore, data structures required to map the buffered values to their respective CDFG nodes are generated.

Based on the scheduled input, output and arithmetic operations as well as the targeted CGRA model, the context information required to let the CGRA execute the current application is generated (Step 8). The CMem content for PEs, C-Box, CCU, and the peripheral buffers described in Sect. 4.2 is generated as Java object model at this stage. In Step 9, this context information is exported into C structures as part of the CGRA API for the host processor (see Sect. 5.3). Besides the context data, the *C-API generator* exports more scheduling details about the RegFile allocation to hide the mapping of inputs, parameters, and constants to certain PEs from the host application. Steps 7 to 9 allow to use any CGRA composition feasible with the generic model.

Finally, the C-API is combined with the software part of the CAMeL-View application and fed into the ARM compiler (Step 10). The resulting binary is downloaded to the host processor and executed on one ARM Cortex-A9 core. The other core is interfacing the control terminal and does not need to be reprogrammed when modifying the target application.

Listing 1.1. Minimal usage example for the CGRA API

```
1  uint8_t nextCycle = 0;
2  void handler(void *data) {nextCycle = 1;}
3  void main() {
4    cgra_setupData.logLowerAddr = 0x14000000;
5    cgra_setupData.logUpperAddr = 0x147FFFFF;
6    cgra_setupData.logIncrement =    0x1000;
7    cgra_setupData.mainPeriod    =    100000;
8    cgra_setup();
9    cgra_onSyncIn(handler)
10   cgra_changeStateRun();
11   while (1) if (nextCycle) {
12     nextCycle = 0;
13     cgra_updateRuntimeParameters();
14     for (int i=0; i<CGRA_LOG_RESULT_COUNT; i++)
15       printf("%f\n", (float*) cgra_readLogData(i));
16     cgra_stepLogWindow();
17   }
18 }
```

5.3 CGRA API

The software API for the host processor provides methods to configure the CGRA, to register interrupt handlers, to start and stop the periodic execution of the accelerated application kernel, to transfer runtime data to the CGRA, and to read result and log data from the OCM and DDR memory. All transfers from the host processor to the CGRA exploit the Cortex-A9 Direct Memory Access controller. They are combined to AXI burst transfers as far as possible. Both mechanisms are transparent to the API user.

A minimal usage example is shown in Listing 1.1. After defining the boundaries of the circular log buffer in the DDR memory region (Lines 4 to 6) and the number of clock cycles per control cycle (Line 7), all configurations (i.e. context data and initial RegFile values) are transferred to the CGRA in Line 8. In Line 9, the interrupt handler for the sync_in pulse is registered and the control cycle is started in Line 10. After each sync_in pulse, all runtime parameters modified by the control terminal (i.e. on the second ARM core, not shown in Listing 1.1) are transferred to the CGRA in Line 13. A dirty flag mechanism is used to avoid superfluous parameter transfers. Furthermore, one parameter update might result in multiple AXI transfers, if this parameter is scheduled to multiple PEs inside the CGRA. The mapping of parameters to (multiple) AXI addresses is based on the tables exported by the C-API generator. Finally, after reading the log data received from the CGRA during the last application cycle (Line 15), the API-internal pointer to the current window in the circular log buffer has to be forwarded (Line 16).

5.4 CGRA Verification

The integration of the CGRA into an SoC, the parallel execution of the PEs, the parallel execution of host processor and CGRA, and the communication between both units over three independent AXI ports provide a large number of possible errors calling for verification support. Based on the generator framework described above, two helpful features were integrated into the CGRA toolflow.

First, a testbench generator was implemented to simplify RTL verification using Modelsim. This generator combines the outputs of the both CGRA toolchains, i.e. the Verilog code for the CGRA composition and the C Code including the CGRA API implementation and the configuration for a certain application model. Using the Modelsim Direct Programming Interface to mimic the AXI transfers, the whole configuration and runtime data exchange of the CGRA can be simulated without modifying any other detail on the hardware or software level. Thus, only a simple C-like test file has to be generated manually to verify the CGRA execution on RTL.

Second, the Verilog generator of the composition toolchain was extended to add all code necessary for propagating any nested signal to the CGRA toplevel, where it can be connected to the Xilinx Logic Analyzer for runtime observation. This debug signal propagation can handle regular expressions within its path specifications, which is very helpful when analyzing similar structures such as the ALU output of all PEs or the CMem outputs within different modules.

6 Evaluation

In this section, the proposed CGRA-based hardware accelerator is evaluated in terms of resource utilization, clock frequency, tool runtime and application execution time. Therefore, the CGRA is integrated into a Xilinx XC7Z045-2 SoC, as detailed in Sect. 4.2.

6.1 Synthesis Results

To analyze the scalability of the accelerator, CGRAs with different numbers of PEs are generated and synthesized. Table 1 details the composition settings common for all of these CGRAs. They are chosen such that all example applications used for the performance evaluation in Sect. 6.3 can be mapped to those CGRAs. The CGRAs were configured to operate on single precision floating-point numbers. As shown in Fig. 9, each PE is connected with its eight neighbors in a matrix structure with horizontal and vertical wrap-around. This matrix star toroidal interconnect was chosen as the best performing solution among the regular interconnects that do not lead to significant drops in clock frequency [10]. Heterogeneous interconnects and PE operator selections could improve the CGRA performance, but this is beyond the scope of this paper.

Figure 10 details the LUT, DSP, and BRAM utilization (left axis) and the minimum clock cycle period (right axis) for different CGRA configurations using Vivado 2017.3. As expected, the resource usage increases significantly when increasing the number of PEs. The LUTs are the limiting resource and allow for a 5×5 PE configuration. The clock frequency is relatively stable and never falls significantly below 100 MHz.

Table 1. Common CGRAs settings. Operators are annotated with their single precision floating-point latency (cycles).

Operators	ADD(8), SUB(8), MUL(8), DIV(38), OR(1), NEG(1), ABS(1), SGN(1), SQRT(54), IFLT(4), IFGT(4), SIN(36), COS(36), ASIN(37)
PE Interconnect	Matrix Star Toroidal
RegFile	256 entries (32 bit each)
C-Box Size	64 entries
CMem Size	8192 entries
I/O Buffer Size	32 entries

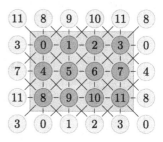

Fig. 9. Interconnect topology: 4×3 matrix star toroidal

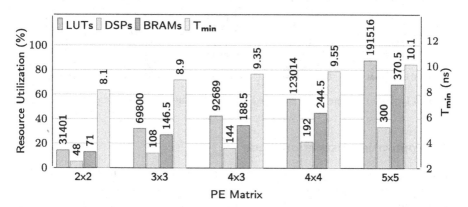

Fig. 10. Vivado 2017.3 performance results for XC7Z045-2 target. The value above each bar refers to the absolute of either LUTs, DSPs, or BRAMs

6.2 Tool Execution Time

As described in Sect. 3, one goal of this project is to minimize the time required to map control algorithms to the accelerator. To evaluate the tool runtime, several CAMeL-View applications have been mapped to the 4×3 CGRA discussed in Sect. 6.1. As shown in Fig. 11, the CDFGs to be handled by the scheduler range from several dozen nodes for a simple mechanical pendulum to more than 10 000 nodes for the model of a vehicle suspension system (i.e. half axle). The Java Tools described in Sect. 5.2 were executed on an AMD Ryzen 5 1600X processor running at 3.7 GHz. Figure 11 details the measured runtime averaged over 100 executions. For the smaller CDFGs, the file I/O dominates, but the overall runtime is negligible. The runtime of the scheduler and context generator increases significantly with the CDFG size. However, providing a complete configuration within 35 s for the largest example is still two orders of magnitude faster than generating a corresponding FPGA bitstream.

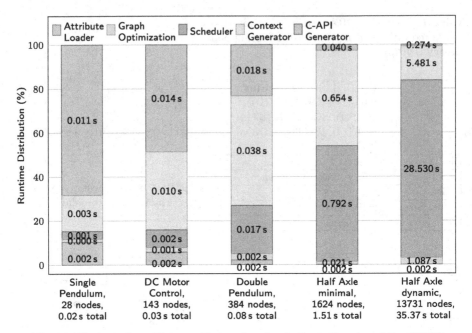

Fig. 11. Tool runtime: The specified node value indicate the size of the CDFG

6.3 Application Execution Time

The time required to execute a single control cycle is limiting the integration step size and is thus considered the main performance metric. The average execution time of one cycle on the ARM Cortex-A9 processor (running at 800 MHz) *after* cache initialization is taken as the performance baseline. The control algorithms already used in Sect. 6.2 are run out of CAMeL-View, which uses the GCC compiler with an O2 optimization. Those applications are not using sensors or actuators, as this comparison should focus on the computational performance of the architecture itself. Figure 12 lists the execution time of these applications on the ARM processor in the labels below the application names.

Those applications were mapped to the 5 × 5 CGRA, since it is the largest possible composition identified in Sect. 6.1. As shown in Fig. 12, the CGRA outperforms the ARM processor for all investigated applications by up to 2.23×.

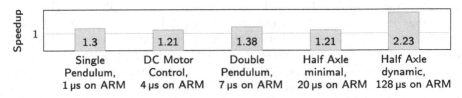

Fig. 12. CGRA speedup of application execution time compared to ARM Cortex-A9.

7 Conclusion

This contribution presented a CGRA-based hardware accelerator for control engineering applications and its integration into a Xilinx Zynq SoC. It executes a complex mechatronic model more than twice as fast as an ARM Cortex-A9. The overall CGRA configuration toolflow is fully integrated into the CAMeL-View development environment and maps even larger models to a given CGRA composition within a few seconds.

Future work will optimize the CGRA core and scheduler (e.g. interleaved operations, pipelining and resource sharing for similar operations). Heterogeneous PE operator sets and irregular interconnects will be exploited and alternative CGRA architectures and scheduling strategies will be investigated.

Acknowledgements. This research was funded by the German Federal Ministry for Education and Research with the funding ID 01 IS 15020 and supported by iXtronics.

References

1. Cong, J., Huang, H., Ma, C., Xiao, B., Zhou, P.: A fully pipelined and dynamically composable architecture of CGRA. In: IEEE International Symposium on Field-Programmable Custom Computing Machines, pp. 9–16 (2014)
2. dSpace: DS5203 - FPGA programmable per application (2018)
3. Fathoni, M.F., Wuryandari, A.I.: Comparison between Euler, Heun, Runge-Kutta and Adams-Bashforth-Moulton integration methods in the particle dynamic simulation. In: International Conference on Interactive Digital Media, pp. 1–7, December 2015
4. Fricke, F., Werner, A., Shahin, K., Huebner, M.: CGRA tool flow for fast runtime reconfiguration. In: Voros, N., Huebner, M., Keramidas, G., Goehringer, D., Antonopoulos, C., Diniz, P.C. (eds.) ARC 2018. LNCS, vol. 10824, pp. 661–672. Springer, Cham (2018). https://doi.org/10.1007/978-3-319-78890-6_53
5. Ho, C.H., et al.: Performance evaluation of a DySER FPGA prototype system spanning the compiler, microarchitecture, and hardware implementation. Energy (mJ) **5**(10), 15 (2015)
6. iXtronics: Mechatronics, tools & technologies. http://www.ixtronics.com
7. Lee, D., Jo, M., Han, K., Choi, K.: FloRA: coarse-grained reconfigurable architecture with floating-point operation capability. In: International Conference on Field-Programmable Technology, pp. 376–379, December 2009. https://doi.org/10.1109/FPT.2009.5377609
8. Ruschke, T., Jung, L., Hochberger, C.: A near optimal integrated solution for resource constrained scheduling, binding and routing on CGRAs. In: IEEE International Parallel and Distributed Processing Symposium Workshops, pp. 213–218 (2017)
9. Ruschke, T., Jung, L., Wolf, D., Hochberger, C.: Scheduler for inhomogeneous and irregular CGRAs with support for complex control flow. In: IEEE International Parallel and Distributed Processing Symposium Workshops, pp. 198–207, May 2016
10. Wolf, D., Ruschke, T., Hochberger, C.: Amidar project: lessons learned in 15 years of researching adaptive processors. In: International Symposium on Reconfigurable Communication-centric Systems-on-Chip, July 2018

Exploiting Reconfigurable Vector Processing for Energy-Efficient Computation in 3D-Stacked Memories

João Paulo C. de Lima[1(✉)], Paulo C. Santos[1], Rafael F. de Moura[1], Marco A. Z. Alves[2], Antonio C. S. Beck[1], and Luigi Carro[1]

[1] Informatics Institute, Federal University of Rio Grande do Sul, Porto Alegre, Brazil
jpclima@inf.ufrgs.br
[2] Department of Informatics, Federal University of Paraná, Curitiba, Brazil

Abstract. Although Processing-in-Memory (PIM) architectures have helped to reduce the effect of the memory wall, the logic placed inside 3D-memories still faces the large disparity between DRAM and CMOS logic operations. Thereby, for a broad range of emerging data-intensive applications, the Functional Units (FUs) are usually underutilized, especially when the application presents poor temporal-locality. As applications demand irregular processing requirements on the different parts of their execution, this behavior can be used to reconfigure energy-reduction techniques, either by scaling frequency or by power-gating functional units. In this paper, we present the application-dependable characteristics that enable dynamic usage of energy-reduction techniques without performance degradation for highly constrained PIM designs. The experimental results show that the exploration of a reconfiguration mechanism can improve PIM system energy efficiency by 5× and also can effectively benefit both memory-intensive and compute-intensive applications.

Keywords: Processing in Memory ·
Reconfigurable vector architectures · Energy-efficiency

1 Introduction

The 3D-stacking process has emerged as a solution for mitigating the memory-wall problem. In recent years, the emergence and feasibility of 3D-stacking technology have opened up opportunities in both architectural and chip design fields. Supported by these new trends, Processing-in-Memory (PIM) concept has emerged as a prominent approach to improve performance and reduce the energy of modern systems. This approach keeps closer processing and data by taking advantage of logic layer available on 3D-stacked memories to compute data directly in the memory device. Nevertheless, the design of 3D-stacked PIM devices still faces challenges related to costs, retention characteristics, and business decisions. The main issue resides on the thermal dissipation challenges that

© Springer Nature Switzerland AG 2019
C. Hochberger et al. (Eds.): ARC 2019, LNCS 11444, pp. 262–276, 2019.
https://doi.org/10.1007/978-3-030-17227-5_19

happen when stacking Dynamic Random Access Memory (DRAM) layers on top of processor layers. [1]. A second issue involves customizing the DRAM dies for each processor chip, which introduces design and supply-chain complexity that would increase the overall manufacturing cost [2].

Although PIM architectures have reduced the effects of the memory wall, the processing logic placed inside 3D-memories still faces the disparity of latencies between DRAM and CMOS logic operation. The average latency for DRAM access is typically tens of times higher than the time of a Functional Unit (FU) operation under the same constraints, and even worse for the most recent technology nodes. This fact implies that the processing unit can potentially spend more time in idle mode and increase power density depending on the arithmetic intensity. The degree of utilization of FUs relies on data reuse and the computational intensity inherent from the workload.

Furthermore, the majority of the applications can present a mix of compute-bound and memory-bound behavior [3]. Thus, the variability of application's demand for processing power and the latency disparity between operations on DRAM and FUs can be used to reduce energy consumption, and also help with the inherited thermal dissipation problems of the 3D-stacked PIM architectures. To do so, a special mechanism must detect the fluctuations in the application needs for FU resources. Further, this mechanism must reconfigure the PIM architecture to dynamically match the current demand for processing power and keep the maximum memory bandwidth achievable by each application part based on some decision heuristic. A reconfiguration process should dynamically adapt the number of FUs or perform a frequency scaling operation ideally without performance penalties. Adjusting the number of working FUs implies that highly parallel and bigger operations can be split into smaller and sequential ones. Thus, both the idle time and the energy consumption of unused FUs could be minimized.

This paper opens up a discussion on the use of reconfigurability in vectorial PIM architectures to provide energy-efficiency and overcome technical issues, rather than limiting the effects of reconfiguration to performance-oriented goals. The main contributions of this paper are:

1. The use of reconfigurability to minimize thermal power dissipation challenges in 3D-stacked PIM architectures.
2. The identification of application characteristics to match processing power to the maximum bandwidth achievable by each application.
3. A reconfigurable mechanism for dynamically reducing the number of active FUs as the application demands, which varies the processing power of PIM logic and finds a near-optimal point to the energy consumption.

The rest of this paper is organized as follows: in Sect. 2 a general overview of 3D-stacked PIM is presented, as well as its constraints and feasibility challenges are discussed. In Sect. 3, hardware and software aspects of reconfiguration on vector processors are discussed, and some examples are shown to highlight the benefits of reconfiguration. The experimental setup and methods used to validate the proposed method are described in Sect. 4 and the results are presented in

Sect. 4.3. Finally, some related works are listed in Sect. 5 and final considerations are made in Sect. 6.

2 Background

In this section, a general overview of fundamental concepts related to 3D-stacked memories and Processing-in-Memory (PIM) architectures are presented. Next, a brief discussion about 3D-PIM architectures design feasibility and constraints is promoted to situate the proposed approach realm.

2.1 3D-Stacked Processing-in-Memory

By connecting Dynamic Random Access Memory (DRAM) memory dies stacked on top of a logic layer using dense Through-Silicon Via (TSV), high-density 3D memories can provide higher capacity, bandwidth, and lower access latencies compared to traditional DRAM modules. The most diffused and recent examples of 3D-memory usage in the industry are the Micron's Hybrid Memory Cube (HMC) [4], and AMD/Hynix's High Bandwidth Memory (HBM) [5]. Figure 1 illustrates the internal organization of a generic 3D-stacked memory. For HMC and HBM, the 3D memory layout is composed of several DRAM layers, each one containing multiple banks.

The stacked arrangement of DRAM layers is split vertically into *vaults*. Each vault comprises a region of DRAM layers and a logic layer connected by an independent group of TSV and controlled by a vault controller. Each vault controller manages its own DRAM banks independently. Thus, it is possible to operate on a 3D-memory with both vault-level and bank-level parallelism. Following the last HMC specification [4], it can be seen that the memory module can have either four or eight DRAM dies and one logic layer all stacked within a memory cube. The cube has 32 vaults with their respective vault controllers. Each vault controller can manage independently 16 memory banks. The HMC can achieve up to 320 GB/s of bandwidth distributed along four serial link interfaces.

In addition to the emerging of 3D-stacked memories, the increasing demand for computational resources by data-intensive applications leveraged and reintroduced the PIM research field. As the usage of PIM devices alleviates the memory bottleneck, the natural application domain covers current big-data processing. Also, PIM reduces energy consumption and accelerates applications execution time avoiding the data movements back and forth along the memory hierarchy. Moreover, PIM can exploit both the high memory bandwidth, more massive Data Level Parallelism (DLP) and vault-level parallelism when coupled with 3D-stacked memories.

There are several architectural PIM design approaches in the literature. For commodity, and according to [1], they can be classified into two main categories based on the central processing element type present in the logic layer: General Purpose Processor (GPP)-like cores and dedicated logic circuits. The former group adopts the replication of conventional GPPs into the logic layer. This PIM

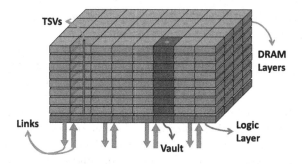

Fig. 1. 3D-stacked memory layout comprising of eight DRAM layers and a base logic layer connected by TSVs and vertically organized in vaults.

processing element type takes advantage in programmability since it inherits the commodity software development tools such as MPI and CUDA. On the other hand, processing elements built based on dedicated circuitry often rely on replication of Functional Unit (FU) elements, which, in turn, achieves high DLP, memory bandwidth, and computational power [6].

2.2 Constraints and Feasibility of 3D-Stacked PIM

Although 3D-stacked PIM is feasible for a broad range of application domains, some design challenges must be faced when considering a 3D memory PIM project. The designers have to deal with power, area and energy constraints for the logic layer to effectively implement the PIM architecture.

According to [1], the power budget related to the logical layer available in the last generation of HMC comprises 11W. However, this constraint can be even smaller if thermal aspects are taken into consideration, reducing it to mere 8.5 W. Regarding area, for an HMC design with a capacity of 8 GB distributed along eight DRAM layers, 16 memory banks and 32 vaults, the area available in the logic layer corresponds to 144 mm^2. Thus, taking into consideration all the physical and technological aspects involved in the logic layer project design, the most suitable PIM processing element type for 3D-stacked memories is that one based on FUs replication [1]. Moreover, FU-centered PIM design with vector operations capabilities can exploit both the entire bandwidth available and provide high DLP, while fitting in the logic layer constraints.

3 Reconfigurable Execution

There are several possibilities to be explored in a PIM architecture design when concerning about energy consumption. Even following the power and area constraints related to 3D logic layer, some aspects intrinsic from DRAM technology cannot be changed. Although PIM reduced the memory walls, the time spent to perform a memory access to a DRAM is still tens of times higher than the time required to process the data in the FUs. So, exploring such inherent character-istics in PIM designs can lead to an energy consumption reduction.

Recent proposals of PIM architectures rely on multiple homogeneous pro-cessing units, and most of them have in common a high number of FUs. For example, we will examine groups of Single Instruction Multiple Data (SIMD) units organized into several Vector Processing Units (VPUs). Thus, sizing the number of FUs to exploit the high internal bandwidth requires an analysis of the area and power costs. Floating point units, for instance, are generally required in basic applications and have a high cost regarding area and power [7]. Energy savings can be achieved by (a) selecting how many units will execute a code por-tion on compile time (b) dynamically scaling frequency or by (c) reconfiguring the data path to turn on/off FUs when they are not used for a long time.

3.1 Application Classification

The SIMD units with fixed width and frequency cannot satisfy different process-ing utilization requirements of various applications. Even a single application can have a variable processing power pattern during execution time [8]. PIM based on SIMD units are a natural choice for many data-intensive workloads [9–11], as this combination can benefit both memory-intensive and compute-intensive applications. Some known metrics can identify the compute intensity and cost of memory access, such as:

1. **Memory access distance:** indicates a fraction of cycles where pipeline could be stalled due to demand for load or store instructions. As kernel code por-tions with poor-temporal locality may cause a miss throughout the cache hierarchies, the major part of such cycles may be spent due to DRAM latency accesses [12].
2. **Arithmetic intensity and cost of instruction:** indicates how many SIMD operations are made in sequence, and the cost in cycles of each instruction. For instance, floating point division takes 20 cycles, while typical bit-wise operations are made in 1 cycle.
3. **Memory parallelism:** the predominance of regular memory access patterns, either by vault-level and bank-level parallelism, reduces the average memory access latency. Thus, the reduced and stable latency can be used to create a pipeline for data stream workloads [13,14].

Either a compiler or a HW mechanism can identify such metrics. As past studies already extracted these characteristics on compile time, a compiler-based tool with hardware information should be suitable for that task. This compiler tool can analyze basic blocks based on the costs of instructions and memory accesses to foresee the arithmetic intensity. To better illustrate this analysis, two basic blocks of common kernels with irregular processing power demands are presented in Listing 1.1. The first basic block (*BB0*) performs a data copy operation from one region of the memory to another, and the second basic block (*BB1*) executes the dot product of two vectors.

In the *BB0*, the whole basic block consists of PIM load and store instructions, which implies that no processing power of SIMD units is needed and all FUs can be turned off. In contrast to the *BB0*, the *BB1* has 14 PIM instructions between the second load instruction and the next memory access in the loop. For instance, the 14 instructions take 52 cycles, or 41.6 ns using the default period (0.8 ns) of the HMC's logic layer, to be completed. As 14 SIMD instructions take 41.6 ns considering 256-byte SIMD units, this represents about 20 GFlops. In order to not hurt the total execution time, the maximum processing power must be kept the same. However, the number of FU per SIMD unit can be significantly reduced without performance degradation, while improving the energy of computation.

In this paper, we rely on a compiler that identifies and offloads instructions to a PIM device as presented in [15]. Then, we test this heuristic to find the optimal point regarding energy-efficiency in a case study architecture. Some alternatives, such as vector size and Dynamic Voltage Frequency Scaling (DVFS) are considered. However, the need for a fine-grain reconfigurability leads to changes in the execution mechanism that will be presented in Sect. 3.3.

Listing 1.1. Example of an assembly code snippet with two different basic blocks.

```
.BB0:
        PIM_256B_LOAD    VPU_0_Reg_0 , pimword ptr [rax]
        PIM_256B_LOAD    VPU_0_Reg_1 , pimword ptr [rax + 256]
        PIM_256B_STORE   pimword ptr [rbx] , VPU_0_Reg_0
        PIM_256B_STORE   pimword ptr [rbx + 256] , VPU_0_Reg_1
        add      rbx , 256
        add      rax , 256
        inc      rcx
        cmp      rcx , 16384
        jne      BB0

.BB1:
        PIM_256B_LOAD    VPU_0_Reg_1 , pimword ptr [rax]
        PIM_256B_LOAD    VPU_0_Reg_2 , pimword ptr [rbx + 4*rcx]
        PIM_256B_VFMUL   VPU_0_Reg_1 , VPU_0_Reg_2 , VPU_0_Reg_1
        PIM_256B_VFADD   VPU_0_Reg_0 , VPU_0_Reg_0 , VPU_0_Reg_1
        PIM_256B_VSHUF64x2  VPU_0_Reg_1 , VPU_0_Reg_0 , VPU_0_Reg_0 , 0x3feec
        PIM_256B_VFADD   VPU_0_Reg_0 , VPU_0_Reg_0 , VPU_0_Reg_1
        PIM_256B_VSHUF64x2  VPU_0_Reg_1 , VPU_0_Reg_0 , VPU_0_Reg_0 , 0x1f4
        PIM_256B_VFADD   VPU_0_Reg_0 , VPU_0_Reg_0 , VPU_0_Reg_1
        PIM_256B_VSHUF64x2  VPU_0_Reg_1 , VPU_0_Reg_0 , VPU_0_Reg_0 , 0xe
        PIM_256B_VFADD   VPU_0_Reg_0 , VPU_0_Reg_0 , VPU_0_Reg_1
        PIM_256B_VSHUF64x2  VPU_0_Reg_1 , VPU_0_Reg_0 , VPU_0_Reg_0 , 0x1
        PIM_256B_VFADD   VPU_0_Reg_0 , VPU_0_Reg_0 , VPU_0_Reg_1
        PIM_256B_PSHUFFLE  VPU_0_Reg_1 , VPU_0_Reg_0 , 0xffffffffeeffeec
        PIM_256B_VFADD   VPU_0_Reg_0 , VPU_0_Reg_0 , VPU_0_Reg_1
        PIM_256B_PSHUFFLE  VPU_0_Reg_1 , VPU_0_Reg_0 , 0xffffffffeedf4e5
        PIM_256B_VFADD   VPU_0_Reg_0 , VPU_0_Reg_0 , VPU_0_Reg_1
        PIM_256B_STORE   pimword ptr [rcx] , VPU_0_Reg_0
        add      rax , 256
        add      rbx , 256
        add      rcx , 256
        inc      r12
        cmp      r12 , 16384
        jne      BB1
```

3.2   Vector Size Identification on Compiling Time

Regarding vectorization, traditional open-source compilers like GCC and commercial compilers such as ICC have different approaches to identify vectorization possibilities. Considering the most aggressive compiler flags which enable vectorization, different schedulings for vectorial instructions are related for GCC and ICC assembly codes. The ICC tends to use only vectorial instructions for a given set of elements if their operations can be converted into vectorial versions. When the number of elements is not an exact multiple of the available vector sizes, ICC issues masked vectorial instructions for those that do not fit entirely in a vector unit. On the other hand, GCC issues as many vector instructions as possible for a specified vector width and scalar instructions for the remaining vector operands. However, none of the state-of-the-art compilers perform an efficient analysis regarding energy consumption in vector operations. Memory-intensive applications could have their processing power reduced without performance degradation by selecting fewer VPUs and turning off the idle ones. Moreover, the number of Load/Store Units impacts the maximum memory bandwidth achievable by an application, which reflects applications where the memory bounds the execution time, rather than the number of processing elements.

3.3   Dynamic Reconfiguration of Execution Mechanism

In a typical vector processor, as the degree of compute-boundness of an application decreases, a significant amount of static energy is lost to keep a great number of FUs in active mode. In applications that are mostly memory-bounded, the full width of a large SIMD unit is used for a few cycles. This fact causes low utilization rate and ineffective energy spendings to keep them in idle mode, mainly when the architecture supports large SIMD units. As the number of active FUs is reduced, the spatial operations of a SIMD instruction can be pipelined in a few number of FUs, and they can be completed with a small penalty of a few more cycles per instruction. As basic blocks may admit a variable increase of the latency of modifying instructions, no performance degradation can be perceived, since the processing latency is masked by the memory access latency in a loop.

A straightforward change in the control unit and data-path of an usual SIMD unit is needed to provide variable width of this unit on the execute stage. Figure 2 presents a possible implementation of a VPU to have a single SIMD instruction pipelined using different factors of two. In this mechanism, the original VPU has 32 active FUs, and Fig. 2A presents 16-FUs setup for compute-bounded basic blocks. For memory-bounded application the SIMD unit can be reconfigured to 2-FUs setup. These different setups provide a fine-grain reconfigurability of SIMD instructions with low cost of reconfiguration. Thus, the PIM device can change this configuration at each basic block or even at each instruction. Further, energy savings are achieved, since static power is avoided by turning off some FUs that would spend more if they were on. The analysis to find the near-optimal setup has also to take into consideration the trade-off between cumulative static energy and execution time.

4   Experimental Setup

In this section, we present the methodology and tools used to evaluate our mechanism.

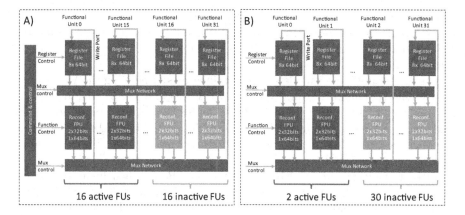

Fig. 2. Example of two reconfiguration setups. Figure A presents half of the total functional units in active mode, thus being able to compute 128 B per cycle. Figure B represent a more constrained processing power capable of executing 8 Bytes per cycle

4.1 The PIM Architecture for a Case Study

The micro-architecture Recon gurable Vector Unit (RVU) [11] was chosen as case study architecture to support our experiments. Accordingly to [1], within a range of recent proposal 3D-stacked PIM architectures, RVU not only fits in the power and area constraints related to HMC logic layer but also is capable of exploring higher memory bandwidth and DLP when compared to others state-of-art PIM architectures. A RVU module comprises a set of 32 × 8-byte multi-precision FUs, a Finit State Machine (FSM) to control the flow of RVU instructions and a 8 × 256-byte register file. For the HMC, each *vault* has one RVU module that can operate independently in a parallel fashion. Thus, RVU provides up to 8192-byte FU capacity of vectorial processing and can reach a peak compute power of 2.5 TFLOPS.

The RVU Instruction Set Architecture (ISA) extends the original Intel Advanced Vector Extensions (AVX) keeping compatibility with legacy x86 host instructions allowing a hybrid PIM code style. When the host processor fetches a RVU instruction, it is treated as a store operation and sent to the PIM device to be executed. RVU instructions can deal with operand sizes varying from 4 Bytes to 256 Bytes at once. Additionally, RVU instances can aggregate their execution to deal with bigger instructions ranging from 256 Bytes to 8192 Bytes at once.

4.2 Simulation Method

To experiment and evaluate the proposed techniques, the RVU architecture was implemented for simulation and tests on GEM5 Simulator [16] as presented in [17]. Since RVU extends AVX, and the Intel x86 host processor offloads RVU instructions to HMC, GEM5 was adapted to support both AVX and RVU instructions. For compiling the source code application tests and generating the binaries, Processing-In-Memory cOmpiler (PRIMO) [15] was used as a support compiler tool. Table 1 summarizes the setup simulated, it comprises an Intel *Skylake* micro-architecture as the host processor and an HMC RVU capable module as main memory.

The energy and power models were obtained by synthesizing the VPU design provided by [1]. This vector unit contains 32×32 bits and 32×64 bits, integer and float-pointing FUs (adders and multipliers), an $8 \times 32 \times 64$ bits register file, and a FSM able to represent a single RVU instance. Supported by Cadence RTL Compiler tool, we extracted area, dynamic and static power for this implementation using 32 nm process technology.

Further, we use a subset of BLAS routines, STREAM benchmark and other miscellaneous kernel applications to represent different kernels behaviors, ranging from mostly memory-bounded to mostly compute-bounded kernels. We varied the number of active FUs from 32 to a single FU, which is given by the #FUn labels in the following charts. Regardless of the data operands present in the benchmarks, a single FU can operate on either 2×32-bit operands or 64-bit operand at a time.

Table 1. Baseline system configuration.

Intel Skylake Microarchitecture
4GHz; AVX-512 Instruction Set Capable; L3 Cache 16MB;
8GB HMC; 4 Memory Channels;
HMC
HMC version 2.0 specification;
Total DRAM Size 8GBytes - 8 Layers - 8Gbit per layer;
32 Vaults - 16 Banks per Vault; 4 high speed Serial Links;
RVU
1.25GHz; 32 Independent Functional Units; Integer and Floating-Point Capable;
Instructions from 4Bytes to 4096Bytes;
32 Independent Register Bank of 8x256Bytes each;
Latency (cycles): 1-alu, 3-mul. and 20-div. integer units;
Latency (cycles): 5-alu, 5-mul. and 20-div. floating-point units;
Interconnection between vaults: 5 cycles latency;

4.3   Results and Discussion

Figure 3 presents normalized memory bandwidth and processing power achieved by PIM logic to process kernels with different behaviors. Figure 3a depicts a pure streaming behavior where the number of FUs does not impact on the total processing power, neither the average memory bandwidth. As this kernel application is not compute-intensive, the memory bandwidth stands out when the application makes use of the largest load/store instructions available. In contrast to Stream Scale, the Polynomial Solver Equation shows an opposite behavior to streaming applications, as shown in Fig. 3c. The largest vector widths reach both the highest values of memory bandwidth and processing power. In this case, not only memory bandwidth is required by the application, but also the processing power, which is achieved by the two reconfiguration setups (#FU32 and #FU16). It is possible to notice that the combination of memory- and compute-bound characteristics are found in the Bilinear Interpolation kernel. As shown in Fig. 3b, the discrepancy of bandwidth and FLOPS is only observed on the setups #FU1. One can notice that increasing the vector width also increases the memory bandwidth, thus allowing the use of few FUs to reach the maximum FLOPS.

Figure 4 shows speedup and energy results for the same kernels presented in Fig. 3. To ease the comparison with other designs, the absolute values for each baseline are given in the chart area (Fig. 4). The streaming-like application in Fig. 4a shows that bandwidth limits the speedup. The reconfiguration setup with fewer FUs is enough to consume data and obtain the same performance of the setups with more FUs. To reach a higher performance, more VPUs are required to allow larger load operations. However, this implies that more hardware resources (register file, FSM, and FUs) will be kept in idle mode wasting static power, thus reducing the energy efficiency of those configurations. Similarly, Fig. 4c can reach the highest performance for different reconfiguration

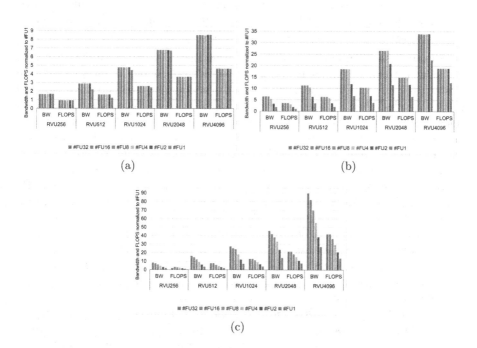

Fig. 3. Total memory bandwidth and processing power for applications with different processing requirements. (a) Stream Scale, (b) Bilinear Interpolation and (a) Polynomial Solver

setups, except for the #FU1. In Fig. 4d, different points can reach the low energy consumption of computation. However, as aforementioned, this application combines memory and compute-bound behavior, which means that the most efficient points will occur when a better compromise between memory bandwidth and processing power. Compute-intensive kernels are profoundly impacted by the number of FUs available in SIMD units, as presented in Fig. 4e. Although the highest performance is reached by using the RVU4096 with setups #FU32 or #FU16, the most energy efficient configuration is achieved by using the setups #FU16 and #FU8.

Despite Fig. 4 has presented different energy consumption and performance points separately, a better metric to show the efficiency of the reconfiguration is the Energy Delay Product (EDP). Figure 5 presents the EDP results of several kernel applications. All columns were obtained by running the largest vector width (RVU4096) and varying the reconfiguration setups. One can notice that memory-bound applications must use fewer FUs to obtain significant energy efficiency. On the other hand, compute-bound applications require higher FLOPS, which is ruled by the number of FUs selected in the reconfiguration.

5   Related Work

There are several works related to exploring energy reduction techniques. The studies mostly associated with PIM architectures, reconfigurable processors and reconfigurable vectorial machines are presented in this section.

Processing-in-Memory: In [18], it is proposed an offload candidate mechanism which can be implemented as a compiler technique. The basic idea is to statically estimate the memory bandwidth savings by whether moving or not blocks of code to be processed near the memory based on dynamic system conditions such as current bandwidth utilization. DRAMA (DRAM-Accelerator) [19] proposes a PIM architecture where the host processor can offload computation and data-intensive operations to Coarse-Grain Recon gurable Arrays (CGRAs) stacked on top of DRAM devices. Similarly, [20] presents Heterogeneous Reconfigurable Logic (HRL), a reconfigurable array for Near-Data Processing (NDP) systems. HRL combines both coarse-grained and fine-grained logic blocks and uses specialized units to support irregular data layouts in analytics workloads effectively. The study represented in [21] reports huge performance speed-up on basic operators of data analytic processing. This PIM architecture achieves significant energy-efficiency by placing SIMD-enabled ARM cores on each HMC *vault*, although it does not support floating point operations and neither presents a technique or optimization to make better use of SIMD units. The work of [10] presents an in-memory resistive design of a general-purpose SIMD co-processor. They claim to allow better scalability and performance compared to a CMOS SIMD processor. However, the main drawback resides on the significantly high power density and low endurance inherent of Resistive Random Access Memories (ReRAM).

Reconfiguration for Energy Reduction: In [22], the authors present a fine grain power-gating technique to cope with future leakage power problem. This

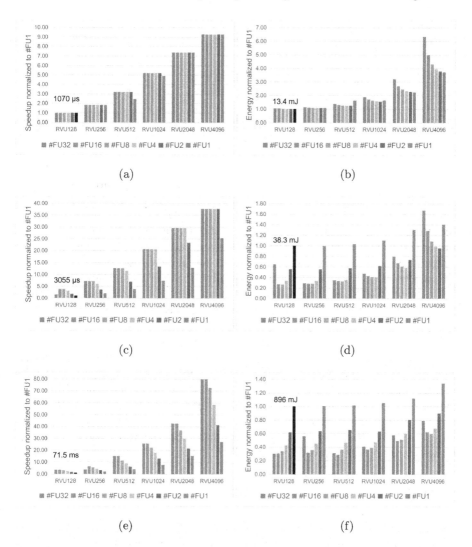

Fig. 4. Speed-up and energy consumption in three applications. (a) and (b) Stream Scale, (c) and (d) Bilinear Interpolation, and (e) and (f) Polynomial Solver Equation

technique can be applied to a CGRA and can reduce up to 48% in real applications. In a different manner, the study of [23] describes a dynamic voltage switching technique to reduce energy dissipation of dynamically reconfigurable processors. This technique dynamically changes the supply voltage of each processing element at the context-by-context basis. However, the energy overhead due to voltage switching hinders the energy reduction, and a mapping optimization was necessary to enable up to 12.5% of total energy savings.

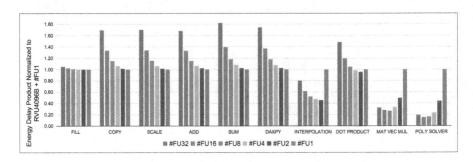

Fig. 5. Energy Delay Product (EDP) results for several application kernels

Reconfigurable Vectors: In [24], the authors propose Softbrain, a reconfigurable vectorial machine for accelerating stream-dataflow applications. Softbrain comprises a control core to generate stream commands, a set of stream-engines to transfer data with memories, and a deeply-pipelined reconfigurable dataflow composed of CGRAs for parallel computation. Regarding regular architectures, [25] proposes an integrated vector scalar mechanism coupled into an ARM microarchitecture core. Their proposed design reuses scalar FUs to provide the execution for vectorial instructions. The main component is a block-based model of implementation that groups vectorial computational operations to execute them in a coordinated manner. ARM Scalable Vector Extension (SVE) defines a SIMD unit able to operate on up to 2048-bit registers, and the SIMD unit defined by the Vector Extension of RISC-V up to 1024-bit registers. However, no physical implementation using the largest size is available yet, and no information regarding power-gating techniques driven by the application's demands on these large registers was found.

6   Conclusions and Future Work

This paper presented a discussion introducing the necessity for the adoption of reconfiguration techniques in vectorial Processing-in-Memory (PIM) architectures to improve energy efficiency. We demonstrated that identifying and taking advantage of the deviations in the compute-intensity to reconfigurable the current PIM architecture can lead to energy savings. To do so, the reconfigurable mechanism must be able to estimate intrinsic applications characteristics. Our simulation results show that, for a set of memory-bounded applications, the number of Functional Units (FUs) on does not interfere in the system performance so that energy savings can be achieved. On the other hand, compute-bounded applications have their memory bandwidth as FLOPS dictated by the biggest number of FUs active. As future works, compiler and hardware techniques for application profiling and PIM reconfiguration will be studied.

Acknowledgment. This study was financed in part by the Coordenação de Aperfeiçoamento de Pessoal de Nível Superior - Brasil (CAPES) - Finance Code 001, and by the Serrapilheira Institute (grant number Serra-1709-16621).

References

1. de Lima, J.P.C., Santos, P.C., Alves, M.A., Beck, A., Carro, L.: Design space exploration for PIM architectures in 3D-stacked memories. In: International Conference on Computing Frontiers, pp. 113–120. ACM (2018)
2. Hu, X., Stow, D., Xie, Y.: Die stacking is happening. IEEE Micro **38**(1), 22–28 (2018)
3. Awan, A.J., Brorsson, M., Vlassov, V., Ayguade, E.: Performance characterization of in-memory data analytics on a modern cloud server. In: 2015 IEEE Fifth International Conference on Big Data and Cloud Computing (BDCloud), pp. 1–8. IEEE (2015)
4. Hybrid Memory Cube Consortium. Hybrid Memory Cube Specification Rev. 2.0 (2013). http://www.hybridmemorycube.org/
5. Lee, D.U., et al.: 25.2 A 1.2 V 8 GB 8-channel 128 GB/s high-bandwidth memory (HBM) stacked DRAM with effective microbump I/O test methods using 29 nm process and TSV. In: 2014 IEEE International Solid-State Circuits Conference Digest of Technical Papers (ISSCC), pp. 432–433, February 2014
6. Zhu, Q., et al.: A 3D-stacked logic-in-memory accelerator for application-specific data intensive computing. In: International 3D Systems Integration Conference (2013)
7. Chen, T., et al.: DianNao: a small-footprint high-throughput accelerator for ubiquitous machine-learning. ACM SIGPLAN Not. **49**(4), 269–284 (2014)
8. Mittal, S.: A survey of techniques for improving energy efficiency in embedded computing systems. arXiv preprint arXiv:1401.0765 (2014)
9. Nair, R., et al.: Active memory cube: a processing-in-memory architecture for exascale systems. IBM J. Res. Dev. **59**(2/3), 17-1 (2015)
10. Morad, A., Yavits, L., Kvatinsky, S., Ginosar, R.: Resistive GP-SIMD processing-in-memory. ACM Trans. Archit. Code Optim. (TACO) **12**(4), 57 (2016)
11. Santos, P.C., Oliveira, G.F., Tome, D.G., Alves, M.A.Z., Almeida, E.C., Carro, L.: Operand size reconfiguration for big data processing in memory. In: 2017 Design, Automation Test in Europe Conference Exhibition (DATE), March 2017
12. Keramidas, G., Petoumenos, P., Kaxiras, S.: Cache replacement based on reuse-distance prediction. In: 25th International Conference on Computer Design, ICCD 2007, pp. 245–250. IEEE (2007)
13. Ding, W., Guttman, D., Kandemir, M.: Compiler support for optimizing memory bank-level parallelism. In: Proceedings of the 47th Annual IEEE/ACM International Symposium on Microarchitecture, pp. 571–582. IEEE Computer Society (2014)
14. Sura, Z., et al.: Data access optimization in a processing-in-memory system. In: Proceedings of the 12th ACM International Conference on Computing Frontiers, p. 6. ACM (2015)
15. Ahmed, H., et al.: A compiler for automatic selection of suitable processing-in-memory instructions. In: Design, Automation and Test in Europe Conference and Exhibition (DATE) (2019)
16. Binkert, N., et al.: The gem5 simulator. ACM SIGARCH Comput. Archit. News **39**, 1–7 (2011)

17. Santos, P.C., de Lima, J.P.C., Moura, R.F., Alves, M.A., Beck, A., Carro, L.: Exploring IoT platform with technologically agnostic processing-in-memory framework. In: Proceedings of the Intelligent Embedded Systems Architectures and Applications Workshop. IEEE (2018)
18. Hsieh, K., et al.: Transparent offloading and mapping (TOM): enabling programmer-transparent near-data processing in GPU systems. ACM SIGARCH Comput. Archit. News **44**(3), 204–216 (2016)
19. Farmahini-Farahani, A., Ahn, J., Compton, K., Kim, N.: Drama: an architecture for accelerated processing near memory. Comput. Archit. Lett. **14**(99), 26–29 (2014)
20. Gao, M., Kozyrakis, C.: HRL: efficient and flexible reconfigurable logic for near-data processing. In: 2016 IEEE International Symposium on High Performance Computer Architecture (HPCA), pp. 126–137. IEEE (2016)
21. Drumond, M., et al.: The mondrian data engine. In: 2017 ACM/IEEE 44th Annual International Symposium on Computer Architecture (ISCA), pp. 639–651. IEEE (2017)
22. Saito, Y., et al.: Leakage power reduction for coarse grained dynamically reconfigurable processor arrays with fine grained power gating technique. In: International Conference on Engineering and Computer Education (2008)
23. Yamamoto, T., Hironaka, K., Hayakawa, Y., Kimura, M., Amano, H., Usami, K.: Dynamic V_{DD} switching technique and mapping optimization in dynamically reconfigurable processor for efficient energy reduction. In: Koch, A., Krishnamurthy, R., McAllister, J., Woods, R., El-Ghazawi, T. (eds.) ARC 2011. LNCS, vol. 6578, pp. 230–241. Springer, Heidelberg (2011). https://doi.org/10.1007/978-3-642-19475-7_24
24. Nowatzki, T., Gangadhar, V., Ardalani, N., Sankaralingam, K.: Stream-dataflow acceleration. In: 2017 ACM/IEEE 44th Annual International Symposium on Computer Architecture (ISCA), pp. 416–429. IEEE (2017)
25. Stanic, M., et al.: An integrated vector-scalar design on an in-order ARM core. ACM Trans. Archit. Code Optim. (TACO) **14**(2), 17 (2017)

Automatic Toolflow for VCGRA Generation to Enable CGRA Evaluation for Arithmetic Algorithms

André Werner[1], Florian Fricke[1(✉)], Keyvan Shahin[1], Florian Werner[1], and Michael Hübner[2]

[1] Chair for Embedded Systems, Ruhr-University Bochum, 44801 Bochum, Germany
{andre.werner-w2m,florian.fricke,keyvan.shahin,
florian.werner}@ruhr-uni-bochum.de
[2] Chair for Computer Engineering, B-TU Cottbus-Senftenberg,
03046 Cottbus, Germany
michael.huebner@b-tu.de
https://www.esit.rub.de
https://www.b-tu.de/en/computer-engineering-group

Abstract. The work, presented in this paper has been carried out within an EU-funded project with the name EXTRA, aimed at creating an environment to generate, configure and evaluate user-customizable Coarse-Grained Reconfigurable Array (CGRA) architectures, called VCGRA. The tools provide a fully automatic development and evaluation platform for a VCGRA architecture including synthesis and execution of the VCGRA with its corresponding hardware configuration and the required interfaces on an FPGA platform. Furthermore, it also provides the necessary software modules for data transmission between the processing system (PS) and the VCGRA on reconfigurable hardware. In this paper, the part of the "VCGRA Toolflow" which is responsible to provide the generation of the VCGRA hardware's FPGA-bitstream from a specification is discussed. Especially the generation of the VCGRA hardware, the automatic creation of the required interfaces and the evaluation of the improvements are presented. The toolflow is planned to be an open source project, providing hardware developers with a framework to create extensions for the VCGRA architecture, and to make them accessible for software developers. Many aspects of the hardware can be customized, including the functions provided by the Processing Elements and the communication infrastructure as well as the target platform integration. Furthermore, software developers from the EDA domain are enabled to provide, integrate and evaluate algorithms for application mapping.

Keywords: CGRA · Dynamic reconfiguration · Toolflow ·
FPGA overlays

© Springer Nature Switzerland AG 2019
C. Hochberger et al. (Eds.): ARC 2019, LNCS 11444, pp. 277–291, 2019.
https://doi.org/10.1007/978-3-030-17227-5_20

1 Introduction

Coarse-Grained-Reconfigurable-Arrays (CGRA) are application-specific accelerators and can be based on ASICs or FPGAs. In general, these consist of Processing Element (PE) nodes and an infrastructure for communication between these nodes. CGRAs can provide huge advantages, when implemented on FPGAs and combined with General-Purpose-Processors (GPP), which are needed, because CGRAs can exploit parallelism very well, but lack some flexibility when control-flow has to be processed. For CGRAs, in comparison to fine-grained FPGA-fabrics, the granularity of both, the Processing Elements' operations, and the communication infrastructure cannot be controlled on bit-level, like in traditional FPGA architectures. This reduces the level of flexibility, but also lowers the effort for creating configurations (CAD-process) and for reconfiguring the functionality at run-time, due to the reduced size of the bitstreams and the lower complexity of the system's state. Many different approaches for coarse-grained compute architectures have been proposed, e.g. in [5,9,12], most of them suited for specific tasks and providing significant speedups, nevertheless most architectures did not have commercial success. The reason for the commercial failure can be due to different reasons: First of all, these specific architectures have great advantages, but only for a limited number of applications, so the additional effort required cannot always be justified. Furthermore, both the creation and the configuration are in many cases much less supported by well-engineered tools than this is the case with less efficient but more widespread architectures (e.g. DSPs or GPGPUs). For this reason, a toolchain covering both, the generation of the CGRA as an overlay architecture on top of commercial FPGA architectures, as well as the tools for deriving configurations for the overlay architectures from algorithm-descriptions in high-level programming languages have been developed.

Throughout the last decades, various overlay architectures with different granularity regarding to specific application's requirements have been proposed by the academic community.

In general, FPGA-based architectures, that can parameterized to implement a certain type of application, is called an FPGA overlay. Compared to the low level FPGA realizations, these architectures make it easier to implement a certain type of application, without the need to engage with complicated and time consuming FPGA design process. In 2012, ZUMA [1] has been introduced as an "FPGA-on-an-FPGA" overlay. The architecture has been published as open source, and therefore provides the general benefits of overlays, such as bitstream compatibility, independent of different vendor tools and physical FPGA hardware. Besides this approach, overlays for coarse grained architectures have been developed and presented within the last decade. QUKU [10] for instance, consists of a grid of cycle-by-cycle reconfigurable PEs and interconnects. The authors of [2] described the design of an architecture for the pipelined execution of data flow graphs (DFG). It consists of a mesh of overlay cells with functional units and nearest-neighbour-connections as routing logic. Intermediate Fabrics (IF) [3,11] enable near-instant placement and routing of applications. The authors of

IF showed a 700x improvement in compilation time compared to vendor tools at the cost of approximately 40% extra resources in [11]. In [7], the authors considered the properties of the underlaying architecture to increase the throughput of the overlay. They achieve a reduction of almost 70% in the overlay tile requirement compared to there considered overlay architectures and kernel throughputs of almost 60 GOPS.

In analogy to the architectures presented, our architecture is called "Virtual Coarse-Grained Reconfigurable Array" (VCGRA). Like the other overlay architectures mentioned, it exists as an intermediate level between the accelerated algorithm and the FPGA-hardware. A first draft of the architecture's structure has been presented in [4]. It still consists of alternating levels of Processing Elements and so-called Virtual Channels (VCH), which control the dataflow. In contrast to the other presented CGRA architectures, many aspects are configurable during design time and built automatically by the toolchain depicted in Fig. 1: The size and the shape of the array which includes the number of inputs and outputs, the widths of inputs and outputs, the number of array layers and the number and functionality of Processing Elements for each layer. The bitwidth of the arithmetic units and the connections as well as the operations, which are provided by the PEs, can also be adjusted at design time whereas the connections within the layers and the operations carried out by the PEs are run-time-(re)configurable. The toolflow, which is depicted in Fig. 1 also covers the generation of the configuration bitstreams for an VCGRA instance to enable fast dynamic reconfiguration during run-time. To ease the usage of the overlay, the hardware generation part of the toolflow generates the FPGA-configuration-bitstream of this architecture, including a wrapper, providing the interface to e.g. an embedded CPU within a System-on-Chip (SoC) as well as the required HW/SW interface. The software part of the toolchain takes the parameters of the VCGRA-architecture and the description of the algorithm as input and creates the configuration for the overlay architecture. Furthermore, a template for a Linux application is provided and adapted for running the hardware-accelerated application on the target system.

Taken together, for accelerating compute intensive applications on huge datastreams coarse-grained arrays can be a valuable addition to a GPP or a GPGPU. The fact, that the structure as well as the compute units can be tailored to the application's demands, enables the adaption of a generic CPU to a specific application domain by using CGRA-based accelerators. The next section covers the motivation to create the above mentioned kind of architecture and the toolchain.

2   Motivation

Our first motivation to create a CGRA architecture is based on the idea to evaluate the concept of Dynamic Circuit Specialization (DCS, [6]) on a powerful architecture, that is capable to host accelerators for applications from the High-Performance Computing (HPC) domain. The concept behind DCS is the rapid adaption of hardware accelerators to the values of specific inputs, which act more like parameters of the module than rapidly changing input data. The concept can be compared to the constant propagation technique, which is used in modern Just-In-Time compilers. Basically, a specialized implementation of a hardware function is created by treating specific inputs as constant for a period of time and optimizing the implementation for these specific values. As soon as the specific inputs change, a new implementation has to be created. Applying this technique to real hardware designs is supported by the so called TLUT/TCON toolflow, proposed by researchers from Ghent University [8,13]. The TLUT/TCON toolflow has some requirements for the code to be processed: The code must be available in VHDL without vendor-specific constructs, furthermore the inputs to be used must be identified in the code by special comments. Secondly, while developing the architecture, the goal was to enable the usage of FPGA-based accelerators to a wider community without deep knowledge in hardware development, e.g. software developers for HPC applications. This needs to ensure, that the overlay architecture is synthesizable using an arbitrary vendor toolchain. Furthermore, the generation of the overlay and its configuration has to be fast and user friendly for a high acceptance in the scientific community.

Having in mind, that the overlay had to fulfil the demands of the TLUT/TCON toolchain and that it is to be used by non-hardware-experts, the decision to develop a highly automated toolflow has been taken. This paper presents the improvements in the hardware-generation part of the toolchain, that have been introduced since our last publication [4] and also the evaluation of the improved architecture and tools. The part responsible for the generation of configuration bitstreams for the overlay architecture in this toolchain (depicted in the right branch of Fig. 1) is not in the scope of this paper.

3 VCGRA Toolflow

The VCGRA toolflow aims to provide a fully automatic development and evaluation platform for a Virtual Coarse Grained Reconfigurable Array architecture. It includes synthesis and execution of the hardware architecture with its corresponding hardware configuration, and the required interfaces on a suitable target platform. Furthermore it provides the necessary software modules for data transmission between the processing system and the VCGRA instance. The majority of the toolchain has been written in Python3, some modules use TCL or C++. It primarily consists of four sub modules, which can be executed in parallel or sequentially. As an open source project, hardware specialists shall provide extensions for functions of the Processing Elements or interconnects of Processing Elements as well as target platform integration while software developers may provide and integrate algorithms for application mapping for instance. The parameters for the toolflow are the application itself, currently limited to a directed acyclic graph representation, parameters of the target platform, currently limited to Xilinx Zynq devices as well as parameters for the virtual coarse grained architecture. The description of an application is performed at a higher level of abstraction by using a directed acyclic graph representation, because this

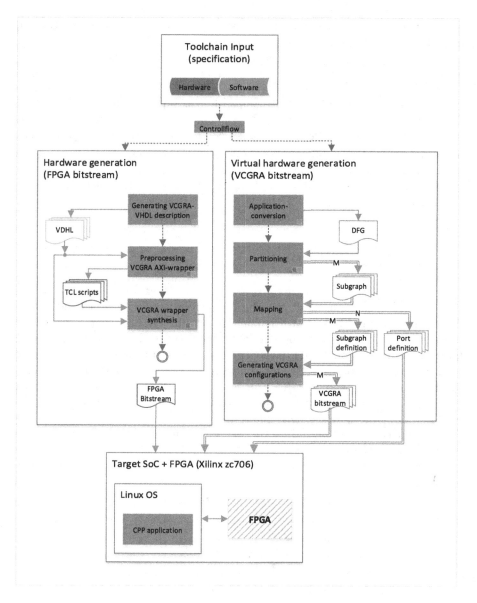

Fig. 1. Complete toolflow from pre-definitions to an executable application

will enable a wide usage of the approach, and also acceptance by non-specialists in hardware development. Moreover, it enables the community, with the first publicly available tool-chain, which provides the feature of dynamic and partial reconfiguration of a CGRA on several layers and hardware overlay together, a platform for further research in the domain of dynamic and partial reconfiguration. For the target devices, there is no restriction to a specific vendor target platform, since the backend tools for the physical FPGA can be substituted, while the VCGRA tool chain remains on top.

As one can see in Fig. 1, the toolflow is separated into a "Software Branch" mainly used to generate the configuration bitstream for a VCGRA instance for a special application and the "Hardware Branch" mainly used to generate and synthesize a VCGRA instance defined by the input parameters of the tool chain. The "Software Branch" is outside the scope of this paper. The "Hardware Branch" consists of a VCGRA generator tool to build the VCGRA instance concerning the given input parameters, a VCGRA wrapper tool to create the *AXI4*-interface as well as a parameterizable TCL-script library to automatically build and synthesize the VCGRA instance for the chosen target platform. Before the start of the description of the "Hardware Branch" in details, the paper outlines a VCGRA's components in the following section.

4   VCGRA Architecture

The VCGRA introduced in this article is a multi-layer architecture, in which each layer of re-configurable Processing Elements is connected to the next layer using a re-configurable Virtual Channel. To use this VCGRA core, in order to execute a desired application or algorithm, the functionality of each PE in each layer has to be configured and the VCHs has to be set to connect the outputs of each PE to the appropriate PE in the next layer. By using these configurations, the functionality of the VCGRA can be changed during run-time after each batch of data is processed by it. The VCGRA consists of four main types of sub-modules, namely, the *Processing Elements*, the *Virtual Channels*, the *Pipeline Stages*, and the *Synchronization Module*. These modules are described in the following subsections.

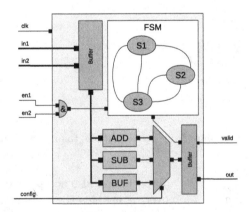

Fig. 2. Overview processing element

4.1   Processing Elements

A Processing Element takes two operands as inputs and produces an output. The functionality of each Processing Element is set, using its input configuration bits. In the example shown in Fig. 2, it uses two configuration bits per Processing Element to select between three different operations: addition, multiplication, and simply buffering the first input. The number of operation is not limited to these three types. The current version of the tool chain supports five arithmetic operations: Addition, subtraction, multiplication, division, greater, and equal. A Processing Element also takes an enable bit for each input and produces a valid signal indicating that the data processing is completed. This valid signal is passed to the next VCH, from there to the enable inputs of the next layer of Processing Elements and ultimately to an output synchronization module, to be used as an indicator when the VCGRA's work is done and the ultimate outputs are valid. The bitwidth of a Processing Elements' data-path can be set by the VCGRA generation tool before implementation. As also shown in Fig. 2, the input and output values are buffered. The input values are processed only if both enable bits indicate a valid input on each data input port. The output is buffered, because the calculation time for implemented task may differ and the following layer of a Virtual Channel only works as combination logic without any data buffering.

4.2   Virtual Channels

The Virtual Channels, illustrated in Fig. 3, are layers of re-configurable switches, controlling how the VCGRA inputs or the outputs of the current layer of the Processing Elements are connected to the next layer of Processing Elements. The goal is to realize a certain functionality using the VCGRA core via configuring each Processing Element's operation and how they are connected using Virtual Channels. The design of Virtual Channels in this work allows any possible pattern of connecting two layers of Processing Elements together. The Virtual Channels are composed entirely from combinational logic and do not increase the overall latency.

4.3   Pipeline Stages

The Pipeline Stages, also shown in Fig. 3, are integrated in the input and output of each Virtual Channel to buffer all the incoming and outgoing data of each layer of Processing Elements. The Pipeline Stages are configurable in a sense that they can be turned on or bypassed using the pipeline configuration bits. Thus, the user can individually turn each stage of pipelines on or off, to control the throughput and latency of the VCGRA core at run-time. Separating these pipeline stages from VCHs also makes it possible for the generator, to completely neglect putting a whole pipeline stage when it is not needed or due to trade-off preferences and conserve the FPGA resources consumed by the overall design.

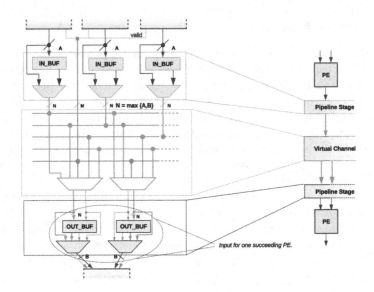

Fig. 3. Overview virtual channel with pipeline stages

4.4   Output Synchronization

This sub-module receives all the valid signals generated in different paths, for different outputs, and generates the signal showing when all the outputs of the VCGRA core are valid. Using configurable mask bits, one can neglect the state or validity of individual outputs, in the generation of the final valid signal for the whole core to synchronize data transmission with a PS.

5   VCGRA Interface Wrapper

After the generation of the VCGRA core, an interface wrapper is generated to feed the data and configurations in, and deliver the results out of the core. In this work, *AXI4-Lite* and *AXI4-Stream* interfaces were developed and tested for communicating with the VCGRA core.

5.1   AXI4-Lite Wrapper

The *AXI4-Lite* interface consists of four different ports: data, PE-configuration, VCH-configuration and a configuration for the synchronization sub-module (mask-configuration). As the names of the interfaces already outline, one port is used to process data input and data output while the other three ports handle the configuration process. Thus, the data interface is configured as an input/output port, while the other three ports handle only input functions. We define an input or output from the VCGRA point of view.

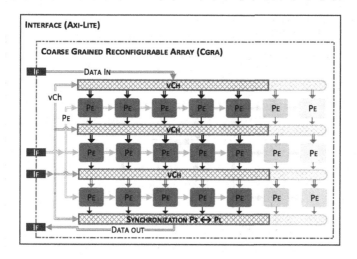

Fig. 4. *AXI4-Lite* wrapper for a Vivado block design

The base for the interface is the *AXI4-Lite* template generated from Xilinx Vivado tool chain. Further details on the creation of the wrapper are described in Sect. 6.1. For the data interface, a user programmable slave register (*slv-register*) handles exactly one port for a datum input or output. As an example: Consider a VCGRA instance, which consists of five data inputs, five parameter inputs and three data outputs. The first ten slv-registers configured as inputs – the five data registers followed by the five parameter registers respectively – while the last three registers are configured for data output. Therefore, the *AXI4-Lite* port for data is configured for thirteen 32 bit wide slv-registers. The number of slv-registers for the configuration crucially depends on an VCGRA instance's features. One register is 32 bits wide. Thus, the number of necessary registers is

$$\#\text{SlvReg} = \text{roundup} \left(\frac{\text{sum of configuration bits}}{32} \right) \qquad (1)$$

The *sum of configuration bits* includes all bits for a VCGRA instance's PEs, VCHs and its mask configuration. The advantage of using *AXI4-Lite* ports, is the usability from a processing system, because by creating the templates by Vivado, also the necessary accessing functions and addressing offsets are generated. At the negative side, the *AXI4-Lite* protocol does not support bursts or streaming capabilities. Thus, frequent data transfers or reconfigurations are inefficient via this interface. In [4] the results showed that almost 50% of the execution time for a small VCGRA including twelve PEs and three VCH is used for data transfer for both, configuration and processing data. Moreover, the bitwidth of a slv-register is always set to 32 bit. The design wastes a lot of area, if the data bitwidth differs from 32 bits. As a result, an *AXI4-Stream* interface is developed which

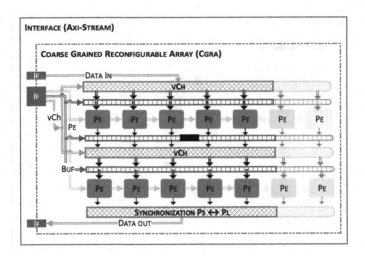

Fig. 5. *AXI4-Stream* wrapper for a Vivado block design

is presented in the next section. Figure 4 illustrates the described design as a
schematic overview.

5.2 AXI4-Stream

As mentioned in the previous section, *AXI4-Lite* interface has drawbacks in this
project, leading to the throughput of the whole VCGRA being bottle-necked by
how fast the data can be written and read back to and from inputs and outputs
respectively. As mentioned *AXI4-Lite* has no burst mode, so for the VCGRA
to be able to start working, the configurations and input data registers should
be written one by one, using many single transactions. The same can be said
for reading back the results from the VCGRA. To overcome these restrictions,
another interface wrapper with *AXI4-Stream* protocol was developed. One of
the reasons for choosing the *AXI4-Stream* interface is the speed it can deliver
the data and configurations to and from the VCGRA core. With its streaming based mechanism, *AXI4-Stream* can deliver data chunks as big as the data
bus width, every clock cycle till the end of a full data package. This widens
the data transmission bottleneck and increases the overall processing speed and
wastes less time for transmission of data to and from the VCGRA compared
to the *AXI4-Lite* interface. Another thing about *AXI4-Stream* is, it essentially
gives the same data transmission speed as the *AXI4-Full* burst mode, but with
lower complexity, less number of signals and less resource utilization. The only
downside is unlike *AXI4-Lite* and *AXI4-Full* it is not easy to interact from a
processing system. However it will be shown how the interaction between the
ARM processor on Zynq, and the VCGRA *AXI4-Stream* can be carried out. As

shown in Fig. 5 There are three instances of *AXI4-Stream* port, two slave ones for data input and configurations and one master port for data output. The input and output data buffers are fed and feeding the *AXI4-Stream* input and output ports. The *AXI4-Stream* configuration port, streams the data into the configuration buffer. When the full configuration packet is loaded into the buffer, it gets divided into VCH configurations, PE configurations, pipeline configurations and the output mask configurations. The way each part of the VCGRA can be configured using these configuration information was mentioned in Subsects. 4.1, 4.2, 4.3 and 4.4. What should be noted is that a new configuration packet should only be transmitted (or rather its transmission be finished) after the VCGRA is done processing the input data, because reconfiguration of the VCGRA will be done instantly as soon the last word in the configuration packet is received via the *AXI4-Stream* port and if the VCGRA is still processing the data at that time, this reconfiguration will disrupt the results for the current batch of input data. It should also be noted that the VCGRA will start processing the input data as soon as the last word of input packet is received via *AXI4-Stream* data port.

6   Toolflow Submodules for Hardware Generation

6.1   VCGRA Creator

The VCGRA creator consists of two main parts: the VCGRA generator and the wrapper designer. The generator is introduced in [4]. Therefore, only the improvements will be described here. Many parts of the VCGRA generation tools have been improved and made more flexible, but most of the changes are internally. Worth to mention is the adaption to a newly created *AXI4-Stream* interface and the introduction of a more flexible Virtual Channel design. Within the process of integrating the *AXI4-Stream* Wrapper into the generator, many parameters of the hardware were moved into an external VHDL module, which also eases the adaption of existing or the creation of further interfaces. The generator now allows the generation of the optimized Virtual Channels, which splits the monolithic design from the old version into a pure combinational module, which just handles the signal routing and separates modules for the buffers. This design decision makes modifications to the channels more targeted and furthermore allows the buffers to be bypassed for special application scenarios. One big improvement is the new interface, which allows the CLI-based control of all functions of the tool. Additionally, the tool can now read the VCGRA specifications and write it to JSON-files. Overall it can be said that many aspects of the tool have been adapted and improved to the new possibilities, especially the improvements in the new interface, but most of the changes concern details.

6.2   AXI4-Wrapper Designer

AXI4-Lite Wrapper Designer. The wrapper designer currently supports VCGRA designs with *AXI4-Lite* interface. It consists of two main parts: A

TCL-script generator for Vivado to create the *AXI4-Lite* template files for an Intellectual Property (IP) block, which are then additionally adapted by the second part regarding the properties of the ports of the VCGRA entity. Four files are created by the TCL-script and copied into the a target directory, which can be specified by a second parameter: An *AXI4-Lite* root file, a data port file as well as a configuration port file for each configuration port of the VCGRA entity respectively (refer Sect. 5.1 and Fig. 4 for interface details). The major parameter for the Python-based tool is the VCGRA entity. Therefore, the VHDL file is parsed for the number of data inputs and outputs, parameters, and the configuration signals for PEs, VCH and the synchronization function. With these information, the *AXI4-Lite* template file for the data port is adapted as follows:

(a) For the number of input ports the VCGRA contains, output ports with the same bitwidth are added to the entity of the *AXI4-Lite* interface. The same is processed as inputs for the number of VCGRA data outputs.
(b) The slv-registers for inputs and outputs are configured to perform only one of these functionalities.
(c) The slv-registers are mapped to its corresponding *AXI4-Lite* entity ports while also adapting the 32 bit fixed bitwidth of the slv-registers to the bitwidth of the VCGRA data ports.

For the three *AXI4-Lite* configuration ports left, the slv-registers are concatenated until the number of required configuration bits is reached for each configuration port. The entities of the interfaces also get an additional output port with the bitwidth of the corresponding configuration port from a VCGRA instance. The entity of a VCGRA instance is added as a component to the *AXI4-Lite* root file and afterwards all ports are connected. The last step is an update of the generated IP-block by adding the VCGRA files of the instance to the IP-block repository. Besides the mentioned *AXI4-Lite* ports, the IP-block consists of a clock port and two additional control ports to start the VCGRA and to recognize a finished calculation (*Ready* signal).

AXI4-Stream Wrapper Designer. The big difference of the *AXI4-Stream* Wrapper Designer in comparison to its counterpart is its simplicity due to the independence of the *AXI4-Stream* wrapper from the target platform, since it has been written in pure VHDL. Furthermore, all the parameters for configuring the wrapper and the VCGRA have been moved to one single VHDL file. In addition, TCL scripts are also provided which combine the generated VHDL files from the VCGRA Designer and the *AXI4-Stream* Wrapper Designer to a Vivado project. The script can be used to generate a bitstream for a desired FPGA platform in the Vivado IDE, using the generated VHDL modules. To ensure both, the correct transmission of data between the PS and the VCGRA, and the correctness of the VCGRA functionality another TCL script is provided. This script exports the bitstream into a Xilinx SDK project, builds a demo application for testing the VCGRA with the *AXI4-Stream* Wrapper and executes it on the target platform.

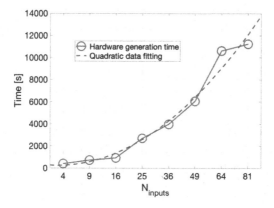

Fig. 6. Generation time for VCGRA hardware depending on the number of inputs

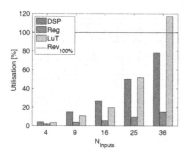

Fig. 7. Resource utilization by category

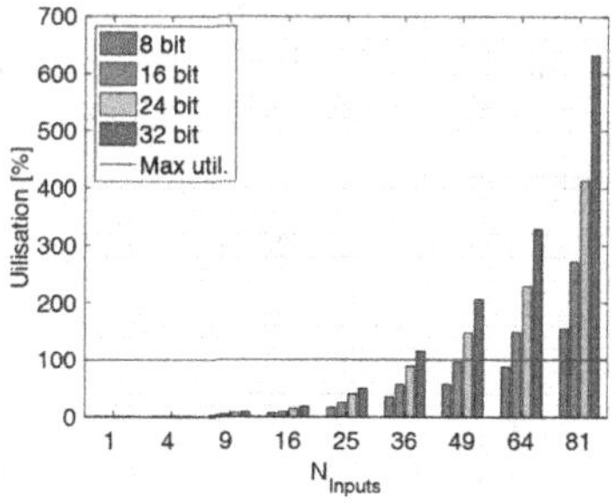

Fig. 8. Utilization dependence on number of inputs and their bitwidth

7   Toolflow Benchmarking

In this section the evaluation results of the hardware-generation branch of the toolchain are presented and the empirical execution times for different toolflow runs are shown. The generation of the configuration and the VCGRA bitstream is the main goal of this work. An important aspect of evaluation is the relationship between the size of the algorithms to be implemented and the resulting time required to build the VCGRA architecture. Figure 6 shows the relation between VCGRA hardware generation time and the number of inputs. The width of the VCGRA is given by the number of inputs (N_{inputs}) whereas the number of layers is given by $ceil(log2(N_{inputs}))$. By using a quadratic data fitting, it is shown that the time is related to $N_{inputs} \times log2(N_{inputs})$, which is the number of PE's in the architecture.

Also the FPGA utilization can be shown depending on the number of inputs and the width of inputs, which are among the most important factors impacting the utilization. The platform for testing the resource utilization is the Xilinx ZC706 board. Figure 8 shows the overall utilization depending on the number

Time: $t_{\text{complete}} = t_{\text{config}} + t_{\text{data}} + t_{\text{process}} + t_{\text{overhead}}$ [ns]

Type	t_{config}	$t_{\mu,\text{data}}$	$t_{\mu,\text{process}}$	t_{overhead}
VCGRA-Lite	$1.23 \cdot 10^5$	$9.67 \cdot 10^4$	$3.01 \cdot 10^3$	$2.96 \cdot 10^9$
VCGRA-Stream	$7.84 \cdot 10^4$	$5.01 \cdot 10^4$	$3.51 \cdot 10^3$	$1.80 \cdot 10^9$

Fig. 9. Performance test

of inputs and for different input bitwidths. Figure 7 shows the amount of each FPGA resource used depending on the number of inputs, when all the inputs have 32 bit bitwidth. Regarding the performance of the VCGRA, a test was done with a convolution filter, as the application. The kernel size is 5×5 and a VCGRA with 25 × 6 PEs and the input image size is 400 × 400. As expected the one with *AXI4-Stream* have better performance compared with to the *AXI4-Lite* version, however this difference is not as much as one may expect and the reason is that the bottleneck here is the ARM core on the Zynq that needs to prepare the data to be sent on these interfaces to the VCGRA. It can be said that a large portion of the time, the VCGRA core remains idle simply because the processor can not keep up to send the data to it. The results of this performance test can be seen in Fig. 9.

8   Conclusion and Outlook

The improvements to a tool-chain for generating an application-specific CGRA architecture are introduced in this article. Since the last version, all the tools have been updated and improved for modularity and also to be as automated as possible. The main contribution of these improvements is the *AXI4-Stream* wrapper, which has been developed in pure VHDL, to improve the throughput and to reduce the latency of the data transmission to and from the VCGRA core. For full control, the interface has been completely developed using VHDL and can be tailored based on the requirements of the wrapped VCGRA. As can be seen from the benchmark, the overall performance improvements are lower than expected. A deeper analysis showed, that the low transfer rate was only partially caused by the *AXI4-Lite* interface of the last version, and another bottleneck remains in the communication on the processing system side. For this reason, this problem is processed and alternatives for optimizing the data exchange between a software application on the PS and the VCGRA are evaluated and are considered as possible future works in this project. This evaluation is eased due to the improved tool-chain and the VCGRA-specific handwritten interface, which makes it possible to completely monitor the functionality correctness of internal signaling. In future work we plan to improve the hardware of the VCGRA, especially the external interfaces to the processing system. Furthermore the inner functionality of the Processing Elements is also a point which we work on, as improvements directly effect the resource utilization, throughput and the latency of the whole architecture.

References

1. Brant, A., Lemieux, G.G.F.: ZUMA: an open FPGA overlay architecture. In: 2012 IEEE 20th International Symposium on Field-Programmable Custom Computing Machines, pp. 93–96, April 2012. https://doi.org/10.1109/FCCM.2012.25
2. Capalija, D., Abdelrahman, T.S.: A high-performance overlay architecture for pipelined execution of data flow graphs. In: 2013 23rd International Conference on Field programmable Logic and Applications, pp. 1–8, September 2013. https://doi.org/10.1109/FPL.2013.6645515
3. Coole, J., Stitt, G.: Intermediate fabrics: virtual architectures for circuit portability and fast placement and routing. In: 2010 IEEE/ACM/IFIP International Conference on Hardware/Software Codesign and System Synthesis (CODES+ISSS), pp. 13–22, October 2010. https://doi.org/10.1145/1878961.1878966
4. Fricke, F., Werner, A., Shahin, K., Huebner, M.: CGRA tool flow for fast runtime reconfiguration. In: Voros, N., Huebner, M., Keramidas, G., Goehringer, D., Antonopoulos, C., Diniz, P.C. (eds.) ARC 2018. LNCS, vol. 10824, pp. 661–672. Springer, Cham (2018). https://doi.org/10.1007/978-3-319-78890-6_53
5. Hartenstein, R.: Coarse grain reconfigurable architecture (embedded tutorial). In: Proceedings of the 2001 Asia and South Pacific Design Automation Conference, ASP-DAC 2001, pp. 564–570. ACM, New York (2001)
6. Heyse, K., Davidson, T., Vansteenkiste, E., Bruneel, K., Stroobandt, D.: Efficient implementation of virtual coarse grained reconfigurable arrays on FPGAS. In: 2013 23rd International Conference on Field programmable Logic and Applications, pp. 1–8, September 2013
7. Jain, A.K., Maskell, D.L., Fahmy, S.A.: Throughput oriented FPGA overlays using DSP blocks. In: 2016 Design, Automation Test in Europe Conference Exhibition (DATE), pp. 1628–1633, March 2016
8. Kulkarni, A., Stroobandt, D.: How to efficiently reconfigure tunable lookup tables for dynamic circuit specialization. Int. J. Reconfigurable Comput. **2016**, 1–12 (2016)
9. Lee, D., Jo, M., Han, K., Choi, K.: FloRA: coarse-grained reconfigurable architecture with floating-point operation capability. In: International Conference on Field-Programmable Technology, FPT 2009, pp. 376–379, December 2009
10. Shukla, S., Bergmann, N.W., Becker, J.: QUKU: a two-level reconfigurable architecture. In: IEEE Computer Society Annual Symposium on Emerging VLSI Technologies and Architectures (ISVLSI 2006), pp. 6-pp, March 2006. https://doi.org/10.1109/ISVLSI.2006.76
11. Stitt, G., Coole, J.: Intermediate fabrics: virtual architectures for near-instant FPGA compilation. IEEE Embedded Syst. Lett. **3**(3), 81–84 (2011). https://doi.org/10.1109/LES.2011.2167713
12. Thomas, A., Rückauer, M., Becker, J.: HoneyComb: a multi-grained dynamically reconfigurable runtime adaptive hardware architecture. In: 2011 IEEE International SOC Conference (SOCC), pp. 335–340, September 2011
13. Vansteenkiste, E., Al Farisi, B., Bruneel, K., Stroobandt, D.: TPaR: place and route tools for the dynamic reconfiguration of the FPGA's interconnect network. IEEE Trans. Comput.-Aided Des. Integr. Circ. Syst. **33**(3), 370–383 (2014)

Architectures

Rem: A Reconfigurable Multipotent Cell for New Distributed Reconfigurable Architectures

Ludovica Bozzoli◉ and Luca Sterpone(✉)◉

Politecnico di Torino, Turin, Italy
{ludovica.bozzoli,luca.sterpone}@polito.it

Abstract. Recently, the usage of the reconfigurable computing devices has seen a sharp increase in many application fields. Several reconfigurable architectures have been proposed in the last decades, with different levels of granularity and complexity and SRAM-based Field Programmable Gate Array (FPGA) remains the target support to develop reconfigurable architectures. However, even if FPGA is an established technology, it is not fully optimized for detailed partial run time reconfiguration. In fact, FPGAs reconfiguration granularity is large, even if single resources are configured by few bits, since the amount of data to be re-loaded inside the configuration memory for small changes is huge. Considering that the major bottleneck of reconfiguration is the excessive reconfiguration time, which is proportional to the number of bits to be reconfigured, when reconfiguration involves few basic resources, such architecture leads to a considerable overhead.

In this paper, we propose a new reconfigurable computing architecture that implement distributed reconfiguration at the lowest granularity to maximize flexibility and scalability. This is obtained providing to the basic reconfigurable functional unit the ability to reconfigure itself and the neighbor units. In fact, each cell, beside functioning as Logic, Memory and Connectivity can also trigger reconfiguration for itself and for given portion of the array of cells. To show the feasibility and the advantages of our idea, we designed and implemented a Reconfigurable Multipotent Cell, ReM. The results obtained with the implementation of benchmark circuits on this architecture confirm the advantages in terms of reconfiguration time.

Keywords: FPGA · Reconfigurable architectures · Reconfiguration time · Reconfigurable array

1 Introduction

In the last decades, the adoption of the Reconfigurable Computing device has seen a sharp increase. This is because Reconfigurable Systems increasingly provide opportunities to fulfill the growing needs of flexibility and performance in several applications, such as signal processing, cryptography, arithmetic, scientific computing, and networking. In fact, the capability of dynamically allocate resources at run-time has become so attractive for several reasons: it allows to implement time-space partitioning

© Springer Nature Switzerland AG 2019
C. Hochberger et al. (Eds.): ARC 2019, LNCS 11444, pp. 295–304, 2019.
https://doi.org/10.1007/978-3-030-17227-5_21

and consequently space saving, to extend product life exploiting fault recovery techniques or to enhance application performance by adapting computational effort to payload variations [1].

In literature, two main categories of systems can be identified: coarse-grained and fine-grained architectures according to the data width processable by the smallest reconfigurable basic unit. Considering the granularity with respect to the smallest functional unit data width and computational capability, FPGAs present a fine level of granularity since its basic tile elaborate at the bit level [2, 3].

Anyway, the reconfiguration granularity can be seen more specifically in terms of atomic reconfigurable unit. i.e., the smallest addressable configuration memory segment. If FPGA granularity is seen from this point of view, it is fine only virtually, because its smallest reconfigurable memory unit is the Frame, a very long bit word. In fact, even if single resources like Look-up Tables (LUTs), Flip- Flops (FFs) and Routing segments are controlled by few bits, when they have to be reconfigured, a large number of bits should be re-loaded inside the configuration memory [4]. This is due to the current FPGA architecture, which is implemented as a two layers system. In fact, on the *top* of the configurable logic layer there is the configuration memory layer, which replicate the regular FPGA structure but is not atomically addressable. For instances, in Xilinx 7 Series device the smallest addressable memory segment is 3,232 bits wide and its bits are configuring (partially) different resources, even physically distant in reconfigurable physical layer [4, 5]. Considering that the major bottleneck of reconfiguration is the excessive reconfiguration time, which is strongly dependent from the number of bits to be reconfigured, this architecture became a limit, especially when the reconfiguration should be performed frequently and for small portion of the design.

In this paper we propose a different reconfigurable computing model with the aim to give more flexibility and to minimize reconfiguration time by re-thinking the reconfiguration mechanism itself. We suggest an architecture in which configuration settings and reconfigurable resources are tidily coupled instead of being separated in two different layers.

The key idea of this work is to implement the reconfiguration in a distributed manner at the lowest granularity to maximize flexibility, scalability, parallelization and concurrency. This is obtained providing to the basic reconfigurable functional unit the ability to reconfigure itself and the neighbor units. In fact, each cell, beside functioning as Logic, Memory and Connectivity can also trigger reconfiguration for itself and for given portion of the array of cells.

To show the feasibility and the advantage of our idea, both in terms of reconfiguration time and flexibility, we also present the design of a Reconfigurable Multipotent Cell, that we called ReM, as a possible implementation for the basic unit of the computational model we propose.

Furthermore, to confirm the feasibility of our approach we implement the physical layout of a ReM Cell and we map several benchmark circuits with ReM architectural model, showing a significant reduction in terms of reconfiguration bits and time.

The rest of the paper is organized as follows: Sect. 2 provide the Background and the Motivations behind the work, in Sect. 3 the principles of the suggested computational model are clarified presenting the Multipotent Reconfigurable Cell. In Sect. 4 the results of the ReM Implementation and Layout are provided with an evaluation of circuits implementation on its architecture, while in Sects. 5 Conclusions and Future Works are provided.

2 Background and Motivations

In the last decades, the growth of computational demand in several applications fields, such as signal and image processing, security and cryptography, pattern recognition and matching, networking and routers, has resulted in various emergent architectures, and among them the Reconfigurable Computing one is among of the most promising [1, 6, 7].

In fact, reconfigurable computing has experienced a period of rapid development and several alternative architectures have been proposed. According to the granularity of the basic computational unit, reconfigurable devices have been classified in two main categories: fine-grain and coarse-grain. Fine-grain Reconfigurable architectures show higher configuration capabilities but higher area overhead with respect to coarse-grain ones. Complex arithmetic functions and sophisticated sequential control result less convenient for fine-grain cells. However, increasing the granularity size results in a strong reduction of the flexibility. Coarse Grain Reconfigurable Architectures (CGRAs) can be grouped in three macro categories: Hybrid Architectures, Arrays of Functional Units and Arrays of Processors [2].

A Hybrid Architecture combines a processor with a reconfigurable fabric as a computational support to speed-up the computations, such as MorphoSys and DAPDNA [8, 9].

In Functional Array, computation is managed by a large number of Reconfigurable Functional Units which process algorithms already partitioned in a sequential flow of configurations to be dynamically configured. In this architecture the on-chip control processor is absent, and the dynamic reconfiguration is controlled by the configuration manager which do not perform any calculation. Among this category, XPP and MATRIX Architectures can be mentioned [10, 11].

Arrays of Processors instead allow great flexibility since they consist in scalable architecture made of simple processors with local memory and dedicated interconnect. What is dynamically configured in this case is the interprocessor communication network. RAW and picoArray belong to this category [12, 13].

On the opposite corner of the reconfiguration granularity there is the concept of Filed Programmable Transistor Arrays (FPTAs) in which the programmability is at the level of transistor characteristic. In these devices the dimension and the type of Transistor can be chosen at run-time to accommodate the increased variability of individual device characteristic. Even if this is an attractive concept, it is feasible only at the cost of large area overhead. Some examples of FPTA are PAnDA and PTA architecture [14, 15].

Even if both CGRA and FPTA are interesting computational architectures most of them have never been employed in real case scenarios and remain academic models. In fact, FPGA remains the golden reconfigurable computing architecture, because its granularity level provides a reasonable trade-off between Complexity and Flexibility.

Furthermore, several application merging FPGAs portions embed with a fixed process general purpose processor are recently emerged, such as Stretch S6000 [16] and Menta eFPGA augmented CPUs [17]. In fact, to meet the variation in standards or algorithms, which require to accordingly modify the accelerators, a new alternative to highly customized VLSI macros is the use of reconfigurable custom-size embedded FPGAs.

Despite their granularity and their applicability, what all these architectures have in common is that their reconfiguration relies on a two layers mechanism: configuration settings for the programmable resources (resource layer) are stored in the configuration memory layer. Furthermore, reconfiguration is typically scheduled and managed by a dedicated agent such as a microprocessor or a configuration manager.

In fact, there are several approaches to perform Reconfiguration, both form the point of view of the configuration interface and the portion of bitstream to reconfigure. Typical interfaces are the Serial Configuration Mode and JTAG Partial Reconfiguration, which have a slow transmission speed due to the interfaces hardware characteristics. Faster interfaces are the parallel port configuration interfaces (i.e., Xilinx SelectMAP) and the FPGA internal configuration approach, which exploits the available Internal Configuration Access Port (ICAP) [4, 18].

The frame is the smallest addressable memory segment in configuration memory, thus reconfiguration time is directly proportional to the number of downloaded frames. Scrubbing is the classic method adopted when the whole FPGA needs to be reconfigured; in this case, all the configuration memory frames are re-written. On the other hand, the typical partial reconfiguration approach allows configuring only the configuration frames belonging to the target Reconfigurable Region (RR). On both cases, all the configuration frames are transmitted into the FPGA's configuration memory independently from their content: thus, even empty frames are downloaded. A Capillary (C) approach has been proposed [4] in order to download exclusively the used frames, reducing the reconfiguration time [19].

What is important to notice is that even if the Basic Functional Unit of the FPGA, elaborates at bit level its bitstream description is not compact: the entire basic unit uses 128 bits in vertical that span over 68 frames along the horizontal axes. In details, 26 frames subsection are used for the routing while the remaining 10 for LUTs and Control Logic. Thus, to change the settings of one LUT, which are described by few bits, all the frames these bits belong should be reconfigured. For Xilinx 7 Family FPGAs, the length of a Frame is 3,232 bits [5].

Considering this overhead and adding the one related to the Reconfiguration Mechanism, if the goal is to perform small changes in the design, the current architecture can result penalizing.

This is the reason why we suggest a different architectural model for fine-grained reconfigurable device, to implement the reconfiguration in a distributed manner and to providing to the basic reconfigurable functional unit the ability to reconfigure itself and the neighbor units to maximize flexibility, scalability, parallelization and concurrency.

3   The ReM Cell Architecture

The key idea of the ReM Cell Architecture is to have as basic unit of a computing system a cell that is as simple as possible and that can easily switch between multiple functionalities according to its content and the one of the neighbors. In Fig. 1 the functional scheme of the ReM Cell is reported. Circuits implementation is obtained by exploiting several ReM Cells organized in a 2-dimensional array.

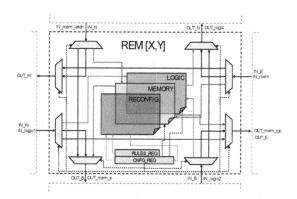

Fig. 1. Overall functional ReM Cell Architecture.

Since ReM is the basic element of a reconfigurable computing system, the state available for the cell are the primitives one for calculation: Logic, Memory, Connectivity and Reconfiguration. For each one of these functionalities, several modes are available, according to few bits. In fact, one of the main efforts in building the cell has been focused in find the most synthetic way to encode different states to use the minimum number of bits. The string of bits to dynamically reconfigure the cell behavior consist of just 8 bits. Other 3 extra bits are needed in the reconfiguration unit to define the Update Rules, i.e., the rules on which reconfiguration propagate for each cell as well as all the states of the cell, as it will be clarified in the following paragraphs.

3.1   Connectivity

Each Cell has one input and one output on each side. Each one of them can act as a pure interconnect point or as an input/output for each functionality. In fact, the setting of each input and output multiplexer defines where the signal should go, and thus, implicitly, which block is active inside the cell. To have a light structure and do not increase complexity, not each direction is reachable from each port. The selectivity of the communication has been realized keeping in mind which are the most probable links to implement functions, as it will be clarified in the following paragraph.

To define Cell Connectivity and thus also the state, only 5 bits are required (Fig. 2a). The available connections are: Straight (North to South and vice versa, East to West and vice versa), Knee (North to West, South to East, East to North and West to South) and connection to activate and connect Logic and Memory.

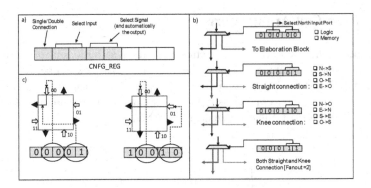

Fig. 2. ReM connectivity.

Furthermore, there is the possibility to activate at the same time both Straight and Knee to allow each input port to have fanout equal to two, as showed in Fig. 2b. Furthermore, as showed in Fig. 2c, to increase routability, it is possible to activate two independent orthogonal connections in the same Cell. It has been obtained adding the Single/Double connection bit (the most significant one). When it is equal to one, the two couple of bits are both interpreted as port index, and the Straight connection of that ports are implicitly activated at the same time, as showed in Fig. 2c.

3.2   Computation

Elaboration features are two: Logic and Memory. The bits configuring the Elaboration features are 3 and they will be interpreted as settings of Memory or Logic according to the value of the 5 bits devoted to configuring connections. In fact, if the bits are activating the input and, automatically the output, of the Memory or the one of the Logic, the 3 bits will be automatically interpreted respectively according to the Memory or the Logic Encoding. On the other hand, if the 5 Connection bits are activating simple routing these 3 bits will be not considered. The logic block receives two inputs, produce one output and consists in one NAND gate, one NOR gate in parallel and a NOT on their output, all connected to inputs, output and between them with some multiplexer and demultiplexer. Thus, according to the 3 configuration bits, the cell can be programmed in 8 different modes: AND, NAND, OR, NOR, NOT Input1, NOT Input2, Buffer Input1 and Buffer Input 2. To link with the previously mentioned selectivity if the connections, it is important to notice that the connectivity configuration has been contrived in order to facilitate the cascade of logic operations and to easily add sequential behavior.

The memory block consists instead of an Edge Triggered Flip-Flop and a Level Sensitive Latch, which are again connected with the input and the output of the block by means of multiplexers and demultiplexers. According to the configuration bits, the input signal can be sent to one of the two sequential elements or bypass both of them and forward or to the output or the Reconfiguration Block. This last possibility is the one that allows the cell to trigger its own reconfiguration or neighbor reconfiguration.

It is again important to notice as the connectivity of Memory functionality has been contrived to make easier to insert sequential behavior in logic function (Memory output to the left side), to cascade several logic elements to produce Flip-Flop Chains and to receive Latch enable signal (North Input Latch).

3.3   Reconfiguration

The key innovation of the developed Reconfigurable Architecture is that the Reconfiguration management is embed inside the cell itself instead of being dislocated on a higher level. The effective implementation of the Reconfigurable Block follows the scheme reported in Fig. 3.

We distinguish between two kinds of reconfiguration: the Static one, when the succession of the possible states of the Cell is known and statically determined, and the Dynamic one, in which the scheduling of the states is not known a priori. The first one sees the Configuration Engine as a Finite State Machine. The second kind of reconfiguration, even if the Architecture has been contrived in order to support it in the future, has not been completely defined yet. Anyway, the shift from Static to Dynamic Reconfiguration should conceptually be like the shift from Finite State Machine to Pushdown Automata, as it will be clarified soon. In both cases, Cell reconfiguration can be triggered from the Cell itself, and from the two cells on its sides.

In fact, it has tree separated inputs and 2 separated outputs, beside the 4 inputs and output of the Cell described in Paragraph 1 of this chapter.

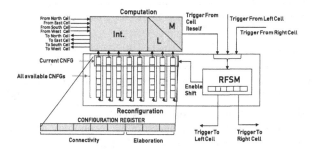

Fig. 3. Reconfiguration mechanism.

This is due to the fact that Reconfiguration should be triggered in any moment, so it should be independent from the current configuration of the Cell and especially from the activation of its input and outputs. In the Static Reconfiguration, the circular buffers are filled at the start-up with the possible configurations that are going to be taken from the Cell. When the reconfiguration is triggered from one of the three possible inputs, the Finite State Machine will enable the change of states in the cell itself, in the one on the left, in the one in the right, or in any combination of them, according to the content of the register of the Sub-Configuration Register. The content of this register defines the 'Update Rules' and in the Static Reconfiguration it is written only once at the start up. The Update Rules basically define the rules according with the reconfiguration propagates in the Array of Reconfigurable Cells. For the Static Configuration considered 3 bits are enough to define all possible states. In the Dynamic one, the complexity of the Reconfiguration Block will be higher: the number of bits required to the update rules will increase as well as the inputs of this block, and the circular buffers will become more similar to a small RAM, but we leave the design and the discussion on the trade-off between complexity and flexibility as future developments.

4 Experimental Results

In this section the result of the placement and routing of the ReM Cell itself with standard cells are provided, to demonstrate the implementability of this architecture.

Then, the results about the implementation of several benchmark circuits on ReM architecture are shown in order to highlight the benefit of the proposed approach.

A VHDL model of ReM cell has been realized in order to evaluate its implementability. To make a fair comparison with FPGA basic unit in this section only the part relative to the reconfigurable resource is considered. In fact, since no information are available about the configuration memory size and distribution in the Xilinx FPGA, the reconfiguration Module of ReM is neglected.

The ReM Cell design has been synthesized using the full 45 nm NangateOpenCell Library with Design Compiler. The area obtained is equivalent to 251 Nand Gate, which considering the target Library corresponds to a total logic area of 200.298 μm^2.

The ReM netlist has been used to obtain the cell layout. In order to obtain a first estimation of the area (no constraints or optimization has been applied) and to confirm the routability of the circuit has been used the PDD_Place&Route tool [20] developed in Politecnico di Torino.

The ReM Placement and Route consists in 190 Standard Cells, 131 Nets composed by 274 segments, distributed in 12 Routing Metal Layer.

The 190 Standard Cells of the basic layout, organized in a 13 × 16 Greed, occupy an area of 207.063 μm^2, value which is compliant with the one provided by Design Compiler considering the additional space dedicated to routing.

To further evaluate the proposed architecture the technology mapping of the first 6 benchmarks of the ITC'99 Set [21] has been obtained.

Since a custom tool for the purpose is not already available, to obtain the resources utilization Design Compiler has been used. In order to compute the needed ReM Cells, each design has been synthesized omitting all the NangateOpenCell Library Gates except for the ones available in ReM (AND2_X1, NAND2_X1, OR2_X1, NOR2_X1, INV_X1, and Memory Elements). In this manner, the amount of required ReM Cells in Memory and Logic Mode is accurately obtained. The number of ReM Cell in Connection Mode has been extracted interpolating the information provided by Design Compiler about edges and nets with the routability provided by the ReM Cell in Connectivity Mode.

Furthermore, a comparison with the same benchmarks implemented on the FPGA (Xilinx ZYNQ7020) in terms of resources and Reconfiguration Time has been made. The summary of this comparison is reported in Table 1. As is possible to guess, the ReM Implementation pay a bit in terms of resources usage, even if a fair comparison is difficult because no information is available about the area occupied by the FPGA Configurable Logic Block and Switch Matrix. But considering the Reconfiguration Time, the ReM approach is considerably faster. In fact, if we consider the Capillary Reconfiguration Approach [4], in which only the used frame for a design are reconfigured, the reconfiguration time is enormous, since each Frame needs about 10 ms to be reconfigured. With ReM Architecture instead the whole circuit can be reconfigured within a clock cycle with the systolic propagation of a Reconfiguration Trigger. The ReM Configuration times are computed with a working frequency of 10 MHz.

Table 1. Implementation results on ZYNQ and reconfiguration time comparison

ITC'99 benchmarks	ZYNQ7020					ReM		
	LUT	FF	Routing	Cnfg. bits	Cnfg. time [ms]	ReM cells	Cnfg. bits	Cnfg. time [ms]
b01	5	5	101	84032	∼260	95	757	0,0001
b02	4	4	72	71104	∼220	62	497	0,0001
b03	15	30	420	158368	∼490	372	2974	0,0001
b04	112	66	2140	429856	∼1330	1060	8483	0,0001
b05	84	34	1985	1383296	∼4280	1340	10718	0,0001
b06	8	9	187	145440	∼450	152	1214	0,0001

5   Conclusions and Future Works

In conclusion a new Reconfigurable Computing Paradigm has been developed, which consists in exploiting Reconfiguration in a distributed manner at the lowest granularity, providing to the basic reconfigurable functional unit the ability to reconfigure itself and the neighbor units to maximize flexibility, scalability, parallelization and concurrency. We also provide a proof of concept of our idea by implementing a physical model of the ReM Cell, which is a basic reconfigurable element which can behave as Logic, Memory, Connection and Reconfiguration Trigger. Finally, we demonstrate the benefits in terms of reconfiguration time.

Several future developments spreads, such as trying to make a fair comparison with FPGA area by investigating the real area used by FPGA resources, From the theoretical point of view we will further investigate the trade-off between granularity, area and reconfiguration time by and suggesting different version of Reconfigurable Basic Element. In parallel we will work on the realization of a tool chain to easy circuits implementation and evaluation on ReM architecture. In the future we also plan to a realize a real device with or technology architecture.

References

1. Tessier, R., Pocek, K., DeHon, A.: Reconfigurable computing architectures. Proc. IEEE **103** (3), 332–354 (2015)
2. Ul-Abdin, Z., Svensson, B.: Evolution in architectures and programming methodologies of coarse-grained reconfigurable computing. Microproces. Microsyst. Embed. Hardw. Des. **33**, 161–178 (2009)

3. Hartenstein, R.: Trends in reconfigurable logic and reconfigurable computing. In: 9th International Conference on Electronics, Circuits and Systems, Dubrovnik, Croatia, vol. 2, pp. 801–808 (2002)
4. Xilinx User Guide: 7 Series FPGAs Configuration. UG470, v1.11, pp. 1–176, 27 September 2016
5. Bozzoli, L., Sterpone, L.: COMET: a configuration memory tool to analyze, visualize and manipulate FPGAs bitstream. In: ARCS Workshop 2018, 31st International Conference on Architecture of Computing Systems, Braunschweig, Germany, pp. 1–4 (2018)
6. Hai, Y., Zhao, X., Liu, Y.: Reconfigurable computing availability and developing trends. In: 2015 11th International Conference on Computational Intelligence and Security, CIS, Shenzhen, pp. 138–141 (2015)
7. DeHon, A., Wawrzynek, J.: Reconfigurable computing: what, why, and implications for design automation. In: Proceedings 1999 Design Automation Conference (Cat. No. 99CH36361), New Orleans, LA, USA, pp. 610–615 (1999)
8. Singh, H., Lee, M.H., Lu, G., Kurdahi, F.J., Bagherzadeh, N., Filho, E.M.C.: MorphoSys: an integrated reconfigurable system for data-parallel computation-intensive applications. IEEE Trans. Comput. **49**, 465–481 (2000)
9. DAPDNA-2 Dynamically Reconfigurable Processor product brochure. IPFlexInc., 13 March 2007
10. XPP III Processor Overview: (XPP-III_overview_WP.pdf), 13 March 2008
11. Mirsky, E., DeHon, A.: MATRIX: a reconfigurable computing architecture with configurable instruction distribution and deployable resources. In: Proceedings of IEEE Symposium on FPGAs for Custom Computing Machines, pp. 157–166, April 1996
12. Taylor, M.B., et al.: Evaluation of the RAW microprocessor: an exposed-wire-delay architecture for ILP and streams. In: Proceedings of 31st International Symposium on Computer Architecture, ISCA (2004)
13. picoArray: ASIC processing power with DSP flexibility, PC102 datasheet, 8 December 2004
14. Walker, J.A., Trefzer, M.A., Bale, S.J., Tyrrell, A.M.: PAnDA: a reconfigurable architecture that adapts to physical substrate variations. IEEE Trans. Comput. **62**(8), 1584–1596 (2013)
15. Langeheine, J., Becker, J., Folling, S., Meier, K., Schemmel, J.: A CMOS FPTA chip for intrinsic hardware evolution of analog electronic circuits. In: Proceedings of Third NASA/DoD Workshop on Evolvable Hardware, EH-2001, Long Beach, CA, USA, pp. 172–175 (2001)
16. Neumann, B., von Sydow, T., Blume, H., Noll, T.G.: Design flow for embedded FPGAs based on a flexible architecture template. In: 2008 Design, Automation and Test in Europe, Munich, pp. 56–61 (2008)
17. MENTA eFPGA-augmented RISC CPUs (website). http://www.menta.fr/efpga_cpu.html
18. Heiner, J., Collins, N., Wirthlin, M.: Fault tolerant ICAP controller for high-reliable internal scrubbing. In: IEEE Aerospace Conference, pp. 1–10 (2008)
19. Sterpone, L., Bozzoli, L.: Fast partial reconfiguration on SRAM-based FPGAs: a frame-driven routing approach. In: Voros, N., Huebner, M., Keramidas, G., Goehringer, D., Antonopoulos, C., Diniz, P.C. (eds.) ARC 2018. LNCS, vol. 10824, pp. 319–330. Springer, Cham (2018). https://doi.org/10.1007/978-3-319-78890-6_26
20. Sterpone, L., Du, B.: SET-PAR: place and route tools for the mitigation of single event transients on flash-based FPGAs. In: Sano, K., Soudris, D., Hübner, M., Diniz, P.C. (eds.) ARC 2015. LNCS, vol. 9040, pp. 129–140. Springer, Cham (2015). https://doi.org/10.1007/978-3-319-16214-0_11
21. Corno, F., Reorda, M.S., Squillero, G.: RT-level ITC'99 benchmarks and first ATPG results. IEEE Des. Test Comput. **17**(3), 44–53 (2000)

Update or Invalidate: Influence of Coherence Protocols on Configurable HW Accelerators

Johanna Rohde[(✉)][iD], Lukas Johannes Jung, and Christian Hochberger

Department of Electrical Engineering and Information Technology,
Computer Systems Group, TU Darmstadt, Darmstadt, Germany
{rohde,jung,hochberger}@rs.tu-darmstadt.de

Abstract. Configurable hardware accelerators offer the opportunity to execute compute intense parts of applications with a higher performance and a higher energy efficiency as in pure software execution. One important component in such accelerators is the memory access to the system memory. Typically, this is realized through a cache hierarchy. In this contribution, we implement two different cache coherence protocols in two different configurable HW accelerators on real hardware. Using multiple benchmarks, we evaluate the influence of the cache coherence protocol on the execution time of the accelerators. As a result, we show that the Dragon protocol performs better than the MOESI protocol.

1 Introduction

Hardware (HW) accelerators have the potential to substantially improve the performance of software systems. In Field Programmable Gate Arrays (FPGA), HW accelerators can be customized for the application. In Coarse Grained Reconfigurable Arrays (CGRA), the application is mapped to the existing resources of the array. Both types of accelerators have in common that they need a regular processor to execute the software parts that were not mapped to the accelerator. Also, both accelerator types are highly dependent on the efficiency of memory accesses from the accelerator to the main memory. Multiple accesses should be possible at the same time in order to provide a maximum degree of parallelism. This is achieved by using multiple caches that can be accessed in parallel. These caches in turn get their data either from a secondary cache level or from the main memory. Additionally, these caches have to be kept in a coherent state.

Cache coherence has been a major research topic in the area of multi-core CPUs. Different protocols have been proposed and investigated. Nevertheless, in the use case of HW accelerators a stronger correlation and more locality of the access patterns can be expected.

In this contribution, we study the effect of two different cache coherence protocols on the efficiency of data caches for HW accelerators. We measure the execution times of different applications on the two accelerator types using the MOESI protocol and the Dragon protocol. It turns out that the Dragon protocol performs better than MOESI.

© Springer Nature Switzerland AG 2019
C. Hochberger et al. (Eds.): ARC 2019, LNCS 11444, pp. 305–316, 2019.
https://doi.org/10.1007/978-3-030-17227-5_22

The remainder of this paper is structured as follows. Sections 2 and 3 discuss related work and the two coherence protocols. It is followed by a description of the different machine concepts and an evaluation using multiple application oriented benchmarks is shown in Sect. 5. Finally, we give a conclusion in Sect. 6.

2   Related Work

Most reconfigurable accelerators do not use a typical multi cache system. Some approaches like DySer [6] rely on the memory subsystem of the host processor to load data from the memory. While this approach eliminates the need of cache coherence protocols, this is a major bottleneck of the accelerator [6].

Plasticine [8] streams data from the memory directly into the accelerator using Pattern Memory Units. This is very efficient but it can only be done with a priori knowledge of the memory access patterns. Similarly, [3] uses Global Data Transfer Units to load data from the offchip memory into the accelerator.

In [7] a single dual port cache is used in the accelerator but the cache of the host processor has to be flushed and invalidated when the accelerator starts execution. The accelerator cache uses write-through, no-allocate strategy to ensure coherence.

LegUp is a relatively well known high level synthesis (HLS) tool to create application specific hardware accelerators. Their cache consists of a single memory which is connected to processor and accelerators likewise. This eliminates the need to implement a coherence protocol. Furthermore, they take advantage of the dual port feature of BRAMs found on FPGAs. In order to increase the number of ports, they either use multi-pumping (MP) or a live value table (LVT) [2]. MP time multiplexes the BRAM blocks using a clock of higher frequency. Therefore, the number of ports that can be created by this technique is limited. The LVT approach replicates the BRAM multiple times increasing the area with $O(n^2)$ and n being the number of ports. This leads to an enormous area consumption for systems with many caches.

In [13] the authors automatically generate multi-cache systems with caches of varying size using spare BRAM resources on the FPGA. Nevertheless, they assume a direct mapped cache architecture with fixed line size and never take into account the effect of the implemented coherence protocol.

3   Cache Coherence Protocols

3.1   MOESI Protocol

The MOESI protocol is an invalidation based protocol developed to maintain coherent data over any number of caches. It consists of five states: *Modified, Owned, Exclusive, Shared* and *Invalid*. Each cache line can either be valid or invalid. If it is valid, it can either be shared or exclusive and it can either be modified or unmodified. Therefore, the Modified state is also exclusive, the Owned state is modified and shared while the Exclusive and the Shared states are both unmodified. For further information see [11].

Compared to simpler protocols, the Owned state allows to share dirty cache lines. The dirty value is only written back when the cache line is replaced.

This type of protocol is called *invalidation based* since one cache will invalidate a shared line in all other caches before writing to it. Therefore, the cache line will be transitioned from the Shared or Owned state into the Modified state in the writing cache, while being transitioned into the Invalid state in every other cache.

3.2 Dragon Protocol

The main issue with the MOESI protocol is that upon a (shared) write access, a notification is sent and all other caches holding that line will invalidate their copy. If the data is needed later on, it has to be reloaded.

The Dragon protocol [1] tries to avoid these reloads by not invalidating the cache line in all other caches upon a write access. Instead, the new value is directly sent with the notification. The Dragon protocol is therefore *update based*.

Consequently, Dragon has the same states as MOESI. However, when one cache writes to a shared cache line, that cache line is transitioned to the Owned state instead of the Modified state while all other cashes maintain their copy in the Shared state. The update can be done in the background and no delay is needed if no other requests are posted on the bus during that time.

3.3 Comparison

Table 1 shows different events that delay an access to the cache. In order to show the advantages and disadvantages of these two protocols, it is best to compare these events.

Case (1a) is inevitable while case (1b) can only happen when an invalidation based protocol such as MOESI is used. The Dragon protocol would not cause this event since the value would be updated directly and the line would remain in a valid state.

The occurrence of case (2) is inevitable for both coherence protocols.

Table 1. MOESI vs Dragon delay events

	Event	Reason	MOESI invalidate	Dragon update
(1a)	L1 Miss	Line was never read	•	•
(1b)		Line was invalidated by another cache	•	
(2)	Write back	Replaced cache line was in state Owned or Modified	•	•
(3a)	Bus congestion	Two caches write to a shared cache line alternatingly in quick succession	•	•
(3b)		One cache writes to a shared cache line in quick succession		•

Case (3a) causes delays in both caches. For MOESI each write access will invalidate the cache line in all other cache and the data has to be reloaded for the next access. When Dragon is used, the updates congest the coherence bus. Therefore, they cannot be done in the background any more. The same holds for Dragon in case (3b). However, this case cannot occur when MOESI is used because the first write access invalidates the cache line in all other caches.

In conclusion, one can say that using the Dragon protocol will reduce the miss rate because a shared line will be updated instead of invalidated. At the same time depending on the access pattern the cache latencies might increase when a single cache is repetitively writing a shared cache line. However, the occurrence of delay types (3a) and (3b) can be minimized by reducing the number of shared lines in the system.

4   Accelerator Concepts

We implemented cache based memory interfaces into a CGRA based (Sect. 4.1) and an FPGA based (Sect. 4.2) accelerator architecture.

4.1   CGRA Based Accelerator

In the AMIDAR system a CGRA based accelerator whose configurations can be created and loaded at runtime is used [14]. AMIDAR is a token-based Java processor which is tightly coupled to the accelerator. The accelerator is shown in Fig. 1a. It consists of an array of Processing Elements (PE, white and green), a context control unit (red) and the Condition Box (C-Box, yellow).

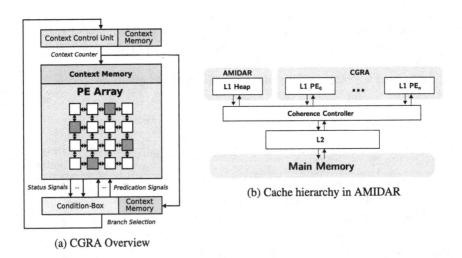

(a) CGRA Overview

(b) Cache hierarchy in AMIDAR

Fig. 1. CGRA architecture and memory hierarchy of the AMIDAR system (Color figure online)

Each PE can execute one instruction per clock cycle provided by the context memories (blue). New configurations for different kernels are created and loaded at runtime to adapt to the program flow. No user interaction in any way is needed at this point.

In order to accelerate arbitrary applications with irregular access patterns, several PEs are equipped with memory interfaces (green) which can load data from the memory on demand via caches.

Figure 1b shows the cache hierarchy in AMIDAR. Cache lines can be exchanged between both L1 and L2 caches in one clock cycle. The cache properties using the DDR3 memory of the Nexys Video board as main memory are shown in Table 2. Note that in the AMIDAR processor, the cache is addressed indirectly via an object handle and an offset, referred to as virtual addressing. This technique is limited to object oriented programming languages where pointer arithmetic is not allowed [12].

Access Classification and Distribution. When a kernel is mapped onto the CGRA, a combined placer and scheduler [10] maps each memory access to a PE. Depending on this decision, the number of shared cache lines varies. As a result, the quality of the mapping algorithm directly influences the performance of the kernel.

As explained in Sect. 4.1, the cache in the AMIDAR system is virtually addressed using an object handle as base address and an offset. Since the absence of aliasing can easily be proven in most cases, it can be assumed that memory accesses with the same base address are more likely to cause cache conflicts than memory accesses with different base addresses.

In order to minimize those cache conflicts, the scheduler tries to classify memory accesses and distributes them to the PEs in a manner that memory accesses with the same base address are mapped to the same PE. In the following, this processes will be called ACD (Access Classification and Distribution).

ACD is done with the help of a list for each base address in the kernel. The list contains all PEs on which an access with the corresponding base address was scheduled. The following heuristic is used when binding the memory access instructions to the PEs:

1. Find all memory accesses with the same base address
2. If there are more than twice as many read accesses than write accesses, there are no restrictions in order to exploit parallelism.
3. If not, each access in this class has to be mapped to a PE which is already in the list of the corresponding base address (if possible).
4. Update the list as follows when an access is mapped:
   - Add PE to the list if the current access is a read access
   - Add PE to the list and remove all other PEs if the current access is a write access

Note, that this heuristic will improve the cache access times but at the same time this might lead to longer schedules since less operations can be parallelized.

Table 2. AMIDAR and PIRANHA cache properties (see Figs. 1b and 2)

	AMIDAR/CGRA	PIRANHA
L1 Core Cache	64 KB, 32 Byte/8 Word per Line Virtually addressed, 4-Ways	8 KB, 16 Byte/8 Word per Line 4-Ways
L1 Acc. Cache in sum	16 KB, 32 Byte/8 Word per Line Virtually addressed, 4-Ways	16 KB, 16 Byte/8 Word per Line 4-Ways
L2 Cache	256 KB, 32 Byte/8 Word per Line Virtually addressed, 4-Ways	Non-existent
L1 miss Latency		
read		
... from other L1 Cache	5+ Cycles	4+ Cycles
... from L2 Cache	10+ Cycles	Non-existent
... from main memory	48+ Cycles	36+ Cycles

4.2 Application Specific Accelerator

Application specific accelerators are created at compile time and are directly integrated into the system. Their advantage is that the accelerators and the surrounding architecture such as the cache system can be tailored to the specific needs of the application.

PIRANHA. The Plugin for Intermediate Representation ANalysis and Hardware Acceleration (PIRANHA) can be used to automatically generate application specific hardware accelerators while compiling the system's firmware with the GCC [5]. It can be integrated into any System-on-Chip (SoC) kit for FPGAs that uses the GCC to compile the firmware. The idea is to take advantage of the fact that systems deployed on FPGAs can be newly synthesized after each change to the firmware giving the opportunity to insert additional application specific hardware.

Currently, PIRANHA is mainly used with the SpartanMC, an 18-bit SoC-kit designed to get the optimum use of the internal structures of an FPGA [4]. The toolchain automatically integrates the plugin into the compiler. The key concept is that code analysis, loop selection and accelerator generation run completely transparently. The firmware developer neither has to indicate which parts of the code to accelerate nor what assumptions about code can be made.

PIRANHA accepts a parameter that indicates the number of available memory ports to the accelerators. During operation scheduling this number serves as a resource constraint on how many concurrent memory accesses can be scheduled in one time step.

Decoupling memory operations is a non trivial task for the C language due to pointer aliasing. Therefore, most memory accesses can only be performed out of order or in parallel when it can be proven at compile time that they never refer to the same memory address. This is usually the case when both operations access different elements of the same array. Two read operations are always independent of each other.

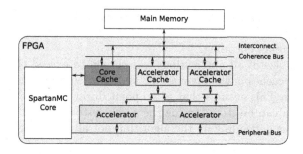

Fig. 2. Interconnect between softcore, hardware accelerator and caches

The memory accesses are assigned to memory ports after scheduling. PIRANHA uses the GCC internal algorithms to calculate a base address object for every memory access instruction that follows a regular access pattern [9]. The algorithm tries to bind memory access with the same base address to the same port in order to reduce the number of shared lines in the cache. In comparison to the ACD method, this binding algorithm is not executed during scheduling but afterwards. Therefore, it is not possible to prevent shared cache lines by forcibly scheduling memory accesses of the same array to the same port in different time steps. Furthermore, due to pointer aliasing, two memory accesses with different base addresses can still refer to the same data.

Cache Integration. Figure 2 shows the interconnect between softcore, hardware accelerators and data caches. The accelerators are connected to the processor as peripherals. Live-in and live-out variables are transferred using the peripheral bus. Accelerators and the SpartanMC core use different types of caches. Only one accelerator can be active at a time. Therefore, they can share the access to all accelerator caches. Coherence is maintained over the coherence bus.

Note that the coherence bus is able to transfer a whole line in parallel. This increases the efficiency of the system. The cache properties using the DDR3 memory of the Nexys Video board are shown in Table 2.

5   Evaluation

The cache coherence strategies will be evaluated with three applications:

The **Mandelbrot** calculation contains a compute heavy inner loop that calculates i values of a complex valued sequence for each pixel in a picture. It uses a random access pattern for the color lookup and a linear access pattern to store the colors of the pixels.

The **AES-256** application encrypts and decrypts a given byte array. Therefore, many memory accesses have a regular access pattern and arrays are changed in place.

In the **JPEG** encoder many different kernels with different characteristics are computed ranging from color space transformation over discrete cosine transformation to Huffman encoding.

The problem size of all applications was chosen to exceed the cache size of the combined L1 caches in the SpartanMC system as well as the L2 cache of the AMIDAR system. This ensures that at no point during runtime the entire data of the application can be stored inside the cache system. Nevertheless, it has to be considered that depending on the algorithm not all data is used at the same time.

5.1 Preselection of Cache Parameters

Basically, it would be possible to sweep over all available parameters for the cache design. Yet, this would span a huge search space and it would take an unbearable time to evaluate. Thus, we try to make reasonable choices for some of the parameters.

Experiments with the cache line size have shown that with a line size of 8 words in both accelerator types the best performance was gained. Smaller or larger line sizes had a negative effect on almost all test cases. Thus, we fixed the line size to 8 words.

Varying the cache size in total might change other influence factors. Nevertheless, we found that beyond 16 KB cache size these effects are no longer relevant. At the same time this cache size seems to be reasonable. Thus, we fixed the cache size to 16 KB.

Eventually, we analyzed the effect of different associativities. Comparing 1, 2, and 4-way caches, we found that 4-way caches always performed at least as good as the others, which could be expected. At the same time, the timing of these 4-way caches in the accelerator was still within the limits of the other system components. Thus, the only mentionable drawback of a 4-way configuration is the relatively small hardware overhead (more comparators for the tag). Consequently, we fixed the associativity to 4.

As a result of this preselection, the following parameters will be swept: number of caches (between 1, 2 and 4) and the coherence protocol. In case of the CGRA based accelerator, additionally we evaluated the usage of ACD.

5.2 Evaluation of Application Specific Accelerators

All three benchmarks were executed on the SpartanMC in order to evaluate the impact of the coherence protocol in a system with application specific accelerators. The system was synthesized for an Artix-7 FPGA on the Nexys Video board. This board includes a 512 MB DDR3 memory which was used as main memory. A baseline was created by executing each benchmark without any accelerators present.

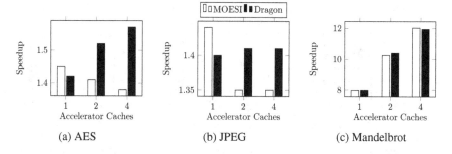

Fig. 3. Comparison of the speedup for a total cache size of 16 KB and line size of 8 words executed on the SpartanMC with application specific accelerators

Figure 3 compares the speedup for MOESI and Dragon. It can be seen that MOESI outperforms Dragon as long as there is only a single accelerator cache connected to the system. This is not surprising since the processor is idling while the accelerator is running. Therefore, it is more beneficial to invalidate a line the first time it is written.

Once there is more than one accelerator cache present, Dragon outperforms the MOESI protocol. As explained in Sect. 4.2, PIRANHA is currently not able to efficiently classify memory instructions in order to reduce the number of shared writes to the cache system. Therefore, the system benefits from directly updating a shared line.

The evaluation also shows that the coherence protocol has close to no effect on the Mandelbrot benchmark. The implementation of the benchmark has two arrays: the color lookup table, which is read only, and the output picture, which is write only. Due to the unroll factor of 4, all ports can be fully exploited. The coherence protocol does not have any influence on read only data, since the data is never invalidated. Furthermore, the delay to access a write only array simultaneously from multiple ports is almost identical for MOESI and Dragon since both protocols demand a single coherence access either to request and invalidate or to update the line.

The last thing to note is that the JPEG performs best when a single cache and MOESI is used. This is due to the fact that the algorithm is hard to decouple. Therefore, the additional memory interfaces have a low utilization and it is better to use a single bigger cache.

5.3 Evaluation of CGRA Based Accelerators

For the CGRA a cycle accurate simulator was used and a design space exploration sweeping the parameters presented in Sect. 5.1 was done.

Figure 4 shows the speedups for AES, JPEG and Mandelbrot with and without ACD. The baseline is an execution of the applications on the AMIDAR system without CGRA acceleration. In Mandelbrot the difference between the different coherence strategies is negligible for the same reasons presented in

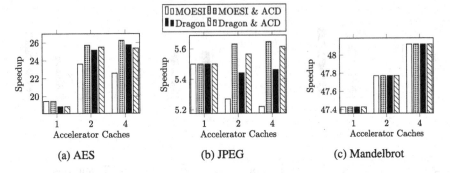

Fig. 4. Comparison of the speedup for a total cache size of 16 KB and line size of 8 words executed on AMIDAR with reconfigurable accelerator

Sect. 5.2. When just one cache is used, MOESI is better or results at least in the same performance and ACD has no effect as all memory accesses will be mapped to the one cache anyways. When more than one cache is present, Dragon performs better for both, AES and JPEG, when no ACD is used. When ACD is used, MOESI is slightly better in all cases.

A more detailed evaluation was made using 24 benchmarks[1] in two different sizes. A thorough discussion is omitted here, but the key findings are be given in the following.

When only one cache is present, the cache lines are only shared with the cache of the host processor. Updating shared cache lines brings no benefit but only slows down the execution. Therefore, MOESI outperforms Dragon in this case.

For CGRAs with more than one cache and without ACD, Dragon is always better than MOESI because written values are updated directly in the other caches.

ACD increases the performance in both Dragon and MOESI. Yet, ACD cancels the advantages of Dragon. Therefore, MOESI with ACD is slightly better because MOESI blocks unnecessary cache line sharing with the cache in the host processor.

As a conclusion of both system evaluations we can say that if there is just one cache in the CGRA MOESI is better than Dragon and ACD is unnecessary. If there is more than one cache, Dragon is better if ACD cannot be used. If ACD is used both protocols have a similar performance while MOESI has a slight advantage if there are fewer caches in the CGRA. The more caches are added, the better Dragon performs.

---

[1] AES, Blowfish, DES, IDEA, RC6, Serpent, Skipjack, Twofish, XTEA, BLAKE256, CubeHash512, ECOH256, MD5, RadioGatun32, SHA1, SHA256, SIMD512, ContrastFilter, GrayscaleFilter, SobelFilter, SwizzleFilter, ADPCMdecode, ADPCMencode, JPEG.

6   Conclusion

In this contribution, we have investigated the influence of different coherence protocols on the efficiency of the memory subsystem of two accelerator architectures. In summary, we found that the number of useful memory ports is dependent on the nature of the accelerator and the thoroughness of the memory access analysis. In contrast, the Dragon coherence protocol is always the better choice, if more than one cache is used. In case the memory accesses can be classified and distributed, the Dragon protocol does not have an advantage over MOESI, but in all other cases, the Dragon protocol leads to a better performance.

References

1. Archibald, J., Baer, J.L.: Cache coherence protocols: evaluation using a multiprocessor simulation model. ACM Trans. Comput. Syst. **4**, 273–298 (1986)
2. Choi, J., Nam, K., Canis, A., Anderson, J., Brown, S., Czajkowski, T.: Impact of cache architecture and interface on performance and area of FPGA-based processor/parallel-accelerator systems. In: FCCM 2012, April 2012
3. Cong, J., Huang, H., Ma, C., Xiao, B., Zhou, P.: A fully pipelined and dynamically composable architecture of CGRA. In: FCCM 2014, May 2014
4. Hempel, G., Hochberger, C.: A resource optimized processor core for FPGA based SoCs. In: 10th Euromicro DSD Conference on Architectures, Methods and Tools, August 2007
5. Hempel, G., Hochberger, C., Raitza, M.: Towards GCC-based automatic soft-core customization. In: 22nd International Conference on Field Programmable Logic and Applications (FPL), August 2012
6. Hoy, C., et al.: Performance evaluation of a DySER FPGA prototype system spanning the compiler, microarchitecture, and hardware implementation. In: 2015 IEEE International Symposium on Performance Analysis of Systems and Software (ISPASS), Philadelphia, PA, pp. 203–214 (2015). https://doi.org/10.1109/ISPASS.2015.7095806
7. Paulino, N.M.C., Ferreira, J.C., Cardoso, J.M.P.: Trace-based reconfigurable acceleration with data cache and external memory support. In: 2014 IEEE International Symposium on Parallel and Distributed Processing with Applications, August 2014
8. Prabhakar, R., et al.: Plasticine: a reconfigurable architecture for parallel patterns. In: Proceedings of the 44th ISCA, ISCA 2017. ACM (2017)
9. Rohde, J., Hochberger, C.: Using GCC analysis techniques to enable parallel memory accesses in HLS. In: Fourth International Workshop on FPGAs for Software Programmers, FSP 2017, September 2017
10. Ruschke, T., Jung, L.J., Wolf, D., Hochberger, C.: Scheduler for inhomogeneous and irregular CGRAs with support for complex control flow. In: 2016 IPDPSW, May 2016
11. Solihin, Y.: Fundamentals of Parallel Multicore Architecture. Chapman and Hall/CRC, Boca Raton (2015)
12. Vijaykrishnan, N., Ranganathan, N.: Supporting object accesses in a Java processor. IEE Proc. Comput. Digital Tech. **147**(6), 435–443 (2000)

13. Winterstein, F., Fleming, K., Yang, H., Wickerson, J., Constantinides, G.: Customized caches in application-specific memory hierarchies. In: 2015 International Conference on Field Programmable Technology (FPT), December 2015
14. Wolf, D.L., Jung, L.J., Ruschke, T., Li, C., Hochberger, C.: AMIDAR project: lessons learned in 15 years of researching adaptive processors. In: 2018 13th International Symposium on Reconfigurable Communication-centric Systems-on-Chip (ReCoSoC), July 2018

Design Frameworks and Methodology

Hybrid Prototyping for Manycore Design and Validation

Leonard Masing$^{(\boxtimes)}$, Fabian Lesniak, and Jürgen Becker

Institute for Information Processing Systems, Karlsruhe Institute of Technology,
Karlsruhe, Germany
{leonard.masing,fabian.lesniak,juergen.becker}@kit.edu

Abstract. The trend towards more parallelism in information processing is unbroken. Manycore architectures provide both massive parallelism
and flexibility, yet they raise the level of complexity in design and programming. Prototyping of such architectures helps in handling this complexity by evaluating the design space and discovering design errors.
Several system simulators exist but they can only be used for early software development and interface specification. FPGA-based prototypes
on the other hand are restricted by available FPGA resources or expensive multi-FPGA prototyping platforms. We present a hybrid prototyping approach for manycore systems that consists of an FPGA-part and
a virtual part of the architecture on a host system. The hybrid prototyping requires less FPGA resources while retaining its speed advantage
and enabling flexible modeling in the virtual platform.
  We describe the concept, provide an analysis of timing accuracy and
synchronization of the FPGA with the Virtual Platform (VP) and show
an example in which the hybrid prototype is used for feature development
and evaluation of a scientific manycore architecture. The hybrid prototype allows us to evaluate a 7×7 architecture on a Virtex-7 XC7VX485T
FPGA board which otherwise could only fit a reduced 2×2 design of our
architecture.

Keywords: Hybrid prototyping · Manycore · Virtual Platforms

1 Introduction

The trend towards more and more cores on a single chip has been predicted for
many years, yet even today we still see only few real manycore architectures
present in academia and industry. This is mostly due to major challenges in the
programmability of such architectures. Yet the development of a manycore hardware architecture itself, its feature selection, composition and micro-architecture
is not trivial. A major role regarding performance and fulfillment of other non-
functional properties is played by the interconnect and the memory architecture.
Their impact is much more severe in a manycore, compared to traditional single,
dual or quad-core architectures. Towards a scalable interconnect backbone for
manycore architectures, Networks-on-chip (NoC) solutions have emerged. These

© Springer Nature Switzerland AG 2019
C. Hochberger et al. (Eds.): ARC 2019, LNCS 11444, pp. 319–333, 2019.
https://doi.org/10.1007/978-3-030-17227-5_23

NoC, while simple in concept, have increased in complexity over the years in order to offer QoS guarantees, low power, safety, security, etc. Yet many new concepts are evaluated purely on abstract software simulators, leaving actual hardware implementations of novel NoC extensions and concepts a rare case. This is especially true for large manycore architectures, since they are difficult to develop and prototype. However, real hardware implementations are an important factor in strengthening a concepts credibility and help integrating useful approaches into other architectures. The reason why there are so few implementations is often simply the extra effort that has to be spent on developing a concept as an actual hardware block, compared to doing so in an abstract software simulator. However, there is also the problem of prototyping, debugging and evaluation of a hardware implementation. This problem is exceedingly more difficult in the context of NoCs and manycore: Huge architectures that do not fit into a single FPGA and that do not scale well in hardware simulation.

In this paper we introduce and investigate hybrid prototyping, i.e. a combination of FPGA and Virtual Platforms (VP), in the context of manycore design. At first, the current state-of-the-art in manycore prototyping is illustrated and the existing shortcomings are discussed. Afterwards the concept of hybrid prototyping for manycore architectures is introduced and its benefits highlighted. The detailed design and implementation that is applied to a scientific manycore architecture is shown afterwards. Furthermore, the synchronization and delay among the domains of the hybrid prototype is analyzed. Finally, the hybrid prototyping is evaluated based on a NoC extension of said manycore architecture.

2   Traditional Manycore Prototyping

Besides high-level synthesis based on functional descriptions in OpenCL, SystemC or even plain C which slowly gains more attraction, the typical way for hardware design is still based on Hardware Description Languages (HDL) like VHDL or Verilog and their extensions. The common approach for evaluation, debugging and verification of HDL code is the use of hardware simulators. These simulators provide cycle accurate simulation of all signals present in a design. A large benefit of such simulators is the fact that any design change can be recompiled rather quickly. Furthermore, all signals in the design can be monitored and observed at cycle-level granularity. On the other hand, simulations on such a detailed level are rather slow. Simulation time directly correlates with the design size, i.e. the amount of signals that need to be simulated. Thus, in the case of a manycore, it becomes unfeasible to simulate the whole hardware platform together with the applications running on it. Instead, typically testbenches are used which test only small components of a platform. However, this often leads to unrealistic scenarios or uncovered corner cases, causing design failures in real hardware. Furthermore, it is impossible to evaluate and compare implementation performance in any real use-case scenario.

An alternative to pure software based hardware simulators is FPGA prototyping. Using FPGA for prototyping is sometimes also seen as an enhancement or extension to hardware simulation, labeled simulator acceleration. Field programmable gate arrays have a long history in hardware prototyping besides also being a target technology for hardware implementation and deployment in many different application domains [11]. FPGA prototyping allows clock frequencies of up to a few hundred MHz and it provides fully parallel hardware execution, in contrast to sequential execution in any software simulator. This allows high performance and good scalability with growing design size. However, this scalability is limited by the available resources on an FPGA. In fact, a single resource such as LUT, FF or BRAM that exceeds its limit prevents the placement of the whole design. Additionally, the more resources are in use, the less likely it is for the tools to provide good routing to allow high clock frequencies. Even though FPGAs are growing in size each generation, no single FPGA can currently host a full manycore design with hundreds of cores on its own. A common approach for prototyping a manycore architecture is thus based on a multi-FPGA prototyping platform. Such prototyping systems typically host a fixed number of FPGAs connected via high-throughput and low-latency interconnection cables or boards. Partitioning a manycore architecture onto multiple FPGAs as shown in Fig. 1 typically uses the NoC-links between routers (R) to separate the design at the FPGA boundaries. However, the links which cross FPGA boundaries typically cannot be operated with the same delay as FPGA-internal links, resulting in restrictions for the design and potentially even different timing behavior. Furthermore, there is always an overhead when connecting pins for the FPGA interconnect and doing delay calibration among all signals on such a link. Another drawback of FPGA prototyping is the large time for synthesis and place & route, especially in big designs. Changing any configuration, fixing a bug or implementing a new feature requires a new synthesis which can easily take several hours to finish. The time is further increased if timing and mapping constraints are difficult to fulfill and require further optimization steps by the synthesis tools.

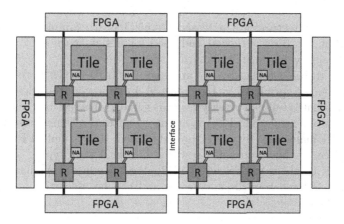

Fig. 1. A manycore partition onto a multi-FPGA prototyping system.

3   Related Work

Since the performance of manycores largely depends on the on-chip interconnect, a large amount of research on the design and prototyping of manycore architectures focuses specifically on NoCs. The authors of [5] present AdapNoC, a flexible FPGA-based NoC simulator. The authors also provide a thorough comparison about the state of the art regarding NoC simulators. Major distinctions among FPGA-based simulators are made based on virtualization techniques, traffic generation and the decoupling of simulator and network.

All NoC simulators have to provide some form of traffic generation which can either be synthetic or real traffic (typically trace-based). The authors in [14] decouple the simulator from the simulated architecture and use C-based traffic generation on the host while in [7] the traffic generation is handled by a soft-core on the FPGA.

In [10], Papamichael introduces a virtualization technique on FPGAs, which allows much larger designs than the available resources would normally allow. In this approach, the NoC architecture is split into several virtual regions that run on a single physical instance of such a region. Thus, the logic of the region exists just once and only the state holding elements must be duplicated to exist physically for each virtual region. A similar virtualization approach on FPGAs, targeted towards cores of a Multicore instead of the interconnect is presented in [12].

All these approaches lack the availability of a full manycore architecture including the processing elements, I/O, memories etc. Prototyping such full manycore architectures suffers from the sheer size and complexity much more than pure interconnect simulators/emulators. Software based approaches using instruction set simulators (ISS) may achieve high execution speeds and allow rather simple architecture modelling, yet they always face the issue of accuracy loss, not being a physical implementation. Furthermore, software simulators work by sequential execution, which results in bad scalability when the dimensions of the emulated architectures are increased. Gem5 [3] is an example of a full-system simulator that has been extended and used for design-space explorations and proof-of-concept evaluations in manycore architectures.

Attempts to bring full manycore architectures onto FPGA were made with the introduction of Formic [8] by Lyberis et al. In their work they describe a new FPGA board that is tailored exactly towards a manycores resource requirements. However, a lot of boards and FPGA in an interconnected scheme are still required to host a full manycore. Synopsys provides their HAPS multi-FPGA boards that have recently been extended towards a hybrid prototyping approach in conjunction with their Virtualizer tool [2]. We introduce a similar approach, however it is tailored towards manycores and can be used with any available FPGA board.

Table 1. Resource cost comparison of example components present in a manycore architecture.

	LUT	FF	Mux	BRAM
1 LEON3 core	8797	2583	96	16
1 Tile (5 Cores)	61572	27949	733	132
1 Aethereal router [4]	2658	N/A	N/A	N/A

4   The Hybrid Prototyping

In this paper we investigate the hybrid prototyping, which is essentially a fusion of software based virtual platforms (VPs) and FPGA prototyping, for manycore and NoC design. The application of a hybrid prototype is motivated by the observation that the full level of detail is not always needed in every component when developing a manycore. The approach is similar to the concept of testbenches for small sub-components when designing hardware in cycle accurate simulators. In this case however, the goal is to execute real applications and prototype the full manycore architecture, yet not every component at the same level of detail. As such, we propose to implement a part of the architecture on an FPGA, while modelling the remaining part in a virtual platform. This allows us to have more FPGA resources for the components we want to investigate while creating a prototype that encompasses a much larger manycore architecture in total.

An analysis of the area consumption of a CPU that is available as synthesizable HDL description and a multi-CPU tile that is typically part of a manycore architecture is shown in Table 1. The core is a LEON3 processor from Gaisler Research including 32 KB/64 KB I/D L1 caches, a typical tile consists of 5 cores, local bus, network interface and debug link. As it can be seen, the LUT requirements are the limiting factor for the cores and tiles. Based on the resources available on the XC7V2000T (1,222M LUTs and 2,443M FFs), we could theoretically fit a full design consisting of 17 tiles and routers. In comparison, there are resource utilization numbers of the aethereal NoC available as provided in [4] which hint towards a theoretical number of 459 routers fitting on the XC7V2000T. While these theoretical numbers can't be achieved in an actual synthesis due to placement constraints, this estimation demonstrates the impact of mapping only a subset of an architecture to the FPGA.

Based on these area observations, we present two major scenarios for manycore prototyping. The first scenario implements a spatial fragment of the architecture (i.e. several tiles including their NoC routers) on the FPGA, while modeling the remaining tiles and routers in a virtual platform. This approach is shown in Fig. 2. The connection between FPGA and virtual platform is located between two routers in the NoC, i.e. a physical router on the border of the FPGA that is connected to a neighboring router in the virtual platform. The interface between the physical router on the FPGA and the virtual router on the host PC will be described in detail later. In this setup, the focus is on the investigation of the tiles, which are prototyped with full FPGA accuracy but can send and

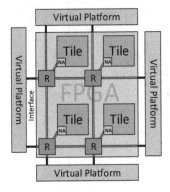

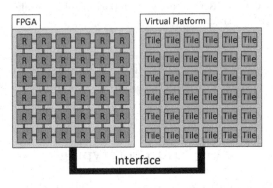

Fig. 2. Scenario 1: a subsection of the manycore is implemented in the FPGA

Fig. 3. Scenario 2: the NoC is implemented physically, tiles reside in the virtual platform

receive their data to respectively from a much larger architecture. This allows the modeling of different load scenarios, access latencies over the NoC, I/O and large background memory on the host system.

The second scenario (Fig. 3) is focused on the network-on-chip interconnect itself. In this scenario, a full NoC and all its physical links are implemented on the FPGA, while the tiles including the network interface is modeled in the virtual platform. The connection between FPGA and VP is thus at the local port of each router at which point the data is transferred to the host and processed by a virtual network interface and the virtual tiles. This scenario allows us to investigate much larger NoC architectures under real application traffic, provide resources (e.g. memory, I/O) that might not be available on the FPGA itself and enables modeling of different (end to end) network protocols in the virtual platform (e.g. shared memory versus message passing). Since the "cut" between FPGA and VP is on regular NoC links and the local port/link typically behaves exactly the same as the links between two routers, both scenarios can be handled by the same physical interface implementation and only require different modeling on the VP side.

5   Implementation

Figure 4 shows the full hybrid prototyping scheme. On the left we see the Host-PC, on which the virtual platform and the application code running within the platform resides. The virtual platform can also be abstracted on a functional level by the use of a communication library that handles the access to the FPGA. The virtual platform uses a direct access to a PCIe driver for the physical interface to the FPGA. On the right we see the FPGA part, that is split into three components: The fragment of the manycore architecture that is prototyped (i.e. the two scenarios), a NoC Interface which collects/distributes and prepares all the data from/to the NoC, and the host interface that includes the PCIe.

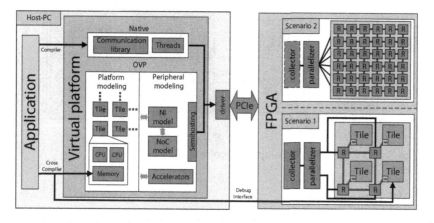

Fig. 4. The full hybrid prototyping architecture

5.1 Host Interface

The requirements for the FPGA-host interface are low latency data transfers and high potential throughput so that large manycore architectures with high network load can be handled. We choose PCIe for this task since it offers the best performance in comparison to any other typically available interface between FPGA and host-PC. The PCIe interface is clocked with 250 MHz and offers 128 bit width for the data transfers. Data is transferred via DMA requests into a ringbuffer in the main memory on the host PC. The main memory hosts two separated ringbuffers, one for the receiving and one for the sending side.

5.2 NoC Interface

The NoC interface as shown in Fig. 5 is responsible for collecting all the data from the NoC towards the VP, and distributing the data from the VP to the NoC. For this task we introduce a Dummy Network Interface (DNI) that is able to handle the communication with the routers. All dummy NIs are connected to one of the parallelizers, which bundle the data streams of multiple NIs into 128 bit packets that are used by the PCIe Interface. A configurable amount of dummy NIs can be connected to a parallelizer, yet with a typical NoC Link bandwidth of 32 bit that are converted to 128 bit, we choose four dummy NIs for each parallelizer. The parallelizer also adds a header to each packet which indicates the ID of the router and the virtual channel on which a packet arrived. The parallelizers are connected to a collector. This unit contains dual clock FIFOs which allow an arbitrary configuration of the clock frequency of the NoC, while keeping the PCIe Interface at maximum clock speed for best performance. The collector is then connected to the Host Interface, that contains a Xilinx PCIe core.

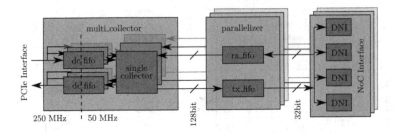

Fig. 5. Components of the NoC interface

5.3   SW Interface

When data is copied from the FPGA into the host memory via DMA, an interrupt is raised to notify the user-space software. We implemented a specific driver that takes care of the low-level tasks for communication of user-space software with the FPGA design. The driver can reserve memory ranges in the host memory, initialize the PCIe device and setup DMA and interrupts. It creates a character device with the following syscalls: open, close, read, write, ioctl, poll. The driver makes sure that only valid data is read and supports both blocking as well as non-blocking calls. This interface allows the creation of user-space libraries and applications that directly work on the driver in order to send and receive data to, respectively from the FPGA.

5.4   VP Interface

In order to prototype a full manycore system, all the components that are not placed on the FPGA need to be modeled on the host. As an example, according to scenario 2 we place the NoC interconnect on the FPGA while modeling the network interface and the tiles in a virtual platform. In order to be fully binary compatible, we require an Instruction Set Simulator (ISS) as well as a modeling and platform generation framework for arbitrary components like the network interface, memories and local interconnects within a tile. One existing framework that fulfills these goals is Open Virtual Platforms (OVP) [1]. OVP contains processor models for many different ISA, allows platform and system generation and the generation of peripherals that can be modeled to behave exactly like real hardware with fully compatible interfaces to the software. These peripherals also allow the use of a semihosting functionality, which gives access to host resources including drivers. Through semihosting we can access the low level SW-Interface and our PCIe driver, process the data within the modeled peripheral and make load/store accesses to data in the memories of the virtual platform.

6   Timing Accuracy Analysis

Fully cycle accurate operation as in a HDL simulator is only provided on the FPGA part of the hybrid prototype. The host part including the virtual platform works on instruction accurate processor models and fixed delay peripherals. This means that the hybrid prototype is inherently not a fully timing accurate model of a real hardware synthesized manycore, since it does not consider processor pipelines, memory access times and any other elements that are part of the VP. As motivated earlier, this is often perfectly fine when focusing on a single aspect of the whole architecture, using the hybrid prototype for functional testing, validation and debugging. However, there are situations in which a certain level of timing accuracy is desirable for the whole prototype, mostly considering design space exploration and performance evaluations. We will focus on analyzing the synchronization of the two domains of the hybrid prototype: FPGA and VP. However, the authors in [13] show that it is also possible to bring accuracy to virtual platforms, at the cost of execution speed that is lowered by a factor of 150–170. In the following, we investigate the timing delays induced by the two different domains and describe approaches for bringing certain levels of timing accuracy into the hybrid prototype.

We identify three different modes of operation regarding synchronization of the two domains of the hybrid prototyping:

- Fully-synchronous stepping
- Pseudo-synchronous operation
- Delta-based execution.

The Fully-synchronous stepping refers to a mode of operation in which all elements in both domains progress one cycle and synchronize before the next cycle is processed. This mode has been investigated in many publications in the past when coupling HDL simulators, typically used for testbenches, with FPGA prototypes that run the design under test. The authors in [6] give an overview of existing techniques and present an optimization based on events and net clustering. Such an approach can be adapted for virtual platform execution that is proposed in this paper, however it would completely defeat the purpose of providing fast evaluation speeds and is thus not considered a valid option.

The second mode of operation, labeled Pseudo-synchronous operation, does not use any direct synchronization and thus does not provide the same behavior as a fully cycle-accurate execution. Instead, it balances the speeds of both domains in order to allow similar execution patterns compared to the fully synchronous mode. This mode tries to avoid two imbalances:

- The FPGA running too fast, resulting in situations where a request towards the FPGA is handled before another request takes place, resulting in loss of resource contention scenarios that might happen in synchronized execution.
- The VP running too fast, resulting in request clogging in the FPGA which might not have happened in a synchronized execution.

Realization of this mode requires that the hybrid prototype is running at defined speeds in both domains, for example by scheduling the VP elements so that they are sequentially executed to match the FPGA clock speed. This can be achieved by inserting sleep cycles after all elements have sequentially processed for a time

slot. Another issue that needs to be addressed is the delay that is introduced by
crossing the domains between FPGA and VP. The shortest possible request that
crosses the domain and triggers a response is the critical part in this regard. In
our scientific manycore architecture, the shortest request that crosses boundaries
is a remote read operation. In a full hardware implementation it takes 9 cycles for
input processing in the network interface, 5 cycles for bus and memory access of
a single word, and another 9 cycles for output processing. Providing an accurate
remote read thus requires that within 23 cycles on the FPGA, the dummy NI
can transfer the request to the host and retrieve the data in time. We analyze the
delays of the domain crossing between FPGA and VP in Table 2. FPGA to Host
and Host to FPGA both encompass the parallelizer, collector and PCIe interface
as described earlier. They represent the delay between a packet being sent to the
local dummy NI via the NoC, till the processed PCIe packet is located in the
ringbuffer in the host memory. The software delays encompass the interrupt and
the packet processing on the host, including the access to the virtual platform.
We use the Linux RT (real time) patch on the latest kernel to avoid large delays
due to the regular linux scheduler. As we can see, the software is the major
source of delay. The biggest issue is not the average delay but instead the fact
that there are some outliers with a much larger delay than average. These outliers
were vastly improved by the use of the RT patch, yet they are still four times
larger than the mean delay. In order to provide in-time requests over the domain
crossing in accordance with the presented findings, we can run the VP and the
FPGA design at lower frequencies. This does not affect the performance of the
Host-interface on the FPGA since it operates in its own clock domain.

Table 2. Delay measurements for the domain crossing

Domain	Mean	SD	Min	Max
FPGA to Host	0.52 μs	0.04 μs	0.39 μs	1.49 μs
Software	4.46 μs	0.74 μs	3 μs	24 μs
Host to FPGA	1.54 μs	0.33 μs	1.28 μs	7.24 μs
Sum	6.52 μs	1.11 μs	4.67 μs	32.73 μs

The last mode retains a global synchronization that is valid in any task driven
model of computation like Kahn process networks. The general assumption is
that the FPGA is inherently accurate and any interaction with the VP is based
on timestamps taken from an accurate clock counter in the FPGA. When data
from the NoC is collected by the dummy NI, the global clock counter is sampled
and attached to the PCIe packet towards the host. In the VP on the host, each
data that was updated via the NoC is linked to such a timestamp. When a
consuming task is triggered by that data, the VP starts processing and takes
the timestamp as a baseline, adding its processing time to the timestamp. When
processing in the VP triggers another event (i.e. message over the NoC), the new

timestamp will be added to the data transfer towards the FPGA. In the FPGA, the timestamp is used to delay packet injection into the network until the global clock counter reaches the provided timestamp. While this mode does come with some limitations as to the model of computation and requires the FPGA part to be slowed down so that the VP is always able to run ahead (to avoid a situation in which a request is sent to the FPGA that should have been injected at a global clock cycle earlier than the current clock cycle), it also provides a fast and accurate execution aside from the inaccuracies of the virtual platform itself, which are out of scope here.

7 Use-Case Evaluation

The hybrid prototyping approach was devised in order to evaluate and develop new features for a scientific manycore architecture with a special focus on the NoC interconnect. As a first use case we select a previous work about a NoC extension for low latency shortcuts that was presented in [9]. The NoC extension specifically targets long distance, multi-hop traffic and thus requires large NoC dimensions to be beneficial. The concept was first implemented and evaluated on a cycle-accurate SystemC simulator since large manycore/NoC designs did not fit any available FPGA. A HDL based implementation was presented, yet it could only be verified in HDL simulation testbenches and small application fragments. With the proposed hybrid prototyping we were able to bring the implementation onto a single FPGA and use it for verification, bug detection and feature optimization. We show the gained insights and results in the following.

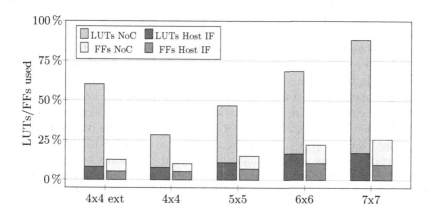

Fig. 6. The resource consumption of the NoC (the design under test) and the host interface including the NoC interface.

In our example setup we use a Xilinx Virtex-7 XC7VX485T evaluation board connected to a regular Intel PC with 8xPCIe 2.0 as a host system. The resource overhead that accompanies the hybrid prototyping can be seen in Fig. 6. As we can see, in a 4×4 NoC design 7.7% of the total available LUT and 5.2% of total FF on the FPGA were used by the host interface, compared to 20.6% of LUT and 4.9% of FF used for the NoC itself. The host interface thus adds an overhead of 37% LUT to the design under test in a 4×4 meshed NoC. Since the figure shows that LUT are the limiting factor, we can ignore the overhead in FF. A comparison with the more complex, multi-layer design of the extended NoC router in a 4×4 NoC shows that in more complex routers the overhead is even less significant. When looking at larger NoC sizes, we can see that the NoC IF and the PCIe part scale better than the NoC itself, resulting in an overhead of 24% in a 7×7 design.

Table 3. Run time of the blackscholes trace on NoC prototypes from different prototyping domains, each representing a 4×4 NoC.

Hybrid prototype	SystemC sim	HDL sim
179 s	1 d 2 h	10 d 8 h

For determining the prototyping speeds, we analyze the runtime of a simple benchmark application in our available implementations: SystemC, HDL simulator and FPGA. We choose a trace of the network traffic that was generated from the blackscholes algorithm, mapped onto several tiles of a 4×4 architecture. We selected a 4×4 architecture since the HDL simulator does not scale well and would take an unreasonable amount of time for a larger mesh. For a fair comparison we use the exact same input trace in all three variants. However, by including a suitable VP, the hybrid prototype can also natively execute the algorithm in contrast to the other methods. We use SystemC version 2.3, ModelSim SE-64 10.0d for the HDL simulation and Vivado 2017.3 for FPGA synthesis. The results are shown in Table 3. The FPGA was able to execute the whole trace via the communication library and the PCIe interface in 179 s. The SystemC simulator took 93 678 s (1 day 2 h) based on a cycle accurate model of our NoC that contains some simplifications and is not synthesizable. The Modelsim simulation took a total of 927 047 s (10 days 8 h). The design was based on the same HDL description that was synthesized onto the FPGA, minus the PCIe interface and the collector logic but instead with a testbench that reads the traces of the blackscholes benchmark. The runtime difference is enormous and highlights the benefits of hybrid prototyping besides the ability to execute the same code as on a physical platform and the modeling advantages of the VP. The gap will increase even more to a point where it is completely unfeasible when the designs grow larger or include the processors, memory, etc. in the HDL simulation and SystemC models.

Compared to a HDL simulator, the hybrid prototype requires synthesis of the FPGA part and thus induces some extra time for re-synthesis when design changes are made. We show the measured times for a hybrid platform in Table 4. To put these numbers in comparison, we also show the build duration required

to re-synthesize an architecture containing the same amount of tiles for a large
multi-FPGA prototyping platform. As it can be expected, these numbers are
much larger since the multi-FPGA platform hosts a design containing the full
tiles and thus much more logic needs to be synthesized. Depending on the mapping onto the multiple FPGA, the build durations may be decreased by utilizing
more parallelism (i.e. synthesizing all FPGAs in parallel), if enough computing power is available. However, this will improve the build duration even in
the best case scenario at most by a factor that is equivalent to the amount
of FPGA boards in such a system. Considering this, the hybrid prototype can
be re-synthesized much more quickly and allows higher tile counts even on a
smaller FPGA board (Virtex-7 XC7VX485T for the hybrid prototype versus the
Virtex-7 XC7V2000T of the multi-FPGA platform).

Table 4. Build duration for a commercial Multi-FPGA platform and the proposed
hybrid prototype.

Prototyping platform	Tile count	Build duration
Multi FPGA	4	5 h 51 m
	16	23 h 24 m
Hybrid	4	20 m
	16	42 m
	49	1 h 19 m

Using the hybrid prototype with our use-case NoC extension helped us to
detect several bugs and design issues that would have gone unnoticed without.
We were able to reproduce most of the observed issues in small HDL testbenches
after analyzing the behavior on the FPGA. However, we even found an issue
with a wrongly written assert statement, that was ignored in HDL simulation
but caused issues in the FPGA design. Since asserts are deleted by the tools in
synthesis, some critical assignments were incorrectly deleted due to a missing
semicolon. The synthesis gave a waring about ignoring the assert but gave no
hint that actually a large chunk of code was deleted. The HDL simulator on
the contrary simply evaluated the assert as true and scheduled the assignments
correctly.

8   Conclusion

In this paper, we use hybrid prototyping for design and validation of manycore
and NoC architectures. Our approach allows the prototyping of large architectures with full FPGA accuracy and speed for critical components at much lower
cost compared to large FPGA-clusters while giving additional flexibility for the
traffic generation and protocol implementation thanks to the virtual platform.
We also present an investigation into timing accuracy and timing delays of such

an approach and showcase its application for the feature development and evaluation of a scientific manycore architecture.

Acknowledgment. This work was supported by the German Research Foundation (DFG) as part of the Transregional Collaborative Research Center Invasive Computing [SFB/TR 89].

References

1. Open Virtual Platforms (OVP). http://www.ovpworld.org/
2. Synopsys Hybrid Prototyping Solution. https://www.synopsys.com/verification/virtual-prototyping/virtualizer/hybrid-prototyping.html
3. Binkert, N., et al.: The gem5 simulator. ACM SIGARCH Comput. Archit. News **39**(2), 1 (2011). https://doi.org/10.1145/2024716.2024718
4. Goossens, K., Bennebroek, M., Hur, J.Y., Wahlah, M.A.: Hardwired networks on chip in FPGAs to unify functional and configuration interconnects. In: Second ACM/IEEE International Symposium on Networks-on-Chip, NOCS 2008. IEEE, April 2008. https://doi.org/10.1109/nocs.2008.4492724
5. Kamali, H.M., Hessabi, S.: AdapNoC: a fast and flexible FPGA-based NoC simulator. In: 2016 26th International Conference on Field Programmable Logic and Applications, FPL. IEEE, August 2016. https://doi.org/10.1109/fpl.2016.7577377
6. Kwon, Y.S., Kyung, C.M.: Performance-driven event-based synchronization for multi-FPGA simulation accelerator with event time-multiplexing bus. IEEE Trans. Comput.-Aided Des. Integr. Circ. Syst. **24**(9), 1444–1456 (2005). https://doi.org/10.1109/tcad.2005.852035
7. Lotlikar, S., Pai, V., Gratz, P.V.: AcENoCs: a configurable HW/SW platform for FPGA accelerated NoC emulation. In: 2011 24th International Conference on VLSI Design. IEEE, January 2011. https://doi.org/10.1109/vlsid.2011.46
8. Lyberis, S., et al.: Formic: cost-efficient and scalable prototyping of manycore architectures. In: 2012 IEEE 20th International Symposium on Field-Programmable Custom Computing Machines. IEEE, April 2012. https://doi.org/10.1109/fccm.2012.20
9. Masing, L., Srivatsa, A., KreB, F., Anantharajaiah, N., Herkersdorf, A., Becker, J.: In-NoC circuits for low-latency cache coherence in distributed shared-memory architectures. In: 2018 IEEE 12th International Symposium on Embedded Multicore/Many-core Systems-on-Chip (MCSoC). IEEE, September 2018. https://doi.org/10.1109/mcsoc2018.2018.00033
10. Papamichael, M.K.: Fast scalable FPGA-based Network-on-Chip simulation models. In: Ninth ACM/IEEE International Conference on Formal Methods and Models for Codesign, MEMPCODE 2011. IEEE, July 2011. https://doi.org/10.1109/memcod.2011.5970513
11. Rodriguez-Andina, J., Moure, M., Valdes, M.: Features, design tools, and application domains of FPGAs. IEEE Trans. Ind. Electron. **54**(4), 1810–1823 (2007). https://doi.org/10.1109/tie.2007.898279
12. Saboori, E., Abdi, S.: Hybrid prototyping of multicore embedded systems. In: 2013 IEEE Conference Publications on Design, Automation & Test in Europe Conference & Exhibition (DATE) (2013). https://doi.org/10.7873/date.2013.330

13. Schreiner, S., Gorgen, R., Gruttner, K., Nebel, W.: A quasi-cycle accurate timing model for binary translation based instruction set simulators. In: 2016 International Conference on Embedded Computer Systems: Architectures, Modeling and Simulation, SAMOS. IEEE, July 2016. https://doi.org/10.1109/samos.2016.7818371
14. Wang, D., Lo, C., Vasiljevic, J., Jerger, N.E., Steffan, J.G.: DART: a programmable architecture for NoC simulation on FPGAs. IEEE Trans. Comput. **63**(3), 664–678 (2014). https://doi.org/10.1109/tc.2012.121

Evaluation of FPGA Partitioning Schemes for Time and Space Sharing of Heterogeneous Tasks

Umar Ibrahim Minhas$^{(\boxtimes)}$(ID), Roger Woods(ID), and Georgios Karakonstantis

Queen's University Belfast, Belfast, UK
u.minhas@qub.ac.uk

Abstract. Whilst FPGAs have been integrated in cloud ecosystems, strict constraints for mapping hardware to spatially diverse distribution of heterogeneous resources at run-time, makes their utilization for shared multi tasking challenging. This work aims at analyzing the effects of such constraints on the achievable compute density, i.e the efficiency in utilization of available compute resources. A hypothesis is proposed and uses static off-line partitioning and mapping of heterogeneous tasks to improve space sharing on FPGA. The hypothetical approach allows the FPGA resource to be treated as a service from higher level and supports multi-task processing, without the need for low level infrastructure support. To evaluate the effects of existing constraints on our hypothesis, we implement a relatively comprehensive suite of ten real high performance computing tasks and produce multiple bitstreams per task for fair evaluation of the various schemes. We then evaluate and compare our proposed partitioning scheme to previous work in terms of achieved system throughput. The simulated results for large queues of mixed intensity (compute and memory) tasks show that the proposed approach can provide higher than $3\times$ system speedup. The execution on the Nallatech 385 FPGA card for selected cases suggest that our approach can provide on average $2.9\times$ and $2.3\times$ higher system throughput for compute and mixed intensity tasks while $0.2\times$ lower for memory intensive tasks.

Keywords: Cloud environments · Data centers · Space sharing

1 Introduction

Cloud computing offers users ubiquitous access to a shared pool of resources, through centralized data centres. With increasing device sizes and efficiency for high performance computing, there has been an increased interest in recent times to integrate Field Programmable Gate Arrays (FPGAs) in data centres [5,11]. However, their architecture and programming environment presents a different resource sharing model when compared to software programmable accelerators.

The challenge lies in sharing the device space by accommodating multiple heterogeneous tasks at one instance of time. Heterogeneous tasks in our context

© Springer Nature Switzerland AG 2019
C. Hochberger et al. (Eds.): ARC 2019, LNCS 11444, pp. 334–349, 2019.
https://doi.org/10.1007/978-3-030-17227-5_24

are defined by heterogeneity in resource utilization (compute, memory, logic) and execution time. Optimization of system's resource utilization in time and space when executing these tasks in a shared environment is a challenging task, leading to suboptimal compute density and system throughput.

In software-based systems, a runtime approach can map a task to any portion of underlying hardware. This together with *microsecond* latency context switching between tasks, provides flexible sharing of resources. For FPGAs, the tasks are custom designed and mapped spatially on the device off-line. This, along with the reconfiguration overhead associated with task initiation, places extra constraints for efficient utilization of FPGA resources [9].

A common way of sharing the FPGA space is to partition it into partially reconfigurable regions (PRRs) which can be configured independently in time and partially in space. Flexibility in space is partial as incoming tasks can only be placed in one of the statically defined PRR via dynamic partial reconfiguration (DPR) at runtime. This means that tasks with diverse resource needs are mapped to the same homogeneous PRR which may result in inefficient resource utilization. To address this challenge, researchers have looked at providing more flexibility in space using heterogeneous PRRs and multiple bitstreams for a single task [3]. Although this approach increases the system throughput via intelligent off-line and runtime PRR design, the same intrinsic idea of mapping more than a single task to the same PRR still may lead to inefficient resource utilization.

This work first analyses the effect on compute density due to constraints imposed by PRR. To achieve this, we create multiple bitstreams per tasks for ten real high performance computing (HPC) tasks, for domains such as graph analytics, dense linear algebra, scientific computing, etc., allowing exposure of the area-throughput trade-off. This design space exploration (DSE) allows us to estimate the average utilization of heterogeneous resources (Logic Cells, DSPs, BRAMs) in a homogeneous PRR. Furthermore, along with the help of an exhaustive simulator, the DSE allows us to gauge the effect on system *speedup* for various PRR optimizations of runtime scheduling using real HPC tasks.

Secondly, we also evaluate an alternative approach to PRR by hypothesizing that a higher compute density can be achieved via static partitioning and mapping (SPM) of heterogeneous bitstreams. The SPM looks to provide complete spatial independence as heterogeneous tasks can be mapped to custom designed regions utilizing all of the resources on the FPGA. This only provides partial time independence, however, as tasks sharing the FPGA need to be reconfigured and executed at the same time, resulting in stalling by the longest running task.

Thirdly, our work compares both approaches while varying system design parameters. To achieve this, the simulator allows scheduling of large task queues with varying execution times to estimate average system *speedup*. Moreover, implementation of selected cases on an actual FPGA allows us to analyze the constraints of both approaches when targeting compute or memory intensive tasks, and report on performance in terms of System Throughput (STP), a metric defined specifically for multi-task workloads processing. The above mentioned DSE and PRR optimisations enable a fair comparison of both approaches.

The results show that SPM can provide a higher compute density while allowing for bitstreams generation from a higher level Open Computing Language (OpenCL) representation. SPM can be complemented with data center workload characterization [1] to select the best approach for varying environments. Statically generated high compute density bitstreams fit well with the idea of providing users with a library of optimized IPs allowing tasks to access the FPGA resource as a service (Amazon Marketplace for Amazon FPGA Image).

We first discuss the motivation of this work based on previous studies in Sect. 2. We then present our implementation and evaluation methodology in Sect. 3 and our detailed experimental evaluation in Sect. 4 followed by conclusions in Sect. 5.

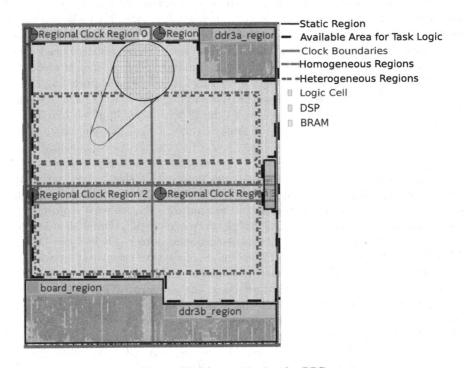

Fig. 1. FPGA partitioning for PRR

2　Background and Motivation

Cloud services are being used by range of users with diverse computing requirements which vary with task size and type [16]. In FPGA, the compute versus memory intensity of the task, suggests the need for FPGA sharing by heterogeneous tasks in order to achieve maximum system utilization. For sharing, the FPGA is partitioned into rectangular PRRs which are configured typically with a new bitstream via DPR, independently of the processing going on in other PRRs [17]. This provides independence in time to each PRR, such that a task A running in a PRR can be instantly replaced by task B, when task A finishes.

The design of PRRs is challenging since the spatial distribution of various types of resources on FPGA is not uniform or homogeneous (Fig. 1). The whole FPGA can be represented as a matrix, with dimensions $X \times Y$, of tiles where each tile, $x_i y_j$, represents a resource type; logic cell, DSP block or BRAM. Resources of same type form the columns, y_{dsp}, y_{bram}, etc., of a matrix where each row, x_i, contains at least 1 tile involving all type of resources. Furthermore, the FPGA is divided into multiple clock regions across both the vertical and horizontal axes, where the crossing of the region boundary requires custom logic implementation.

Now since the tasks are physically mapped to this diverse distribution of resources, their relocation at runtime is challenging, particularly along the horizontal axis [6]. For more complex mappings, modern bitstream relocation techniques [14] allow for relocation from one region to another vertically only, due to the column-based FPGA architecture, whilst permitting routing of interface connections and clock. However, such a relocation scheme cannot happen from a non-clock crossing region to a clock crossing region and vice versa. Thus, relocation is only possible among homogeneous regions along the y-axis and at discrete starting points with a step size equal to height of clock regions (Fig. 1), in line with work on partially reconfigurable systems for independent tasks [17].

These mapping constraints require PRRs to be majorly homogeneous and along the y-axis which may lead to inefficiency in resource utilization by heterogeneous tasks. Firstly, after omission of the static area used for memory interconnects near I/O pins and other hard static logic, the homogeneous region along the y-axis can be as low as 60% area of the FPGA [17]. The concept is explained in Fig. 1 where the marked boundaries represent the total available area and area distribution for homogeneous PRRs and heterogeneous PRRs (discussed in Sect. 3.2) after considering static resources and clock regions. In this case, PRR area is limited to 80 rows of resources compared to total 128 rows of FPGA along the vertical axis, with further limitations on horizontal axis. Secondly, within the rectangular boundaries defined for any task, the actual area being allocated to task may be lower than the area available in that region, namely 38%–51% [18] which is similar to our own implementation of HPC tasks (Sect. 4). This is worsened in case of fixed PRRs due to diverse spatial placement of different types of resources.

Whilst mapping optimizations using PRRs is well researched [3,17], for the first time, this work intends to analyze the effect on compute density caused by the constraints of PRRs and inefficient utilization of resources when mapping heterogeneous tasks. Firstly, we create a large design space using a range of real high performance computing tasks while exposing the area-throughput trade-off, using the biggest selection of the most relevant HPC tasks to date [4,15]. This allows us to quantify the heterogeneity in resource utilization by modern workloads when mapping to FPGA and to project the need for heterogeneous mapping. The DSE also allows us to quantify various existing PRR optimizations in literature using a range of real workloads.

We then propose SPM of tasks in heterogeneous regions as a mean to achieve higher compute density. Although the technology has supported this approach, this is the first time it has been analyzed from a high level perspective for use in space sharing FPGAs in data centers. The approach aims to provide complete spatial independence for highly optimized mapping on account of partial time independence. Time independence is partial as all tasks need to be reconfigured at the same time. We aim to quantify this and comment on design parameters that affect system performance. Finally, we fairly compare both approaches using the DSE on a flexible simulator as well as real hardware execution measurements.

3   Implementation and Evaluation Methodology

In this section, we describe multiple aspects of the design environment (Fig. 2). In particular, we start with multiple bitstreams generation for each task and then define the optimizations applied to PRR mapping. Finally, we briefly define our simulator and metrics used for evaluation.

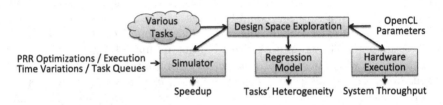

Fig. 2. Summary of implementation and evaluation methodology

3.1   Multiple Tasks' Bitstreams with Area-Throughput Trade-Off

A key goal is to generate multiple hardware bitstreams of the same task that provide a *speedup* corresponding to the resources used. Using an area-throughput curve, this allows for precise quantification of the variation in compute density with resource utilization due to different partitioning strategies.

To achieve this, we make use of the OpenCL framework for heterogeneous parallel programming that both provides abstraction of parallelism and a high level DSE model for tuning the underlying hardware mapping. In addition to OpenCL, we use general high level synthesis parameters, to scale the task over multiple parallel compute units *(CUs)*; multiple pipelines can be defined via a Single Instruction Multiple Data *(SIMD)* parameter, whilst the key compute intensive loops can be unrolled via the UNROLL *(U)* parameter. For some tasks, we vary task-specific parameters such as block size or number of rows, where these define the parallel processing of a defined parameter size. All these parameters allow scaling of the underlying hardware by varying the number of custom parallel data paths for each task.

3.2   Partially Reconfigurable Regions Mapping Optimizations

Using the same created design space, we can quantify the various optimizations presented in earlier studies and which are important to fairly compare PRR with SPM. The optimizations are mainly targeted at avoiding segmentation, causing vacant regions of FPGA, by varying the sizes of used bitstreams. Basic PRR mapping generates homogeneous regions as well as a single bitstream for each task corresponding to that region. Among the optimizations, the first one is called Elastic resource allocation which looks at adjacent PRR regions. If they are free, the approach attempts to fit larger bitstreams of the same task in this combined region, thus replacing·the current task bitstream with a larger one to gain a *speedup* [17].

Another way to increase mapping flexibility is to partition the FPGA into heterogeneous PRRs which offer different number of resources [3,5]. The tasks are then custom designed for one of the PRRs. Heterogeneous PRRs can be defined by including a different ratio of each heterogeneous resource type. However, in our case, the device size is not big enough to benefit from such an approach, so we define heterogeneous PRRs by varying the number of each type of resources while their relative ratios remain the same (Fig. 1). We define the areas on top of homogeneous regions which means it can either be configured as homogeneous or heterogeneous, allowing flexibility in mapping options from the generated design space. Another optimization that is made possible by heterogeneous PRRs is using smaller (contracted) bitstreams for tasks when none of the original bitstream can be fit into a region [3].

Finally, we provide simulated results for continuous y-axis, i.e. the hypothetical performance gains that can be made if the bitstream relocation step size is reduced to a single *row* by future technology support. At present, this can be achieved by generating multiple bitstreams, equal to the number of *rows* within each clock region, by varying starting y-coordinates for each unique bitstream.

3.3   Runtime Simulator and Hardware Implementation

The key configurable parameters and functional blocks of the runtime simulator are summarized in Fig. 3. The DSE provides the bitstreams' characteristics such

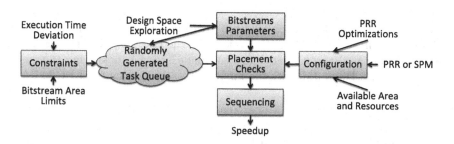

Fig. 3. Runtime simulator

as area and resource utilization, and relative speedup. This along with tasks' parameters, such as their execution time and limitation on resource utilization of bitstreams as per the available resources, is used to generate a task queue which is then fed into task placement and sequencing modules. For evaluation of average *speedup*, these modules then treat the task queue mapping as a rectangle fitting problem with configurations set for continuous y, homogeneous and heterogeneous PRRs along with other mapping optimizations or use SPM, while keeping under the overall available resources. As for the sequencing of tasks, we use a basic first fit heuristic which takes the task queue and tries to fit tasks in incoming sequence.

For evaluation of compute density on hardware, the bitstreams for SPM have been generated using Intel OpenCL SDK for FPGA, and all tasks run at the same frequency. This, however, is not a limitation of design as varying frequencies can be used for statically generated task cores. Also for PRR evaluation, OpenCL is used to generate the intermediate design files and constraints file, then modified to include bounding rectangular regions, as per defined PRRs for logic placement before generating the final bitstream. Similar efforts were used to map the largest possible bitstream configurations both for PRR and SPM within their respective area constraints.

3.4 Metrics

Assessing the system performance of a multi-task workload running in parallel on a single hardware is challenging as the performance of individual tasks may not entirely relate to system performance. We use two different metrics for simulated and hardware results to have a comprehensive assessment. First, simulation of large task queues allows us to project average *speedup*, measured as variation in execution time of complete queue. Secondly, for measuring compute density, we use various configurations of bitstreams of same tasks implemented on hardware which consume varying execution times to process the same data size, as well as allow to share FPGA with different number of tasks. We then use the STP metric [7] as defined by:

$$STP = \sum_{i=1}^{n} NP_i = \sum_{i=1}^{n} \frac{C_i^{SP}}{C_i^{MP}} \qquad (1)$$

where NP is each task's normalized progress defined by the number of clock cycles it takes in single (C_i^{SP}) task mode when the task has all of the resources of FPGA, compared to multi (C_i^{MP}) task mode, when it is sharing the space with other tasks. Here, n defines the number of tasks sharing the FPGA.

3.5 Evaluated Tasks

We have considered a number of tasks belonging to various computing dwarfs [2] and application domains with varying ratio of compute and memory operations.

(a) *Page Rank (PR)* is a graph analysis algorithm used for link analysis of web pages, social networks, etc. [13].

(b) *Alternative Least Squares (ALS) based Collaborative Filtering* is a verified approach based on the aggregated behavior of large number of users used to develop recommender systems for commercial domains such as Netflix [19].

(c) *Lower Upper Decomposition (LUD)* is an important dense linear algebra used for solving systems of linear equations with reduced complexity [4].

(d) *Binomial Option Pricing (BOP)* is a key model in finance that offers a generalized method for future option contract evaluation and for options with complex features [12].

(e) *Breadth First Search (BFS)* is a challenging and important graph traversal algorithm forming the basis of many graph-processing workloads [4].

(f) *3 Dimensional Finite Difference Time Domain (FDTD)* is an important numerical method for electromagnetic propagation modeling in space [10].

(g) *Sparse Matrix Vector Multiplication (SpMV)* is an important sparse linear algebra algorithm used in scientific applications and graph analytics, etc. [8].

(h) *Matrix Matrix Multiply (SGEMM)* is used in various compute intensive algorithms and benchmarks [8].

(i) *Video Downscaling (VD)* is used by a range of media streaming services for real-time bandwidth reductions [10].

(j) *Needleman-Wunsch (NW)* is a bioinformatics optimization algorithm used for protein sequence alignment [4].

Table 1. Use cases characteristics where the step size is $2\times$, unless otherwise specified.

Use case	Dwarf	Data size	Bitstreams scaling	Speedup
PR	Sparse linear algebra	Pages: 64K	(CU: 1,2,4) × (U: 1, 2, 4)	6×
ALS	Sparse linear algebra	Users: 4K	(CU: 1, 4) × (U: 1, 4)	2×
BOP	Structured grids	Options: 2K	CU1 × (U1, U2, U4, U8, U16); CU2 × U16; (CU: 3, 4, 5) × U8	21×
BFS	Graph traversal	Nodes: 64K	U: 1–16	5×
SpMV	Sparse linear algebra	X × Y: 4K × 4K	U: 1–32	190×
FDTD	Structured grids	X × Y × Z: 512 × 512 × 1K	Block size: 1–16	13×
LUD	Dense linear algebra	X × Y: 4K × 4K	CU1 × (U: 1–16); (CU: 2, 3) × U16	18×
VD	Structured grids	Resolution: 4K	Parallel rows: 1–32	8×
SGEMM	Dense linear algebra	X × Y: 4K × 4K	SIMD1 × (U: 1–64); SIMD4 × (U: 32–64)	204×
NW	Dynamic programming	X&Y: 4K	Block size: 2–128	33×

Table 2. Average resource utilization when using PRRs

Resource	Custom regions		Homogeneous PRRs	
	Avg. Util.	Min./Max. Util.	Avg. Util.	Min/Max Util.
Logic	52.54%	30.36%/79.40%	37.12%	18.47%/61.19%
Block RAM	60.56%	15.49%/95.82%	45.05%	10.07%/91.91%
DSPs	32.33%	0.0%/97.0%	26.30%	0.0%/97.0%

3.6   System Hardware

The DSE has been accomplished via Intel OpenCL SDK for FPGAs v 16.1, performed on a Nallatech 385 with an Intel Stratix V GX A7 FPGA chip and 8GB DDR3 memory. The A7 chip has 234,720 ALMs, 256 DSPs as well as 2,560 M20K BRAM blocks. The runtime simulations are performed via Python v3.3.7.

4   Results and Analysis

Our implementation of real tasks is given in Table 1. Besides providing real area numbers for spatial mapping problem, the implementation provides area-throughput graphs for HPC tasks. To measure the *speedup*, the baseline throughput, corresponding to the lowest area bitstream, is defined by the serial pipelined benchmark implementation. The maximum throughput is defined by the largest bitstream, limited by FPGA resources. We have generated 4–9 bitstreams per task providing 2–204× maximum *speedup* compared to slowest bitstream with *speedup* for each task mentioned in Table 1. The table also mentions the parallelization used for each task, such as number of compute units, unrolling of main computing loop, using SIMD pragma for work items parallelism and data block size variation where elements in a block are executed in parallel and relate to resources utilized in mapping. The generation of multiple bitstreams is a key step in evaluating the mapping strategies as we discuss in coming sections.

4.1   Analysis of Heterogeneous Tasks

Using the DSE, we analyse the heterogeneity in resource utilization by tasks. We mainly focus on three resources, Logic cells, DSPs and BRAMs and evaluate the inefficiency in resource utilization caused by the rectangular and fixed size shapes of PRRs resulting in homogeneous regions. We present percentage utilization of resources from two perspectives.

The first case calculates percentage resource utilization compared to the bounding box where dimensions are custom defined for each bitstream, as per bitstream's resource requirements. We use all of the bitstreams which are smaller than the largest PRR. The second case deals with percentage utilization compared to the PRRs available on the FPGA. We use 4 sizes of heterogeneous PRRs (Fig. 1).

In total, there are 80 *rows* of FPGA that can be configured as a single region (PRR-1) or a set of two homogeneous regions of 40 *rows* each (PRR-2). We define two more heterogeneous PRRs, namely 30 (PRR-3) and 50 (PRR-4) *rows*, based on the sizes of generated bitstreams. Note that either the homogeneous or heterogeneous PRRs can be used at a single instance of time.

We select bitstreams for each task that would maximize the resource utilization in each of 4 PRRs, i.e. up to 4 bitstreams per task and give average percentage resource utilization by these bitstreams compared to their respective PRRs. The measurements in Table 2 show that due to the homogeneous nature of PRRs, the logic, DSP and BRAM utilization is limited to 37%, 26% and 45% on average.

4.2 Runtime Simulation

In this section, we use our simulator to analyse various mapping strategies. Firstly, we examine the *speedup* achieved by various improvements on the PRR mapping, as explained in Sect. 3.2. We use three different mapping strategies, namely the continuous *y*-axis, heterogeneous PRRs and homogeneous PRRs and their respective bitstreams (Fig. 1). Please note that this is a study of resource utilization efficiency of various mapping approaches and does not consider data transfers from host CPU memory to DRAM memory on the FPGA board. Furthermore, the DRAM to FPGA on-chip memory transfers are not considered as bottlenecks for simulation purposes, but their effect is discussed in more detail in next section using real execution on hardware.

The runtime scheduler performs Elastic and Contract optimizations, as explained in Sect. 3.2. We use the actual measured relative throughput of various bitstreams of tasks to calculate the new execution time of tasks. For Contract, we found out that if the difference in *speedup* for a smaller bitstream replacing the bigger is too large, the total execution time increases rather than decrease. Thus, we limited the allowed *speedup* degradation for smaller bitstreams to 5×.

The graphs in the Fig. 4 show the *speedup* achieved for various configurations. Generally, Elastic is more useful with gains up to 1.24× whereas the best gain for Contract is 1.05×. Optimizations benefit more on heterogeneous mapping to tackle segmentation, hence, the gain is negligible for our case of only two heterogeneous regions while no gain is achieved for homogeneous regions.

Next we investigate gains made by SPM in comparison to PRR. For the SPM, we either use the same region as used for PRR (Homogeneous Regions in Fig. 1) and call it Partial Static or use all of the available area for task logic (Fig. 1) and call it Whole Static. This approach helps to differentiate between the *speedup* achieved by heterogeneous mapping in the same region as well as the gains made by the availability of extra logic when mapping statically.

As the results in Fig. 5 show, a key finding is that SPM gives on average 4.6× higher throughput, measured in terms of total execution time for a set size of tasks queue. A 2.4× *speedup* is achieved via heterogeneous mapping while the rest is achieved via use of higher resource availability. The results show that if the *y*-axis can be made continuous, then a throughput gain of 2× can be achieved.

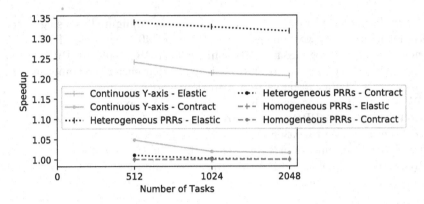

Fig. 4. *Speedup* achieved by optimization of PRR mapping on various bitstreams

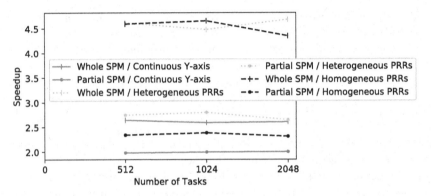

Fig. 5. *Speedup* achieved by SPM versus PRR mapping

So far, the reported *speedup* numbers have considered an ideal scenario for SPM by considering all of the tasks sharing the FPGA at any time, have same execution time. This is not the case for real workloads. Next, we vary the execution time of tasks and report on *speedup* achieved. We use a uniform distribution for execution time and vary the range of distribution.

The results shown in Fig. 6 depict a surprising trend. Even with increasing range of execution time by up to 32× (beyond this range a reconfiguration overhead would become negligible for most tasks), the *speedup* decreases but remains higher than 3×. This is because on average, the device under test may be used by 3 or less tasks using SPM, as constrained by the size of FPGA and tasks bitstreams. Thus, a task may stall up to two tasks or a maximum of about 50% resources with an average much lower than that. Stalls by smaller tasks are overcome by the higher average compute density and gains made when the longest running task is not the smallest. However, to gauge the effect of the approach on bigger devices, we estimate the *speedup* possible by increasing the size of available resources while keeping the size of tasks' bitstream the same.

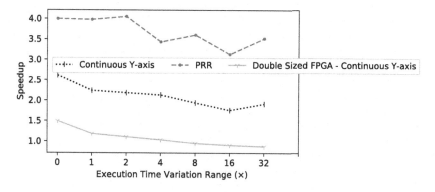

Fig. 6. *Speedup* variation of SPM with variation in execution times (Tasks = 1024)

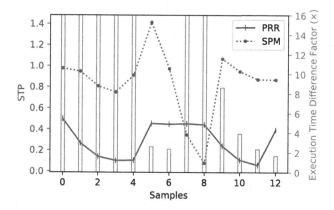

Fig. 7. STP variation with data sizes for 2 compute intensive tasks - MM and LUD

The results show that for a device double the size, the gains drop below 1 for an execution time variation greater than 4×. Such a study can help optimize the number of tasks that may be shared at a single instance of time.

4.3   Evaluation on Hardware

A key limitation of using SPM is the need to generate each multi-task heterogeneous bitstream separately. This limitation can be overcome partially by benchmarking cloud and data center workloads to estimate the frequency and data sizes of incoming tasks [1]. This can help decide the combination of tasks that may be shared on a single FPGA as well as the percentage resource allocation for each task. These decisions, apart from helping with a higher resource utilization on-chip, result in minimizing bottlenecks in off-chip resources, such as DRAM access. To analyze this further, as well as provide numbers for throughput for real hardware execution, we discuss some of the extreme cases below using the STP metric defined in Sect. 3.4.

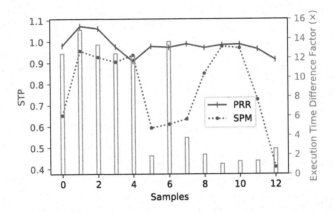

Fig. 8. STP variation with data sizes for 2 memory intensive tasks - ALS and PR

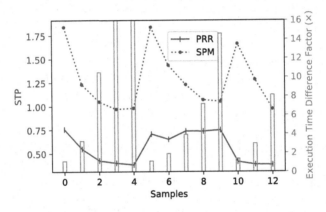

Fig. 9. STP variation with data sizes for one compute and one memory intensive tasks - LUD and PR

In terms of resource utilization, SPM resulted on average 60%, 59% and 129% higher logic, BRAM and DSP utilization compared to PRR. Furthermore, Figs. 7, 8 and 9 show the achieved STP for PRR and SPM for two compute, memory and mixed (one compute/one memory) intensive tasks, respectively. The graphs also show the difference in factor between the execution times of both tasks on the second y-axis. In our experiments, the execution time between both tasks varied by up to 5108×, 14× and 361× for compute intensive, memory intensive and mixed tasks. Note that for SPM, NP for each task is calculated using the time for longest running task.

STP for PRR stays relatively uniform with variation in data sizes while for SPM it generally reduces with increase in difference of individual execution times. The results show that for compute intensive and mixed tasks, SPM performs on average 2.9× and 2.3× better than the PRR mapping, respectively.

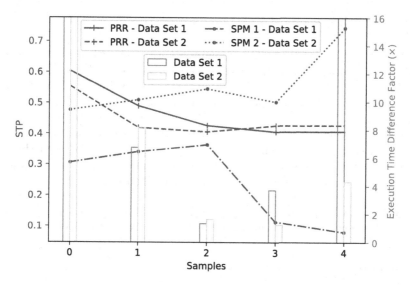

Fig. 10. STP variation for PRRs and static designs for two configurations using four tasks - SPMV, NW, LUD, PR

For memory intensive tasks, the increase in resource utilization did not result in a performance increase. This is because the for memory intensive tasks, the increase in throughput via higher utilization of on-chip compute resources is limited by external memory access latency and bandwidth. For memory intensive tasks, PRR has 1.25× higher STP on average than the SPM.

Finally, for all cases, the trend for SPM is not entirely dependent on the variation in execution time of tasks sharing the FPGA. This is because it also depends on the percentage resource utilization as well as the NP of the longest running task. To explain this further, we present another set of results where we have 4 tasks sharing the FPGA. However, we focus on a single task, LUD, and use two different SPM configurations. In SPM 1, LUD has a minimum number of resources while in SPM 2, it is allocated more such that it has a 10× higher individual NP in SPM 1 compared to SPM 2. Furthermore, we select data sizes for the rest of the tasks such that their execution time is similar to each other. We then vary the data size of LUD (size of square matrices from 128 to 1024 in steps of 2×). The resulting STP presented in Fig. 10 shows that for the SPM 1, the PRR performs 1.9× better than the SPM while for SPM 2, the SPM performs 1.2× better than PRR for the same data sizes of LUD. Also even for the second case, SPM performs worse for first sample projecting that sharing 4 tasks on this size of an FPGA reduces the average system throughput.

5 Conclusion

This work analyses the constraints of mapping bistreams of heterogeneous tasks to FPGA at runtime and their effect on compute density when using partially reconfigurable regions for space shared multi-task processing. Static partitioning and mapping of tasks to achieve higher *speedup* and system throughput is proposed and several aspects of each approach are evaluated via design space exploration using a range of HPC tasks, a comprehensive simulator and evaluation on hardware. Static partitioning provides up to 2.9× higher system throughput and facilitates a completely software based implementation of a multi-task computing environment without requiring low level support for PRR.

Acknowledgment. The work was supported by the European Commission under European Horizon 2020 Programme, grant number 6876281 (VINEYARD).

References

1. Abdul-Rahman, O.A., Aida, K.: Towards understanding the usage behavior of Google cloud users: the mice and elephants phenomenon. In: International Conference on Cloud Computing Technology and Science. IEEE (2014)
2. Asanovic, K., et al.: The landscape of parallel computing research: a view from Berkeley. Technical report, Technical Report UCB/EECS-2006-183. EECS Department, University of Berkeley (2006)
3. Charitopoulos, G., Koidis, I., Papadimitriou, K., Pnevmatikatos, D.: Run-time management of systems with partially reconfigurable FPGAs. Integr. VLSI J. **57**, 34–44 (2017)
4. Che, S., et al.: Rodinia: a benchmark suite for heterogeneous computing. In: International Symposium on Workload Characterization. IEEE (2009)
5. Chen, F., et al.: Enabling FPGAs in the cloud. In: Conference on Computing Frontiers. ACM (2014)
6. Enemali, G., Adetomi, A., Seetharaman, G., Arslan, T.: A functionality-based runtime relocation system for circuits on heterogeneous FPGAs. IEEE Trans. Circ. Syst. II: Express Briefs **65**(5), 612–616 (2018)
7. Eyerman, S., Eeckhout, L.: System-level performance metrics for multiprogram workloads. IEEE Micro **28**(3), 42–53 (2008)
8. Gautier, Q., et al.: An OpenCL FPGA benchmark suite. In: 2016 International Conference on Field-Programmable Technology. IEEE (2016)
9. Huang, M., et al.: Programming and runtime support to blaze FPGA accelerator deployment at datacenter scale. In: Symposium on Cloud Computing. ACM (2016)
10. Intel: Developer zone. Intel FPGA SDK for OpenCL (2018). https://www.intel.com
11. Minhas, U., et al.: NanoStreams: a microserver architecture for real-time analytics on fast data streams. IEEE Trans. Multi-Scale Comput. Syst. (2017)
12. Minhas, U.I., Woods, R., Karakonstantis, G.: Exploring functional acceleration of OpenCL on FPGAs and GPUs through platform-independent optimizations. In: Voros, N., Huebner, M., Keramidas, G., Goehringer, D., Antonopoulos, C., Diniz, P.C. (eds.) ARC 2018. LNCS, vol. 10824, pp. 551–563. Springer, Cham (2018). https://doi.org/10.1007/978-3-319-78890-6_44

13. Page, L., et al.: The PageRank citation ranking: bringing order to the web (1998)
14. Pham, K.D., Horta, E., Koch, D.: BITMAN: a tool and API for FPGA bitstream manipulations. In: Design, Automation & Test in Europe Conference & Exhibition, pp. 894–897. IEEE (2017)
15. Sengupta, D., et al.: Scheduling multi-tenant cloud workloads on accelerator-based systems. In: Supercomputing Conference. IEEE (2014)
16. Vaishnav, A., Pham, K.D., Koch, D.: A survey on FPGA virtualization. In: International Conference on Field Programmable Logic and Applications (2018)
17. Vaishnav, A., Pham, K.D., Koch, D., Garside, J.: Resource elastic virtualization for FPGAs using OpenCL. In: International Conference on Field Programmable Logic and Applications (2018)
18. Vipin, K., Fahmy, S.A.: Architecture-aware reconfiguration-centric floorplanning for partial reconfiguration. In: Choy, O.C.S., Cheung, R.C.C., Athanas, P., Sano, K. (eds.) ARC 2012. LNCS, vol. 7199, pp. 13–25. Springer, Heidelberg (2012). https://doi.org/10.1007/978-3-642-28365-9_2
19. Zhou, Y., Wilkinson, D., Schreiber, R., Pan, R.: Large-scale parallel collaborative filtering for the netflix prize. In: Fleischer, R., Xu, J. (eds.) AAIM 2008. LNCS, vol. 5034, pp. 337–348. Springer, Heidelberg (2008). https://doi.org/10.1007/978-3-540-68880-8_32

Invited Talk

Third Party CAD Tools for FPGA Design—A Survey of the Current Landscape

Brent E. Nelson[✉]

NSF Center for Space, High-Performance, and Resilient Computing (SHREC),
Department of Electrical and Computer Engineering, Brigham Young University,
Provo, UT, USA
brentnelson@byu.edu

Abstract. The FPGA community is at an exciting juncture in the development of 3rd party CAD tools for FPGA design. Much has been learned in the past decade in the development and use of 3rd party tools such RapidSmith, Torc, and IceStorm. New independent open-source CAD tool projects are emerging which promise to provide alternatives to existing vendor tools. The recent release of the RapidWright tool suggests that Xilinx itself is interested in enabling the user community to develop new use cases and specialized tools for FPGA design. This paper provides a survey of the current landscape, discusses parts of what has been learned over the past decade in the author's work with 3rd party CAD tool development, and provides some thoughts on the future.

Keywords: Computer-aided design · CAD · FPGA · Digital circuits

1 Introduction

Traditionally, the CAD tools for compiling HDL designs onto FPGAs have been available only from the FPGA vendors themselves. However, a number of 3rd party research CAD tools have also been created over the years to provide functionality lacking in the vendor tools. One example of such lacking functionality is specialized analysis of physically implemented designs for fault mitigation purposes.

Recently, interest in 3rd party tools has accelerated with a number of publicly available open source CAD tools emerging for use with FPGA devices from a variety of vendors. The purpose of this paper is to provide a survey of some of these 3rd party tool efforts, including tools developed over the past decade as well as some recently emerged (and emerging) tools in this space.

This work was supported in part by the I/UCRC Program of the National Science Foundation within the NSF center for Space, High-performance, and Resilient Computing (SHREC) under Grant No. 1738550.

© Springer Nature Switzerland AG 2019
C. Hochberger et al. (Eds.): ARC 2019, LNCS 11444, pp. 353–367, 2019.
https://doi.org/10.1007/978-3-030-17227-5_25

First, a three-part taxonomy is developed with the goal of categorizing various tools in this space, while illustrating some of the considerations for such tools. For each category in the taxonomy, a selection of prior work is described. Next, a more in-depth review is then given of RapidSmith, Tincr, Rapidsmith2, and Maverick—tools from the taxonomy's categories and which were developed in the Configurable Computing Laboratory at Brigham Young University. In the context of these tools some lessons learned and ramifications for future work are described. Finally, some recent alternative tool efforts from other sources are described followed by conclusions[1].

2   Taxonomy

A taxonomy regarding 3rd party FPGA CAD tools is described in this section, and which may be useful for discussing the various tools created over the years. The taxonomy has three categories including (1) Architecture and CAD Research Tools, (2) Cooperative CAD Tool Frameworks, and (3) Stand-Alone, Vendor-Independent Tools. These three tool categories will be discussed in terms of two basic criteria:

Criteria 1. How dependent are tools from a given category on existing vendor tools to complete their tasks? Do they require vendor tools for some tasks or are they able to run completely independently?

Criteria 2. What is the level of *reverse engineering* of the FPGA device that is required for the tool's development and operation? I use the term *reverse engineering* loosely here and include, among other things for example, the work required to understand and support all of the operating modes and parameterization of the various soft- and hard-IP blocks included on the die, the work required to read and write file formats required to interoperate with vendor tools, etc.

2.1   Category 1: Architecture and CAD Research Tools

The principal example of this first category is VTR and VPR which, for many years, have provided the platform of choice for the evaluation of proposed or new FPGA architectural features. Additionally, they have provided an important platform for researching and demonstrating new CAD algorithms and tools.

In general, the research uses of VTR/VPR have not been targeted at commercial FPGA devices but rather have been used to study hypothetical FPGA devices. The CAD tools included in VTR/VPR can readily be adapted to map designs onto these devices, thus providing the ability to predict the impact a

---

[1] Missing from the discussion in this paper are the myriad tools which provide high-level design paradigms and functionality such as domain specific languages or HLS tools. Also missing are tools such as floorplanning tools and PR management tools. Rather, the focus here is on physical design tools, specifically the steps of synthesis through bitstream generation.

new feature might have on an FPGA device and on applications mapped to that device in terms of performance, area, and power.

With regards to Criteria 1, the VTR/VPR tool suite typically requires no interaction with vendor CAD tools since it does not target commercial FPGA devices. This eliminates the need to export designs from and import designs back into vendor tools. With regards to Criteria 2, there is similarly no need to exhaustively analyze commercial devices to create such tools. Rather, much of the complexity and power of VTR/VPR comes from its ability to model new FPGA architectures, the ability to rapidly re-target its toolchain to these new architectures, and the strong modelling provided in the toolset for predicting performance, area, power consumption, etc.

2.2 Category 2: Cooperative CAD Tool Frameworks

Tools in the second category of this taxonomy focus on targeting commercial FPGA devices. The goal with such tools has not necessarily been to create fully vendor-independent CAD tool flows, but rather to provide a way for 3rd party CAD tools to create, analyze, and modify designs in ways not supported by the vendor tools. These tools are called *Cooperative CAD Tool Frameworks* because they cooperate with vendor tools, performing only certain portions of the flow and relying on the vendor tools for other portions.

Examples of tools in this category include RapidSmith, Torc, and Rapid-Smith2 (the first two operate with ISE and the last with Vivado). These tools have proven useful in cases when the vendor tools cannot (or will not) perform specialized functions required for a particular application or use model.

As one example of the need for this category of tools, consider the area of circuit reliability and in particular, the use of Triple Modular Redundancy (TMR). Here, circuit triplication and voting circuits are used to protect a design against single event upsets, the assumption being that a single configuration memory bit fault cannot cause erroneous results. This assumption, however, is incorrect—the routing multiplexors of at least some FPGA's are structured such that a single configuration bit corruption can easily defeat TMR by affecting signals in more than one of the triplicated circuit copies. The solutions proposed in [2] and [3] are to detect these single points of failure and then physically re-place and/or re-route portions of the circuit to eliminate them—operations which require custom 3rd party physical design and analysis tools.

With respect to Criteria 1, Cooperative CAD Tool Frameworks rely, at a minimum, on the ability to export designs from the vendor flow and then re-import designs back into that flow—i.e. they are not intended to function as complete stand-alone flows by themselves. As a result, a given tool in this category need not address the entire flow but may provide very limited functionality focused on a specific issue. As will be seen later, this has made such tools extremely valuable for many research groups and projects. And, in many instances, it can greatly simplify the creation of such a specific tool since it does not need to implement the entire flow.

Criteria 2 represents a challenge in the creation of such tools. Since these tools typically need to be prepared to accept *any* vendor-generated design, they must support at least the import and export of *all* device features (even if they don't allow them to be manipulated using an API). This is because the vendor tools, as a part of their normal operation, will produce designs which use all device features This may require substantial effort to understand the many configuration options associated with the many IP blocks embedded in the device as well as other device issues such as BEL and site route-throughs, router-based LUT pin permutations, cell/BEL dynamic pin mappings, etc.

2.3   Category 3: Stand-Alone, Vendor-Independent Tools

This third category of tools focuses on providing a replacement for vendor tools by compiling HDL designs to commercial FPGA devices without vendor tool involvement. The IceStorm project was the earliest and, to date, the most notable example of this class of tool. It provides a reverse engineered bitstream for the iCE40 FPGA, along with a complete Verilog-to-bitstream tool flow for that FPGA. At the time of the writing of this paper, a variety of other tools in this category are beginning to emerge (as evidenced by projects visible on Github). Some of these are mentioned later.

With respect to Criteria 1, the stand-alone CAD tools in this category have no need for regular interactions with vendor tools. But, they typically require the assistance of vendor tools to initially develop a device description database. But, once such development is complete they can operate independently of commercial tools. Interestingly, Category 3 tools have less stringent requirements, in some ways, than Category 2 with regards to commercial device support, something which may initially sound counter-intuitive. Since they are not designed to consume designs produced by vendor tools (but rather create designs anew themselves), they need not initially support every device feature. While it may be undesirable to not support all FPGA device functionality in this way, it does

Table 1. Summary: 3rd party FPGA CAD tools taxonomy

	Pros	Cons
Cat. 1	Support what-if studies for both CAD tools and architectures	Doesn't target commercial devices
Cat. 2	Is not a full tool flow. Provides framework for 3rd party special-purpose tool development. Has found widespread use in a variety of research projects	Is not a full tool flow. Must suport import/export of all device features
Cat. 3	Provides full tool flow, replaces vendor tools. Need not support *all* device features	Requires completing full tool flow including bitstream generation. Lower QOR than vendor tools?

provide a pathway an incremental development path, where some device features are not initially supported. Ultimately, however, Category 3 tools provide the entire flow, and therefore don't have the ability to rely on vendor tools like Category 2 tools do and this is their most notable characteristic.

Table 1 summarizes this taxonomy. Note that for Category 2 tools, the phrase *"Is not a full tool flow."* is listed as both a *pro* and a *con*, in accordance with the description from above. In the following sections a series of 3rd party CAD tools are described in more detail, providing some insights into the considerations associated with creating such tools.

3 Rapidsmith

RapidSmith is a Category 2 tool (Cooperative CAD Tool Framework) which emerged from the HMFlow project in 2010. The goal of the HMFlow project [12] was to investigate rapid prototyping methods, specifically by reducing the time required for the edit-compile-debug loop in FPGA design. The approach taken in HMFlow was to mimic the IC design flow where pre-compiled (and physically implemented) circuit modules are assembled (placed and interconnected) to form the final design. The benefit of such a flow comes from the need for the tool to place and route relatively few modules and interconnecting wires. But, this macro placement and routing requires a custom CAD tool and RapidSmith was developed to support that need.[2] The resulting HMFlow tool flow was able to demonstrate more than 70x CAD tool speedups over ISE, with the resulting design clock rates being approximately 75–90% of those produced by ISE.

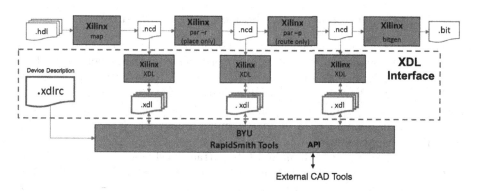

Fig. 1. RapidSmith usage model

The Xilinx ISE toolset provides a textual design and device description file format called XDL. As shown in Fig. 1, RapidSmith reads and writes XDL files

---

[2] The Torc tool [19] was developed at approximately the same time as RapidSmith and the two tools are similar in many ways. Interestingly, both tool suites have their roots in a common joint research project between their respective development teams.

and so is able to manipulate Xilinx ISE designs. ISE's .xdl file format describes a design as a collection of *instances* which correspond to Xilinx sites such as SLICE, IOB, and BRAM blocks. Instances in a .xdl file can be placed or unplaced. Attribute strings within instances are used to describe the configuration of the site's contents: LUT equations, internal routing MUX settings, etc. Nets are used to interconnect instance pins and can be either unrouted or routed. If routed, the net's physical route is described by a list of the PIPs making up the physical route.

The .xdlrc file format, also provided by ISE, describes the contents and structure of a specified FPGA device. It is very detailed, representing every tile, site, wire, and PIP in the entire device. This combination of both .xdl and .xdlrc files supports the creation of 3rd party CAD tools with the ability fully analyze and manipulate Xilinx designs and map them onto arbitrary Xilinx devices.

The use model for RapidSmith as illustrated in Fig. 1 provides the ability to export a design from ISE (as a .xdl file) at multiple points in the ISE flow. It also processes the huge .xdlrc files produced by ISE into compact device representations called *device files*. It then provides an API into those exported design and device files so that tools can be written against that API to perform a variety of analysis and circuit implementation functions.

RapidSmith is best characterized as a 3rd party CAD tool *framework* since it provides few, if any, complete analysis or implementation tools itself (beyond a collection of demonstration programs). Rather, the goal with RapidSmith was to provide an infrastructure for both ourselves and others to develop their own custom CAD tools on top of.

3.1   RapidSmith Adoption in the Research Community

RapidSmith was open-sourced at SourceForge in approximately 2010 and has served as the foundation for a large number of custom CAD tools created by others, a sampling of which is given in this section. [21] used it to rapidly create SoC designs on FPGAs from system specifications. [14] used it to implement the relocatable and dynamically reconfigurable modules of their Dreams framework while [15] implemented a bidirectional mapping framework, StML, between RTL and FPGA primitives with it.

In [5], researchers used RapidSmith to extract hard macros from a netlist as part of their dynamic and partial reconfiguration framework. [9] used it as part of a VPR-based design flow targeting Xilinx devices. And, [10] used it to embed logic analyzers into placed and routed circuits, avoiding the need to re-implement the entire design.

In the area of FPGA reliability, [4] used RapidSmith to modify LUT equations and re-purpose carry chains to mask faults while [1] used it to create hard macros of test configuration circuits for an online integrity test of the FPGA's components. In [24], the authors developed a fault-tolerant placement algorithm with it and [16] used it to correlate bitstream frame addresses to the reconfigurable module located at that frame for use in their fault tolerant soft-core processer system. In [17], it served as the basis of a soft-error vulnerability analysis framework for Virtex 5 FPGAs, including a visualization tool for identifying vulnerable areas. Finally, in the area of FPGA security, RapidSmith was used in [18] to insert a denial of service trojan (post synthesis) into an FPGA and [11] used it to create a digital to analog converter on the FPGA's power rails as a side-channel attack demonstration.

RapidSmith has thus found relatively widespread use within the research community. At the time of the writing of this paper, it has been downloaded more than 5,100 times, a surprising number given the relatively small niche it occupies.

The RapidSmith experience demonstrated to us the strong desire in the research community for 3rd party FPGA physical design tools. A second takeaway is that the advantages and disadvantages of the RapidSmith tool correspond, in large part, with the characteristics of XDL. The XDL representation is fairly simple, and therefore RapidSmith is correspondingly straightforward to use. However, XDL was best suited for describing designs at the *slice* level—it contains no explicit representation of individual cells (LUTs, FFs, . . .) internal to an instance. Rather, their existence must be *inferred* from XDL's attribute string settings, a clumsy and part-family-specific process. RapidSmith is thus most useful for applications which analyze and manipulate designs at the slice level.

4   Vivado, Tincr, and RapidSmith2

With the introduction of Vivado, the XDL tool disappeared. Vivado, however, provided a Tcl facility for interacting with its design representation. Vivado represents a design as a netlist of cells which may be placed onto physical BELs - a much lower level of representation than in XDL. This both simplifies and complicates a number of issues surrounding 3rd party CAD tool development.

An initial evaluation of the capabilities of Vivado's Tcl interface and its suitability as a replacement for RapidSmith demonstrated that its low performance and lack of memory management (specifically, garbage collection) made it unsuitable for this use. While not unexpected, that work quantified and demonstrated its limitations [22,23].

The Tincr project was then initiated to determine whether a Tcl script could extract sufficient information from Vivado to produce a device description in the .xdlrc format. The .xdlrc format was chosen since existing tools which work with .xdlrc would be able to support newer Vivado-only devices without modification as a result. And, importantly, we were able to produce 7-Series .xdlrc files from Vivado and compare them with the original 7-Series XDLRC files produced by ISE for verification purposes.

Tincr [23] is thus a Tcl library of routines, one portion of which produces .xdlrc files by querying the Vivado device representation and outputting an equivalent .xdlrc representation. Once it was verified for 7-Series devices, Tincr was then used to demonstrate the generation of .xdlrc files for Ultrascale devices, demonstrating the viability of Tincr-generated .xdlrc for devices beyond those supported by ISE.

Going beyond the production of .xdlrc files, however, Tincr also generates a large set of meta-data regarding Xilinx devices and cell libraries never available with XDL, and thus overcomes some key limitations mentioned above with regards to RapidSmith. This information is encapsulated in .xml files associated with a .xdlrc file and includes, among other things (1) an explicit representation of the Xilinx cell library, (2) information on the legal mappings of cells to BELs, (3) cell pin to BEL pin mappings, (4) cell properties, (5) alternate site types present in devices, and (6) information on legal route-through locations. None of this information was available with XDL, but is essential for performing subsite design manipulations such as packing cells into sites, an example of an operation which is terribly difficult to do using RapidSmith and its XDL representation. This meta-data is created by Tincr and supplied to external tools as a set of XML files as shown in the top-center of Fig. 2.

4.1   Design Export from Vivado: Tincr/VDI

The VDI (Vivado Design Interface) project was then initiated to complete the system by providing for the export and import of complete design data between Vivado and an external representation. It uses Tincr to extract the needed information and package it as a specialized checkpoint file, called a RapidSmith Checkpoint (RSCP) file, and which contains the logical design (EDIF netlist) plus physical placement and routing information for the design's cells and wires. This checkpoint information is shown in the center portion of Fig. 2. This checkpoint, coupled with the XML meta-data described above and the XDLRC-based device file representation (also described above), provides all the data needed for an external tool to fully manipulate Vivado designs.

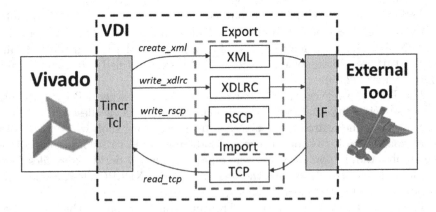

Fig. 2. VDI: Vivado design and device export/import

A number of challenges were encountered in extracting all needed design data from Vivado, for which solutions were developed as a part of the Tincr and VDI projects and which are documented in [23] and [20]. A few examples are given here. (1) A first issue is route-throughs, which are instances where the router will use an unoccupied BEL or an entire unoccupied site for routing purposes. Route-throughs are not represented in Vivado's logical netlist for the design. (2) The logical representation for VCC/GND nets does not match their physical implementation. (3) The Xilinx cell library contains both cells which are primitives as well as cells which are macros made up of primitives. These issues (and others) require special handling in order to import and export designs from Vivado.

Reimporting a design back into Vivado using Tcl has its own set of challenges as well. For example, when a cell is placed onto a BEL in a site, Vivado seems to immediately route that site's internals. Surprisingly, the order of placement of cells onto BELs inside a slice matters—doing so in the wrong order (?) will cause Vivado to reject legal placements [20] (and changing the order of the placement directives solves the problem). That is, Vivado seems to be able to easily *paint itself into a corner* from which it cannot emerge. Thus, a specific ordering for placing cells (determined through experimentation) must be observed.

Most importantly, however, importing designs back into Vivado through the Tcl interface is a slow process, taking many minutes or even hours for large designs. Thus, while useful for a variety of applications, Tincr/VDI not suitable for applications requiring rapid re-import of designs. See [20] for more details on the development of these tools.

4.2   RapidSmith2

RapidSmith2 is new version of RapidSmith, modified to work with Tincr/VDI-produced designs[3]. Like RapidSmith, it processes .xdlrc files to create highly compressed device files for its use. But unlike RapidSmith, it does not use .xdl files but rather reads and writes its own checkpoint file formats.

A number of other features distinguish it from RapidSmith. Its design representation more closely reflects that of Vivado—its logical model represents the design as a network of cell objects placed onto BELs. This makes it straightforward to do design analyses and modifications inside sites. This is in contrast to the XDL approach of RapidSmith where attribute strings had to be interpreted to infer the cell- and BEL-level structure of the design. Additionally, the XML meta-data generated by Tincr (described above) and a large collection of higher-level abstractions in its API (such as structured route tree objects) make RapidSmith2 better suited for creating tools which manipulate designs at the cell/BEL level. In particular, the RSVPack project [6] which investigated packing algorithms using RapidSmith2 would not have been practical using RapidSmith and XDL.

---

[3] RapidSmith2, Tincr, and VDI are all available open-source at GitHub.

4.3   Tincr, VDI, and RapidSmith2 - Discussion

A major lesson learned from the Tincr/VDI/RapidSmith2 experience were the difficulties encountered, an understanding of which may provide guidance to future projects targeting Xilinx FPGA devices. The author estimates that the RapidSmith2 development effort was more than an order of magnitude larger than the RapidSmith effort.

This can be attributed to two things. Vivado and its Tcl interface was more difficult to work with than ISE, was more buggy, and yet was more powerful than ISE and its XDL. Additionally, the work of [6,8] in creating a packer illustrated a number of complexities associated with targeting recent Xilinx FPGAs. The structure of a Xilinx 7 Series slice is complex and irregular, in contrast to the comparatively interconnect-rich and regular structures usually targeted by VPR. Many special-case rules regarding legal packings for this irregular structure had to be discovered and created before even a rudimentary packing tool could be tested. There is thus a significant barrier to entry for the creation of tools such as RapidSmith2 that work at the sub-site level. In spite of these challenges, the benefits of a tool such as RapidSmith2 to be able to work at the level of intra-site design manipulation have been significant (if not for the faint-of-heart).

5   RapidWright

RapidWright [13] is a recently released Xilinx CAD tool framework which promises to support the creation of 3rd party FPGA design tools for use with Vivado. It fits most closely into the Cooperative CAD Tool Frameworks category of the taxonomy above. That is, it exports/imports designs to/from Vivado and provides an API to manipulate those designs. In this respect it closely parallels the operation of RapidSmith and Torc. In fact its heritage (code base and authorship) derive, in part, from the original RapidSmith tool.

RapidWright natively (and very rapidly) reads and writes Vivado Design Checkpoints, and thus overcomes a shortcoming of previous tools which were relatively slow due to their reliance on XDL or Tcl for import and export. And, the promise is that it should track Vivado updates and support all future Xilinx devices as a part of its operation.

Two demo applications of RapidWright are included in its distribution: (1) building an IP integrator design with pre-implemented blocks and (2) creating the physical design for a high speed SLR crossing circuit for UltraScale+. Both of these demonstrate its API's support for the creation of physical design tools, similar in spirit to the tools described above.

Interestingly, RapidWright itself is not actually a 3rd party, open source tool. It was developed by and is supported by Xilinx and much of its functionality is distributed only in compiled code form. In these respects, it is similar to normal vendor-supplied tools. In spite of these characteristics, however, one could argue that RapidWright will likely become the Cooperative CAD Tool Framework of choice for creating 3rd party tools in the future (especially those requiring physical design capabilities). This is due to its support for all Vivado design and device features and its planned ability to support future Xilinx device families. It is the author's hope that an active user community will develop around RapidWright to encourage its further development and to create new and novel 3rd party tools. Finally, of great interest, recent presentations made by Xilinx [29] (see especially pp. 76–80), under the title "Open Source Community Call for Action", now actively encourages the user community to participate in the development of new usage models and associated CAD tools for Xilinx FPGAs.

6   Maverick

Leaving Category 2 tools and moving to Category 3, the recent Maverick project at Brigham Young University investigated the feasibility of creating a fully stand-alone CAD tool flow for Xilinx devices. The Maverick flow is based on several existing and new tools including Yosys [26] for synthesis, RapidSmith2-based tools [6,7,20,23] for packing/placement/routing, and the Project X-Ray tools [27] for bitstream generation.

Maverick targets partial reconfiguration (PR) regions within a static design on an FPGA. To do so it first uses the Vivado PR flow to create a bitstream for a full-chip static design containing a PR region. It then is able to compile Verilog designs into partial bistreams and configure those into that PR region in a running design.

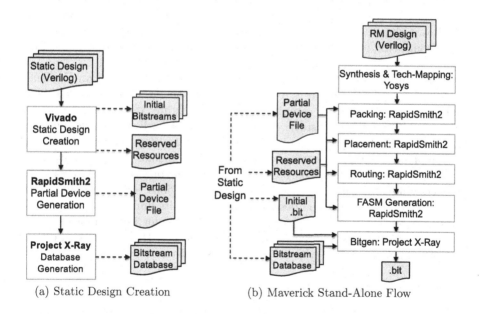

(a) Static Design Creation   (b) Maverick Stand-Alone Flow

Fig. 3. The Maverick flow

Figure 3(a) shows how an initial static design is created using Vivado's PR flow. This initial step (which must be done only once for each such static design)

is done using a combination of Vivado's PR flow and Tincr/VDI. The results of this step include: (a) an initial bitstream for the static design, (b) a list of resources within the PR region used by the static design and which the remainder of the flow must avoid (these are created by the Vivado PR flow and must be noted), (c) a partial device representation for RapidSmith2 which describes the device contents which lie within the PR region, and (d) a bitstream database for the device of interest (generated by the Project X-Ray tools and used in the creation of partial bitstreams for the PR region, see next section for details). These products are shown passing from left to right in the figure.

Once this initial step is done, the actual Maverick flow can be run as shown in Fig. 3(b), which compiles Verilog designs to partial bistreams for the PR region *without any interaction with or support from Vivado*—it is a truly stand-alone, untethered flow. The result of the Maverick flow is a partial bitstream which targets the PR region in the original static design. This may then be dynamically configured into the programmed FPGA's PR region.

Because the Maverick flow targets only PR regions, care must be taken for it to interoperate with static designs created by Vivado's PR flow. In particular, the Vivado PR flow creates partial routes that connect the static portion of the design with the PR region at special locations called *partition pins*. These partition pins typically lie inside the PR region, meaning partial routes enter the PR region from the static region and must be avoided by the PR compilation tools. In addition, Vivado at times will simply run static routes *through* the PR region and these must also be avoided by the PR compilation tools. A key step in Fig. 3(a) is thus to generate a list of these reserved routing resources to prevent them from being used by the Maverick placement and routing tools later in the flow.

This stand-alone portion of Maverick has been demonstrated on Digilent's PYNQ-Z1 board. The entire CAD flow runs on the PYNQ's embedded ARM processors and is used to compile and then configure Verilog designs into a PR region in the FPGA's static design. For a set of basic Verilog designs that might be designed as part of an introductory digital systems course, the Maverick compilation flow consumed just over 200 MB of memory, demonstrating the extremely small footprint achievable for the tool. Ongoing Maverick work being pursued will test it with larger designs, larger PR regions, and even multiple PR regions within a single static design to understand its limitations and possible use cases. Such a system opens up new possibilities for autonomous systems which are able to create, implement, and program new HDL designs onto their own programmable fabric without any outside assistance.

7   Other Category 3 Tools

Additionally, the IceStorm project (mentioned previously) has demonstrated the feasibility of creating a complete external CAD flow for the Lattice iCE40 FPGA device. And, due to its relatively small memory footprint, not only does it run on conventional workstations but a version of it has been demonstrated running on a Raspberry Pi as well [25].

Recently, a variety of other open-source projects have appeared on the Internet, all related to the creation of Category 3 stand-alone FPGA CAD tools. They represent an exciting development and, hopefully, an acceleration of work in the area of 3rd party CAD tools for FPGA devices. I note that the recent "Workshop on Open Source Design Automation (OSDA) 2019", held in conjunction with the DATE conference is another encouraging sign in this direction.

One example recent tool effort is Project X-Ray [27], the website of which states that it "contains both tools and scripts which allow you to document the bit-stream format of Xilinx 7-series FPGAs". And, as of the time of the writing of this paper, partial bitstream databases for one or more devices can be found in the prjxray-db Github repository. Note that Project X-Ray figures prominently in the Maverick flow described above—a modified version of it is the tool which converts the placed-and-routed circuit description created by the RapidSmith2 tools of the Maverick flow into a final partial bitstream.

As another example, the nextpnr tool [28] "aims to be a vendor neutral, timing driven, FOSS FPGA place and route tool". Its website states that it currently supports two Lattice families and further states the authors hope to see Xilinx 7 Series devices supported in the future.

8 Conclusions

The FPGA community seems to be at an exciting juncture in the development of 3rd party CAD tools for FPGA design. Much has been learned in the past decade in the development of 3rd party tools such as have been described in this paper. And, activity surrounding 3rd party CAD tool development within the FPGA community seems to be accelerating. As the efforts outlined above mature and gain traction, many more design tools possibilites will hopefully be available to users of FPGA devices. The result, undoubtedly, will be the creation of new use cases across a spectrum of application domains and the development of many new and exciting tools for users.

References

1. Abdelfattah, M., et al.: Transparent structural online test for reconfigurable systems. In: 2012 IEEE 18th International On-Line Testing Symposium (IOLTS), pp. 37–42, June 2012. https://doi.org/10.1109/IOLTS.2012.6313838
2. Cannon, M., Keller, A., Wirthlin, M.: Improving the effectiveness of TMR designs on FPGAs with SEU-aware incremental placement. In: 2018 IEEE 26th Annual International Symposium on Field-Programmable Custom Computing Machines (FCCM), pp. 141–148, April 2018. https://doi.org/10.1109/FCCM.2018.00031
3. Cannon, M.J., Keller, A.M., Rowberry, H.C., Thurlow, C.A., Pérez-Celis, A., Wirthlin, M.J.: Strategies for removing common mode failures from TMR designs deployed on SRAM FPGAs. IEEE Trans. Nuclear Sci. 1 (2018). https://doi.org/10.1109/TNS.2018.2877579

4. Das, A., Venkataraman, S., Kumar, A.: Improving autonomous soft-error toler-ance of FPGA through LUT configuration bit manipulation. In: 2013 23rd Inter-national Conference on Field Programmable Logic and Applications (FPL), pp. 1–8, September 2013. https://doi.org/10.1109/FPL.2013.6645498

5. Gantel, L., Benkhelifa, M., Lemonnier, F., Verdier, F.: Module Relocation in heterogeneous reconfigurable systems-on-chip using the Xilinx isolation design flow. In: 2012 International Conference on Reconfigurable Computing and FPGAs (ReConFig), pp. 1–6, December 2012. https://doi.org/10.1109/ReConFig.2012.6416763

6. Haroldsen, T., Nelson, B., Hutchings, B.: Packing a modern Xilinx FPGA using RapidSmith. In: 2016 International Conference on ReConFigurable Computing and FPGAs (ReConFig), pp. 1–6, November 2016. https://doi.org/10.1109/ReConFig.2016.7857180

7. Haroldsen, T., Nelson, B., Hutchings, B.: RapidSmith 2: a framework for BEL-level CAD exploration on Xilinx FPGAs. In: Proceedings of the 2015 ACM/SIGDA International Symposium on Field-Programmable Gate Arrays, FPGA 2015, pp. 66–69. ACM, New York (2015). https://doi.org/10.1145/2684746.2689085

8. Haroldsen, T.D.: Academic packing for commercial FPGA architectures. Ph.D. thesis, Brigham Young University (BYU), Provo, Utah (2017). https://scholarsarchive.byu.edu/etd/6526

9. Hung, E., Eslami, F., Wilton, S.: Escaping the academic sandbox: realizing VPR circuits on Xilinx devices. In: 2013 IEEE 21st Annual International Symposium on Field-Programmable Custom Computing Machines (FCCM), pp. 45–52, April 2013. https://doi.org/10.1109/FCCM.2013.40

10. Hutchings, B.L., Keeley, J.: Rapid post-map insertion of embedded logic analyz-ers for Xilinx FPGAs. In: 2014 IEEE 22nd Annual International Symposium on Field-Programmable Custom Computing Machines (FCCM), pp. 72–79, May 2014. https://doi.org/10.1109/FCCM.2014.29

11. Hutchings, B.L., Monson, J., Savory, D., Keeley, J.: A power side-channel-based digital to analog converterfor Xilinx FPGAs. In: Proceedings of the 2014 ACM/SIGDA International Symposium on Field-Programmable Gate Arrays, FPGA 2014, pp. 113–116. ACM, New York (2014). https://doi.org/10.1145/2554688.2554770

12. Lavin, C., Padilla, M., Lamprecht, J., Lundrigan, P., Nelson, B., Hutchings, B.: HMFlow: accelerating FPGA compilation with hard macros for rapid prototyp-ing. In: 2011 IEEE 19th Annual International Symposium on Field-Programmable Custom Computing Machines (FCCM), pp. 117–124, May 2011. https://doi.org/10.1109/FCCM.2011.17

13. Lavin, C., Kaviani, A.: RapidWright: enabling custom crafted implementations for FPGAs. In: 2018 IEEE 26th Annual International Symposium on Field-Programmable Custom Computing Machines (FCCM), May 2018

14. Otero, A., de la Torre, E., Riesgo, T.: Dreams: a tool for the design of dynamically reconfigurable embedded and modular systems. In: 2012 International Conference on Reconfigurable Computing and FPGAs (ReConFig), pp. 1–8, December 2012. https://doi.org/10.1109/ReConFig.2012.6416740

15. Peterson, D., Bringmann, O., Schweizer, T., Rosenstiel, W.: StML: bridging the gap between FPGA design and HDL circuit description. In: 2013 International Conference on Field-Programmable Technology (FPT), pp. 278–285, December 2013. https://doi.org/10.1109/FPT.2013.6718366

16. Pham, H., Pillement, S., Piestrak, S.J.: Low-overhead fault-tolerance technique for a dynamically reconfigurable softcore processor. IEEE Trans. Comput. **62**(6), 1179–1192 (2013). https://doi.org/10.1109/TC.2012.55
17. Sari, A., Agiakatsikas, D., Psarakis, M.: A soft error vulnerability analysis framework for Xilinx FPGAs. In: Proceedings of the 2014 ACM/SIGDA International Symposium on Field-Programmable Gate Arrays, FPGA 2014, pp. 237–240. ACM, New York (2014). https://doi.org/10.1145/2554688.2554767
18. Soll, O., Korak, T., Muehlberghuber, M., Hutter, M.: EM-based detection of hardware trojans on FPGAs. In: 2014 IEEE International Symposium on Hardware-Oriented Security and Trust (HOST), pp. 84–87, May 2014. https://doi.org/10.1109/HST.2014.6855574
19. Steiner, N., Wood, A., Shojaei, H., Couch, J., Athanas, P., French, M.: Torc: towards an open-source tool flow. In: Proceedings of the 19th ACM/SIGDA International Symposium on Field Programmable Gate Arrays, FPGA 2011, pp. 41–44. ACM, New York (2011). https://doi.org/10.1145/1950413.1950425
20. Townsend, T.J.: Vivado design interface: enabling CAD-tool design for next generation Xilinx FPGA devices. Master's thesis, Brigham Young University (BYU), Provo, Utah, July 2017. https://scholarsarchive.byu.edu/etd/6492
21. Wenzel, J., Hochberger, C.: RapidSoC: short turnaround creation of FPGA based SoCs. In: 2016 International Symposium on Rapid System Prototyping, RSP 2016, Pittsburg, PA, USA, 6–7 October 2016, pp. 86–92 (2016). https://doi.org/10.1145/2990299.2990314
22. White, B., Nelson, B.: Tincr—a custom CAD tool framework for Vivado. In: 2014 International Conference on ReConFigurable Computing and FPGAs (ReConFig14), pp. 1–6, December 2014. https://doi.org/10.1109/ReConFig.2014.7032560
23. White, B.S.: Tincr: integrating custom CAD tool frameworks with the Xilinx Vivado design suite. Master's thesis, Brigham Young University (BYU), Provo, Utah, December 2014. https://scholarsarchive.byu.edu/etd/4338
24. Wirthlin, M., Jensen, J., Wilson, A., Howes, W., Wen, S.J., Wong, R.: Placement of repair circuits for in-field FPGA repair. In: Proceedings of the ACM/SIGDA International Symposium on Field Programmable Gate Arrays, FPGA 2013, pp. 115–124. ACM, New York (2013). https://doi.org/10.1145/2435264.2435286
25. Wolf, C., Amesberger, D., Humenberger, E.: icoBoard (2016). http://icoboard.org/
26. Wolf, C., Glaser, J.: Yosys - a free Verilog synthesis suite. In: Proceedings of Austrochip, October 2013
27. Wolf, C., McMaster, J., Altherr, R., Ansell, T., et al.: Project X-ray (2018). https://github.com/SymbiFlow/prjxray/
28. Wolf, C., Milanović, M., Shah, D., Bazanski, S., Gisselquist, D., Hung, E., et al.: nextpnr (2018). https://github.com/YosysHQ/nextpnr
29. Xilinx: Conversation with Xilinx Research Labs, pp. 76–80 (2018). https://www.xilinx.com/content/dam/xilinx/imgs/developer-forum/2018-silicon-valley/XUP-Conversations-with-Xilinx-Research-Labs.pdf

Convolutional Neural Networks

Filter-Wise Pruning Approach to FPGA Implementation of Fully Convolutional Network for Semantic Segmentation

Masayuki Shimoda[✉], Youki Sada, and Hiroki Nakahara

Tokyo Institute of Technology, Tokyo, Japan
{shimoda,sada}@reconf.ict.e.titech.ac.jp, nakahara@ict.e.titech.ac.jp

Abstract. This paper presents a hardware-aware sparse fully convolutional network (SFCN) for semantic segmentation on an FPGA. Semantic segmentation attracts interest since for self-driving car it is important to recognize road and obstacles in pixel level. However, it is hard to implement the system on embedded systems since the number of weights for the SFCN is so large that embedded systems cannot store them using limited on-chip memory. To realize good a trade-off between speed and accuracy, we construct an AlexNet-based SFCN which has no skip connections and deconvolution layers to reduce the computation costs and the latency. Furthermore, we propose a filter-wise pruning technique that sorts the weights of each filter by their absolute values and prunes them by a preset percent filter-by-filter from a small order. It is more suitable for the hardware implementation since the number of computation of each filter becomes equal. We trained the AlexNet-based SFCN by using Camvid image dataset and implemented on Xilinx zcu102 evaluation board. The results show that the FPGA system is 10.14 times faster than a mobile GPU one, and its performance per power consumption is 24.49 times higher than the GPU counterpart.

Keywords: FPGA · Fully convolutional network ·
Sparse neural network · Semantic segmentation

1 Introduction

In recent years, convolutional neural networks (CNNs) [1] achieve state-of-the-art performance, and they are widely used for computer vision tasks, such as object classification, object detection, and semantic segmentation. Among them, semantic segmentation is a fundamental task in image processing that performs pixel-wise classification, as shown in Fig. 1. It has been increasingly required in a variety of embedded systems such as robots, self-driving cars, and drones.

For good performance of the task, some CNNs incorporate additional convolutional layers, new components, and a new architecture. The resulting models are so complicated and big that they are not suitable for resource-limited embedded systems, such as FPGAs. To deal with it, [2] proposes a small network for

© Springer Nature Switzerland AG 2019
C. Hochberger et al. (Eds.): ARC 2019, LNCS 11444, pp. 371–386, 2019.
https://doi.org/10.1007/978-3-030-17227-5_26

Input   Output

Fig. 1. Example of semantic segmentation using CamVid dataset.

road segmentation, and its FPGA implementation meets a real-time processing requirement. In exchange for the FPGA realization by the proposed small model, it can deal with road class only, and therefore the implementation challenges of the task for many categories still remain. To deal with the problem, we propose a filter-wise weight sparse fully convolutional network (SFCN) based on AlexNet [3]. The model has no skip connections and deconvolution layers, and it leads to a considerable reduction in the buffer size for the feature maps, the number of memory accesses, and the computation cost. Additionally, the filter-wise pruning is applied to our model, and the filters in a layer of the resulting model have the same number of nonzero weights. It means that since the number of convolutional computation for each filter in a layer is the same, the circuitry runs efficiently. Our contributions are as follows.

1. We suggest an AlexNet-based SFCN on an FPGA. While our model has fewer parameters and is a very smaller network than conventional ones, its accuracy is practical.
2. We propose a filter-wise pruning technique that sorts weight parameters by their absolute values and then prunes them by a preset percent from a small order. Our technique realizes higher sparse model without accuracy degradation than previous work [4].
3. Our model is evaluated on an FPGA to investigate area requirement. As far as we know, this is the first FPGA implementation of a multi-class semantic segmentation system.
4. We compare our system on an FPGA with on a mobile GPU in term of speed, power, and power efficiency. As for frame per second (FPS), the FPGA realization is 10.14 times faster than the GPU one.

2   Related Works

2.1   Semantic Segmentation

Fully Convolutional Network (FCN) [5] generates a coarse label map from input images by a pixel-wise classification, and the map is resized into input image size by a bi-linear interpolation, then we obtain a more fine-grained label map.

SegNet [6] incorporates skip connections during deconvolution to improve performance for small objects using middle-level features. Pyramid Scene Parsing Network (PSPNet) [7] adopts a pyramid pooling module which applies pyramid pooling to feature maps, extracts features from them, and concatenates their futures to deal with multi-scaling objects. In addition, PSPNet uses resizing function provided by OpenCV as an upsampling layer. ICNet [8] uses various resolution input to go through the corresponding networks and combine them using a cascade feature fusion unit.

Since their networks are not suitable for embedded systems due to their network size and complexity, we modify the model structure. The resulting model is a feed-forward architecture model which has no skip connections and replace deconvolution layers into a resizing function as an upsampling layer. By removing them, the circuitry does not need to have their buffers and decreases memory access significantly with low accuracy degradation, which means that our proposed network is more suitable for embedded systems.

2.2 Sparseness Approach for Weight Memory Reduction

Since the modern CNN requires a large number of weight parameters, an FPGA on-chip memories cannot store the all parameters. To deal with it, there are two varieties of sparseness (pruning) methods for after training and during training.

As for pruning during training, [9] proposed a gradual pruning method that increases a weight pruning ratio using binary mask variable. [10] uses sparse various dropout for both dense and convolutional layers to realize high sparsity. [11] reduces the rank of the parameter matrices in each layer.

On the other hand, there are many works for pruning after training, and the representative one is deep compression [4] which combined quantization, weight pruning, and Huffman coding method together, obtaining 3–4 times speedup. Neuron pruning [12] shows that pruning neurons instead of edges (weights) realizes high sparse model, maintaining the sequential memory access. For the hardware of SIMD architecture, [13] proposes SIMD-aware weight pruning which provides high parallelism using a specific format, such as compressed sparse rows (CSR) format.

We propose a filter-wise pruning which eliminates weights filter-by-filter by a preset percent from a small order after training, since it is able to train faster than pruning while training counterparts from our experiments. Figure 2 shows the learning curves of both pruning while training and pruning after training models when using our technique. The pruning after training converges faster than the during training one. We consider that the pruning after training type is more suitable for our technique.

3 Preliminary

We employ three metrics which are often used to measure performance. Let n_{ij} is a #pixels of class i predicted as class j, n_{class} is a number of class to recognize.

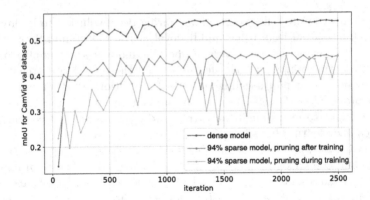

Fig. 2. Learning curve of both pruning after training and pruning while training models when using a filter-wise pruning. Note that we used a polynomial shift for scheduling learning rate.

The metrics are as follows.
Pixel-wise accuracy (Pixel-wiseAcc):

$$\frac{\sum_{i=1}^{n_{class}} n_{ii}}{\sum_{i=1}^{n_{class}} \sum_{j=1}^{n_{class}} n_{ij}} = \frac{Accurate\ area}{All\ area}$$

Mean class accuracy (mClassAcc):

$$\frac{1}{n_{class}} \sum_{i=1}^{n_{class}} \frac{n_{ii}}{\sum_{j=1}^{n_{class}} n_{ij}} = \frac{Area\ predicted\ as\ class\ i}{Truth\ area\ of\ class\ i}$$

Mean intersection over union (mIoU):

$$\frac{1}{n_{class}} \sum_{i=1}^{n_{class}} \frac{n_{ii}}{\sum_{j=1}^{n_{class}} (n_{ij} + n_{ji}) - n_{ii}}$$

4   Fully Convolutional Network

4.1   Definition

A fully convolutional network (FCN) is a variation of convolutional neural networks (CNNs) which consists of convolutional layers only. It can deal with any size input data. To perform classification, FCNs uses 1×1 convolutional layer instead of dense layer.

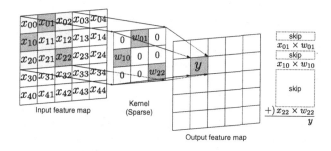

Fig. 3. Sparse convolutional operation.

4.2 Convolutional Operation

Let i be i-th layer, $X^i(x, y, ch)$ be an input feature map value at (x, y, ch) coordinates in i-th layer, $W^i(x, y, ch)$ be a weight value, w_{bias} be a bias, $S^i(x, y)$ be an intermediate variable, $f_{act}(s)$ be an activation function, and $Z^i(x, y)$ is an output feature map. The $K \times K$ 2D convolutional operation at (x, y) coordinates in $(i+1)$-th layer is as follows:

$$S^{i+1}(x, y) = w_{bias} + \sum_{ch=0}^{N_i-1} \sum_{r=0}^{K-1} \sum_{c=0}^{K-1} X^i(x+r, y+c, ch) \times W^{i+1}(r, c, ch) \quad (1)$$

$$Z^{i+1}(x, y) = f_{act}(S^{i+1}(x, y)),$$

where N_i is a number of input feature maps, ch, r, c are coordinates of depth-axis, x-axis, and y-axis, respectively. The input is multiplied by a weight and the resulting sum is applied to the activation function, or MAC (multiply-accumulation) operation. In this paper, we use the rectified linear unit (ReLU) functions as the activation function. As shown in Expr. (1), when $K = 1$, it performs classification corresponding to the part of input images.

4.3 Sparse Convolutional Operation

Figure 3 illustrates a sparse convolutional operation. After a pruning technique is applied, many weight values become zero. To store such weight parameters formed in the sparse matrix to block RAMs (BRAMs) efficiently, we employ coordinate (COO) format. Figure 4 shows the COO format overview. The arrays, *row*, *col*, *ch*, and *data* store its row, column, channel indices, and nonzero weight values of the sparse matrix, respectively. Since our proposed pruning technique realize high sparse ratio, the overhead of additional memory requirement (*row*, *col*, and *ch* arrays) is small compared with that for nonzero weights. When COO format is introduced, the sparse convolutional operation at (x, y) coordinates is formulated as follows.

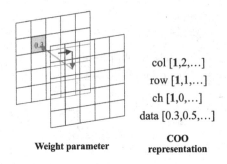

col [1,2,...]
row [1,1,...]
ch [1,0,...]
data [0.3,0.5,...]

Weight parameter   **COO representation**

Fig. 4. COO representation of weight parameters.

$$S^{i+1}(x,y) = w_{bias} + \sum_{i=0}^{N-1} X^i(x + row_i, y + col_i, ch_i) * data_i$$

$$Z^{i+1}(x,y) = f_{act}(S^{i+1}(x,y)),$$

where N is a number of nonzero values, $data_i$ is a weight value, and col_i and row_i are column and row indices, respectively.

4.4   AlexNet-Based Sparse Fully Convolutional Network

In recent years, many models for semantic segmentation are proposed. However, these models are so complex and deep that their FPGA implementations are not feasible. Therefore, we investigate an FPGA-aware model with high accuracy and propose an AlexNet-based model as shown in Table 1. Batch normalization (BN) [14] is conducted after each convolutional layer. To realize high accuracy, we removed the last max pooling layer and decided the low sparse ratio for the pixel-wise convolutional layers. While other models employ deconvolution layers, we replaced it with bi-linear function on a host processor, as shown in Fig. 5, since the deconvolution layers incur many memory accesses and do not affect the accuracy significantly. Table 2 shows a comparison with the other model. Our model achieves comparable performance in floating-point precision. Therefore, we employ our floating-precision model as a baseline model.

5   Filter-Wise Pruning by Using Distillation

As for related works, pruning techniques are applied to the weight parameters of each layer. However, considering an FPGA implementation, they are not suitable since if the sparse ratio of each filter varies significantly (in other words, there is a big difference between the number of nonzero values in certain two filters, as shown in Fig. 6), we should adjust the circuitry to the worst case. This means that all filters except for the worst case filter should conduct wasteful calculation. To address the problem, we propose a filter-wise pruning by using distillation

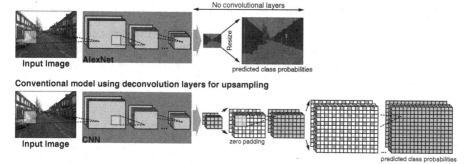

Fig. 5. AlexNet-based FCN, using resize function instead of deconvolutions.

Table 1. The sparse ratio of our AlexNet-based model

Layer	#In. F.maps	#Out. F.maps	In. F.Size	Kernel size	Stride	Padding	Zero weight ratio
Hardware part:							
Conv	3	64	480 × 360	11 × 11	4	0	21,888/23,232 (94.2%)
MaxPool	64	64	119 × 89	3 × 3	2	0	-
Conv	64	64	59 × 44	5 × 5	1	2	96,320/102,400 (94.1%)
MaxPool	64	64	59 × 44	3 × 3	2	0	-
Conv	64	128	29 × 22	3 × 3	1	1	69,376/73,728 (94.1%)
Conv	128	128	29 × 22	3 × 3	1	1	138,624/147,456 (94.0%)
Conv	128	128	29 × 22	3 × 3	1	1	138,624/147,456 (94.0%)
Conv	128	128	29 × 22	1 × 1	1	0	13,184/16,384 (80.5%)
Conv	128	11	29 × 22	1 × 1	1	0	1,067/1,408 (75.8%)
Software part:							
Resize	11	11	22 × 29	-	-	-	-
Total	−	−	-	-	-	-	479,083/512,064 (93.6%)

Table 2. Comparison with existing results on CamVid dataset.

	SegNet [6]	Ours
Params [M]	1.425	0.515
Pixel-wiseAcc	84.0%	77.6%
mClassAcc	54.6%	65.9%
mIoU	46.3%	45.0%

that weights of each filter are sorted by absolute amount, and then eliminates them by a preset percent of the total from a small order. The details of our proposed technique procedure are as follows:

(1) Train floating-point precision model
(2) The pre-trained weights of each filter are sorted by its absolute value

378   M. Shimoda et al.

(3) Prune their small value ones by a preset percent per each filter
(4) Retrain their nonzero weights by using distillation

By following the above procedure, sparse ratios of each filter are the same, which leads to improvement of its implementation circuitry performance. In our experiments, we set the pruning percent 94% for convolutional layers, and 80% or 75% for pixel-wise convolutional ones, as shown in Table 1.

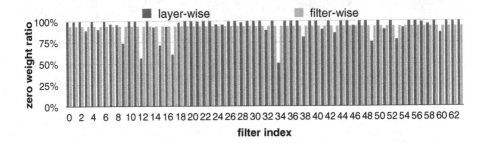

Fig. 6. Filter-wise zero weight ratio of the 1st convolutional layer.

5.1 Distillation Scheme for Retraining

Distillation [15] is a compression technique that can obtain a small model by using the class probabilities produced by the cumbersome model as "soft targets". Some works apply the knowledge distillation to both object classification [16] and object detector [17]. In this paper, we exploit it to semantic segmentation tasks to obtain a high sparse model using the dense model. The sparse model can acquire high accuracy by using not only ground truth, which is called "hard targets", but cumbersome dense model as "soft targets". We introduce following two losses to accelerate convergence and also get higher accuracy. In our training method, two types of training losses are defined.

(1) Hard targets: Soft-max cross entropy loss
    We use pixel-wise cross entropy loss between the predicted class probabilities produced by sparse model and the ground truth, which is defined by

$$L_{sft} = -\frac{1}{H_{in}W_{in}} \sum_{ch=0}^{n_{class}-1} \sum_{x=0}^{W_{in}-1} \sum_{y=0}^{H_{in}-1} \log\left(\sigma\left(s_{x,y}\right)_{ch}\right) p_{ch,x,y}$$

$$\sigma\left(s_{x,y}\right)_{ch} = \frac{\exp(s_{ch,x,y})}{\sum_{k=0}^{n_{class}-1} \exp(s_{k,x,y})},$$

where H_{in}, W_{in} denotes input image size, $\sigma(s_{x,y})_0, \ldots, \sigma(s_{x,y})_{n_{class}-1}$ are predicted class probabilities. n_{class} is equal to 11 for the CamVid dataset, and $p_{ch,x,y} \in \{0, 1\}$ are the ground truth class probabilities.

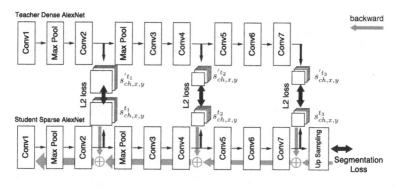

Fig. 7. Pruning method using distillation.

(2) Soft targets: Mean squared losses
For soft target loss, we use mean squared losses between feature maps of sparse model and dense model.

Therefore, the total loss is defined by

$$L = \frac{1}{M} \sum_{j=0}^{M-1} \frac{\alpha_j}{C_j H_j W_j} \sum_{ch=0}^{C_j-1} \sum_{x=0}^{W_j-1} \sum_{y=0}^{H_j-1} \left(s_{ch,x,y}^{t_j} - s_{ch,x,y}^{'t_j} \right)^2 + \beta L_{sft},$$

where M represents a number of feature maps to apply distillation, α_j, β are hyper parameters to balance learning rate, s, s' is feature map of sparse model and dense model, and L_{sft} is soft-max cross entropy loss. In our experiment, we set M 3, which means that the soft target loss uses output feature maps of "conv1", "conv2", and "conv7" as shown in Fig. 7.

Finally, we get 40.53% [mIoU] without "soft targets" and 44.90% [mIoU] with both soft and hard ones, while the weights are pruned by 93.6%. This means only 0.14% [mIoU] drop from the dense model.

6   Implementation

Figure 8 shows the overall circuitry. The design consists of buffer parts for parameters and convolutional block (CB) part, which forms task-level pipeline architecture. All parameters such as weights and biases area loaded into on-chip buffers from DDR3 memory. After that, the processor sends an input image to the design, and the convolutional operations are performed on the first CB. The output feature maps are sent to the ping-pong buffer in the next CB, to be read to compute the next layer operation. Finally, the outputs of the last CB (7-th CB) are sent to the ARM processor to resize them into the given input size by using OpenCV software. Weight parameter matrices are stored to on-chip memory as COO format. Filter-wise pruning can be stored on the on-chip memory (BRAM), thereby implying that this circuitry achieves better power performance.

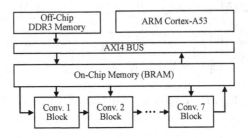

Fig. 8. Overall architecture.

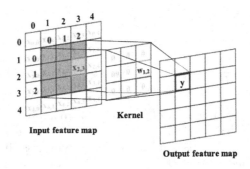

Fig. 9. Absolute and relative localization. The convolutional operation counter has the absolute localization of the top-left pixel in the kernel, such as (y, x) = (1, 1) and the COO decoder contains relative localization denoted in blue (col, row, ch) = (2, 1, 0). (Color figure online)

6.1   Convolutional Block

Figure 10 shows a CB circuitry. It consists of a COO decoder, a COO counter, a counter for convolutional operation, a ping-pong buffer for feature maps, sequential MAC units, and a processing element (PE) for both BN and ReLU. The COO counter counts up to the number of nonzero weight parameters of each filter, and the number is fed into the COO decoder which outputs corresponding relative address, or col, row, and channel values. After that, to fetch values from feature map memory, the absolute address is calculated using both the relative addresses and the convolutional counter which outputs both row and column of the localization at which the convolution is performed. As shown in Fig. 9, the localization of convolution, (y, x) is (1, 1), and the relative address, (col, row,

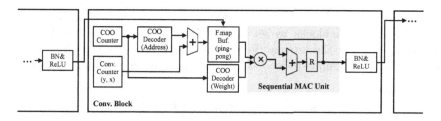

Fig. 10. Convolutional block.

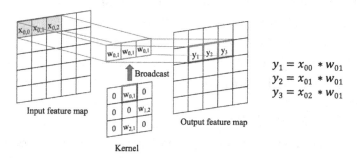

$$y_1 = x_{00} * w_{01}$$
$$y_2 = x_{01} * w_{01}$$
$$y_3 = x_{02} * w_{01}$$

Fig. 11. SIMD convolutional operation.

ch) is $(2, 1, 0)$. Therefore, the absolute localization of corresponding feature map value is $(y+col, x+row, ch) = (3, 2, 0)$. The fetched value and the weight are fed into sequential multiply-accumulate (MAC) unit, followed by PE for BN and ReLU. Finally, the output is stored to the ping-pong buffer for the next CB computation. In our experiments, the calculations in the CB use half-precision floating-point representation.

In our experiments, we modify the above CB circuitry to improve the execution speed. Figure 11 shows the behavior of a SIMD CB which has several sequential MAC units, and Fig. 12 shows the circuitry. Several successive feature map values along to width-axis are fetched simultaneously, and a corresponding weight is broadcast to all sequential MAC units to realize parallel computing. Their outputs are fed into the PE for both BN and ReLU. The resulting values are output sequentially, and sent to the next CB. The configured parallel number

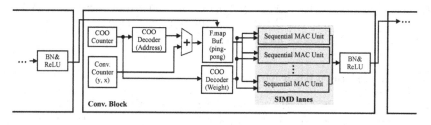

Fig. 12. SIMD Convolutional block.

is shown in Table 3. Since 1st and 2nd CB perform convolution on large images than their successive blocks, we set the parallel number of 1st and 2nd CB bigger number to improve the latency differences among all CB. In addition, we use array partition technique to load several feature map values simultaneously.

Table 3. SIMD configuration for 300×225 images.

	Conv. 1	Conv. 2	Conv. 3	Conv. 4	Conv. 5	Conv. 6	Conv. 7
#SIMD lanes	300	37	19	19	19	19	19

7   Experimental Results

7.1   Accuracy Comparison

In our experiments, both Chainer [18] and ChainerCV [19] deep learning frameworks train our dense and sparse models, and we use CamVid [20] dataset which is one of the popular datasets of the semantic segmentation task for self-driving cars to evaluate our model performance. The image size is set $(height, width) = (360, 480)$, and the number of the categories is 11.

Table 4 shows accuracy comparison results. Our sparse model achieved the dense model performance. The results imply that by using our technique, its resulting model has high zero weight ratio with very few accuracy degradation. Figure 13 presents some examples of both our model outputs and ground truth images.

7.2   FPGA Implementation

We implemented our model for various image sizes on an FPGA and investigated their resulting areas by using Xilinx Inc. SDSoC 2018.2 with a timing constraint of 99.9 MHz. We used a Xilinx Inc. Zynq UltraScale+ MPSoC zcu102 evaluation board, which is equipped with a Xilinx Zynq UltraScale+ MPSoC FPGA (ZU9EG, 68,520 Slices, 269,200 FFs, 1,824 18 Kb BRAMs, 2,520 DSP48Es). Table 5 shows an implementation results. Since our design uses ping-pong buffer for feature maps and array partition to increase memory bandwidth, the utilization of the BRAM is a dominant part. Due to the above reason, our circuitry cannot realize larger image size than $(300, 225)$.

7.3   Comparison with a Mobile GPU

We compare the FPGA with a Jetson TX2 GPU (NVIDIA Corp.) on the basis of both frame per second (FPS) and power consumption. Note that we used the same sparseness CNN for both platforms to fair comparison. In this paper the

Table 4. Semantic segmentation result

	Dense model	Sparse model
Zero Weight Ratio	-	93.6%
mIoU	45.04%	44.90%
mClassAcc	65.92%	61.62%
Pixel-wiseAcc	77.64%	79.38%
Sky	85.58%	85.78%
Building	53.36%	60.80%
Pole	8.85%	8.28%
Road	86.51%	84.15%
Pavement	63.66%	59.26%
Tree	57.26%	60.66%
Sign symbol	12.75%	16.41%
Fence	16.88%	13.56%
Car	63.20%	61.46%
Pedestrian	21.75%	19.01%
Bycyclist	25.65%	24.53%

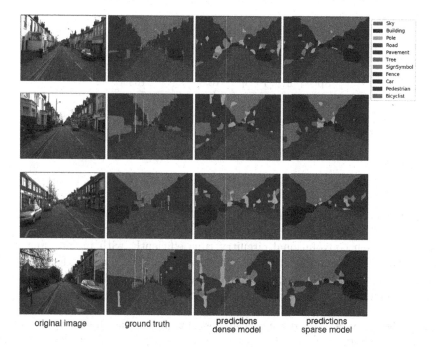

original image   ground truth   predictions dense model   predictions sparse model

Fig. 13. Example of inference results using the test dataset.

Table 5. Implementation on an FPGA for various image sizes (utilization of the zcu102 evaluation board). Note that, SDSoC 2018.2 obtains the following results.

Image size	120 × 90	180 × 135	240 × 180	300 × 225
18 Kb BRAM	224(12.28)	432(23.68)	779(42.71)	1,123(61.57)
DSP48E	183(7.26)	252(10.00)	333(13.21)	390(15.48)
FF	41,957(7.65)	59,865(10.92)	77,122(14.07)	100,508(18.34)
LUT	50,654(18.48)	66,416(24.23)	83,864(30.60)	105,060(38.33)
mIoU	29.23%	35.91%	40.79%	42.62%

power consumption is defined as dynamic one, and the Chainer framework is used for the GPU board. The comparison results are shown in Table 6. As for dynamic power consumption, the GPU system was 2.9 W, while the FPGA consumed only 1.2 W. Thus, it reduced power consumption by 1.7 W. As for performance on average, the GPU achieved 16.3 FPS, whereas the FPGA achieved 165.4 FPS, which means that only our proposed one meets a real-time processing (30 FPS). In terms of performance per power consumption (FPS/W), the FPGA was 24.49 times higher than the mobile GPU. From these results, our system is more suitable for FPGA.

Table 6. Comparison with a mobile GPU with a 300 × 225 image size

Platform	Mobile GPU	FPGA
Device	Jetson TX2	zcu102
Clock freq. [GHz]	1.3	0.1
Speed [avg. FPS]	16.3	165.4
Power [W]	2.9	1.2
Efficiency [FPS/W]	5.6	137.9

8   Conclusion

We presented a SFCN made by the filter-wise pruning technique. By using the proposed method, the generated model is more suitable for embedded systems since each convolutional circuitry runs efficiently with maintaining high sparse ratio. From our experiments, our model achieved good performance on the CamVid dataset and outperform its GPU system in term of both speed and power efficiency.

Acknowledgments. This research is supported in part by the Grants in Aid for Scientific Research from JSPS, and the New Energy and Industrial Technology Development Organization (NEDO). In addition, thanks are extended to the Xilinx University Program (XUP), the Intel University Program, and NVidia Corp. for their support.

References

1. Lecun, Y., Bengio, Y., Hinton, G.: Deep learning. Nature **521**(7553), 436–444 (2015)
2. Lyu, Y., Bai, L., Huang, X.: Real-time road segmentation using LiDAR data processing on an FPGA. In: 2018 IEEE International Symposium on Circuits and Systems (ISCAS), pp. 1–5, May 2018
3. Krizhevsky, A., Sutskever, I., Hinton, G.E.: Imagenet classification with deep convolutional neural networks. In: Proceedings of the 25th International Conference on Neural Information Processing Systems - Volume 1, NIPS 2012, pp. 1097–1105. Curran Associates Inc., USA, (2012)
4. Song, H., Mao, H., Dally, W.J.: Deep compression: compressing deep neural network with pruning, trained quantization and huffman coding. CoRR, abs/1510.00149 (2015)
5. Shelhamer, E., Long, J., Darrell, T.: Fully convolutional networks for semantic segmentation. IEEE Trans. Pattern Anal. Mach. Intell. **39**(4), 640–651 (2017)
6. Badrinarayanan, V., Kendall, A., Cipolla, R.: SegNet: a deep convolutional encoder-decoder architecture for image segmentation. IEEE Trans. Pattern Anal. Mach. Intell. **39**(12), 2481–2495 (2017)
7. Zhao, H., Shi, J., Qi, X., Wang, X., Jia, J.: Pyramid scene parsing network. In: 2017 IEEE Conference on Computer Vision and Pattern Recognition (CVPR), pp. 6230–6239, July 2017
8. Zhao, H., Qi, X., Shen, X., Shi, J., Jia, J.: ICNet for real-time semantic segmentation on high-resolution images. In: Ferrari, V., Hebert, M., Sminchisescu, C., Weiss, Y. (eds.) ECCV 2018. LNCS, vol. 11207, pp. 418–434. Springer, Cham (2018). https://doi.org/10.1007/978-3-030-01219-9_25
9. Zhu, M., Gupta, S.: To prune, or not to prune: exploring the efficacy of pruning for model compression. CoRR, abs/1710.01878 (2017)
10. Molchanov, D., Ashukha, A., Vetrov, D.: Variational dropout sparsifies deep neural networks. arXiv preprint arXiv:1701.05369 (2017)
11. Alvarez, J.M., Salzmann, M.: Compression-aware training of deep networks. In: Advances in Neural Information Processing Systems, pp. 856–867 (2017)
12. Fujii, T., Sato, S., Nakahara, H., Motomura, M.: An FPGA realization of a deep convolutional neural network using a threshold neuron pruning. In: Wong, S., Beck, A.C., Bertels, K., Carro, L. (eds.) ARC 2017. LNCS, vol. 10216, pp. 268–280. Springer, Cham (2017). https://doi.org/10.1007/978-3-319-56258-2_23
13. Yu, J., Lukefahr, A., Palframan, D., Dasika, G., Das, R., Mahlke, S.: Scalpel: customizing DNN pruning to the underlying hardware parallelism. In: Proceedings of the 44th Annual International Symposium on Computer Architecture, ISCA 2017, pp. 548–560, New York, USA. ACM (2017)
14. Ioffe, S., Szegedy, C.: Batch normalization: accelerating deep network training by reducing internal covariate shift. arXiv preprint arXiv:1502.03167 (2015)
15. Hinton, G., Vinyals, O., Dean, J.: Distilling the knowledge in a neural network. arXiv preprint arXiv:1503.02531 (2015)
16. Gao, J., Li, Z., Nevatia, R., et al.: Knowledge concentration: learning 100k object classifiers in a single CNN. arXiv preprint arXiv:1711.07607 (2017)
17. Chen, G., Choi, W., Yu, X., Han, T., Chandraker, M.: Learning efficient object detection models with knowledge distillation. In: Guyon, I., et al. (eds.) Advances in Neural Information Processing Systems, vol. 30, pp. 742–751. Curran Associates Inc. (2017)

18. Tokui, S., Oono, K., Hido, S., Clayton, J.: Chainer: a next-generation open source framework for deep learning. In: Proceedings of Workshop on Machine Learning Systems (LearningSys) in The Twenty-ninth Annual Conference on Neural Information Processing Systems (NIPS) (2015)
19. Niitani, Y., Ogawa, T., Saito, S., Saito, M.: ChainerCV: a library for deep learning in computer vision. In: ACM Multimedia (2017)
20. Brostow, G.J., Fauqueur, J., Cipolla, R.: Semantic object classes in video: a high-definition ground truth database. Pattern Recognit. Lett. **30**, 88–97 (2009)

Exploring Data Size to Run Convolutional Neural Networks in Low Density FPGAs

Ana Gonçalves[1] , Tiago Peres[1] , and Mário Véstias[2](✉)

[1] ISEL, Instituto Politécnico de Lisboa, Lisbon, Portugal
[2] INESC-ID, ISEL, Instituto Politécnico de Lisboa, Lisbon, Portugal
mvestias@deetc.isel.ipl.pt

Abstract. Convolutional Neural Networks (CNNs) obtain very good results in several computer vision applications at the cost of high computational and memory requirements. Therefore, CNN typically run on high performance platforms. However, CNNs can be very useful in embedded systems and its execution right next to the source of data has many advantages, like avoiding the need for data communication and real-time decisions turning these systems into smart sensors. In this paper, we explore data quantization for fast CNN inference in low density FPGAs. We redesign LiteCNN, an architecture for real-time inference of large CNN in low density FPGAs, to support hybrid quantization. We study the impact of quantization over the area, performance and accuracy of LiteCNN. LiteCNN with improved quantization of activations and weights improves the best state of the art results for CNN inference in low density FPGAs. With our proposal, it is possible to infer an image in AlexNet in 7.4 ms in a ZYNQ7020 and in 14.8 ms in a ZYNQ7010 with 3% accuracy degradation. Other delay versus accuracy ratios were identified permitting the designer to choose the most appropriate.

Keywords: Convolutional Neural Network · FPGA · Data quantization

1 Introduction

A CNN consists of several layers in a dataflow structure starting with the input image until the final layer that outputs a classification result. Each layer receives IFMs (Input Feature Map) from the previous and generates OFMs (Output Feature Map) to the next. The main and most common layers are: convolutional, fully connected and pooling.

Convolutional layers are the main modeling blocks of a CNN. For each IFM a 2D convolutional kernel is applied to generate a partial output map. The partial maps and a bias are accumulated to generate an OFM.

The set of 2D kernels form a 3D kernel. Each 3D kernel slides over the IFMs and the convolutions produce an OFM. CNNs consider several kernels at each convolutional layer and so the same number of OFM are produced at each layer.

© Springer Nature Switzerland AG 2019
C. Hochberger et al. (Eds.): ARC 2019, LNCS 11444, pp. 387–401, 2019.
https://doi.org/10.1007/978-3-030-17227-5_27

Convolutional layers may be followed by pooling layers to sub-sample the OFMs to achieve translation invariance and over-fitting. Pooling reduces the size of the feature map by merging neighbor neurons into a single neuron using functions like max or average pooling.

The last layers are usually the fully connected (FC). In a FC layer each neuron is connected to all neurons of the previous layer. The last FC layer outputs the classification probabilities. A nonlinear activation function is applied on every neuron. A common function recently adopted for its simplicity and effectiveness is the Rectified Linear Unit (ReLU) that calculates max(0, activation value).

Several CNNs has been developed with different number and type of layers, and number of kernels. One of the first was LeNet [3] with a total of 60K weights. The model was applied for digit classification with small images. Later, a much larger CNN, AlexNet [10], won the ImageNet Challenge. It consists of five convolutional layers plus three fully connected layers. Different number of kernels with different sizes are applied at each layer with a total of 61M weights requiring a 724 MACC (Multiply-ACCumulate) operations to process images of size $224 \times 224 \times 3$. Other CNN models have followed, like VGG-16 [12], GoogleNet [13] and ResNet [8].

Executing a CNN model (inference) can be done on the same platform used to train it or in an embedded system with strict performance, memory and energy constraints. In a vast set of applications, it is advantageous or necessary to have the inference process near the data input sensor so that important information can be extracted at the image sensor instead of sending the information to the cloud and wait for the answer. Also, in systems where the communication latency and data violations are undesirable, like autonomous vehicles, local processing at the sensor is also desirable.

A common feature of these CNN models is the high number of weights and operations. Due to the limited performance and memory of many embedded platforms it is very important to find architectural solutions to run large CNN inferences in low cost embedded platforms. One approach to achieve such implementations is to reduce the type and size of data without compromising the network accuracy. Size reduction reduces the complexity of arithmetic units and the memory requirements to store feature maps and weights.

In this paper, the focus is on the optimization of LiteCNN [16] for running inference of large CNNs in low density FPGAs (Field-Programmable Gate Arrays) using data size reduction.

The following has been considered for the optimization of LiteCNN:

- Lite-CNN only supports 8 bits dynamic fixed-point. An extended framework based on Caffe [9] and Ristretto [7] was developed to explore other fixed-point sizes;
- LiteCNN modifications are proposed to support generic fixed-point sizes;
- A performance model for LiteCNN was developed to allow design space exploration;

– Tradeoffs among performance, area and accuracy were obtained allowing the designer to choose the most appropriate LiteCNN configuration for a particular CNN model and accuracy.

The paper is organized as follows. Section 2 describes the related work on FPGA implementations of CNNs and optimization methods based on data size reduction. Section 3 describes the flow used to explore data size reduction of CNNs. Section 4 describes the LiteCNN architecture, the modifications necessary to support other data sizes and the performance model. Section 5 describes the results on inference accuracy and area/performance of LiteCNN running well-known CNNs and compare them to previous works. Section 6 concludes the paper.

2   Related Work

Common general processing units achieve only a few hundred GFLOPs with low power efficiency. This performance is scarce for cloud computing and the energy consumption is too high for smart embedded computing. GPUs (Graphics Processing Units) and dedicated processors (e.g. Tensor Processing Unit - TPU) offer dozens of TOPs and are therefore appropriate for cloud computing.

FPGAs are increasingly being used for CNN inference for its high energy efficiency, since it can be reconfigured to adapt to each CNN model.

The first FPGA implementations of CNNs considered small networks [1,2]. A larger CNN was implemented in [19] but only for the convolutional layers.

A few authors considered low density FPGAs as the target device. In [14] small CNNs are implemented in a ZYNQ XC7Z020 with a performance of 13 GOPs with 16 bit fixed-point data. In [5] the same FPGA is used to implemented big CNN models, like VGG16, with data represented with 8 bits achieving performances of 84 GOPs.

In [4] the authors implemented a pipelined architecture in a ZYNQ XC7Z020 with data represented with 16-bit fixed point. The architecture achieves 76 GOPs with high energy efficiency.

Previous implementations on low density FPGAs have performances below 100 GOPs. Previous works [6,11] show that dynamic fixed-point with 8 bits guarantee similar accuracies compared to those obtained with 32-bit floating point representations. In [17] hybrid quantization schema is proposed with different quantizations for different layers targeting edge computing. To deal with this hybrid quantization, the authors propose a pipeline structure with a layer at each pipeline level. The problem is that a pipeline structure requires enough memory to store intermediate feature maps and so it is not adequate for low density FPGAs with scarce memory resources.

Datawidth reduction is essential to implement CNN in target platforms with low on-chip memory and low resources. In this work we consider data bitwidths that can vary between layers and between activations and weights and study the impact of this hybrid quantization over the inference delay, accuracy and hardware resources.

The extended LiteCNN architecture with support for hybrid quantization proposed in this work is able to achieve several hundred GOPs in a low cost FPGA, like the ZYNQ7020, improve the inference delays of the original LiteCNN and of previous works and achieve high area and performance efficiencies. With LiteCNN, we have determined the tradeoffs between area, performance and CNN accuracy. Our solution improves the CNN inference delays of previous works in low density FPGAs with similar network accuracies.

3   Framework for Bitwidth Optimization

We have developed a framework based on Caffe [9] and Ristretto [7] to explore the bitwidth of both activations and weights. Ristretto determines the number of bits to represent data enough to guarantee a maximum error in the precision of the network specified by the user. To explore particular bitwidth sizes, we established a design flow with the following steps:

- The network is initially trained with single precision floating-point;
- Ristretto is applied to the trained network with different precision errors, generating solutions with different datawidths;
- From the results, we extract the fixed-point quantifications from each solution;
- From these values, we create a generic linear model of the quantification parameters (fractional and integer parts of fixed-point quantification);
- From this model we generate architectures with the required number of bits and train them to determine their accuracy.

Usually for a given target hardware architecture some data size configurations are more efficient than others in terms of area/performance. So, we want to explore these more efficient solutions in terms of network accuracy. This design flow permit us to determine the network accuracy for specific data bitwidths.

4   LiteCNN Architecture - 8 Bits

4.1   LiteCNN Architecture

The Lite-CNN architecture consists of a cluster of processing elements (PE) to calculate dot-products, a memory buffer to store on-chip the initial image and the OFMs, one module to send activations and two modules to send and to receive weights to/from the PEs (see Fig. 1).

The architecture executes layers one at a time. The execution of convolutional and fully connected layers work the same because we transform the 3D convolutions in linear dot-products identical to those used in FC layers, to be explained above. Layers are executed the following way:

- Before starting the execution of a layer, the architecture is configured for the specific characteristics of the layer. It also specifies if there is a pooling layer at the output of the feature maps being calculated;

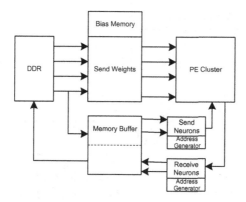

Fig. 1. Block diagram of the Lite-CNN architecture

- The input image and the intermediate feature maps are stored on-chip. Since the layers are executed one at a time, the buffer memory only has to be enough to store the IFM and OFM of any layer;
- For the first convolutional layer, the image is loaded from external memory. For the others, the IFM is already in on-chip memory. At the same time, kernels are read from external memory and sent to the PEs. Besides the weights, the kernel includes the bias value which is stored in the bias memory. Each PE receives one kernel. So, each PE calculates the activations associated with one OFM;
- The initial image or intermediate feature maps in the on-chip memory are broadcasted to all PEs;
- After each calculation of a complete dot product associated with a kernel, all PEs send the output activations back to the receive neurons module that adds the bias and stores the result in the on-chip memory to be used by the next layer. If the layer is followed by pooling, this module saves the activations in a local memory and wait for the other members of the pooling window;
- The process repeats until finishing the convolution between the image and the kernels. After that, the next kernels are loaded from memory and the process repeats until running all kernels of a layer.

The process allows overlapping of kernel transfer and kernel processing. While the PEs process their kernels, in case the local memory is enough to store two different kernels, the next kernels are loaded at the same time. This is fundamental in the fully connected layers where the number of computations is the same as the number of weights.

Also, in case the on-chip memory is not enough to store the whole image and the OFM (usually the first layer is the one that requires more on-chip memory), the image is cut into pieces which are convolved separately.

The PE cluster contains a set of PEs. Each PE (see Fig. 2) has a local memory to store kernels and arithmetic units to calculate the dot product.

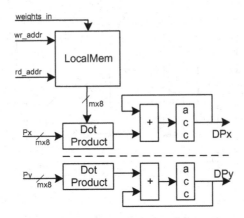

Fig. 2. Architecture of the processing elements

Each PE stores a different kernel and so is responsible for calculating the activations of the output feature map associated with the kernel. This way multiple output feature maps are calculated in parallel. Also, in convolutional layers, the same kernel is applied to different blocks of the IFM and produce different neurons of its OFM. The number of output neurons to be processed in parallel in each PE is configurable. For example, to calculate two activations in parallel it receives two input activations from the feature memory in parallel. This mechanism permits to explore the intra-output parallelism (fully connected layers do not use intra-output parallelism). Finally, weights and activations are stored in groups, that is, multiple weights and activations are read in parallel in a single memory access (e.g., with 8-bit data, a 64 memory word contains eight neurons or weights) permitting to explore dot-product parallelism.

The block *sendWeights* is configured to send kernels to the PE cluster. The block receives data from direct memory access (DMA) units that retrieve data from external memory and send it to the PEs in order. It includes a bias memory to store the bias associated with each kernel.

The *sendNeurons* and *receiveNeurons* blocks are responsible for broadcasting activations from the feature memory to the PEs and receive dot product results from the PEs, respectively. The send neurons module includes a configurable address generator. The receive neurons module implements the pooling layer in a centralized manner.

Previous works use dedicated units to calculate 2D convolutions. The problem is that the method becomes inefficient since the same units have to run different window sizes and are used only for convolutional layers. Lite-CNN transforms 3D convolutions into a long dot product to become independent of the window size. Also, this way, both convolutional and FC layers are executed the same way by the same arithmetic core units.

Pixels of the initial image, activations of feature maps and weights of kernels are stored in order (z, x, y) (see Fig. 3).

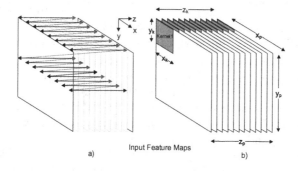

Input Feature Maps
a)   b)

Fig. 3. Reading mode of images, feature maps and weights

Each neuron of an OFM is calculated as a dot product between the 3D kernel of size $x_k \times y_k \times z_k$ and the correspondent activations of the IFM of size $x_p \times y_p \times z_p$ (see Fig. 3b), where z_p is the number of IFMs. The weights of kernel are all read sequentially from memory since they are already ordered. The activations are also read in sequence from memory but after $x_k \times z_k$ activations it has to jump to the next y_k adding an offset to the address of the input feature memory being read. For a layer without stride nor followed by pooling, the offset is $x_p \times z_p$. Formally, the dot product to calculate each step of the convolution is given by:

$$DP_{conv} = \sum_{i=0}^{i=y_k-1} \sum_{j=0}^{j=x_k z_k-1} W_{ix_k z_k+j} \times P_{startAddr+ix_p z_p+j} \qquad (1)$$

where *startAddr* is the address of the first neuron of the block of the IFM being convolved. We use this operation to convolve a kernel with the set of IFMs sliding the 3D kernel along the feature maps. In this process, if a layer is followed by pooling, the output neurons of the pooling set are calculated in sequence and only the final neuron is stored in the OFM buffer. The advantage of our method is that it is independent of the shapes of kernels and weights and layer type. WE just have to configure the address generator properly for each layer.

LiteCNN also implements a method to reduce the number of multiplications by half [16] leading to a considerable reduction in the hardware resources required to implement a convolutional or fully connected layers. Also, the intra-output parallelism used during convolutional layers can be used to batch IFM to be sent to FC layers. This version of LiteCNN supports two parallel lines of computation. Each of these lines can be used to process one of the batched IFM for the FC layers, that is, it supports a batch of two.

We have extended LiteCNN with two modifications to support data sizes different from *activation* × *weight* = 8 × 8. Since we cannot afford having a pipelined datapath with dedicated implementations of each layer, due to low memory resources, we keep the generic layer implementation that is configurable to support each particular layer and extended it to support different data sizes.

In those cases where all layers use the same sizes (e.g., 16×16, 5×5, 8×2), the processing units are configured exactly to execute operations with this size. We kept the memory data bus with 64 bits and so the number of parallel units depend on the size of activations and weights (64/size).

When layers have different data sizes, we store data in their original sizes, but core units are implemented to support the execution of the bigger operands. Therefore, data with smaller dimension are extended to the size of data with the biggest dimension. For example, consider two different representations in the same CNN - 8×4 and 8×2 - the arithmetic units are implemented for 8×4 and 8×2 data is extended to 8×4 to be executed. In this extended version of LiteCNN, cores support multiply-accumulations of data with upto two different data representations whose sizes are configured initially. For example, it can be configured to execute layers with size 8×4 and 8×2, or 8×8 and 8×2. Extending LiteCNN to obtain architecture configurations that support the execution of more than two different data sizes is straightforward but was not considered in this paper.

With this architectural solution using layers with different data representations has no computational advantage, since the number of operations is the same as using the same data sizes, but the data is read and stored from/to memory in their original sizes. So, the method permits to take advantage of using reduced weight sizes to reduce the time to transfer activations and weights from memory. Designing generic arithmetic units was left for future research.

The second modification of the PEs has to do with the method to reduce the number of multiplications. When both activations and weights have the same size, the method is used. Otherwise, the method is less efficient since the multiplications have the size of the bigger parameter (e.g. if 8×4, the size of the multiplications is 9×9). In these cases we adopted and extended for other dimensions the method proposed in [15].

4.2   Performance Model of LiteCNN

The performance model provides an estimate of the inference execution time of a CNN network on the LiteCNN architecture. The model determines the time to process each layer.

Considering convolutional layers, the time to transfer all kernels depends on the number of kernels, $nKernel$, the size of kernels, $kernelSize$, the number of bits used to represent weights, $nBit$ and the memory bandwidth, BW. The total number of bytes, $tByte$, transferred in each convolutional layer is given by Eq. 2.

$$tByte = nKernel \times kernelSize \times \frac{nBit}{8} \qquad (2)$$

The number of cycles to execute a convolutional layer, $conCycle$, is given by Eq. 3.

$$convCycle = \left\lceil \frac{nKernel}{nCore} \right\rceil \times \frac{nConv \times kernelSize}{nMAC} \qquad (3)$$

where $nCore$ is the number of processing elements, $nConv$ is the number of 3D convolutions and $nMAC$ is the number of parallel multiply-accumulations of each PE (intra-output parallelism). From these two equations, the total execution time, $convExec$ depends on the local memory capacities. If local memories of PEs have enough space to store two kernels, than communication and processing of kernels can overlap, otherwise, they must be serialized. Considering an operating frequency, $freq$ de execution time is given by Eq. 5.

$$convExec = \frac{tByte}{BW} + \frac{convCycle}{freq} \qquad \text{without overlap} \qquad (4)$$

$$convExec = max(\frac{tByte}{BW}, \frac{convCycle}{freq}) \qquad \text{with overlap} \qquad (5)$$

For the totally connected layers, the equation to determine the number of bytes to transfer all kernels is the same as Eq. 2. The equation to determine the number of cycles to process the layer is given by:

$$fcCycle = \left\lceil \frac{nKernel}{nCore} \right\rceil \times \frac{kernelSize}{nMAC} \times nParallel \qquad (6)$$

Since in the fully connected layers there is no intra-output parallelism, only one line of parallel MACs of the PE is used. Given the number of intra-output parallel processing lines, $nParallel$, the number of processing cycles is multiplied by this value.

The total execution time of FC layers is similar to 5.

$$fcExec = \frac{tByte}{BW} + \frac{fcCycle}{freq} \qquad \text{without overlap} \qquad (7)$$

$$fcExec = max(\frac{tByte}{BW}, \frac{fcCycle}{freq}) \qquad \text{with overlap} \qquad (8)$$

The total execution of a CNN inference in LiteCNN is the sum of the time to transfer the image to FPGA ($\frac{imageSize(bytes)}{BW}$) plus the time to process each layer. Between layers there is configuration time of the architecture done by the ARM processor of ZYNQ. We have checked the accuracy of the model from the results of LiteCNN 8×8 running AlexNet. The delay obtained with the model is about 1% lower (17.44 ms) against (17.63 ms) of the implementation.

5   Results

We have tested LiteCNN with data size reduction with one small network - LeNet5 - one medium size CNN - Cifar10-full - and one large CNN - AlexNet. Cifar10-full is a network with three convolutional layers and one fully connected layer used to classify images from the CIFAR-10 dataset containing 32×32 color images. All LiteCNN architectures were implemented with Vivado 2017.3 in the ZedBoard with a ZYNQ XC7Z020 and run at 200 MHz.

Table 1. Area occupation for different data size configurations of Lite-CNN

Layer x	4 × 4	5 × 5	6 × 6	16 × 16	8 × 8	8 × 8	8 × 8	8 × 4	8 × 4	8 × 2	2 × 8
Layer y	4 × 4	5 × 5	6 × 6	16 × 16	8 × 8	8 × 4	8 × 2	8 × 4	8 × 2	8 × 2	2 × 2
PEs	64	64	64	32	64	64	64	43	43	40	38
MACC	32	24	20	16	16	16	16	32	32	64	64
LUT	47477	44922	44895	45098	44418	46624	46832	45824	47842	45641	45430
DSP	220	220	220	220	220	220	220	220	220	220	220
BRAM	130	130	130	132	130	130	130	115	115	111	111
Peak GOPs	819	614	512	205	410	410	410	563	563	1024	972

For each CNN we found the relation between delay and accuracy when implemented in LiteCNN. Since LiteCNN is configurable in terms of processing elements, to facilitate the comparison of architectures with different data size configurations, we implemented all architectures with similar areas by changing the number of processing elements (see area results in Table 1).

Table 1 gives the number of PEs and the number of MACC in each PE for a particular implementation of LiteCNN (layer x and layer y lines indicate the size of the operands supported in each implementation). A line with the peak performance was also included. With layers configured with 4 × 4 data sizes the architecture has a peak performance of 819 GOPs and configured with 8 × 2 it has over 1 TOPs of peak performance.

Considering these implementations (with similar areas), we have determined the accuracy (top-1) of the networks (LeNet, Cifar10-full, AlexNet) for different data size configurations and the delay. To avoid long synthesis times of all architectures, we used the performance model to determine the delay (the performance model was verified for the original LiteCNN).

LeNet is a small network and is used for simple number recognition. Therefore, it has high accuracy and executes fast compared to the other larger networks. We have considered data of convolutional layers with the same size and varied the size between convolutional and FC layers (see Fig. 4).

Each architecture configuration is specified by the bitwidth of activations (the same for all layers, specified as A:size) and the bitwidth of weights (can be different across all layers, specified as W:size.. if the same for all layers or W: followed by all sizes of each layer when different).

The fastest solution is obtained with configuration (A:8; W:4442). The reason is that with 2-bit weights in the FC layers, it reduces the high data communication delay of weights in FC layers. In fact, we observe that the increase in delay is related to size of weights in fully connected layers. In terms of accuracy, it increases with the datawidth of activations and weights but the delay increases more than linearly with the increase in accuracy.

Cifar10-Full has 3 convolutional layers and 1 FC layer. The accuracies of Cifar10-Full are lower than that of LeNet because the classification problem is more complex (see Fig. 5).

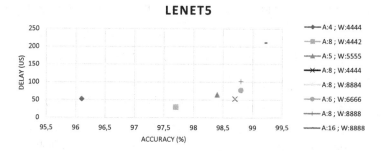

Fig. 4. Accuracy versus delay for different configurations of LiteCNN running LeNet

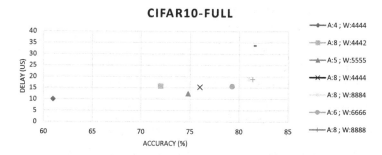

Fig. 5. Accuracy versus delay for different configurations of LiteCNN running Cifar10-Full

The results for Cifar10-Full are slightly different than those for LeNet. The FC layers of Cifar10 are not the bottleneck since the size and number of kernels are close to those of the convolutional layers. Therefore, those configurations with a smaller number of bits for FC weights are not necessarily better; configurations from A:8 W:4444 to A:8 W:8888 have a small variation in delay (around 3 us) for 10% variation in accuracy.

AlexNet is larger and requires more bits to represent data in order to maintain acceptable accuracies. In this case, we considered an hybrid size of weights, that is, two possible sizes of weights in different layers keeping activations with the same size for all layers. The results were compared with state of the art implementations in the ZYNQ board with a low density SoC FPGA - ZYNQ7020. We have also mapped these different configurations of LiteCNN in a ZYNQ7010. As far as we know, this is the first attempt to implement a large CNN in the smallest SoC FPGA of the ZYNQ family from Xilinx (see Table 2).

The results reveal the importance of determining the right bitwidth of data. Moving from the configuration with the highest accuracy (A:16; W:16..) to a configuration with almost the same accuracy (A:16; W:8..) the delay improves 43%. The biggest improvements occur when there is a reduction in the size of the weights. Reducing the activations has a lower impact on the delay with a higher impact on the accuracy.

Table 2. Performance comparison of LiteCNN with previous works in low density FPGAs ZYNQ7020 and ZYNQ7010 SoC FPGAs

Work	Format	Freq (MHz)	Latency (ms)	Acc.
ZYNQ 7020				
[18]	A:16; W:16..	100	71,75	[a]
[14]	A:16; W:16..	125	52,4	[a]
[4]	A:16; W:16..	200	16,7[b]	[a]
LiteCNN	A:16; W:16..	200	33,8	55,6
	A:16; W:8..		19,4	55,5
	A:8; W:8..		17,4	54,4
	A:8; W:82222228		7,4	52,7
	A:4; W:82222228		6,6	49,5
	A:2; W:82222228		5,7	46,5
ZYNQ 7010				
LiteCNN	A:8; W:8..	200	24,8	54,4
	A:8; W:82222228		14,8	52,7
	A:4; W:82222228		12,2	49,5
	A:2; W:82222228		8,3	46,5

[a] Authors assume accuracy close to that obtained with floating-point - 55,9%
[b] With pruning and image batch

Compared to previous works, the proposed architecture improves the delay in more than 50%, except when compared with [4]. However, in this case, the proposed solution uses weight pruning and image batch, which are not considered in our proposal.

With LiteCNN we could map AlexNet in the smallest SoC FPGA from Xilinx - ZYNQ7010 - in a ZYBO board. As expected, inference delays are higher because it has much less resources (less PEs) and since the available on-chip RAM is not enough to hold the image and the first OFM, the image has to be halved and processed separately. The impact in the delay is higher when we reduce the size of the weights since in this case the computation times of the convolutional layers relative to the FC layers increases and the ZINQ7010 implementation has less PEs to calculate convolutional layers. For example, considering configuration (A:8; W:8..) the delay increases 1.4×, while for configuration (A:8; W:82222228) it increases 2×. However, notably, it can run AlexNet in real-time (30 fps).

To better understand the impact of size reduction of activations and weights on the inference delay, we have determined the time to execute convolutional layers and the time to execute FC layers (see Fig. 6).

The execution time of FC layers is higher than that of convolutional layers. The execution time of FC layers is dominated by the communication of weights from external memory. This fact degrades the average GOPs. Reducing the size of

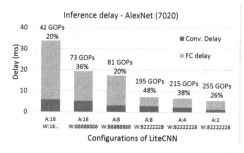
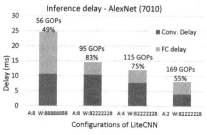

Fig. 6. Execution time of convolutional and FC layers for different configurations of LiteCNN running AlexNet

FC weights improves the real Gops of the architecture. The real Gops improves when LiteCNN is mapped on ZYNQ7010. In this case, the execution time of FC layers is about the same (the memory bandwidth is the same in both FPGAs) and the execution time of convolutional layers increase. So, the implementation in ZYNQ7010 is more efficient.

6 Conclusions

In this work we have developed a framework to explore the design space of bitwidth of activations and weights. LiteCNN was extended to support the execution of layers with different data widths.

The extended LiteCNN with configurable bitwidths improves the performance/area efficiency with a small impact over the inference accuracy of the CNN. This is fundamental for embedded systems with low resources.

We have also observed that weight size reduction has more effect on architecture optimization than activation size reduction since it not only permits to increase the performance/area ratio of the architecture but also reduces the time to transmit FC weights, the performance bottleneck in the execution of CNN models with large FC layers.

We are now studying in more detail the smallest size formats and how to compensate for the accuracy loss by changing the CNN model. We have also started to complement data size reduction with data reduction using techniques like pruning.

Acknowledgment. This work was supported by national funds through Fundação para a Ciência e a Tecnologia (FCT) with reference UID/CEC/50021/2019 and was also supported by project IPL/IDI&CA/2018/LiteCNN/ISEL through Instituto Politécnico de Lisboa.

References

1. Chakradhar, S., Sankaradas, M., Jakkula, V., Cadambi, S.: A dynamically configurable coprocessor for convolutional neural networks. SIGARCH Comput. Archit. News **38**(3), 247–257 (2010). https://doi.org/10.1145/1816038.1815993
2. Chen, Y., et al.: DaDianNao: a machine-learning supercomputer. In: 2014 47th Annual IEEE/ACM International Symposium on Microarchitecture, pp. 609–622, December 2014. https://doi.org/10.1109/MICRO.2014.58
3. Cun, Y.L., et al.: Handwritten digit recognition: applications of neural network chips and automatic learning. IEEE Commun. Mag. **27**(11), 41–46 (1989). https://doi.org/10.1109/35.41400
4. Gong, L., Wang, C., Li, X., Chen, H., Zhou, X.: MALOC: a fully pipelined FPGA accelerator for convolutional neural networks with all layers mapped on chip. IEEE Trans. Comput.-Aided Des. Integr. Circ. Syst. **37**(11), 2601–2612 (2018). https://doi.org/10.1109/TCAD.2018.2857078
5. Guo, K., et al.: Angel-Eye: a complete design flow for mapping CNN onto embedded FPGA. IEEE Trans. Comput.-Aided Des. Integr. Circ. Syst. **37**(1), 35–47 (2018). https://doi.org/10.1109/TCAD.2017.2705069
6. Gysel, P., Motamedi, M., Ghiasi, S.: Hardware-oriented approximation of convolutional neural networks. In: Proceedings of the 4th International Conference on Learning Representations (2016)
7. Gysel, P., Pimentel, J., Motamedi, M., Ghiasi, S.: Ristretto: a framework for empirical study of resource-efficient inference in convolutional neural networks. IEEE Trans. Neural Netw. Learn. Syst. **29**(11), 5784–5789 (2018). https://doi.org/10.1109/TNNLS.2018.2808319
8. He, K., Zhang, X., Ren, S., Sun, J.: Deep residual learning for image recognition. In: 2016 IEEE Conference on Computer Vision and Pattern Recognition, CVPR, pp. 770–778, June 2016. https://doi.org/10.1109/CVPR.2016.90
9. Jia, Y., et al.: Caffe: convolutional architecture for fast feature embedding. arXiv preprint arXiv:1408.5093 (2014)
10. Krizhevsky, A., Sutskever, I., Hinton, G.E.: ImageNet classification with deep convolutional neural networks. In: Proceedings of the 25th International Conference on Neural Information Processing Systems, NIPS 2012, vol. 1, pp. 1097–1105. Curran Associates Inc., USA (2012)
11. Ma, Y., Suda, N., Cao, Y., Seo, J., Vrudhula, S.: Scalable and modularized RTL compilation of convolutional neural networks onto FPGA. In: 2016 26th International Conference on Field Programmable Logic and Applications, FPL, pp. 1–8, August 2016. https://doi.org/10.1109/FPL.2016.7577356
12. Simonyan, K., Zisserman, A.: Very deep convolutional networks for large-scale image recognition. In: Proceedings of the 3rd International Conference on Learning Representations (2015)
13. Szegedy, C., et al.: Going deeper with convolutions. In: 2015 IEEE Conference on Computer Vision and Pattern Recognition, CVPR, pp. 1–9, June 2015. https://doi.org/10.1109/CVPR.2015.7298594
14. Venieris, S.I., Bouganis, C.: fpgaConvNet: mapping regular and irregular convolutional neural networks on FPGAs. IEEE Trans. Neural Netw. Learn. Syst. 1–17 (2018). https://doi.org/10.1109/TNNLS.2018.2844093
15. Véstias, M., Duarte, R.P., de Sousa, J.T., Neto, H.: Parallel dot-products for deep learning on FPGA. In: 2017 27th International Conference on Field Programmable Logic and Applications, FPL, pp. 1–4, September 2017. https://doi.org/10.23919/FPL.2017.8056863

16. Véstias, M., Duarte, R.P., de Sousa, J.T., Neto, H.: Lite-CNN: a high-performance architecture to execute CNNs in low density FPGAs. In: Proceedings of the 28th International Conference on Field Programmable Logic and Applications (2018)
17. Wang, J., Lou, Q., Zhang, X., Zhu, C., Lin, Y., Chen., D.: A design flow of accelerating hybrid extremely low bit-width neural network in embedded FPGA. In: 28th International Conference on Field-Programmable Logic and Applications (2018)
18. Wang, Y., Xu, J., Han, Y., Li, H., Li, X.: DeepBurning: automatic generation of fpga-based learning accelerators for the neural network family. In: 2016 53rd ACM/EDAC/IEEE Design Automation Conference, DAC, pp. 1–6, June 2016. https://doi.org/10.1145/2897937.2898002
19. Zhang, C., Li, P., Sun, G., Guan, Y., Xiao, B., Cong, J.: Optimizing FPGA-based accelerator design for deep convolutional neural networks. In: Proceedings of the 2015 ACM/SIGDA International Symposium on Field-Programmable Gate Arrays, FPGA 2015, pp. 161–170. ACM, New York (2015). https://doi.org/10.1145/2684746.2689060

Faster Convolutional Neural Networks in Low Density FPGAs Using Block Pruning

Tiago Peres[1], Ana Gonçalves[1], and Mário Véstias[2](✉)

[1] ISEL, Instituto Politécnico de Lisboa, Lisbon, Portugal
[2] INESC-ID, ISEL, Instituto Politécnico de Lisboa, Lisbon, Portugal
mvestias@deetc.isel.ipl.pt

Abstract. Convolutional Neural Networks (CNNs) are achieving promising results in several computer vision applications. Running these models is computationally very intensive and needs a large amount of memory to store weights and activations. Therefore, CNN typically run on high performance platforms. However, the classification capabilities of CNNs are very useful in many applications running in embedded platforms close to data production since it avoids data communication for cloud processing and permits real-time decisions turning these systems into smart embedded systems. In this paper, we improve the inference of large CNN in low density FPGAs using pruning. We propose block pruning and apply it to LiteCNN, an architecture for CNN inference that achieves high performance in low density FPGAs. With the proposed LiteCNN optimizations, we have an architecture for CNN inference with an average performance of 275 GOPs for 8-bit data in a XC7Z020 FPGA. With our proposal, it is possible to infer an image in AlexNet in 5.1 ms in a ZYNQ7020 and in 13.2 ms in a ZYNQ7010 with only 2.4% accuracy degradation.

Keywords: Convolutional Neural Network · FPGA · Block pruning

1 Introduction

A CNN consists of a series of convolutional layers where the output of a layer is the input of the next. Each layer generates an output feature map (OFM) with specific characteristics of the input image or of the previous input feature map (IFM). Each feature map is obtained from the convolution of a filter and the IFM. The last layers of the CNN are usually the fully connected (FC) layers that associate a matching probability of the image with one of the classes. Besides convolutional and fully connected layers there may be other layers, like the pooling layer and a non-linear layer (e.g. ReLU).

AlexNet [1], a large CNN, won the ImageNet Challenge. It consists of five convolutional layers plus three FC layers. Different number of kernels with different sizes are applied at each layer with a total of 61M weights requiring a 724 MACC (Multiply-accumulate) operations. Other CNN models have followed, like VGG-16 [2], GoogleNet [3] and ResNet [4].

Executing a CNN model (inference) can be done on the same platform used to train it or in an embedded computing platform with strict performance, memory and energy constraints. In a vast set of embedded applications, it is advantageous or necessary to have the inference process near the data input sensor so that important information can be extracted at the image sensor instead of sending the information to the cloud and wait for the answer. Also, in systems where the communication latency and data violations are undesirable, like autonomous vehicles, local processing at the sensor is also desirable.

A common feature of these CNN models is the high number of weights and operations. Due to the limited performance and memory of many embedded platforms it is very important to find architectural solutions to run large CNN inferences in low hardware density embedded platforms. Recently, a high performance architecture for CNN inference - LiteCNN - was proposed [5]. With a peak performance of 410 GOPs in a ZYNQ7020 FPGA (Field-Programmable Gate Array) it does an inference of AlexNet in about 17 ms.

To improve the processing delay of the inference, pruning (weight cut) can be applied, usually to the FC layers followed by data quantization. The method permits to reduce the number of operations to be performed as well as the memory size to store the weights. The problem of the method is that the sparsity introduced challenges the regular structures of computing datapaths. To reduce the sparsity problem caused by pruning, we propose a block pruning technique in which weights are pruned in blocks. We have studied the impact of pruning and the block size over the performance and area of LiteCNN.

The following has been considered for the optimization of LiteCNN:

- We have implemented a flow based on Caffe [6] and Ristretto [7] to optimize networks using block pruning followed by quantization;
- LiteCNN was upgraded to support the implementation of block pruned CNN;
- A performance model for pruned LiteCNN was developed to allow design space exploration;
- Tradeoffs among performance, area and accuracy were obtained allowing the designer to choose the most appropriate LiteCNN configuration for a particular CNN model.

The paper is organized as follows. Section 2 describes the state of art on FPGA implementations of CNNs and optimization methods based on pruning. Section 3 describes the flow used to explore block pruning and quantization. Section 4 describes the LiteCNN architecture, the modifications necessary to support pruning and the performance model. Section 5 describes the results on inference accuracy and area/performance of LiteCNN running well-known CNNs and compare them to previous works. Section 6 concludes the paper.

2 Related Work

Common general processing units achieve only a few hundred GFLOPs with low power efficiency. This performance is scarce for cloud computing and the energy consumption is too high for embedded computing. GPUs (Graphics Processing Units) and dedicated processors (e.g. Tensor Processing Unit - TPU) offer dozens of TOPs and therefore appropriate for cloud computing.

FPGAs are increasingly being used for CNN inference for its high performance/energy efficiency, because it permits to implement a dedicated hardware architecture for each CNN model. This is an important feature if we want to apply it to embedded computing.

A few authors considered low density FPGAs as the target device. In [8] small CNNs are implemented in a ZYNQ XC7Z020 with a performance of 13 GOPs with 16 bit fixed-point data. In [9] the same FPGA is used to implemented big CNN models, like VGG16, with data represented with 8 bits achieving performances of 84 GOPs. In [10] the authors implemented a pipelined architecture in a ZYNQ XC7Z020 with data represented with 16-bit fixed point. The architecture achieves 76 GOPs with high energy efficiency.

Previous works [11] show that dynamic fixed-point with 8 bits guarantee similar accuracies compared to those obtained with 32-bit floating point representations. This reduction is essential to implement CNN in target platforms with low on-chip memory and low resources. LiteCNN is a configurable architecture that can be implemented in small density FPGAs. The architecture has a peak performance of 410 GOPs in a ZYNQ XC7Z020 with 8-bit dynamic fixed-point data representation for activations and weights. This was a great performance improvement over previous implementations in the same FPGA.

In [12] deep neural networks are compressed using pruning, trained quantization and huffman coding. The techniques are applied on CPU and GPU implementations. Results show that pruning on, e.g., AlexNet results in 91% weight cut without sacrificing accuracy. In [13] pruning is considered to improve CNN execution implemented in FPGA, similar to what is done in [14]. The architecture dynamically skips computations with zeros. The problem is that they keep a dense format to store the matrix requiring to be all loaded from memory. Also, they target high density FPGAs. In [15] the authors use a large FPGA with enough capacity to store all weights on-chip after pruning. This is not possible in low FPGAs with scarce internal memory.

In [16] the pruning is adapted to the underlying hardware matching the pruning structure to the data-parallel hardware arithmetic unit. The method is applied to CPU and GPU. In this paper we propose a similar approach with block pruning. The best block pruning is found and then the hardware architecture is adapted to its size.

We have improved CNN inference in LiteCNN by exploring block pruning in the fully connected layers followed by dynamic fixed-point quantization of all layers. The new LiteCNN architecture keeps the peak performance since we do not skip zero values, but the inference delay was reduced by more than 70% since we have reduced the number of fully connected weights to be transmitted from external memory to LiteCNN, the major performance bottleneck at FC layers.

3   Framework for Data Reduction

A framework to explore the block pruning of weights in fully connected weights followed by data quantization was developed based on Caffe [6] as the main framework and Ristretto for data quantization. The Framework trains the network and generates a file of trained weights.

Pruning can be implemented with different metrics and methods to reduce the number of weights. In this work we have considered the weights magnitude. A percentage of weights whose magnitude is closer to zero is iteratively removed according to the flow in Fig. 1.

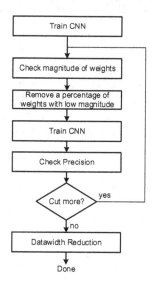

Fig. 1. Network pruning flow

In the first step we train the network or start with a pre-trained network. Then, a percentage of weights with low magnitude (below a predefined threshold) is pruned. The network is trained again with single precision floating-point. We check if the precision allows more pruning. When no more pruning is allowed, we apply Ristretto to reduce the data size. From the results, we extract the fixed-point quantifications for each layer.

Pruning introduces sparsity in the kernels of weights which degrades the performance. Also, introduces an overhead associated with the index information of the sparse vector of weights. To improve the hardware implementation and the performance of pruned networks we introduce the block pruning which performs a coarse pruning with blocks of weights. The method reduces the index overhead data and permits to efficiently use the parallel MACs of the processing units.

The technique permits to prune blocks of weights (similar to what is done in [16]) instead of single weights (see example in Fig. 2).

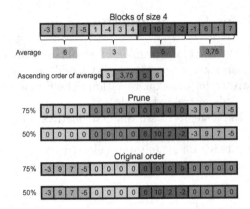

Fig. 2. Pruning method for blocks of four weights

The proposed method determines the average magnitude of a block of weights, sort them and then the blocks with the lowest average magnitude are pruned limited by a pruned percentage. The remaining blocks are stored as a sparse vector where each position contains the block of weights and the index of the next block.

4   LiteCNN Architecture

4.1   LiteCNN Architecture

The Lite-CNN architecture consists of a cluster of processing elements (PE) to calculate dot-products, a memory buffer to store on-chip the initial image and the OFMs, one module to send activations and two modules to send and to receive weights to/from the PEs (see Fig. 3).

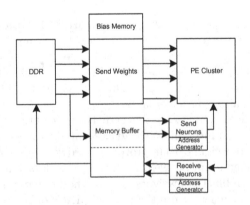

Fig. 3. Block diagram of the Lite-CNN architecture

The architecture executes layers one at a time. The execution of layers work as follows:

- Before starting the execution of a layer, the architecture is configured for the specific characteristics of the layer. It also specifies if there is a pooling layer at the output of the feature maps being calculated;
- The input image and the intermediate feature maps are stored on-chip. Since the layers are executed one at a time, the on-chip only has to be enough to store the IFM and OFM of any layer;
- For the first convolutional layer, the image is loaded from external memory. For the others, the IFM is already in on-chip memory. At the same time, kernels are read from external memory and sent to the PEs. Besides the weights, the kernel includes the bias value which is stored in the bias memory. Each PE receives one kernel. So, each PE calculates the activations associated with one OFM;
- The initial image or intermediate feature maps in the on-chip memory are broadcasted to all PEs;
- After each calculation of a complete dot product associated with a kernel, all PEs send the output activations back to the receive neurons module that adds the bias and stores the result in the on-chip memory to be used by the next layer. If the layer is followed by pooling, this module saves the activations in a local memory and wait for the other members of the pooling window;
- The process repeats until finishing the convolution between the image and the kernels. After that, the next kernels are loaded from memory and the process repeats until running all kernels of a layer.

The process allows overlapping of kernel transfer and kernel processing. While the PEs process their kernels, in case the local memory is enough to store two different kernels, the next kernels are loaded at the same time. This is fundamental in the fully connected layers where the number of computations is the same as the number of weights.

Also, in case the on-chip memory is not enough to store the whole image and the OFM (usually the first layer is the one that requires more on-chip memory), the image is cut into pieces which are convolved separately.

The PE cluster contains a set of PEs. Each PE (see Fig. 4) has a local memory to store kernels and arithmetic units to calculate the dot product in parallel.

Each PE stores a different kernel and so it is responsible for calculating the activations of the output feature map associated with the kernel. This way multiple output feature maps are calculated in parallel. Also, in convolutional layers, the same kernel is applied to different blocks of the IFM and produce different neurons of its OFM. The number of output neurons to be processed in parallel in each PE is configurable. For example, to calculate two activations in parallel it receives two input activations from the feature memory in parallel. This mechanism permits to explore the intra-output parallelism. Finally, weights and activations are stored in groups, that is, multiple weights and activations are

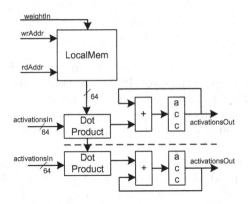

Fig. 4. Architecture of the processing elements

read in parallel in a single memory access (e.g., with 8-bit data, a 64 memory word contains eight neurons or weights) permitting to explore dot-product parallelism.

The block *sendWeights* is configured to send kernels to the PE cluster. The block receives data from direct memory access (DMA) units that retrieve data from external memory and send it to the PEs in order. It includes a bias memory to store the bias associated with each kernel.

The *sendNeurons* and *receiveNeurons* blocks are responsible for broadcasting activations from the feature memory to the PEs and receive dot products from the PEs, respectively. The send neurons module includes a configurable address generator. The receive neurons module implements the pooling layer in a centralized manner.

Most of the previous approaches use dedicated units to calculate 2D convolutions. The problem is that the method becomes inefficient when the same units have to run different window sizes. Lite-CNN transforms 3D convolutions into a long dot product to become independent of the window size. Pixels of the initial image, activations of feature maps and weights of kernels are stored in order (z, x, y) (see Fig. 5).

Each neuron of an OFM is calculated as a dot product between the 3D kernel of size $x_k \times y_k \times z_k$ and the correspondent neurons of the IFM of size $x_p \times y_p \times z_p$ (see Fig. 5b), where z_p is the number of IFMs. The weights of kernel are all read sequentially from memory since they are already ordered. The neurons are also read in sequence from memory but after $x_k \times z_k$ neurons it has to jump to the next y_k adding an offset to the address of the input feature memory being read. For a layer without stride nor followed by pooling, the offset is $x_p \times z_p$.

LiteCNN also implements a method to reduce the number of multiplications by half [5] leading to a considerable reduction in the hardware resources required to implement a convolutional or fully connected layers.

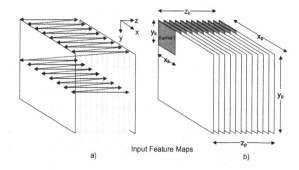

Input Feature Maps

a)

b)

Fig. 5. Reading mode of images, feature maps and weights

We have extended LiteCNN to support pruned FC layers as follows:

- The sparse vectors of weights are sent to the local memory of PEs. The next address index is stored in the parity bits of the BRAMs which were not used in the original LiteCNN. When the size of the index is not enough, we consider extra zero blocks in the middle;
- Activations are sent to the processing elements keeping its dense format and multiply-accumulated by the respective weights. If the activation index corresponds to a zero weight block then its is multiplied by zero keeping the pipeline full.

This solution has no computational advantage, since the number of operations is the same as the case without pruning, but the weight data to be read from memory is considerably reduced. Since the data reduction method is applied in the fully connected layers where the data access is the bottleneck and not the computations, the method permits to achieve high performance improvements, as will been seen in the results. Also, it simplifies the implementation of the PEs permitting to keep the operating frequency and only a small increase in the required hardware resources.

The main modification of the LiteCNN datapath was in the arithmetic core of the PE (see Fig. 6).

Two different datapath modifications are considered. One in which the block size times the quantized datawidth (8 bits) equals 64 (Fig. 6a). In this case, each block has 8 weights the same number of activations received in parallel by the core. The second datapath is when the block size times the quantized datawidth (8 bits) equals 32. In this case, the blocks have only 4 weights and so are read in words of 32 bits. Since the core receives 8 activations in parallel, we read two independent groups of weights from two independent local memories (Fig. 6b).

4.2   Performance Model of LiteCNN

The performance model provides an estimate of the inference execution time of a CNN network on the LiteCNN architecture with block pruning. The model determines the time to process each layer.

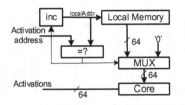

a) Architecture used when (block size x 8) = 64

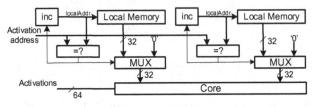

b) Architecture used when (block size x 8) = 32

Fig. 6. Modified datapath of the PE to support weight pruning

Considering convolutional layers, the time to transfer all kernels depends on the number of kernels, *nKernel*, the size of kernels, *kernelSize*, the number of bits used to represent weights, *nBit* and the memory bandwidth, *BW*. The total number of bytes, *tConvByte*, transferred in each convolutional layer is given by Eq. 1.

$$tConvByte = nKernel \times kernelSize \times \frac{nBit}{8} \tag{1}$$

The number of cycles to execute a convolutional layer, *conCycle*, is

$$convCycle = \left\lceil \frac{nKernel}{nCore} \right\rceil \times \frac{nConv \times kernelSize}{nMAC} \tag{2}$$

where *nCore* is the number of processing elements, *nConv* is the number of 3D convolutions and *nMAC* is the number of parallel multiply-accumulations of each PE (intra-output parallelism). From these two equations, the total execution time, *convExec* depends on the local memory capacities. If local memories of PEs have enough space to store two kernels, than communication and processing of kernels can overlap, otherwise, they must be serialized. Considering an operating frequency, *freq* de execution time is given by Eq. 4.

$$convExec = \frac{tByte}{BW} + \frac{convCycle}{freq} \qquad \text{without overlap} \tag{3}$$

$$convExec = max(\frac{tByte}{BW}, \frac{convCycle}{freq}) \qquad \text{with overlap} \tag{4}$$

For the totally connected layers, the equation to determine the number of bytes to transfer all kernels, *tFCByte*, must consider the size of the pruning blocks, *bSize*, and the pruning percentage, *prune*, (see Eq. 5).

$$tFCByte = nKernel \times kernelSize \times \frac{nBit}{8} \times \frac{100 - prune}{100} \times \frac{1 + bSize}{bSize} \quad (5)$$

The equation to determine the number of cycles to process the FC layer is given by:

$$fcCycle = \left\lceil \frac{nKernel}{nCore} \right\rceil \times \frac{kernelSize}{nMAC} \times nParallel \quad (6)$$

Since in the fully connected layers there is no intra-output parallelism, only one line of parallel MACs of the PE is used. Given the number of intra-output parallel processing lines, $nParallel$, the number of processing cycles is multiplied by this value.

The total execution time of FC layers is similar to 4.

$$fcExec = \frac{tFCByte}{BW} + \frac{fcCycle}{freq} \qquad \text{without overlap} \quad (7)$$

$$fcExec = max(\frac{tFCByte}{BW}, \frac{fcCycle}{freq}) \qquad \text{with overlap} \quad (8)$$

The total execution of a CNN inference in LiteCNN is the sum of the time to transfer the image to FPGA and the result from FPGA ($\frac{imageSize+result(bytes)}{BW}$) plus the time to process each layer. Between layers there is negligible configuration time of the architecture to adapt to the layer done by the ARM processor of ZYNQ.

We have checked the accuracy of the model from the results of LiteCNN 8×8 running AlexNet. The delay obtained with the model without pruning is about 1% lower (16.94 ms) against (17.1 ms) of the implementation.

5   Results

We describe the results of the pruning methodology with LeNet, Cifar10-full and AlexNet. All LiteCNN architectures were implemented with Vivado 2017.3 in the ZedBoard with a ZYNQ XC7Z020 and in a ZYBO board with a ZYNQ7010 and run at 200 MHz.

For each CNN we found the relation between block pruning and accuracy. For AlexNet (the larger and most demanding CNN) we have determined the relation between pruning and delay. All results of accuracy are for top-1 classification, since the state-of-the-art works we are comparing also use this metric. Similar tradeoffs were obtained when the top-5 accuracy is used as the metric.

LiteCNN was configured and implemented with 4, 8 and 16 bit dynamic fixed-point (fixed-point numbers in different layers may have different scaling factors), with different block pruning sizes and for each configuration the number of cores was adjusted to obtain a similar area (see the area results in Table 1).

Table 1. Area occupation for different block size configurations of LiteCNN

$Activation \times Weight$	4×4		8×8		16×16	
Block size	8	16	4	8	2	4
PEs	60	64	64	64	38	38
MACC/PE	32	32	16	16	16	16
LUT	47661	47477	47830	43378	45232	43614
DSP	220	220	220	220	220	220
BRAM (36 Kbits)	130	130	130	130	132	132
Peak GOPs	768	819	410	410	243	243

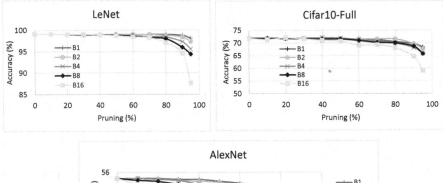

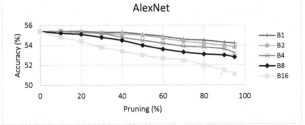

Fig. 7. Variation of accuracy with pruning percentage and block size

The table gives the number of processing elements and the number of MACC in each PE. A line with the peak performance was also included (The peak performance takes into consideration that the architecture reduces the number of multiplications to half).

For each CNN, we have determined the accuracy of the network for different pruning percentages with different block sizes and 8 bit dynamic fixed-point quantization (see Fig. 7, where Bx is the configuration with block size x).

From the results, we observe that the size of the pruning block has a small influence over the accuracy, except for a block of 16. In this worst case, the lost in accuracy is about 4%. Similar results were obtained with 16 bit quantization since the accuracy difference between 8 bit and 16 bit quantizations is small (around 1.5%).

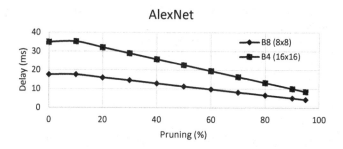

Fig. 8. Variation of delay with pruning percentage for configuration B8 and B4

In order to keep a fair comparison with previous works, we have determined the delay of configurations B8 ($activation \times weight = 8 \times 8$) and B4 ($activation \times weight = 16 \times 16$) for AlexNet for different pruning percentages (see Fig. 8). Pruning has a big impact in the inference delay of AlexNet in LiteCNN since the execution bottleneck of AlexNet is in the fully connected layers because of the huge number of weights to be transferred from external memory. Pruning FC layers reduces the communication time and consequently the whole inference process.

We have also tested with LeNet and Cifar10-Full. With LeNet the delay reduces from 0.1 ms to 0.01 ms when we increase pruning from 10% to 90%. In the case of Cifar10-Full the impact is negligible since the only FC layer of the network has only 2.2% of the total number of weights of the CNN.

We have compared configuration B4 with 16 bit quantization and 8 bit quantization, both with 90% of pruning (1% accuracy loss) with previous works running AlexNet. The overall results are shown in Table 2.

Compared to previous works implemented in the ZYNQ xc7z020, in particular the best implementation from [19], the peak performance and the ratios GOPs/kLUT and GOPs/DSP of LiteCNN are about 2× better and the latency is about 5× better. LiteCNN (8 × 8 configuration) reduces the latency of the original implementation of LiteCNN without pruning (17 ms) to only 5.1 ms with only 1% accuracy loss. This delay allows an inference performance of 196 images/s in a ZYNQ xc7z020.

With LiteCNN we could map AlexNet in the smallest SoC FPGA from Xilinx - ZYNQ7010 - in a ZYBO board. As expected, inference delays are higher because it has less resources (less PEs) and since the available on-chip RAM is not enough to hold the image and the first OFM, the image has to be halved and processed separately. However, notably, it can run AlexNet in real-time (30 fps).

To better understand the impact of pruning of FC weights on the inference delay, we have determined the time to execute convolutional layers and the time to execute FC layers (see Fig. 9). The graph indicates the observed GOPs (and the percentage of peak performance).

Without pruning, the execution time of FC layers is higher than that of convolutional layers. The execution time of FC layers is dominated by the com-

Table 2. Performance comparison of Lite-CNN with other works in low density ZYNQ7020 and ZYNQ7010 SoC FPGAs

Work	Format	Freq (MHz)	GOPs	GOPs/LUT	GOPs/DSP	Latency (ms)	Acc.
ZYNQ 7020							
[17]	16 × 16	100	19	0.35	0.08	71.75	(a)
[18]	16 × 16	150	20	0.38	0.09	—	(a)
[19]	16 × 16	125	38	0.73	0.17	52.4	(a)
[10]	16 × 16	200	80	1.5	0.36	16.7[b]	(a)
[9]	8 × 8	214	84	1.6	0.38	—	53.9
LiteCNN	16 × 16	200	139	3.2	0.63	10.1	53.7
LiteCNN	8 × 8	200	275	6.3	1.25	5.1	53.5
ZYNQ 7010							
LiteCNN	8 × 8	200	275	6.3	1.25	13.2	53.5

[a] Authors assume accuracy close to that obtained with floating-point - 55.9%
[b] With pruning and image batch

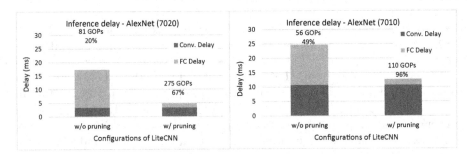

Fig. 9. Execution time of convolutional and FC layers for LiteCNN with and without pruning running AlexNet

munication of weights from external memory. This fact degrades the average GOPs. Pruning FC weights improves the real GOPs of the architecture. The real GOPs improves when LiteCNN is mapped on ZYNQ7010. In this case, the execution time of FC layers is about the same (the memory bandwidth is the same in both FPGAs) and the execution time of convolutional layers increase. So, the implementation in ZYNQ7010 is more efficient.

6   Conclusions

In this work we have proposed block pruning and modified the LiteCNN architecture to support pruned regular networks. The extended LiteCNN with configurable pruning datapath proposed in this work permits to improve the performance/area efficiency while keeping the inference accuracy of the CNN. This is fundamental for embedded systems with low resources.

The results show that block pruning achieves very good accuracies and at the same time simplifies the hardware implementation for regular CNN. We are now studying the relation between pruning and data size reduction.

Acknowledgment. This work was supported by national funds through Fundação para a Ciência e a Tecnologia (FCT) with reference UID/CEC/50021/2019 and was also supported by project IPL/IDI&CA/2018/LiteCNN/ISEL through Instituto Politécnico de Lisboa.

References

1. Krizhevsky, A., Sutskever, I., Hinton, G.E.: Imagenet classification with deep convolutional neural networks. In: Proceedings of the 25th International Conference on Neural Information Processing Systems - Volume 1, NIPS 2012, pp. 1097–1105. Curran Associates Inc., USA (2012)
2. Simonyan, K., Zisserman, A.: Very deep convolutional networks for large-scale image recognition. In: Proceedings of the 3rd International Conference on Learning Representations (2015)
3. Szegedy, C., et al.: Going deeper with convolutions. In: 2015 IEEE Conference on Computer Vision and Pattern Recognition, CVPR, pp. 1–9, June 2015
4. He, K., Zhang, X., Ren, S., Sun, J.: Deep residual learning for image recognition. In: 2016 IEEE Conference on Computer Vision and Pattern Recognition, CVPR, pp. 770–778, June 2016
5. Véstias, M.P., Duarte, R.P., de Sousa, J.T., Neto, H.: Lite-CNN: a high-performance architecture to execute CNNs in low density FPGAs. In: Proceedings of the 28th International Conference on Field Programmable Logic and Applications (2018)
6. Jia, Y., et al.: Caffe: convolutional architecture for fast feature embedding. arXiv preprint arXiv:1408.5093 (2014)
7. Gysel, P., Pimentel, J., Motamedi, M., Ghiasi, S.: Ristretto: a framework for empirical study of resource-efficient inference in convolutional neural networks. IEEE Trans. Neural Netw. Learn. Syst. **29**, 5784–5789 (2018)
8. Venieris, S.I., Bouganis, C.S.: fpgaConvNet: a framework for mapping convolutional neural networks on FPGAs. In: 2016 IEEE 24th Annual International Symposium on Field-Programmable Custom Computing Machines, FCCM, pp. 40–47, May 2016
9. Guo, K., et al.: Angel-Eye: a complete design flow for mapping CNN onto embedded FPGA. IEEE Trans. Comput.-Aided Des. Integr. Circ. Syst. **37**(1), 35–47 (2018)
10. Gong, L., Wang, C., Li, X., Chen, H., Zhou, X.: MALOC: a fully pipelined FPGA accelerator for convolutional neural networks with all layers mapped on chip. IEEE Trans. Comput.-Aided Des. Integr. Circ. Syst. **37**(11), 2601–2612 (2018)
11. Gysel, P., Motamedi, M., Ghiasi, S.: Hardware-oriented approximation of convolutional neural networks. In: Proceedings of the 4th International Conference on Learning Representations (2016)
12. Han, S., Mao, H., Dally, W.J.: Deep compression: compressing deep neural network with pruning, trained quantization and Huffman coding. CoRR, abs/1510.00149 (2015)

13. Nurvitadhi, E., et al.: Can FPGAs beat GPUs in accelerating next-generation deep neural networks? In: Proceedings of the 2017 ACM/SIGDA International Symposium on Field-Programmable Gate Arrays, FPGA 2017, pp. 5–14. ACM, New York (2017). https://doi.org/10.1145/3020078.3021740

14. Albericio, J., Judd, P., Hetherington, T., Aamodt, T., Jerger, N.E., Moshovos, A.: Cnvlutin: ineffectual-neuron-free deep neural network computing. In: 2016 ACM/IEEE 43rd Annual International Symposium on Computer Architecture, ISCA, pp. 1–13, June 2016

15. Fujii, T., Sato, S., Nakahara, H., Motomura, M.: An FPGA realization of a deep convolutional neural network using a threshold neuron pruning. In: Wong, S., Beck, A.C., Bertels, K., Carro, L. (eds.) ARC 2017. LNCS, vol. 10216, pp. 268–280. Springer, Cham (2017). https://doi.org/10.1007/978-3-319-56258-2_23

16. Yu, J., Lukefahr, A., Palframan, D., Dasika, G., Das, R., Mahlke, S.: Scalpel: customizing DNN pruning to the underlying hardware parallelism. SIGARCH Comput. Archit. News 45(2), 548–560 (2017). https://doi.org/10.1145/3140659.3080215

17. Wang, Y., Xu, J., Han, Y., Li, H., Li, X.: DeepBurning: automatic generation of FPGA-based learning accelerators for the neural network family. In: 2016 53rd ACM/EDAC/IEEE Design Automation Conference, DAC, pp. 1–6, June 2016

18. Sharma, H., et al.: From high-level deep neural models to FPGAs. In: 2016 49th Annual IEEE/ACM International Symposium on Microarchitecture, MICRO, pp. 1–12, October 2016

19. Venieris, S.I., Bouganis, C.: fpgaConvNet: mapping regular and irregular convolutional neural networks on FPGAs. IEEE Trans. Neural Netw. Learn. Syst. 30(2), 326–342 (2019)

Author Index

Printed in the United States
By Bookmasters